Report of
THE DEPARTMENT OF THE TREASURY
on the

BUREAU OF ALCOHOL, TOBACCO, AND FIREARMS

Investigation

of

Vernon Wayne Howell

also known as

David Koresh

WITHDRAWN

September 1993

For sale by the U.S. Government Printing Office
Superintendent of Documents, Mail Stop: SSOP, Washington, DC 20402-9328
ISBN 0-16-042025-3

299.93
R299i

DEPARTMENT OF THE TREASURY
WASHINGTON, D.C.

SECRETARY OF THE TREASURY

September 30, 1993

The Honorable William J. Clinton
President of the United States
The White House
Washington, D.C. 20500

Dear Mr. President:

I submit to you the report of the Department of the Treasury's Waco Administrative Review (the "Review").

I established the Review on April 29, 1993, after you directed that Treasury conduct a "vigorous and thorough" investigation of the events leading to the loss of law enforcement and civilian lives near Waco, Texas, on February 28, 1993.

Over the past five months, at my direction, Assistant Secretary for Enforcement Ronald K. Noble has conducted a comprehensive review of the adequacy of the Bureau of Alcohol, Tobacco and Firearms' ("ATF's") procedures, policies, and practices, and whether they were followed during ATF's investigation of Vernon Howell, a/k/a "David Koresh," and his followers. As promised, the Review left no stone unturned in finding out what happened and why.

The Review's final report recounts the events that culminated in the unsuccessful raid of the Branch Davidian Compound and analyzes why the raid ended in the deaths of four courageous ATF special agents, Conway LeBleu, Todd W. McKeehan, Robert J. Williams, and Steven D. Willis.

I know well that no inquiry can bring back any of the lives that were lost near Waco. It is my fervent hope, however, that this review and the changes it will precipitate will prevent the recurrence of such a tragedy in the future.

Sincerely,

Lloyd Bentsen

In Memory of

Conway C. LeBleu

December 23, 1962 - February 28, 1993

Todd W. McKeehan

October 19, 1964 - February 28, 1993

Robert J. Williams

March 1, 1966 - February 28, 1993

Steven D. Willis

December 18, 1960 - February 28, 1993

The Department of the Treasury

Lloyd Bentsen
Secretary

The Waco Administrative Review Team

Ronald K. Noble
Assistant Secretary of the Treasury for Enforcement

Independent Reviewers

Edwin O. Guthman Henry S. Ruth, Jr. Willie L. Williams

Review Team

Lewis C. Merletti
Assistant Project Director

H. Geoffrey Moulton, Jr.
Project Director

David L. Douglass
Assistant Project Director

Kenneth P. Thompson
Special Assistant

Daniel C. Richman
Editor

Andrew E. Tomback
Special Assistant

United States Secret Service

Robert B. Blossman
Special Agent

Colleen B. Callahan
Special Agent

Rafael A. Gonzales
Special Agent

Paul D. Irving
Special Agent

Frederick R. Klare
Special Agent

Joseph A. Masonis
Special Agent

Lewis H. McClam
Special Agent

Dick M. Suekawa
Special Agent

Jennell L. Jenkins
Lead Document Control Assistant

United States Customs Service

Robert L. Cockrell
Special Agent

John J. Devaney
Special Agent

Robert M. Gattison
Special Agent

Susan G. Rowley
Special Agent

Thomas R. Smith
Special Agent

Robert K. Tevens
Special Agent

Ina W. E. Boston
Intelligence Research Specialist

Mary Steinbacher
Correspondence Analyst

Vanessa L. Bolden
Secretary

Internal Revenue Service

Mary C. Balberchak
Special Agent

Kenneth L. Buck
Special Agent

James Rice
Special Investigator

Federal Law Enforcement Training Center

John H. Battle
Instructor/Training Specialist

Office of The General Counsel

Billy S. Bradley
Sarah Elizabeth Jones

DEPARTMENT OF THE TREASURY
WASHINGTON

September 24, 1993

MEMORANDUM FOR SECRETARY BENTSEN

FROM: Robert P. Cesca
Deputy Inspector General

SUBJECT: Department of Treasury's Waco Administrative Review

On April 29, 1993, the Department announced its plans to examine the events leading to the Bureau of Alcohol, Tobacco and Firearms (ATF) execution of search and arrest warrants at the Branch Davidian compound, near Waco, Texas, on February 28, 1993. The purpose of the Department's administrative review was to comprehensively evaluate all aspects of ATF's investigation of David Koresh and the Branch Davidians through and including the events occurring at the compound on February 28, 1993. The review was performed under the leadership and direction of Mr. Ronald K. Noble, Assistant Secretary for the Office of Enforcement. As part of this review, the Department was to analyze and assess whether ATF's procedures, policies, and practices were adequate and whether they were followed up and until the time ATF decided to raid the compound.

In addition, on May 3, 1993, the Department further announced the selection of three independent reviewers to ensure that the Department's administrative review was comprehensively and impartially conducted. These reviewers were selected because of their national prominence, integrity and law enforcement expertise. The reviewers are responsible for providing guidance to the investigation, reviewing the investigative team's findings and providing an independent assessment of the information contained in the final report.

The Office of Inspector General (OIG) was requested to monitor the administrative review for the purpose of providing assurance to the Department that the project plan was complete and properly implemented. Moreover, the OIG was to comment on whether relevant information obtained during the investigation was properly considered and included in the final report.

This memorandum transmits the results of our assessment and provides a level of assurance that the Departmental effort was objective and comprehensively performed. It is our opinion that the administrative review team vigorously and thoroughly examined all significant information surrounding the events leading to ATF's execution of the search warrant at the Branch Davidian compound on February 28, 1993. In addition, the administrative review team's report addresses all the issues that are included in the team's investigative plan. To the best of our knowledge, the review team's findings are consistent with the facts developed and, to the extent possible, accurately reflect the circumstances surrounding ATF's investigation and subsequent raid of the Branch Davidian compound on February 28, 1993.

To arrive at our conclusions, we focused on determining whether

- all appropriate issues were identified for investigation and appropriately considered in the team's planning process;

- the team reviewed pertinent documentation and information obtained by other law enforcement organizations involved in the incident;

- all appropriate individuals were identified and interviewed that could provide insight of the events leading up to ATF's raid and/or the issues being examined;

- all appropriate leads from interviews with ATF agents and management personnel and other relevant persons were properly followed up and satisfactorily resolved;

- external experts were consulted in order to obtain an independent assessment of ATF's planning, training, and execution of the search and arrest warrants;

- input and advice provided by the independent reviewers were properly considered by the project team leaders; and,

- the resultant report reflects the body of information examined and that any conclusions made by the review team are well-founded.

From the outset of the project, we provided our views and comments to the project leadership as we thought would be appropriate. We provided the team with an extensive list of issues and questions that we felt needed to be examined during the course of the administrative investigation. These issues and associated questions were included in the team's investigative plan.

Our opinions are based primarily upon a review of information contained in memoranda of interview from selected interviews with ATF agents involved in the execution of the search warrant; memoranda of interview of selected ATF management personnel; and, the Texas Rangers' investigation of the murders of four ATF agents. In addition, we attended numerous daily team debriefing sessions conducted by project leaders discussing the status of the administrative teams efforts and the required follow-up that should be performed to satisfactorily pursue/resolve issues being examined. These briefing sessions provided an excellent opportunity to gain insight of the quality of the project management and direction and provided a comfort level regarding the integrity of the efforts of the administrative review team.

We also attended the briefings held with the three independent reviewers selected to review the team's findings to judge the quality of the information being provided for use in their assessment of the Treasury's administrative investigation. We believe that the information provided to the reviewers was accurate, based on information obtained at that time by team investigators, and was relevant to the main issues under examination. Additionally, we attended the briefings held with the tactical experts employed to assist in evaluating ATF's tactical operations plan and Special Response Team training. The tactical experts' recommendations have adequately been considered and the results of their reports have been incorporated in the final report.

With regard to the contents of the administrative review team's report, it is our opinion that the report provides an accurate account of the events leading up to the ATF's assault of the Branch Davidian compound. Furthermore, we believe that any conclusions made by the review team have a basis in fact and are consistent with the nature of the findings developed.

During the course of our oversight role, we experienced total cooperation on the part of the project leaders and had unlimited access to the information and documentation compiled by the administrative review team during its investigation. We would like to compliment the team for vigorously and aggressively pursuing this enormous undertaking in order to determine what really happened in Waco, Texas on February 28, 1993. The findings and recommendations in this report should be invaluable to the law enforcement community as a whole and hopefully will serve as a guide for improving how law enforcement approaches the new waves of violent behaviors and the groups that perpetuate them.

TABLE OF CONTENTS

TITLE PAGE	i
MEMO TO THE PRESIDENT	iii
DEDICATION	v
ROSTER	vii
OPINION OF THE INSPECTOR GENERAL	ix
TABLE OF CONTENTS	xiii
TABLE OF FIGURES	xix
INTRODUCTION	1
Project Statement	3
Other Consultants and Experts	4
Investigative Plan	6
Overview	7

PART ONE

Section One: The Probable Cause Investigation	17
Preliminary Information: Initiation of the ATF Investigation of Koresh and his Followers	17
The ATF Investigation and Development of Probable Cause to Arrest Koresh and Search Premises Under his Control	25
Additional Weapons and Explosives Shipments	25
Compliance Inspection of Henry McMahon	26
The Sounds of Machinegun Fire and Explosives	26
Interviews of Former Cult Members	27
Visits from the Texas Department of Protective and Regulatory Services	30
Backgrounds of Compound Residents	31
Reports of ATF Experts	31
The David Block Interview	32

    The Undercover House and Special Agent Rodriguez   33

Section Two: The Decisionmaking Process Leading to Forceful Execution of Warrants   37

    Consideration of Tactical Options   37

        The December 4, 1992, Meeting   37
        The Late December and Early January Meetings   43

    Interviews with Former Cult Members   44
    Intelligence from the Undercover House   51
    The Decision   53
    Development of the Tactical Plan   54
    Additional Intelligence Gathering, Training, and the Briefing of ATF Leadership   64

Section Three: ATF and the Media Prepare for the Raid   67

    The *Waco Tribune-Herald*'s Investigation of David Koresh and Preparation of a Series for Publication   67
    ATF Discussions About the *Tribune-Herald* Investigation and Contacting the Media   68
    The February 1, 1993, Meeting With a *Tribune-Herald* Official   68
    Continued Discussions Between ATF and the *Tribune-Herald*   69
    The *Tribune-Herald* Decision to Publish   70
    The February 24 Meeting With the *Tribune-Herald*   70
    ATF and the Media Prepare for the Raid February 24-27   72

        ATF Raid Preparations: February 24-26   73
        Securing Search and Arrest Warrants   73
        Other Waco Media Learn About the Raid   74
        The Tribune-Herald Notifies ATF of its Decision to Publish on Saturday, and ATF Reacts   75
        ATF Notifies the Treasury Department's Office of Enforcement About the Raid   75
        Saturday, February 27: Media Preparations   76
        Saturday, February 27: ATF Preparations   78

Section Four: The Assault On The Compound.   81

   ATF Agents Assemble   81
   The Media Sets Out To Cover The Raid   82
   Rodriguez Enters The Compound   88
   Rodriguez Reports   89
   The Raid Goes Forward   91
   Activity In The Compound   92
   The Media Covers The Approach Of The Raid Teams   92
   The Helicopter Diversion   95
   The Raid Team Arrives   96
   The Cease-Fire   101

Section Five: Post-raid Events   109

   Aftermath of the Shoot-Out on February 28   109
   The Evacuation of Wounded Agents   109
   The Media and the Shoot-Out   110
   The Failure to Maintain the Perimeter   110
   A Siege Develops and ATF Obtains Assistance from the FBI   112

      Chaos at the Command Post   112
      Initial Relief   113
      The Decision to Bring in the FBI HRT   113
      Hartnett and Conroy Arrive at the Command Post   115

PART TWO

Section One: The Propriety of Investigating Koresh and Other Cult Members and Seeking to Enforce Federal Firearms Laws   119

   ATF Properly Initiated an Investigation of Koresh   119
   Evidence Developed by ATF's Investigation Warranted Application for and Issuance of Search and Arrest Warrants   122

Section Two: Analysis of the Tactical Planning Effort ... 133

    Introduction ... 133

    The Decision to Execute the Warrants by "Raiding" the Compound Was Made Before Other Options Were Fully Exhausted ... 134

        The Decision to Use Force When Executing the Warrants ... 135
        Intelligence Failures and the Failure to Try to Arrest Koresh Off the Compound Followed by an Effort to Execute the Search Warrants ... 136
        A Siege With Koresh Present on the Compound ... 141

    The Decision to Pursue a Raid Option and Develop a Raid Plan ... 142
    Intelligence Failures ... 143

        The "Arms Room" ... 143
        No Guards or Sentries ... 144
        The Men in the Pit ... 145

    No Meaningful Contingency Planning ... 148
    Command and Control Flaws in the Raid Plan ... 152

        The General Command Structure ... 152

    Command and Control on Raid Day ... 154

Section Three: Media Impact on ATF's Branch Davidian Investigation ... 157

    ATF's Efforts to Delay the Publication of the "Sinful Messiah" Series ... 157
    Media Activity Raid Day ... 161

Section Four: The Flawed Decision to Go Forward With the Raid ... 165

    ATF Decisionmakers Understood in Advance that the Raid Had Likely Been Compromised ... 166
    The Lack of a Control Agent ... 167
    Other Intelligence that Could Have Confirmed Rodriguez's Report that Koresh Knew ATF Was Coming ... 168
    Decisionmakers Failed to Realize Unacceptable Risk of Proceeding Without Surprise ... 170
    Handling the Momentum of the Raid ... 173

Section Five: Treasury Department Oversight	177
ATF Notifies Treasury of Impending Operation	177
Discussion	180
Section Six: Operations Security	185
The Investigation	186
The Undercover Operation	186
Pre-raid Logistics	188
The Raid	189
Conclusion	190
Section Seven: ATF Post-raid Dissemination of Misleading Information About the Raid and the Raid Plan	193
ATF Management's Misleading Post-raid Statements	193
The Shooting Review Team	194
Shooting Review Team's Interview of Rodriguez	195
Shooting Review Team's interview of Mastin	195
Shooting Review Team's Report to Hartnett and Conroy	196
Shooting Review Team's Interview of Sarabyn	196
Shooting Review Team's Interview of Cavanaugh	196
Shooting Review Team's Interview of Porter	197
Shooting Review Team's Interview of Chojnacki	197
Hartnett, Conroy and Troy knew surprise was lost	197
ATF's Media Statements After the Shooting Review	198
The Texas Rangers' Reports	200
The Late March and Early April ATF Statements	202
The Significance Of ATF's Misleading Statements	205
The Alteration of ATF's Written Raid Plan	207
The Drafting of the Raid Plan	207
The Alteration of the Raid Plan	208
Inquiries into the Alteration of the Raid Plan	209

Section Eight: National Guard Support   211

    Introduction   211
    ATF's Initial Contact with the Military   211
    ATF's Specific Requests for National Guard Support   213
    Analysis   213

CONCLUSION   215

ACKNOWLEDGMENTS   217

APPENDICES

    APPENDIX A: Letter of Assurance of Chief Willie Williams
    APPENDIX B: Expert Reports
    APPENDIX C: Operations Plans
    APPENDIX D: Chronology of Events
    APPENDIX E: ATF Advisory to the Office of Enforcement
    APPENDIX F: Waco Administrative Review Mission Charter
    APPENDIX G: A Brief History of Federal Firearms Enforcement

TABLE OF FIGURES

Figure One	Map depicting location of Compound and Mag Bag.
Figure Two	Photograph of buried school bus used as firing range and bunker.
Figure Three	Photograph of David Koresh and other Branch Davidians before Roden shoot-out.
Figure Four	Photograph of Ammunition seized from Koresh after Roden shoot-out.
Figure Five	Photograph of Mag Bag taken after execution of search warrant.
Figure Six	Photograph of AK-47 assault rifle.
Figure Seven	Photograph of M-16 assault rifle.
Figure Eight	Photograph of .50-caliber rifle.
Figure Nine	Photograph of typical "pineapple" type grenades.
Figure Ten	Illustration depicting undercover house, Compound, and hay barn.
Figure Eleven	Photograph of main Compound Building (front side.)
Figure Twelve	Photograph of rear of Compound.
Figure Thirteen	Photograph of Mt. Carmel houses before construction of Compound.
Figure Fourteen	Photograph of Mt. Carmel after construction of Compound before demolition of houses.
Figure Fifteen	Diagram of Compound's first level.
Figure Sixteen	Diagram of Compound's second level.
Figure Seventeen	Diagram of Compound's third and fourth levels.
Figure Eighteen	Photograph of Compound designating pit.
Figure Nineteen	Photograph of undercover house.
Figure Twenty	Aerial photograph of command post at TSTC.
Figure Twenty-One	Aerial photograph of Bellmead Civic Center, (staging area).
Figure Twenty-Two	Side view of cattle trailer.
Figure Twenty-Three	Rear view of cattle trailer.
Figure Twenty-Four	Photograph indicating planned deployment for SRTs.
Figure Twenty-Five	Diagram of communications network used for the raid.
Figure Twenty-Six	Organizational chart of national response plan.
Figure Twenty-Seven	Map depicting staging area, Mag Bag, Compound and road blocks.
Figure Twenty-Eight	Map depicting location of media vehicles.
Figure Twenty-Nine	Photograph of Kalashnikov rifle taken after April 19, 1993.

Figure Thirty	Photograph of load-bearing ammunition vests, magazines, and military helmet taken after April 19, 1993.
Figure Thirty-One	Photograph of Compound taken after February 28, 1993.
Figure Thirty-Two	Photograph of Compound designating location of wounded agent Kenny King.
Figure Thirty-Three	Gunshot related deaths and injuries sustained by ATF on February 28, 1993.
Figure Thirty-Four	Non-gunshot related injuries sustained by ATF on February 28, 1993.
Figure Thirty-Five	Deaths and injuries sustained by cult members on February 28, 1993.
Figure Thirty-Six	Photograph of "pineapple" type grenade casings.
Figure Thirty-Seven	Photograph of arms bunker with arsenal of assorted weapons.
Figure Thirty-Eight	Photograph of remains of assault rifle.
Figure Thirty-Nine	Photograph of remains of assault rifle.
Figure Forty	Diagram depicting Rodriguez's undercover contacts with the Compound.

INTRODUCTION

On February 28, 1993, near Waco, Texas, four agents from the Treasury Department's Bureau of Alcohol, Tobacco, and Firearms (ATF) were killed, and more than 20 other agents were wounded when David Koresh[1] and members of his religious cult, the Branch Davidian,[2] ambushed a force of 76 ATF agents. The ATF agents were attempting to execute lawful search and arrest warrants at Mount Carmel, the Branch Davidian Compound. Tipped off that the agents were coming, Koresh and more than 100 of his followers waited inside the Compound and opened fire using assault weapons before the agents even reached the door. This gunfire continued until the Branch Davidians agreed to a cease-fire. The ensuing standoff lasted 51 days, ending on April 19, when the Compound erupted in fire set by cult members after the Federal Bureau of Investigation (FBI) used tear gas to force its occupants to leave. The fire destroyed the Compound, and more than 70 residents died, many from gunshot wounds apparently inflicted by fellow cult members.

In the wake of the tragic events of February 28 and April 19, the Executive Branch, Congress, the media, and the general public raised serious questions about ATF and FBI actions at the Compound. President Clinton promptly directed the Department of the Treasury and the Department of Justice, which are responsible for ATF and the FBI,

---

[1] Born Vernon Wayne Howell on August 17, 1959, Koresh formally changed his name in 1990. According to his court petition, Koresh changed his name because he was an entertainer, and wished to use the name for publicity and business purposes.

[2] The Branch Davidian movement was started by a number of Seventh Day Adventists who believed strongly in the prophecies of the book of Revelation. David Koresh, then named Vernon Wayne Howell, took over leadership of the group in 1987. The Compound residents were extremely devoted to Koresh, and many apparently believed that he was the lamb of God. In the course of this report, the Review has used the term "cult" to refer to Koresh and his followers. The term is not intended and should not be taken as a reference to the Branch Davidian movement generally. The Review is quite aware that "cult" has pejorative connotations, and that outsiders—particularly those in the government—should avoid casting aspersions on those whose religious beliefs are different from their own. The definition of cult in *Webster's Third New International Dictionary* (unabridged) includes: "a great or excessive devotion or dedication to some person, idea or thing" and "a religion regarded as unorthodox or spurious." In light of the evidence of the conduct of Koresh and his followers set out in this report, the Review finds "cult" to be an apt characterization.

respectively, to conduct "vigorous and thorough" investigations of the events leading to the loss of law enforcement and civilian lives. The President's directive resulted in three separate yet coordinated inquiries.

On April 29, Secretary of the Treasury Lloyd Bentsen asked Ronald K. Noble, who was then designated to be Assistant Secretary of the Treasury for Enforcement, to focus on ATF's involvement in the case, from the initiation of its investigation of Koresh and his followers through its unsuccessful effort to execute search and arrest warrants on February 28. At the same time, Attorney General Janet Reno directed Philip B. Heymann, who was then designated to be Deputy Attorney General,[3] to review FBI involvement in the siege of the Compound from early March, when the FBI Hostage Rescue Team took over the law enforcement effort there, through April 19, when the Compound burned. Secretary Bentsen and Attorney General Reno also directed Heymann and Noble to conduct the third inquiry, a joint assessment of federal law enforcement's capacity to handle such dangerous situations as were presented when ATF tried to enforce federal firearms laws at the Compound and when the Branch Davidians refused to surrender after February 28.

All three inquiries were undertaken in a manner designed not to interfere with ongoing criminal investigations and prosecutions resulting from the cult members' conduct. As of September 1993, 12 Compound residents have been indicted on charges including conspiracy to murder federal officers and possessing firearms during a violent crime. Some face additional charges including unlawful possession of machineguns and conspiracy to possess unregistered destructive devices. On September 9, one defendant pleaded guilty to impeding and interfering with the lawful execution of the search warrant by use of a deadly weapon.

Charged by Secretary Bentsen to examine "whether ATF's procedures, policies, and practices were adequate and whether they were followed," Assistant Secretary Noble promised that "no stone would be left unturned in finding out what happened and why." To assure that the Waco Administrative Review, conducted by the Treasury Department, would fulfill its promise of objectivity and comprehensiveness, Secretary Bentsen selected three prominent individuals with extensive expertise in law enforcement and experience in media relations to guide the Review's investigation and report to the public on its findings:

---

[3] Both Noble and Heymann have since been confirmed by the Senate.

- Edwin O. Guthman, a Pulitzer Prize-winning journalist and a professor of journalism at the University of Southern California, is the former national editor of *The Los Angeles Times* and former editor of *The Philadelphia Inquirer*. He also served as press secretary to Robert F. Kennedy when Kennedy was Attorney General and when he was a member of the Senate;

- Henry S. Ruth, Jr. is an attorney who served in the Department of Justice for more than 15 years and who was later chief Watergate prosecutor. Ruth has served on many commissions, including the Special Investigative Commission that examined law enforcement actions in connection with MOVE in Philadelphia;

- Willie L. Williams, Chief of the Los Angeles Police Department since 1991, is a career law enforcement official who, after joining the Philadelphia Police Department in 1964, rose through its ranks to become Commissioner in 1988.

Each of these distinguished reviewers generously agreed to serve without pay, and each will provide a written assessment of the Review's investigation to the Secretary of the Treasury.[4]

Project Statement

The mission of the Treasury Department Office of Enforcement was to conduct a comprehensive inquiry into the ATF operation, from the initiation of its investigation of Koresh's activities through the raid at the Branch Davidian Compound on February 28 and its aftermath. Under the overall supervision of Assistant Secretary Noble, a team of attorneys and law enforcement agents conducted interviews, obtained primary source materials and exhibits, viewed the Compound and other key sites near Waco, and analyzed the materials and information gathered. Based on this investigation, including credibility assessments and circumstantial evidence, the Review made factual determinations and analyzed those facts. Assistant Secretary Noble provided final oversight of the report before its submission to Secretary Bentsen.

The Review's day-to-day operations were supervised by the project director, H. Geoffrey Moulton, Jr., Associate Professor at Widener University School of Law in Delaware, and the assistant project directors, Lewis C. Merletti, Deputy Assistant Director

---

[4] Chief Williams' assessment has been received and is included in Appendix A.

of the U.S. Secret Service, and David L. Douglass, an attorney on leave from Wiley, Rein & Fielding in Washington, D.C. The Review's investigators included 17 senior agents from the Secret Service, the Customs Service, the Internal Revenue Service (both the Criminal Investigation Division and the Internal Security Division), and the Financial Crimes Enforcement Network. These agents, whose names and bureau affiliations are listed at the front of this report, brought to the Review an extraordinary range of investigative and tactical experience from law enforcement and the military. Their collective expertise enabled the Review to conduct a comprehensive examination of ATF's investigation of Koresh.

In addition, the Review was assisted by a computer expert from the Federal Law Enforcement Training Center, an intelligence research specialist from the Customs Service, and clerical support from several Treasury agencies. These agents and other personnel were detailed to the Review full-time. Four other attorneys were also assigned to the Review: two from Treasury's Office of General Counsel, another detailed to Treasury from the Interagency Council on the Homeless, and one who had recently completed a federal district court clerkship.

The investigative team maintained offices at the Department of the Treasury's main building. Access to these offices, the Review's computers, and records compiled by the Review was restricted to ensure the confidentiality and integrity of the investigation.

Other Consultants and Experts

The Review sought technical assistance from several specialists with experience in law enforcement and military operations. For their expertise in tactical command and control, intelligence gathering, and crisis decisionmaking issues, the Review consulted the following:

- Commander George Morrison, a 37-year veteran with the Los Angeles Police Department, with extensive experience planning and executing tactical operations;

- Deputy Chief John Murphy and Lieutenant Robert Sobocienski from the New York City Police Department, the commanding officer and a leading line officer in the department's Special Operations Division, respectively;

- Captain John Kolman, retired from the Los Angeles County Sheriff's Department, who planned and carried out numerous tactical operations in his 23 years with the department and is a founder and director of the National Tactical Officers Association.

- Colonel Rod Paschall, a retired commander of the U.S. Army First Special Forces Group—Delta (Delta Force) and now affiliated with the Office of International Criminal Justice at the University of Illinois at Chicago; and

- Wade Ishimoto, a retired Delta Force intelligence officer, who is currently a manager of Sandia National Laboratories, Albuquerque, New Mexico.

Each of the tactical experts also generously agreed to serve without pay. Each provided the Review with an independent assessment of ATF's operation within their field of expertise. These assessments can be found in Appendix B. The experts had access to all data collected by the investigative team and were free either to request that additional inquiries be pursued or to pursue them on their own.

The Review also received assistance from two weapons experts, William C. Davis, Jr., and Charles R. Fagg, and two explosives experts, Captain Joseph Kennedy, a retired Navy officer, and Paul Cooper. Davis, a registered professional engineer retired from the government, has more than 50 years of federal government and private experience analyzing and designing weapons. Fagg, a mechanical engineer, has more than 30 years of experience analyzing and designing weapons for the federal government and private industry. Kennedy is the former commander of the U.S. Navy Explosive Ordinance Disposal Technology Center in Indian Head, Maryland. Cooper, an explosives expert with Sandia National Laboratories, is well known for his work in the investigation of the battleship *New Jersey* explosion and the Marine barracks bombing in Beirut, Lebanon.

The weapons and explosives experts also served without pay and provided the Review with written reports answering specific questions about whether the materials ATF investigators determined to have been delivered to Koresh and his followers constituted explosives or illegal firearms or whether they are commonly used to produce such items. These reports are also contained in Appendix B.

Treasury Offices of General Counsel and Inspector General

Treasury Department General Counsel Jean Hanson and Assistant General Counsel Robert M. McNamara served as counsel to the Review. The Office of General Counsel secured employment contracts, ensured that the Review complied with the Privacy Act, and the Federal Advisory Committee Act, and provided legal opinions when appropriate during the course of the investigation. The Treasury's Office of Inspector General monitored the Review to ensure that the project plan was complete and implemented properly and that all relevant facts were fully considered and included in this report. In a memorandum to Secretary Bentsen, the Office of Inspector General has concluded that the Review "vigorously and thoroughly examined all significant information surrounding the events leading to ATF's execution of the search warrant at the Branch Davidian Compound" and that "the report provides an accurate account of these events."

Investigative Plan

Even before the Review formally began, the Treasury Department Office of Enforcement directed ATF to gather and provide all information available concerning raid planning and execution.

The process continued throughout the review period, as additional materials were requested and provided to the Review. The Review team also began interviewing ATF agents. Because of allegations that statements by ATF management about the raid did not accurately reflect the understanding of those on the scene, the Review started by interviewing line agents who had been involved in the investigation of the case and the planning and execution of the raid. Before conducting any interviews, peer support counselors briefed the investigative team concerning the reactions they could expect from agents who had lived through the extraordinary trauma of the raid and murders on February 28. Subsequent interviews followed the chain of command, from assistant special agents in charge and special agents in charge, through the ATF director and Treasury Office of Enforcement personnel.

In all, 508 individuals were interviewed between May 17 and the publication of this report. Most interviews were conducted in person, with many lasting more than a full day. As the Review progressed and new facts emerged, agents and attorneys often conducted follow-up interviews.

Throughout its inquiry, the Review took pains to avoid interfering with ongoing investigations and prosecutions being conducted by the Department of Justice into criminal violations by Branch Davidians. The Texas Rangers, deputized as U.S. Marshals for the criminal investigation and prosecution, gave the Review access to their reports, and the Waco U.S. Attorney's Office granted Review investigators access to investigatory materials not restricted by Federal Rule of Criminal Procedure 6(e). Their willingness to share information with the Review was predicated on their trust that the Review would exercise appropriate judgment in determining what information to make public in light of those sensitive investigations and prosecutions.

Overview

First and foremost, the Review's goal was to learn what happened near Waco and to tell the story. The Review tried to explain why the February 28 raid ended in tragedy. In the course of that effort, the investigation confirmed that the rank and file agents of ATF who were sent to enforce federal firearms and explosives laws at the Branch Davidian Compound did their best to perform their assigned tasks and showed dedication and often spectacular courage in the face of murderous gunfire. Unfortunately, the investigation also found disturbing evidence of flawed decisionmaking, inadequate intelligence gathering, miscommunication, supervisory failures, and deliberately misleading post-raid statements about the raid and the raid plan by certain ATF supervisors. Inevitably, the Review's discussion of what went wrong in the operation must refer to certain individuals by name, but the Review sought not to accuse but to explain. This explanation contains lessons that can strengthen the ability of the law enforcement community to deal with similar situations, which unfortunately can be expected to occur.

Part One of this report is a narrative account of the events leading up to and through the raid on February 28. The narrative is divided into five sections, each devoted to one of the major components of the story. Part Two presents the Review's analysis of critical aspects of the events addressed in Part One. An overview of the report structure and content follows.

Part One—The Facts

Section One: The Probable Cause Investigation

Part One, Section One summarizes the ATF investigation of David Koresh and his followers to determine whether there was probable cause to believe that federal firearms laws had been violated. The investigation began when a McLennan County sheriff's deputy asked ATF to look into suspicious United Parcel Service (UPS) deliveries to Koresh and the Branch Davidians. After determining that many such deliveries had been made to the Compound, that the packages contained materials commonly used to manufacture grenades unlawfully, and that Koresh had a violent past, Special Agent Davy Aguilera opened a formal investigation.

Section One describes Aguilera's painstaking effort to piece together evidence of Koresh's accumulation of a formidable arsenal of firearms, including many illegal machineguns and other unlawful destructive devices. Aguilera gathered evidence from many sources, such as records of previous deliveries to Koresh and interviews with a broad range of people, including local law enforcement officers and former cult members. The evidence that Koresh posted guards at the Compound, trained followers to fire the weapons, and believed he would have a violent confrontation with law enforcement indicated strongly that Koresh was prepared to use the arsenal he was amassing. Aguilera learned other disconcerting information about Koresh, including his propensity toward violence and violent rhetoric, his sexual conduct with minors, and his control over the lives and minds of his followers.

Eventually, ATF agents established an undercover house near the Compound, met with Koresh, and corroborated some of the evidence Aguilera had obtained. These contacts with Koresh only confirmed the reports about Koresh's violent nature and his hatred for law enforcement.

Section Two: The Decisionmaking Process Leading to Forceful Execution of Warrants

Part One, Section Two describes ATF's effort to develop a tactical plan to execute a search warrant at the Compound. By fall 1992, ATF's investigation had uncovered sufficient evidence of federal firearms violations to meet the threshold probable cause requirements for a warrant to search the Compound. Anticipating having to apply for warrants and recognizing that executing warrants at the Compound safely would pose a substantial challenge, Aguilera's supervisor, Assistant Special Agent in Charge (ASAC) Chuck Sarabyn of the ATF Houston office, organized a team of tactical planners. The team consisted of several experienced leaders of ATF Special Response Teams (SRTs), all of whom specialized in dynamic, high-risk entries to execute warrants, but only one of whom had participated previously in a tactical operation comparable to the one being contemplated for the heavily armed, fortresslike Compound.

As Section Two sets forth, the planners concluded that their principal options for executing warrants in the face of resistance were either by a siege, which would establish an armed perimeter around the Compound until its residents surrendered, or a raid, a dynamic entry relying on the element of surprise. Although the planners considered trying to lure Koresh away from the Compound, they abandoned the idea quickly because of intelligence reports that Koresh rarely ventured off Compound grounds. The planners rejected a siege because of the physical attributes of the Compound, because of a fear of mass suicide, and because former cult members reported that Koresh had enough food, water, and other resources to withstand a lengthy siege. The planners decided to conduct a raid and developed a tactical plan that hinged on separating the Compound's men from the weapons.

The section then describes how ATF's plan was formulated, the intelligence on which the planners relied, and how the weaknesses of the intelligence went unrecognized. It explains how the plan that ATF developed contained critical flaws.

Section Three: ATF and the Media Prepare for the Raid

Section Three describes how media interest in the Branch Davidian Compound came to hamper ATF's raid planners and commanders. The *Waco Tribune-Herald* began investigating Koresh in April 1992. In October 1992, ATF learned of the *Tribune-Herald* newspaper's investigation. By January 1993, reporters had completed drafting the newspaper's "Sinful Messiah" series, which contained startling revelations about the Branch Davidians' life-style and possession of dangerous weapons.

In January, the raid planners decided to ask the paper to delay publishing the series to ensure the safety of undercover agents and the integrity of the investigation. ATF held two meetings with newspaper representatives in February 1993 and disclosed potential dates for the operation and training. The *Tribune-Herald* did not agree to withhold publishing its series.

The week before the raid, ATF agents made final raid preparations and the *Tribune-Herald* prepared to publish its "Sinful Messiah" series. ATF teams assembled for three days of training at Fort Hood. In addition, ATF opened a command center at Texas State Technical College (TSTC) near Waco and finalized support services with local suppliers and law enforcement. During this time, the *Tribune-Herald* contacted Koresh to get his reaction to its series of articles and implemented new security procedures.

On Wednesday, February 24, ATF rescheduled its raid from Monday, March 1 to Sunday, February 28, because it expected the *Tribune-Herald* to publish its "Sinful Messiah" series on Sunday. However, on Friday afternoon, *Tribune-Herald* officials notified ATF that the series would begin on Saturday morning. The raid planners did not alter their plan, except to have an undercover agent visit the Compound to gauge Koresh's reaction to the first article. Later that Friday, raid planners learned from ATF headquarters in Washington that Treasury officials had directed that the raid not go forward. By Friday evening, however, Treasury officials permitted the operation to proceed after ATF Director Stephen Higgins addressed Treasury's concerns that the operation could be executed safely, and assured that those directing the raid were under express orders to cancel the operation if they learned that its secrecy had been compromised or if those in the Compound had departed from their established routine in any significant way. On Saturday evening, the undercover agent was directed to visit the Compound on Sunday to make sure that the Branch Davidian routine immediately before the raid was normal.

Meanwhile, the *Tribune-Herald* and KWTX, a local television station, learned that ATF was about to raid the Compound. The newspaper, which already knew from its negotiations with ATF that the agency was contemplating a major operation, received a tip as to the precise timing of the raid. KWTX received similar information from a dispatcher with the ambulance service ATF had contracted. By Saturday evening, eight *Tribune-Herald* reporters and three KWTX employees were assigned to be in the Compound area to cover what they believed would be a large ATF operation and a significant local news story.

Section Four: The Assault on the Compound

Section Four recounts the events on the day of the raid. The teams were deployed early that morning: the incident commander, the tactical coordinator and other agents gathered at the command post; the deputy tactical commander, forward observer teams and undercover agents were positioned in the undercover house across from the Compound; and the entry teams assembled at a pre-selected staging area in nearby Bellmead.

At approximately 8 a.m., under the pretext of asking Koresh about the "Sinful Messiah" series, the undercover agent went to the Compound to assess whether the article had incited Koresh to order his followers to take up arms. When the agent arrived, Koresh invited him to join a Bible study session. It appeared that the article had not caused the cult to arm itself. However, unknown to ATF, a KWTX cameraman sent to cover the expected raid became lost on roads near the Compound. A letter carrier, who the cameraman did not realize was one of Koresh's followers, stopped and asked if he needed directions. In the course of their conversation, the cameraman told the letter carrier about the impending raid. The letter carrier went directly to Koresh, called him away from the undercover agent and warned him.

The undercover agent did not hear the warning but Koresh returned to the room upset and shaking. Koresh stated words to the effect that the ATF and the National Guard were coming. Concerned for his safety, the undercover agent immediately left the Compound and reported what had happened to the tactical coordinator, who in turn related it to the incident commander. Failing to appreciate the significance of the undercover agent's report, they ordered the raid to proceed.

The entry teams, concealed in cattle trailers, arrived at the Compound more than 40 minutes after Koresh had received the tip. Koresh used that time to prepare a deadly ambush. As the agents exited the trailers, gunfire erupted from the Compound and cult members threw homemade handgrenades at the agents. In the face of overwhelming firepower the agents displayed extraordinary discipline and courage. The gun battle was waged for almost 90 minutes before a cease-fire could be arranged and the agents were able to withdraw from the Compound.

Section Five: Post-raid Events

Section Five describes the hours immediately following the failed raid and recounts ATF's struggle to restore order to its law enforcement effort. ATF evacuated its wounded and dead agents and withdrew from vulnerable positions around the Compound. But ATF failed to maintain a secure perimeter around the Compound immediately after the shoot-out, which resulted in a deadly confrontation away from the Compound between ATF agents and cult members.

Section Five also explains how ATF's command post deteriorated into near chaos after the raid. Still, various agents made efforts to restore order and accomplish urgent tasks, including negotiating with the cult members to continue the cease-fire and release some children. ATF headquarters personnel arrived at the command post and attempted to restore order and reestablish a secure perimeter around the Compound. As additional ATF Special Response Teams provided immediate relief for their embattled colleagues, ATF asked the FBI Hostage Rescue Team for assistance. The Hostage Rescue Team was mobilized and control of the operation shifted from ATF to the FBI.

Finally, the section reviews how ATF attempted to provide support and counseling for raid participants in the days following the failed raid, and how the media descended on Waco to cover what became an international story.

Part Two—Analysis

Section One: The Propriety of Investigating Koresh and Other Cult Members and Seeking to Enforce Federal Firearms Laws

Part Two, Section One, considers whether ATF properly initiated an investigation of Koresh for suspected violations of federal firearms laws and whether the investigation established probable cause to search the Compound for evidence of such crimes. Based on a review of the evidence, the section concludes that ATF focused properly on Koresh after receiving complaints from local law enforcement officials. Similarly, after reviewing evidence of firearms violations unearthed by the ATF investigation, including Koresh's purchases of weapons and accounts that he was manufacturing weapons illegally on the Compound, the section determines that ATF had a firm basis for searching the Compound and arresting Koresh.

The section also reviews allegations that ATF targeted Koresh because of his religious beliefs and sexual conduct with minors and finds the allegations lacking in merit. The section concludes that ATF focused properly on Koresh because of his propensity toward violence and his ability to control his followers.

Section Two: Analysis of the Tactical Planning Effort

Part Two, Section Two analyzes ATF's tactical planning effort, from the decisionmaking process that led to the choice of a dynamic entry to the development of the raid plan itself. As this section explains, most of the Review's tactical experts agree that the plan had a reasonable chance of success if all of the planners' major assumptions had been correct. If the men in the Compound were working in the pit, separated from the weapons reportedly locked away in the "arms room," and if ATF agents could drive up to the Compound without its residents knowing of the operation until it was too late to offer effective resistance, the warrants might well have been executed without loss of life. But the caveat here is crucial, for significant deficiencies in the tactical intelligence gathering structure, most notably the lack of an agent dedicated to intelligence processing and analysis, resulted in a plan that was based on seriously flawed assumptions.

The problems here lie as much in the planning process as in the plan itself. Not only were the planners too quick to conclude that a massive mid-morning raid was the best possible enforcement option, but they chose a plan whose window of opportunity was much smaller than they realized. The planners also failed to prepare for contingencies that would arise if that window were missed. Against a target as formidable as Koresh, such errors exposed ATF to grievous consequences.

Responsibility for these flaws cannot simply be placed at the feet of those who did the actual planning. Those charged with this mission devoted considerable time and energy to devising a safe and successful operation. They lacked, however, the training, experience, and institutional support necessary for the extraordinary operation they were planning, an operation which was qualitatively as well as quantitatively different from the many smaller enforcement actions each had led successfully in the past. ATF's management never addressed these deficiencies by giving the planners a supportive structure to supplement their own experiences. In addition, ATF's upper management did not actively oversee the development of the tactical plan, even though it involved the mobilization of more than 100 agents—the largest law enforcement effort ever mounted by ATF and one of the largest in the history of civilian law enforcement.

Section Three: Media Impact on ATF's Investigation

Part Two, Section Three analyzes the interaction between ATF and the media before and during ATF's raid on the Branch Davidian Compound. The interest of the media in covering suspected criminal conduct and official responses to it will frequently be at odds with law enforcement's desire to have the advantage of surprise in its activities. Here those interests clashed first before the raid, when ATF was unable to persuade the *Waco Tribune-Herald* to delay publication of its series. Given the substance of ATF's arguments for delay, the *Tribune-Herald*'s decision to go forward with the series is understandable. But had the negotiations been entrusted to those in ATF with more expertise in media relations, an arrangement that would have been more suitable to ATF and the *Tribune-Herald* might have been made.

On the day of the raid itself, media activity in the vicinity of the Branch Davidian Compound tipped off Koresh, allowing him to lay his ambush for ATF agents. KWTX and the *Tribune-Herald* roamed the roads in the vicinity of the Compound for more than an hour before the raid. A cameraman for KWTX told a local letter carrier, whom unbeknownst to him was a cult member, that a raid was imminent. The cult member in turn told Koresh, who then prepared his ambush.

Section Four: The Flawed Decision to Go Forward with the Raid

Part Two, Section Four addresses why ATF's raid commanders proceeded with the raid even though they should have realized that the raid had been compromised. The decision to proceed was tragically wrong, not just in retrospect, but based on what the decisionmakers knew at the time. It is now clear that those decisionmakers had sufficient information from the undercover agent to conclude that the raid had been compromised. They learned that Koresh had proclaimed that neither ATF nor the National Guard would ever get him, and that he had said "They're coming . . . the time has come. They're coming." In addition, the undercover agent told two of the raid commanders that Koresh "knows we're coming." Moreover, the actions and statements of certain raid commanders after hearing the undercover agent's report strongly suggest that they not only had reason to believe, but in fact did believe, that the raid had been compromised. Unfortunately, their response was to hurry up, rather than consult further with the undercover agent, case agent, surveillance agents and raid planners, and carefully assess the likely effect of the tip not only on Koresh but also on the prospects for the raid's success.

Section Four concludes, however, that the flawed decision to go forward was not simply a matter of bad judgment by the raid-day decisionmakers. It was, as well, the product of serious deficiencies in the intelligence gathering and processing structure, poor planning and personnel decisions, and a general failure of ATF management to check the momentum of the massive operation.

Section Five: Operational Security

Part Two, Section Five examines ATF's security practices from the beginning of the investigation through the day of the raid. It discredits certain reports that surfaced shortly after the raid claiming it had been compromised because ATF failed to maintain adequate security measures. Some actions undertaken by ATF, however, failed to preserve the secrecy of their investigation and the timing of the raid. The section examines the security issues and recommends that ATF improve its security practices.

Section Six: Treasury Oversight

The Office of the Assistant Secretary for Enforcement has oversight responsibility for the Bureau of Alcohol, Tobacco & Firearms. Although ATF's planned raid on the Branch Davidian Compound had been under consideration for months, the Office of Enforcement was not advised of the planned raid until fewer than 48 hours before it was to begin. Although the Office of Enforcement's approval was not sought, concerns about the action caused that office to direct that the raid not go forward. ATF then provided assurances that the raid was necessary, carefully planned and designed to minimize the risks to all involved. Based on these assurances the raid was permitted to proceed.

The Office of Enforcement had no regulation or guideline in place at the time of the raid that required ATF to notify it; instead, it relied on the discretion and judgment of ATF's bureau head. The responsibility for ATF's failure to notify the office until fewer than 48 hours before the raid rests with both ATF and the Office of Enforcement. Given how late in the process the office was notified, there was little opportunity for meaningful review or evaluation of ATF's planned operation. The office has instituted new guidelines and regular meetings with enforcement bureau heads to ensure early notification of significant operations that will permit meaningful oversight and review.

Section Seven: ATF Post-raid Dissemination of Misleading Information about the Raid and the Raid Plan

This section describes how in the wake of the tragedy on February 28, the raid commanders and their superiors in the ATF hierarchy endeavored to answer the call for explanations. Although they had access to the facts, critical aspects of the information that they provided to the public were misleading or wrong. In particular, two of the principal raid commanders appear to have engaged in a concerted effort to conceal their errors in judgment. Their conduct had the effect of wrongfully pointing the finger at a line agent as being responsible for the failed raid. And ATF's top management, perhaps out of a misplaced desire to protect the agency from criticism, offered accounts based on those raid commanders' statements, disregarding evidence that those statements were false. The section also examines the role two of the raid commanders played in the misleading alteration of the written raid plan after the raid had failed, and their failure to be candid with the Review when questioned about their role in altering the plan.

Section Eight: National Guard Support

In the aftermath of the raid, questions were raised about the method by which ATF secured the use of National Guard helicopters. Specifically, ATF was accused of misleading the National Guard by falsely representing that evidence of illegal drug activity would be found at the Compound. This section describes how law enforcement agencies can obtain support from the National Guard and how ATF obtained the use of the National Guard helicopters in the operation. The section concludes that, although the standards governing what constitutes a sufficient "drug nexus" to obtain National Guard support need clarification, ATF did not mislead the National Guard or misrepresent the facts concerning the nexus between the proposed raid and evidence of drug violations.

Part One

Section One: The Probable Cause Investigation

Preliminary Information: Initiation of the ATF Investigation of Koresh and his Followers

In late May 1992, Chief Deputy Sheriff Daniel Weyenberg of the McLennan County Sheriff's Department informed the Austin, Texas, ATF office that suspicious United Parcel Service (UPS) deliveries had been received by certain persons residing at the Compound, known as Mount Carmel. The Compound is located a few miles from Waco, which is in McLennan County. Several shipments of firearms worth more than $10,000, inert grenade casings, and a substantial quantity of black powder[5], an explosive, had been delivered to a metal building, known as the Mag Bag, used by Compound residents several miles from the Compound. (See Figure 1.) Because the residents of the Compound were constructing what appeared to be a barracks-type cinder-block structure, had buried a school bus to serve as both a firing range and a bunker (see Figure 2), and apparently were stockpiling arms and other weapons, Deputy Weyenberg asked ATF to investigate.

Special Agent Davy Aguilera of the Austin ATF office immediately began to make inquiries, with the encouragement of Assistant U.S. Attorney Bill Johnston. On June 4, Aguilera debriefed Lieutenant Gene Barber of the sheriff's department about the Compound, and Barber told Aguilera that the sheriff's department had referred the same matter previously to the Waco office of the Federal Bureau of Investigation (FBI).

---

[5] Black powder is an explosive under the federal explosive laws in 18 U.S.C. Chapter 40. See 18 U.S.C. §§841(d) and 844(j). Black powder in quantities of fifty pounds or less intended to be used solely for sporting, recreational or cultural purposes in antique firearms is generally exempt from the regulatory provisions of Chapter 40. See 18 U.S.C. §845(a)(5). Black powder, however, is not exempt from the criminal misuse provisions of 18 U.S.C. §844. Black powder can be combined with aluminum or magnesium powder, items that were delivered to the Compound, to create an enhanced explosive effect. In addition, when black powder is confined in a metal case or container, particularly when it is combined with aluminum or magnesium powder, it can explode violently when detonated, bursting or fragmenting the casing and producing high-velocity fragments.

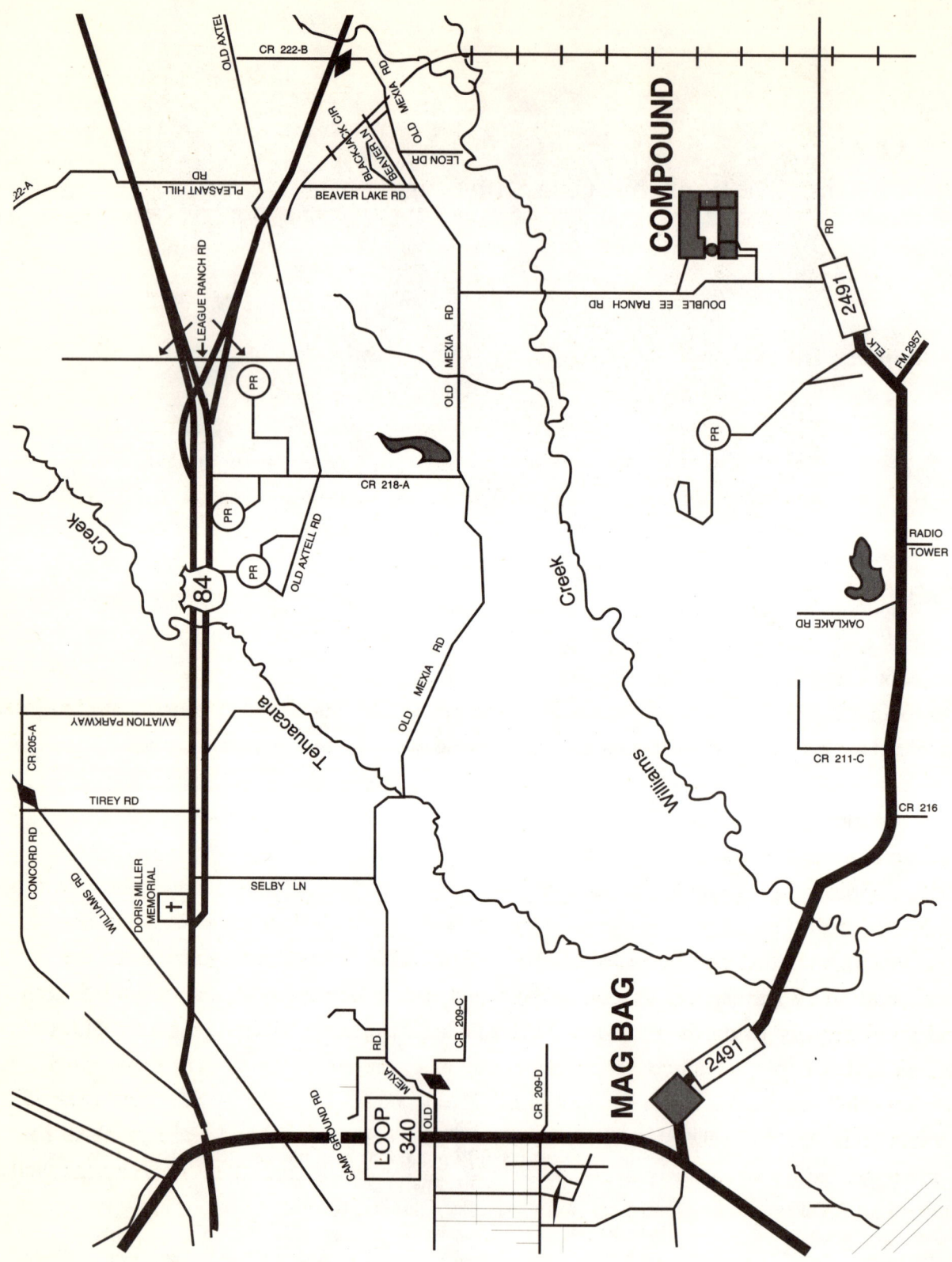

Figure 1: Location of Compound and Mag Bag

Figure 2: Buried school bus used as firing range and bunker (photographed after April 19, 1993 fire).

Although the FBI had formally opened a case, an agent from that office told Aguilera that the FBI was not actively pursuing any investigation.

Barber provided Aguilera with a detailed account of Koresh's alleged attempt to kill George Roden, the Branch Davidian leader whose parents established the Compound in 1959, and how Koresh seized control of the Compound and the Branch Davidians from Roden in 1987. (See Figure 3.) In support of that account, Barber gave Aguilera an "incident report" that had been prepared by the sheriff's department shortly after the confrontation. When deputy sheriffs arrived and ended the shoot-out, they found Koresh and six followers firing their rifles at Roden, who had already suffered a minor gunshot wound and was pinned down behind a tree at the Compound—which was then called "Rodenville." On the day of the shoot-out, Koresh and all of his followers were dressed in combat fatigues, had camouflaged their faces with black greasepaint before going to the Compound, and were armed with shotguns, .22-caliber rifles, and other weapons, as well as more than 3,000 rounds of unspent ammunition. (See Figure 4.)

Figure 3: David Koresh, second from left, posing with other Branch Davidians before the November 1987 shoot-out with George Roden.

Barber also told Aguilera more about UPS deliveries made to the Compound during the preceding months, which consisted of firearms components and materials used to make

Figure 4: Ammunition seized from Koresh and his followers after the November 1987 shoot-out with Roden.

explosives. On each delivery, followers of Koresh, including Steve Schneider, met the UPS driver at the Mag Bag (see Figure 5) and directed him to the Compound, where armed guards often kept watch. There, payment was made, usually in cash.

Using the UPS invoices, Aguilera began contacting firearms dealers and checking national registries to track down the specific firearms, firearms components, and explosives materials received by Koresh and his followers during the past year. After his initial conversation with Aguilera, Barber told Aguilera that the UPS driver delivered to Koresh a large quantity of powdered aluminum metal, a common ingredient in explosives, and 60 ammunition magazines for AR-15 rifles. Barber also related a confidential informant's report that Henry McMahon, a federally licensed firearms dealer who had recently moved to the Waco area from Florida, had recently bragged about selling a large number of

Figure 5: The Mag Bag after execution of search warrant.

weapons, including AK-47s, to Koresh.[6] (See Figure 6.) On June 9, Barber reported that automatic gunfire was heard recently at the Compound.

Aguilera determined that neither Koresh nor any of his followers then known to Aguilera were licensed federal arms dealers or manufacturers or had registered any National

---

[6] An AK-47 is a Soviet-designed selective fire machinegun that was the standard weapon issued to Eastern Bloc military personnel. Semiautomatic copies of the AK-47 (under a variety of model designations, all commonly referred to as AK-47s) were imported and sold commercially in the United States until their importation was prohibited in 1989. Possession of a semiautomatic copy of an AK-47 is legal and does not require registration pursuant to the National Firearms Act. However, a semiautomatic AK-47 can be converted into an illegal machinegun by making modifications to the receiver of the weapon and replacing certain internal parts with commonly available selective fire AK-47 parts.

Figure 6: AK-47 assault rifle.

Firearms Act weapons.[7] Using the shipping invoices, Aguilera also learned that Nesard Gun Parts Company had shipped to Koresh several "M-16 machinegun CAR kits" and several "M-16 machinegun E-2 kits," both of which are often called "conversion kits." Each of these conversion kits, when combined with the lower receiver of an AR-15 semiautomatic rifle, generally constitute all the parts from which a machinegun could be assembled.

Figure 7: M-16 assault rifle.

---

[7] The National Firearms Act, codified in Chapter 53 of Title 26, United States Code, sets out a comprehensive tax and registration system governing the manufacture, transfer and possession of certain firearms. Among other firearms covered by the Act are items classified as "destructive devices," including any explosive, incendiary, bomb, or grenade (26 U.S.C. § 5845(f)), and machineguns (26 U.S.C. §5845(b)). In addition, 18 U.S.C. §922(o) makes it unlawful for any person to transfer or possess a machinegun unless the machinegun was lawfully registered before May 19, 1986, the effective date of the Firearms Owners Protection Act of 1986. Before that Act, it was legal for citizens to make, sell, and possess machineguns as long as they complied with the taxing and registration requirements of the National Firearms Act. Since 1986, no machineguns have been permitted to be manufactured in the United States except those used by government agencies or for export.

An M-16 CAR kit comprises all component parts, with the exception of the lower receiver,[8] for the carbine version of an M-16. (See Figure 7.) The kit includes a complete upper receiver and barrel assembly, buttstock, recoil spring and buffer, M-16 hammer, trigger, disconnector, selector, M-16 automatic sear, pins, springs, trigger guard, magazine release, and bolt hold-open. The parts in the kit can be used with an AR-15 rifle or lower receiver to assemble a machinegun. The M-16 E-2 kit contains a similar set of parts; however, it is geared for use with an M-16 A-2 selective-fire rifle. The parts in the E-2 kit also can be used to convert an AR-15 into a machinegun. Although these kits can be used to maintain M-16 machineguns produced before 1986 and therefore can be sold lawfully, in practice they are commonly used to convert semiautomatic weapons into machineguns. Such kits, of course, only have a lawful, practical utility if the purchaser already owns a registered machinegun. Because neither Koresh nor any of his known followers owned such a registered weapon, Aguilera inferred that the kits Koresh was steadily acquiring were not being used for legal purposes.

On the basis of this information, Aguilera formally initiated a case on June 9, 1992. Within a week, his immediate supervisors and Phillip Chojnacki, the Special Agent in Charge (SAC) of the Houston ATF office, approved this initiation and classified the case as "sensitive," thus ensuring a higher degree of oversight from the SAC and ATF headquarters. ATF regulations classify cases meeting certain criteria as "sensitive" or "significant," and investigating agents are charged with keeping supervising officials informed about those cases. The investigation of Koresh and his followers, which potentially involved a large amount of weapons and explosives in the possession of a potentially volatile group with strong professed religious beliefs, met ATF guidelines for treatment as both sensitive and significant.

The primary violations within ATF's jurisdiction that Aguilera would be pursuing were (1) the illegal manufacture of machineguns from component parts[9] and (2) the illegal

---

[8] A receiver is a part of a firearm that normally houses the barrel and bolt assembly. Many modern military-style rifles are constructed with a horizontal split in the receiver—hence the terms "upper receiver" and "lower receiver." With respect to the AR-15, which has a split-receiver design, the lower receiver, by legal definition, constitutes a "firearm" for purposes of federal firearms laws. See 18 U.S.C. § 921(a)(3)(B).

[9] 18 U.S.C. § 922(o)(1) provides that, save for certain specified exceptions: "it shall be unlawful for any person to transfer or possess a machinegun." The National Firearms Act makes it unlawful for any person other than a qualified manufacturer to make a machinegun without first filing an application to make and register the item with, and receiving approval from, the Secretary of the Treasury. 26 U.S.C. §5822 and

manufacture and possession of destructive devices, including explosive bombs and explosive grenades and the materials necessary to produce such items.[10]

The ATF Investigation and Development of Probable Cause to Arrest Koresh and Search Premises Under his Control

Additional Weapons and Explosives Shipments

Initially, Aguilera focused on the paper trail generated by the weapons and explosives purchased by Koresh and his followers. Aguilera determined that Olympic Arms had recently shipped a substantial quantity of AR-15 parts to the Mag Bag, and he also learned that Henry McMahon had sold more than a dozen AR-15 lower receivers to Koresh a few months earlier. As Aguilera learned from previous investigations, someone with access to metal milling machines and lathes and with the knowledge to use them, can readily convert AR-15 semiautomatic rifles into fully automatic weapons (machineguns)

5861(f). For purposes of Section 922(o) and the National Firearms Act, 'machinegun' means any weapon which shoots, is designed to shoot, or can be readily restored to shoot, automatically, more than one shot without manual reloading, by a single function of the trigger." The term includes "the frame or receiver of any such weapon, any part designed and intended solely and exclusively, or combination of parts designed and intended for use in converting a weapon into a machinegun, and any combination of parts from which a machinegun can be assembled if such parts are in the possession or under the control of a person." 26 U.S.C. §5845(b).

A part not yet assembled into a machinegun can still be illegal if it is (1) "designed solely or exclusively for use in converting a weapon into a machinegun"; (2) a "combination of parts designed and intended for use in converting a weapon into a machinegun"; or (3) "any combination of parts from which a machinegun is assembled" if one person has possession or control of all of the parts. See *United States* v. *Bradley,* 892 F.2d 634, 635 (7th Cir. 1990).

[10] The National Firearms Act makes it unlawful for any person other than a qualified manufacturer to make a destructive device without first filing an application to make and register the item with, and receiving approval from, the Secretary of the Treasury. 26 U.S.C. § 5822 and 5861(f). In addition, the National Firearms Act makes it unlawful to possess any unregistered firearm, including, for example, components that readily could be assembled into a hand grenade or any other destructive device. 26 U.S.C. §§ 5845(a)(8) and (f) and 5861(b), (c), (d) and (e). 18 U.S.C. § 922(a)(1)(A) provides that "[i]t shall be unlawful for any person except a licensed importer, licensed manufacturer, or licensed dealer to engage in the business of importing, manufacturing, or dealing in firearms, or in the course of such business to ship, transport, or receive any firearm in interstate or foreign commerce." 18 U.S.C. § 921(a)(3) defines "firearm" to include, among other things, "destructive devices." In turn, "destructive device" is defined to encompass "any explosive, incendiary, or poison gas bomb or grenade ... [or] ... any combination of parts either designed or intended for use in converting any device into any [of the above destructive devices]." 18 U.S.C. § 921(a)(4). 18 U.S.C. §§ 842(a) and (j) make it unlawful for any person "to engage in the business of importing, manufacturing, or dealing in explosive materials without a license" or "to store any explosive material in a manner not in conformity with regulations promulgated by the Secretary."

similar to M-16 machineguns by using certain key parts legally available, frequently parts designed for use with an M-16. It is worth noting that there is no practical reason to exchange most AR-15 parts on an intact AR-15 weapon for M-16 parts other than for purposes of converting the weapon into a machinegun. The M-16 parts do not improve the performance of the weapon if used in a semiautomatic mode. For example, the AR-15 bolt assembly performs substantially better in a semiautomatic mode than does the M-16 bolt assembly when installed on an AR-15.

Compliance Inspection of Henry McMahon

On July 30, Aguilera, posing as an ATF compliance officer, joined Jimmy Ray Skinner, an ATF compliance officer, to inspect the premises of Henry McMahon, who was doing business as Hewitt Hand Guns out of his home. Aguilera's review of McMahon's records revealed that he had sold 36 firearms to a "Vernon Howell," who was not identified as "David Koresh," and sold others to persons Aguilera knew to be Koresh's followers. Moreover, approximately 65 AR-15 lower receivers reflected in McMahon's inventory records were not in his physical stock. McMahon claimed that these firearms were being stored at the house of his preacher, whom he identified as David Koresh, apparently suggesting that Koresh and Howell were two different persons.

Although McMahon was out of compliance and was therefore subject to fines, Aguilera and the compliance officer ended the audit without imposing any penalties on McMahon to avoid arousing his suspicion. About a month later, Skinner returned and McMahon presented him with receipts and ATF forms reflecting the sale of the missing 65 lower receivers to "Vernon Howell."

The Sounds of Machinegun Fire and Explosives

Further evidence that Koresh and his followers were manufacturing illegal machineguns came when Aguilera interviewed a neighbor who had served in an Army artillery unit and was familiar with the sound of automatic weapons fire. The neighbor reported that since early 1992, he had frequently heard spurts of weapons fire coming from the Compound at night, including .50-caliber (See Figure 8) and automatic weapons fire, and that residents of the Compound had discharged semiautomatics on July 4. In mid-November, a deputy sheriff reported that while on patrol a few days earlier, he had heard a loud explosion at the Compound, accompanied by a large cloud of gray smoke. Neither Koresh nor any of his followers had a license or a permit to use explosives at the Compound.

Figure 8: .50-caliber rifle.

Interviews of Former Cult Members

Aguilera also sought information from former cult members, who gave him some insight into the extraordinary degree to which Koresh dominated the lives of Compound residents. Cult members surrendered all their assets to Koresh and permitted him to have sex with all the female members of the cult. While reports that Koresh was permitted to sexually and physically abuse children were not evidence that firearms or explosives violations were occurring, they showed Koresh to have set up a world of his own, where legal prohibitions were disregarded freely.

In early November, Aguilera interviewed Isabel and Guillermo Andrade, then residing in California, whose two daughters were living at the Compound. They told Aguilera that Koresh had sexual relations regularly with all of the women at the Compound, including girls younger than 16 years of age. "Annulling" the marriages of couples in the cult, Koresh prohibited the men residing at the Compound from having sexual relations with their "former" wives. The Andrades informed Aguilera that Koresh had fathered a child with their daughter Katherine. The child's birth certificate, like the birth certificates of several other children recently born to women residing at the Compound, listed the father as unknown.

In early December 1992, Aguilera interviewed Jeannine Bunds and her daughter, Robyn, both of whom had left the Compound within the past two years, and Mrs. Bunds' son, David, who had left earlier. The three were living in California. Both Mrs. Bunds and her daughter confirmed earlier accounts Aguilera had received about Koresh's sexual domination of female residents of the Compound, including minors. They estimated that Koresh had fathered at least 15 children at the Compound. All three said they had seen Koresh in possession of numerous weapons, including machineguns, and that Koresh had often led cult members in live-fire shooting exercises. The Bundses and other former cult members identified specific weapons they had seen at the Compound from photographs the agents showed them. The Bundses noted that Henry McMahon had participated in some of the shooting exercises.

The Bundses also reported that Koresh frequently directed his followers to maintain an armed guard at the Compound 24 hours a day and that he possessed a loaded firearm at all times. According to Mrs. Bunds, a registered nurse, Koresh on one occasion told her that he was preparing a "hit list" to eliminate former cult members who were complaining to law enforcement authorities and the media about his sexual practices and accumulation of weapons. Mrs. Bunds also mentioned that when she had told Koresh that she was having difficulty with her children, Koresh asked her whether she would kill her children if God asked her to do so. She told him she would not.

Mrs. Bunds told of seeing "pineapple grenades" at the Compound (see Figure 9) and David Bunds remembered seeing Branch Davidians with AK-47s, pump shotguns, revolvers, pistols, and other weapons. David and Robyn related how in June 1992 they had found a machinegun conversion kit at a house in California they had recently taken over from followers of Koresh. Shortly thereafter, several Branch Davidians from the Compound retrieved the kit. David Bunds also related a telephone conversation he had had with his father, Donald, when he called his father at the Compound in spring 1992. Donald Bunds told his son that he was armed and prepared to die for Koresh and that he would resist authorities if they tried to arrest him.

The Bundses' accounts were consistent with information obtained from Poia Vaega, another former resident of the Compound, who had moved to New Zealand. She recalled how Koresh had passed an AK-47 machinegun around to his followers during one of his Bible study sessions and how Koresh regularly had them watch violent war movies that he called "training films" to prepare for "the war to come." Vaega said that both she and her sister, another former cult member, had been subjected on several occasions to physical and

Figure 9: Typical "pineapple" type grenades.

sexual abuse by Koresh and one of his followers before she left the Compound in 1991 and that she had been physically restrained from leaving for more than three months before she gained her freedom. Her account was corroborated by her sister.

In December 1992, Aguilera also began a dialogue with Marc Breault, a former cult member living in Australia, which continued until the ATF raid on February 28, 1993. Breault had already given information about Koresh and the Branch Davidians to Mark England, a reporter for the *Waco Tribune-Herald*. Breault, who left the Compound in 1989, confirmed that Koresh was the undisputed leader of the Branch Davidians and stated that Koresh frequently had sex with minors residing in the Compound and that several minors had given birth to babies fathered by him. Breault also told Aguilera that from time to time Koresh had physically abused children who were younger than three years of age when they cried during his Bible study sessions. According to an affidavit Breault filed in an Australian court, which incorporated affidavits by several other former cult members and which Aguilera obtained, Koresh paddled the children with a wooden paddle until their buttocks were "black and blue all over, so that they even bled." Breault's account, which he confirmed in conversations with Aguilera, was corroborated by other former cult members, including Poia Vaega and members of her family.

Breault also reported that Koresh had posted armed guards around the Compound and instructed them to "shoot to kill" anyone who attempted to enter the gate of the Compound. Many cult members carried firearms, including AK-47s. In fact, according to Breault and the sheriff's department, on one occasion in 1988, a cult member had taken a shot at a newspaper delivery person. Breault also related how Koresh had expressed disdain for gun control laws, frequently proclaiming that he wanted to make machineguns, grenades, and explosive devices at the Compound and bragging how easy it was to convert a semiautomatic weapon into a fully automatic machinegun. In particular, Breault stated that Koresh mocked gun control laws that permitted easy acquisition of all component parts necessary to make a machinegun, yet made possession of either all of those parts or a fully assembled and operable machinegun unlawful. Finally, Breault noted that when Koresh took over the Compound, he told Breault that he had found methamphetamine manufacturing facilities and recipes on the premises. Although Koresh claimed to have turned over these materials to the sheriff's department, according to Breault and the sheriff's department, he never had done so.

Visits from the Texas Department of Protective and Regulatory Services

In light of reports that Koresh might have been engaging in sexual activities with minors, ATF contacted Joyce Sparks, a caseworker with the Texas Department of Protective and Regulatory Services who had been investigating several anonymous reports of the same conduct. Sparks related that, although she had visited the Compound several times in 1992, she had been escorted carefully through the Compound on a staged tour each time. Even though she had not found sufficient reliable evidence to press child or sexual abuse charges against Koresh or any of his followers, she did learn something about Koresh's preparations for an armed struggle.

One child, approximately seven years old, told Sparks that he could not wait to grow up so that he could have a "long gun" as did all the men in the Compound; the boy explained that the men practiced with these weapons regularly. In addition, during one of her guided tours of the Compound, Sparks strayed from the designated path and managed to see the buried school bus. At one end of the bus was a large object riddled with bullet holes, and nearby were at least three "long guns."

In her own dealings with Koresh, Sparks saw a dangerous propensity toward violence. During one of her conversations with him, he proclaimed to her: "My time is coming. When I reveal myself as the messenger and my time comes, what happens will make the riots in L.A. pale in comparison."

Backgrounds of Compound Residents

Aguilera checked the backgrounds of those he identified as current residents of the Compound. He determined that several either had been arrested, convicted, or were under investigation for crimes ranging from fraud to smuggling and narcotics offenses. More than 40 residents were foreign nationals, and many of those were illegal aliens. It is unlawful for either an illegal alien or a person convicted of a crime punishable by more than one year of imprisonment to possess any type of firearm.[11]

Reports of ATF Experts

During December 1992 and January 1993, Aguilera obtained technical assistance from several ATF experts. An ATF firearms expert in Washington, D.C., confirmed that the weapons components Koresh had purchased could be used easily to produce illegal machineguns and that the manner in which Koresh had acquired these components was similar to the method used by other manufacturers of unlawful machineguns investigated by ATF. An explosives expert at the ATF lab near San Francisco reported that several of the items Koresh had received, such as the large quantities of black powder and igniter cord (a burning-type fuse), were explosives requiring proper registration and storage. The explosives expert explained that black powder and inert grenade shells, both of which Koresh had received in substantial quantities, are used commonly by illegal arms manufacturers to produce live explosive grenades. These grenades, in turn, are destructive devices, the possession of which without proper registration is illegal. The explosives expert also informed Aguilera that other chemicals Koresh had obtained were common ingredients in homemade explosives.

Before Aguilera received the written report from the explosives expert in San Francisco, who specialized in evaluating the practical utility of various items used to produce explosives, the explosives expert in Washington, who had a different specialty, told Aguilera that he was unable to conclude that Koresh had accumulated sufficient materials to manufacture explosives. This expert had noted, however, that Koresh could make unlawful explosives by acquiring some additional materials.

The experts also gave Aguilera additional information about the arms dealers who were supplying Koresh. The owner of Nesard Gun Parts Company, Barrington, Illinois,

---

[11] See 18 U.S.C. § 922(g)

who in 1992 had shipped M-16 CAR kits, M-16 E-2 kits, and a grenade launcher to Koresh, had been convicted three years earlier of violations of federal firearms laws. The company had unlawfully supplied one of its customers with AR-15 receivers and certain parts kits that together comprised all the component parts necessary to assemble a "short rifle," a firearm that must be registered pursuant to 26 U.S.C. §§ 5841 and 5845(a)(3). Another of Koresh's suppliers, Shooters Equipment Company, Richland, South Carolina, had been the subject of several ATF investigations, including one that culminated in the seizure of illegal machineguns and silencers in August 1992. At that time, the agents also found large quantities of M-16 and AK-47 machinegun parts and kits to convert AR-15 semiautomatic weapons into unlawful machineguns.

In December, ATF began developing plans for serving the warrants, the "tactical planning" aspect of the investigation. This aspect of the investigation is described in the following section of this report. Aguilera's superiors at the ATF Houston field office directed him to continue developing probable cause for the warrants. Although Assistant U.S. Attorney Johnston was satisfied that probable cause existed in November 1992, it was not until Aguilera and Chojnacki briefed ATF Director Stephen Higgins and ATF Associate Director (Law Enforcement) Daniel Hartnett on February 11 and 12, 1993, in Washington, D.C., that ATF authorized Aguilera to present the information to the U.S. Attorney's Office for the purpose of obtaining the warrants.

The David Block Interview

In late January 1993, Aguilera interviewed David Block, who had been a Branch Davidian from 1981 through June 1992. Block had lived at the Compound for several months before he "escaped." He reported having often seen two Branch Davidians, Donald Bunds, a mechanical engineer, and Jeff Little using a metal milling machine and metal lathe to produce weapons. On several occasions, Bunds also had used an AutoCAD (i.e., computer-aided design) software package—which allows mechanical engineers to design objects by providing a three-dimensional picture and precise measurements of the object being designed—to design a "grease gun." Grease gun is the nickname for the M3 and M3A1 .45-caliber military submachineguns used by American forces during World War II. The parts of this grease gun included a cylindrical tube with a bolt-cocking groove carved into the side and a template to fit around the tube to enable it to be used on the milling machine. Bunds had explained that Koresh wanted him to design a weapon that could be manufactured at the Compound.

Block also recounted that Koresh had asked residents of the Compound how to manufacture grenades and had discussed activating a shipment of inert grenades he had received. Koresh received further technical assistance in spring 1992 when a relative of one of the Branch Davidians, a survivalist with expertise in firearms and explosives, visited the Compound.

Block described the potentially devastating arsenal Koresh was amassing in the Compound. He had seen one high-caliber weapon—either a .50-caliber rifle mounted on a bi-pod or a "British Boys" .52-caliber antitank rifle—and had heard about other .50-caliber weapons stored on the premises. Koresh frequently had expressed interest in converting these high-caliber weapons into unlawful machineguns. Block also had seen approximately 15 AR-15s, 25 AK-47s, several 9mm pistols, and three "streetsweepers." A streetsweeper is a 12-gauge, 12-shot shotgun with a spring-driven drum magazine and folding buttstock. Each time the trigger is released after firing a shot the magazine rotates to position the next shot for firing. Block reported that Koresh would often fire weapons at the Compound's "range" and that he posted armed guards at the Compound every night.

The Undercover House and Special Agent Rodriguez

Aguilera continued to gather information about Koresh's illegal activities even as ATF's focus began to change from building a case to planning an enforcement operation. After ATF established an "undercover house" near the Compound on January 11, 1993 (see Figure 10) one of the undercover agents posted there, Special Agent Robert Rodriguez, began to seek opportunities to visit the Compound and talk to cult members. On January 28, pretending to be interested in purchasing a horse walker that was on the Compound, Rodriguez spoke for the first time with Koresh. Rodriguez, who had read portions of the Bible in preparation for this encounter, discussed the Book of Revelations with Koresh. Koresh showed Rodriguez his motorcycles and invited him to join the cult's Bible study group. Shortly thereafter, Rodriguez attended his first Bible study session.

After a few more visits to the Compound, Rodriguez attended another Bible study session on February 17 and was invited to return the next day. Between Bible study sessions, Rodriguez practiced shooting cans with his rifle near the undercover house in an effort to further pique Koresh's interest. Rodriguez spent three hours in Bible study the next day and emerged with an invitation to shoot with Koresh on the 19th.

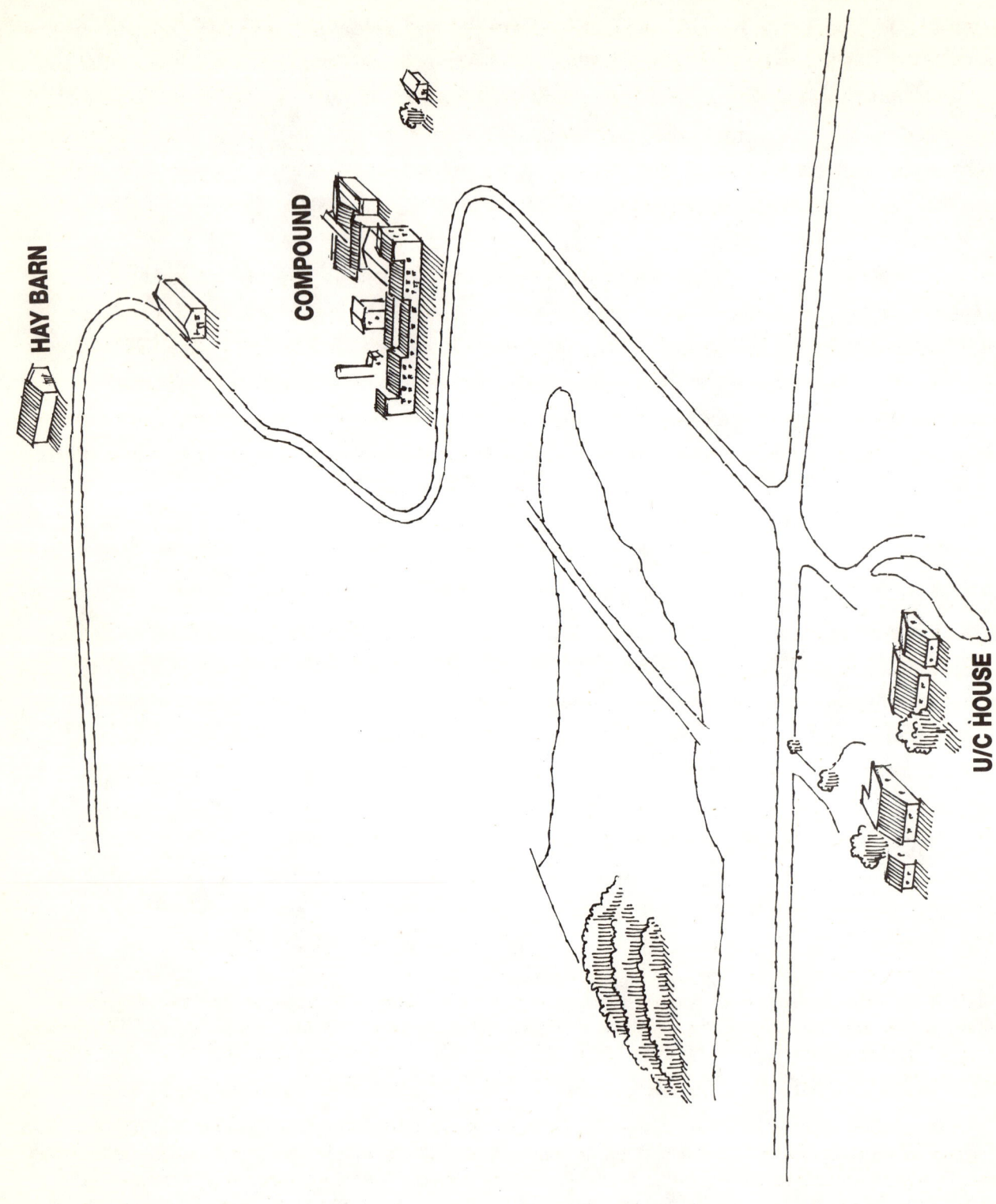

Figure 10: Illustration depicting the undercover house, Compound, and hay barn (not to scale).

Koresh greeted Rodriguez and another agent whom Rodriguez had brought along. Koresh told Rodriguez he had watched him through his binoculars and saw him shooting on the 17th. Koresh brought the agents, both of whom were carrying AR-15 semiautomatic rifles, to the shooting range, and they practiced shooting. Koresh examined in detail and expressed familiarity with Rodriguez's semiautomatic rifle and .38-caliber pistol. Koresh also established himself as an excellent shot and the owner of several weapons, including two Sig-Sauer pistols and a Ruger 10/22-caliber rifle.

Over the next 10 days, Rodriguez visited the Compound several times and often engaged in lengthy conversations with Koresh. During these conversations, Koresh repeatedly confirmed his strong interest in weapons and his disdain for federal laws regulating firearms and explosives. Among other things, Koresh discussed firearms components in great detail, including "hell-fire triggers"[12] and "drop-in sears,"[13] the latter of which are devices used exclusively to convert semiautomatic weapons into machineguns.

Koresh falsely claimed that the possession of an unregistered drop-in sear was lawful as long as the possessor did not also possess an AR-15 rifle. Possession of an unregistered drop-in sear is unlawful regardless of whether the possessor also possesses an AR-15.[14] Nonetheless, he did exhibit profound knowledge of firearms, the nation's gun laws, and methods commonly used to evade those laws. And during a visit Rodriguez made to the Compound on February 23, Koresh showed him a videotape produced by Gun Owners of America, which portrayed ATF as an evil agency that threatened the liberty of U.S. citizens.

---

[12] A "hell-fire trigger" is an external attachment designed to return the trigger to the forward position more quickly after each firing, thus enabling a semiautomatic weapon to be fired more quickly. The device does not enable a semiautomatic weapon to fire as rapidly as a typical machinegun, and its use does not change the classification of a semiautomatic weapon into an unlawful weapon.

[13] A "drop-in sear" is a part or combination of parts placed inside the weapon to convert a semiautomatic weapon into a machinegun. As a rule, the term refers to the "AR-15 drop-in auto sear," which was designed specifically to convert an AR-15 rifle into a machinegun. Because the sear is designed and intended exclusively for use in converting a weapon into a machinegun, it is considered an unlawful machinegun if it was manufactured after 1981 and not registered properly. 26 U.S.C. §§ 5841 and 5845(b); ATF Ruling 81-4.

[14] 26 U.S.C. §§ 5841 and 5845(b); ATF Ruling 81-4.

Part One

Section Two: The Decisionmaking Process Leading to Forceful Execution of Warrants

In late November 1992, Assistant U.S. Attorney Bill Johnston in Waco reviewed evidence that had been developed by ATF and advised Special Agent Davy Aguilera that, although the investigation should be continued, there already was sufficient evidence to meet the threshold of probable cause for a search warrant. Once Aguilera reported Johnston's opinion to Assistant Special Agent in Charge (ASAC) Chuck Sarabyn (Houston), who had been supervising the investigation, tactical planning for an enforcement operation began in earnest.

Consideration of Tactical Options

The December 4, 1992, Meeting

Directing Aguilera to focus his attention on the probable cause investigation, Sarabyn quickly assumed responsibility for tactical planning. Any enforcement action, Sarabyn decided, would require at least one Special Response Team (SRT). Such teams are specially trained groups of ATF agents with expertise in executing difficult tactical missions—principally high-risk warrants. Sarabyn organized a planning meeting to take place in Houston on December 4.

While Sarabyn could not attend the meeting, his superior Phillip Chojnacki, Special Agent in Charge (SAC) of ATF's Houston Division, did attend, along with Ted Royster, SAC of the Dallas Division; William Buford, Resident Agent in Charge (RAC)[15] of the Little Rock ATF office, a co-team leader of the New Orleans SRT, and an Army Special Forces combat veteran; Jerry Petrilli, RAC of the Albuquerque ATF office, team leader of

---

[15] A "RAC" is the resident agent in charge of an ATF field office, who acts under supervision of a larger field division, in this case Houston. Buford was a founder of the ATF SRT program.

the Dallas SRT, and a Marine Corps combat veteran; and James Cavanaugh, ASAC of the Dallas ATF office. Two other ATF agents, Kenny King, a group supervisor in the New Orleans ATF office, co-team leader of the New Orleans SRT, and a Marine Corps combat veteran; and Curtis Williams, a group supervisor in the Houston ATF office and team leader of the Houston SRT, who had five years of experience in the tactical division of the Dallas Police Department; both of whom would later assist in tactical planning, did not attend this meeting.

Each of the planners had extensive experience with ATF, collectively having led hundreds of high-risk raids to search for unlawful weapons. As a group, particularly the SRT leaders who formed the core of the tactical planning team, they had other substantial law enforcement and military experience as well. Only Buford, however, had planned or participated in a tactical operation of the magnitude that eventually would be contemplated for Waco—the 1985 siege by ATF and the FBI of the 360-acre Arkansas compound of the white supremacist group The Covenant, the Sword, and the Arm of the Lord (CSA). To execute a warrant at the heavily armed and fortified CSA compound, which had been surrounded by concealed bunkers and land mines, Buford helped devise a plan that established an armed perimeter around the premises. After three days of negotiations, the besieged group members surrendered, but not before they had destroyed many of their illegal firearms, including silencers and automatic weapons. Buford often recalled this siege while the planners were considering various ways to execute warrants at Koresh's Compound.[16]

At the December 4 meeting, Aguilera briefed the planners about his investigation of Koresh. Based on reports from recent visitors to the Compound, he estimated that 75 people lived at the Compound, including large numbers of women and children, all of whom were fiercely loyal to Koresh and devoted to his religious teachings. Aguilera also reviewed the layout of the 77-acre site, particularly its main structure's fortress-like construction and prominent multistory tower. (See Figures 11 and 12.)[17] After hearing Aguilera describe the challenge they had before them, the planners began to consider what they deemed the two

---

[16] Johnston informed ATF early in the investigation that he would not authorize a search warrant for the Branch Davidian Compound if it was to be executed through a siege-style operation. He, too, feared that a siege strategy would permit Koresh and his followers to destroy evidence and make prosecution more difficult, as happened in the CSA case. Despite Johnston's views, however, ATF's tactical planners seriously considered a siege plan.

[17] The Compound had evolved from a series of free-standing houses. After Koresh took control of the Compound he and his followers dismantled the homes and built the single structure. (See Figures 13 and 14.)

Figure 11: Main Compound building (front side).

Figure 12: Rear of Compound.

Figure 13: Houses on Mt. Carmel site before construction of Compound.

Figure 14: Mt. Carmel site after construction of Compound before houses were dismantled.

principal ways to execute a search warrant: a dynamic entry (raid) or a siege.

Regardless of how the warrant would be executed, ATF's planners decided that execution would be far easier if Koresh were not at the Compound when the agents arrived. Joyce Sparks of the Texas Department of Protective and Regulatory Services had told Aguilera that Koresh rarely, if ever, left the Compound. When they learned this, the planners asked Aguilera to find a way to lure Koresh away from the Compound immediately before the warrant was to be executed. After Aguilera discussed with Sparks her visits to the Compound and Koresh's sexual abuse of minors, the planners suggested that Aguilera inquire whether the Department of Protective and Regulatory Services could schedule a meeting with Koresh on the day of the operation. They also asked whether Koresh could be brought out of the Compound with a grand jury subpoena. Other ways to get Koresh out were also briefly considered, including staging a school bus crash or helicopter crash near the Compound.

Concerned that much of Aguilera's knowledge of the Compound's design and the daily routines of its residents was somewhat dated, Aguilera and Earl Dunagan, acting RAC of the Austin ATF office, recommended that surveillance of the Compound be instituted and that additional information be sought concerning the living arrangements inside, the attitudes of the cult members, the distribution and storage of the cult's weapons and ammunition, and the interior design of the Compound.

At the conclusion of the meeting, Buford, Petrilli, Williams, and King, the leaders of the SRTs that likely would participate in the enforcement action, were assigned to develop a plan for either a siege or a dynamic entry. During tactical planning and on the day of the raid, both Buford and King shared command responsibility for the New Orleans SRT. Sarabyn directed the planning effort, with Buford taking the role of principal tactical contributor. From this point forward, the leaders of the SRTs, who specialized in dynamic entries, would be a driving force in shaping the tactical options and selecting the dynamic entry strategy.

The Late December and Early January Meetings

In late December, the tactical planners met in Austin and reviewed additional information that Aguilera had obtained through his investigation, including reports of interviews of former cult members and new photographs of the Compound. During this time frame, the SRT leaders—Buford, Williams, Petrilli, and King—as well as Sarabyn drove to Waco to survey the Compound. Until this point, the planners thought that a siege would be the best tactical approach, particularly if Koresh could be arrested at a place other than the Compound. After the planners saw the terrain, however, which offered little cover from the dominating Compound, and after considering the injuries that could be inflicted with the long-range, powerful .50-caliber weapons the planners thought Koresh possessed, they began to reconsider this option. Even if a perimeter could be established, they reasoned, it would have to be quite large and therefore difficult to maintain.

In early January, when the tactical planners next convened, they continued to discuss the practicality of imposing a siege if the Branch Davidians resisted the peaceful execution of a search warrant. With an eye toward a siege plan, Sarabyn soon thereafter arranged for ATF to submit a formal request to the Regional Logistics Support Office—the office through which the Department of Defense provides nonoperational military support to civilian law enforcement agencies—for seven Bradley Fighting Vehicles, which were believed to have sufficient armor to withstand .50-caliber fire. The planners, however, were still uncertain about which tactical option was preferable and sought additional information. To this end, pursuant to Aguilera's and Dunagan's recommendation and to address a recent request from ATF's Associate Director (Law Enforcement) Daniel Hartnett for additional evidence to establish probable cause, the decision was made to establish an undercover operation near the Branch Davidian Compound.[18]

Interviews with Former Cult Members

Meanwhile, at the request of the tactical planners, Buford and Aguilera interviewed several former cult members in California. The interviewees—most of whom Aguilera had already spoken with—included Marc Breault, four members of the Bunds family, and David Block. Aguilera and Buford also interviewed Isabel Andrade, who at the time had two daughters living at the Compound. Also interviewed were Sandra Leake and Jaylene Ojena, close friends of the Andrades who were working with them to gain the return of the

---

[18] After the planners shifted their focus to a raid, an ATF military liaison submitted to appropriate military authorities in mid-February a superseding request that did not include the Bradleys. ATF did, however, receive other support from the military, including several flights over the Compound and the Mag Bag to produce aerial reconnaissance photographs, interpretation of the photos, and use of the Thermal Imaging System during flights to identify "hot spots" at the Compound. These flights were directed toward the search for armed guards and drug manufacturing facilities. In addition, the military provided ATF with the Military Operation Urban Terrain training facility at Fort Hood for training purposes and helped ATF set up the facility to resemble the Compound.

Andrades' two daughters. Both Andrade and Ojena had visited the Andrade daughters, Katherine and Jennifer, at the Compound in early November 1992.

These interviews confirmed earlier intelligence concerning the level of weaponry at the Compound. Koresh and his followers were known to fire assault weapons and machineguns, and Block had seen what he believed to be a .50- or .52-caliber weapon mounted on a bipod, as well as several dozen rifles, including AK-47s and AR-15s—many of which he believed were fully automatic.

Where these weapons were stored was not clear. According to Block, Koresh usually kept the weapons next to his room, which he decreed off limits to most Compound residents. From time to time, Koresh would issue AK-47s and other rifles to most of the men and some of the women living at the Compound, and would collect them later. Residents who received "long guns" in this fashion usually kept them under their beds. Block did not know whether Koresh also distributed ammunition; however, he did note that several cult members were allowed to keep their own private small-caliber weapons.

Several members of the Bunds family corroborated Block's account of this intermittent weapons distribution. However, when the Bunds family had last resided at the Compound, the weapons distributed had been less sophisticated, consisting mainly of shotguns and handguns, rather than AK-47s and AR-15s. When interviewed by telephone in New Zealand in mid-November, Poia Vaega, a former cult member with several relatives still living at the Compound said that her husband, another former cult member, "has reason to believe that the guns were stored in the quarters that [Koresh] was sleeping in."

These interviews confirmed the dangers of a dynamic entry or a siege, especially if Koresh was in the Compound to provide leadership when a warrant was executed. Indeed, Aguilera reported, "Block left the cult group because [Koresh] would always remind them that if they were to have a confrontation with the local or federal authorities, that the group should be ready to fight and resist." Similarly, Aguilera's report of his January 8 interview with Breault noted that Koresh would make it a point to emphasize the importance of protecting themselves and that if the cult members were attacked, they would have to arm themselves to defend Koresh and their children. Nonetheless, as far as the former cult members knew, Koresh had not specifically trained his followers to repulse law enforcement officers or other visitors perceived to be hostile.

Several former cult members, most forcefully Breault, noted the distinct possibility that Koresh might respond to a siege by leading his followers in a mass suicide; Breault expressed a particular fear for the children at the Compound. One child who had lived at the Compound told a California police officer, who in turn informed Aguilera, that she had been trained by Koresh and his "Mighty Men"—Koresh's closest and most trusted advisers—to commit suicide in several different ways, including placing the barrel of a handgun in her mouth and pulling the trigger.

Block related that Koresh had accumulated at least a three-month supply of military rations, known as Meals Ready to Eat (MREs), and that the Compound had its own source of well water. This was consistent with the report of Joyce Sparks that during one of her visits she had observed large stores of foodstuffs in the Compound's storage area. Breault and Block emphasized that the Branch Davidians were already familiar with a rudimentary, isolated lifestyle and that the Compound had no indoor plumbing, air conditioning, or heating. The room in which Koresh slept, however, was equipped with air conditioning, heating, a stereo, a television, and other amenities. A siege would thus not impose substantial new deprivations on Koresh's followers.

The former cult members discussed the daily routine and physical layout of the Compound. Block reported that only women and children lived on the second floor and in the large tower—in quarters that Koresh barred the men from entering—and that the tower was not used as a watchtower. The men lived on the first floor of the Compound, in a different section from and a floor below Koresh's "arms room." (See Figures 15-17.) According to Breault and other former cult members, worship services were held between 9:00 and 10:00 a.m. each day, roughly three hours after dawn, after which the men began their day's work (except on Saturday, the Branch Davidian Sabbath).

The agents also learned some details about the work the Compound's men performed daily. McLennan County Deputy Sheriff Weyenberg informed Aguilera that daytime reconnaissance flights over the Compound had revealed men working in a construction pit. When visiting the Compound for two days in early November 1992, Isabel Andrade and Jaylene Ojena also had seen men in the pit building a new structure adjacent to the Compound's main building. (See Figure 18.) For the two months before the raid, the construction pit was an excavated area next to the Compound's southwest corner. The pit was connected to the Compound's front wing by an underground passage constructed from the shell of a buried school bus. The pit was rectangular, about 15 feet deep, 100 feet long, and 45 feet wide. Between mid-January, when the undercover house was established, and

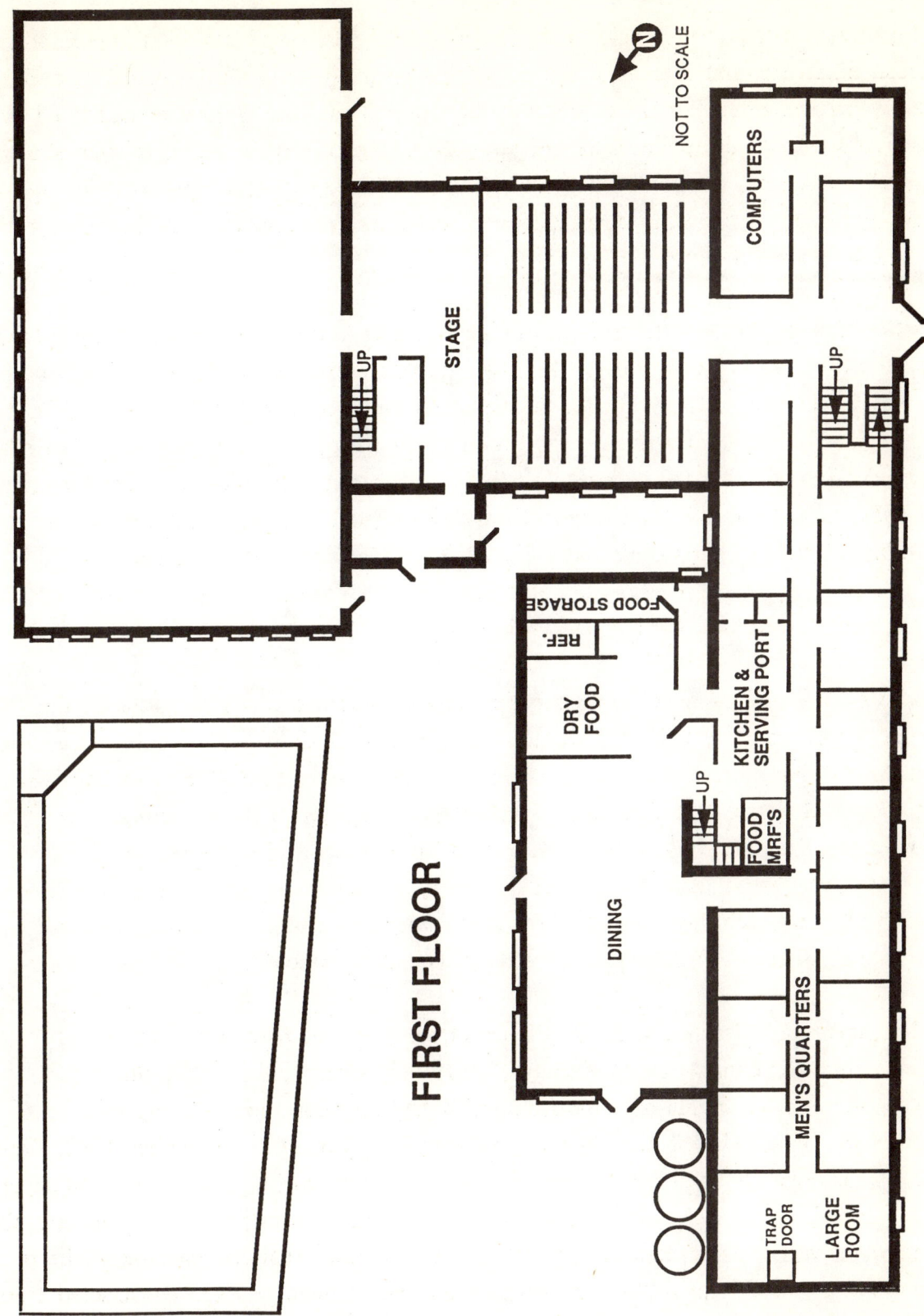

Figure 15: Floor plan of first level based on Block's memory of the Compound's living arrangements.

47

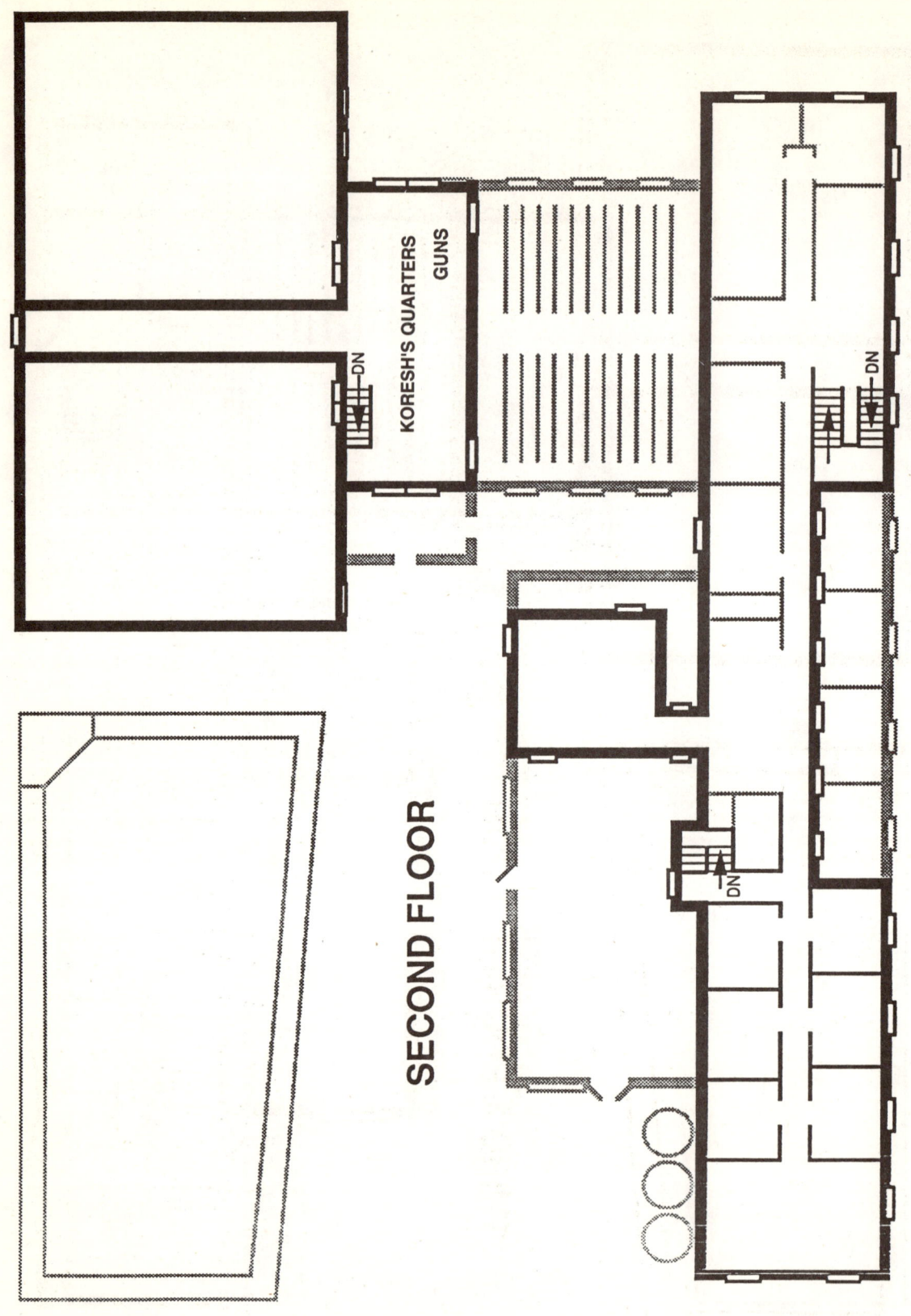

Figure 16: Floor plan of second level based on Block's memory of the Compound's living arrangements.

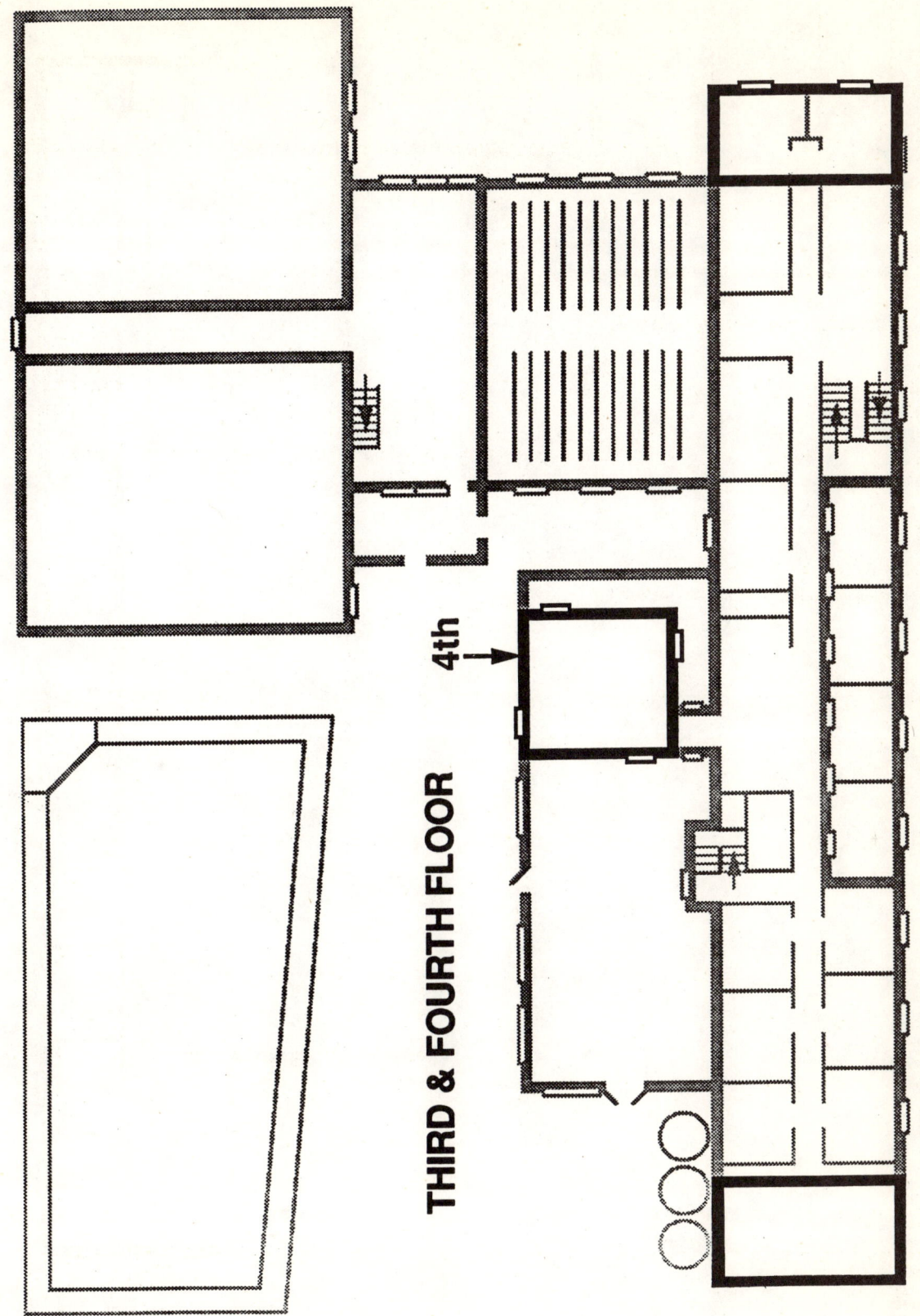

Figure 17: Floor plan of third and fourth level based on Block's memory of the Compound's living arrangements.

Figure 18: Arrow indicates pit (photographed after the raid).

the day of the raid, the men had built a roof covering more than half of the pit.

According to Andrade and Ojena, the men carried no weapons while they worked in the pit. And neither Andrade nor Ojena, outsiders whose only connection to the Branch Davidians was that they were seeking the release of two current cult members, saw any weapons displayed at the Compound. They did report, however, that they were carefully watched and gently kept away from certain areas during their visit.

While the men worked in the pit, the women cared for the children and did household chores. Not every man worked in the pit, however. Some were permitted to go into town, while Steve Schneider and Wayne Martin often stayed inside to work on computers. Koresh's schedule was unpredictable—sometimes he slept past noon, and sometimes he awoke early for services. Block also told the agents that Koresh rarely left the Compound because he feared that he might be arrested by the sheriff's department.

Intelligence from the Undercover House

While Aguilera and Buford were conducting their interviews in California, other agents were busy establishing the "undercover house." By January 11, 1993, the operation was up and running in a vacant house across from the Compound. (See Figure 19.) The house offered agents a clear view of the front of the Compound and of the main road to the Compound. The location also provided a limited view of the construction pit. The house was equipped with basic surveillance equipment, including cameras, a radio scanner, and night-vision devices.

The agents' view of the Compound and its residents was limited, however. Koresh's followers had access to the Compound using a road that led to the rear of the Compound not visible from the undercover house. In addition, Koresh and his followers owned numerous motorcycles, which allowed them to gain access to the Compound without using the roads, thereby avoiding detection by agents.

In the beginning, eight ATF agents manned the house, posing as students from a local technical college. Even though Rodriguez was more than 40 years old when his assignment began, all eight agents were chosen, in large part, for their relatively youthful appearances. The agents were instructed, among other things, to determine whether Koresh maintained an armed guard or a watch at the Compound, to identify, count and photograph cult members and their cars, to identify any counter-surveillance, and to gather further

Figure 19: Photograph of the undercover house.

evidence of firearms violations. Other than being told to pay attention to the routines around the Compound and to gain access to the inside if possible, the agents were not given a firm sense of what information the tactical planners were looking for, nor were they kept abreast of the evolving tactical plan.

During the first eight days, the agents in the undercover house maintained surveillance of the Compound around the clock. However, in the absence of any clear direction or supervision, this vigilance soon broke down, as the agents perceived no significant activity at the Compound and began to disagree among themselves about their respective responsibilities. After staying overnight at the house on January 19, Sarabyn told the agents that they could terminate the effort to maintain 24-hour surveillance and should instead concentrate on significant events only and devote more energy toward infiltrating the Compound.

The agents in the undercover house communicated with the tactical planners primarily by providing surveillance logs, photographs, and videocassettes to a contact agent. Although the agents took hundreds of photographs of the Compound and its residents, many photographs were not developed until long after the raid, and few of the photographs that were developed were reviewed by the tactical planners. Although the Review does not know where the videotapes were kept, the tactical planners never looked at any of them. Finally, once the contact agent obtained the logs and other materials from the undercover agents, no agent was responsible for ensuring that the materials in their original form either were brought to the attention of all tactical planners or analyzed for their benefit.

Using information relayed to them during the first three weeks of the undercover house operation and agents' surveillance logs, the planners concluded that certain routines prevailed among the 75 Branch Davidians who reportedly lived at the Compound. The raid planners concluded that neither armed guards nor sentries were posted at the Compound at any time, that Koresh never left the Compound, and that most of the men worked regularly in the pit, starting at about 10:00 a.m. The planners apparently envisioned that virtually all of the men in the Compound worked in the pit.

The Decision

When the tactical planners met in Houston on January 27-29, Buford reported what he and Aguilera had learned from the former cult members. Sarabyn and the agent who served as the contact with the undercover house related what intelligence was obtained through the undercover agents' surveillance of the Compound. At this time, the tactical planners believed they had sufficient information to choose a tactical option.

Buford, who originally had favored a siege, now rejected this option based on what former cult members told him about Koresh's ability to withstand a siege and the danger of a mass suicide. Buford also noted the tactical difficulty of laying siege to a structure such as the Compound, particularly one with .50-caliber weapons inside. In his view, shared by the other planners, a siege would not succeed quickly, and ATF probably would have to assault the Compound anyway, once public pressure on ATF to resolve the situation grew and the government's patience wore thin. Buford and several other planners warned against any scenario that might result in ATF entering the Compound forcefully, after a prolonged standoff had given Koresh an opportunity to prepare his defenses. Others in the planning group were troubled by the risk of a mass suicide, and based on Buford's experience with the Arkansas siege, they feared that a siege would give Koresh and his followers a chance to destroy evidence of their wrongdoing. All assumed that Koresh would not leave the Compound and would maintain strict discipline over his followers during a siege.

In contrast, Buford and others believed that they could formulate a workable plan for a dynamic entry. If ATF could enter the Compound before weapons could be distributed among cult members, Koresh's arsenal would pose no threat. The critical factor was to separate the men from the weapons. The planners believed this was possible because, according to some cult members, the weapons were kept under lock and key in a room next to Koresh's and were not generally distributed among Compound residents. Neither at this meeting nor during later planning efforts did the tactical planners question the reliability of this dated information from former cult members. In addition, the men routinely worked in the pit, which was at the far end of the Compound away from the arms room, starting at approximately 10:00 a.m. Moreover, relying on surveillance that indicated there were no sentries, which was consistent with Block's recollection that no sentries were posted in the tower, the planners believed that agents could approach the Compound without alerting residents.

Although former cult members claimed that Koresh maintained armed guards, often on a 24-hour basis—a report corroborated by the UPS delivery person—the planners believed the more recent reports from undercover agents that neither guards nor sentries had been observed at the Compound. When Rodriguez and another undercover agent visited the Compound in mid-February to shoot with Koresh, however, Koresh told the two agents that, through his binoculars, he had seen Rodriguez practicing with the same weapon they were now using at the Compound near the undercover house several hundred yards away. Koresh and perhaps other cult members were, therefore, watching the undercover house and the area around the Compound from a vantage point well above ground level—a matter that would have been of some concern to the raid planners. Rodriguez's exchange with Koresh was never documented or made known to any of the tactical planners. In addition, a representative of the National Guard told Aguilera on January 11 that a January 6 night surveillance flight using the Guard's Thermal Imaging System indicated "hot spots" consistent with the posting of sentries or guards outside the Compound.

By the end of the meeting, the tactical planners had reached a consensus that plans should be formulated for a dynamic entry. Despite ATF's early belief that drawing Koresh away from the Compound was central to the success of any operation, intelligence reports that Koresh did not leave the Compound led the planners to abandon efforts to lure Koresh away.

Development of the Tactical Plan

During the next two weeks, outlines of the ATF raid plan were developed by Sarabyn and the SRT leaders who would be involved in the operation—Petrilli, Williams, Buford, and King. The plan was never committed to paper in any detailed form; however, it reflected a shared basic understanding on the part of its creators.

Figure 20: Aerial photograph of command post at TSTC.

Figure 21: Aerial view of Bellmead Civic Center, utilized by ATF as a staging area.

An agent appointed by Sarabyn selected Texas State Technical College (TSTC) as the site for the command post because of its proximity to an airfield for use by the operation's helicopters and because the sheriff's department previously had received cooperation from the airport manager. (See Figure 20.) At the suggestion of local police, the planners selected Bellmead Civic Center as the staging area because of its proximity to the Compound, extensive parking facilities, and ability to accommodate more than 100 people. (See Figure 21.) According to the plan, approximately 75 ATF agents would gather at the staging area early on the day of the raid and leave for the Compound in time to arrive at about 10:00 a.m. The agents would travel approximately 10 miles to the Compound on the main road in cattle trailers, hidden beneath canvas tarpaulins and plywood-reinforced sides. (See Figures 22 and 23.) The planners believed that cattle trailers, which are quite common in Texas, could move a large number of people without attracting attention. Agent Dale Littleton, who had suggested using cattle trailers, had used them in October 1992 to surprise a group of heroin dealers operating from a remote 107-acre ranch in Texas. On that occasion, law enforcement personnel who were concealed in the trailers surprised the subjects and were able to make arrests and execute a search warrant without injury or incident.

In addition to the three SRTs, the trailers would carry three arrest support teams that would be responsible for clearing and securing the perimeter and handling any prisoners. All agents would carry semiautomatic handguns, and some would be equipped with semiautomatic AR-15s or 9mm MP-5 submachineguns. Some of the MP-5s carried by the agents could fire two-shot bursts but none of the MP-5s could fire more than two shots with one trigger pull.

If agents in the undercover house, whose raid-day mission included watching the Compound for changing conditions, did not observe any unusual activities, the cattle trailers would pull in front of the Compound, and the agents would deploy. The helicopters would leave the airfield at the command post, which was approximately three miles from the Compound, on a schedule that would make them arrive shortly before the trailers. There they would provide a diversion by hovering a distance from the Compound before the cattle trailers arrived.

The three SRTs were to arrive at the Compound and surprise the men who were working in the pit, separated from the weapons stored next to Koresh's room. The New Orleans SRT would be responsible for gaining control of the arms room and Koresh's bedroom. Initially, the plan called for part of this team to climb an internal staircase, believed to be located near the front door, and proceed directly to the arms room and Koresh's bedroom. However, because the planners were unable to confirm through Rodriguez's visits to the Compound whether a staircase ran from the front door to those two rooms on the second floor, the plan was changed a few days before the raid.

Figure 22: Side view of second cattle trailer.

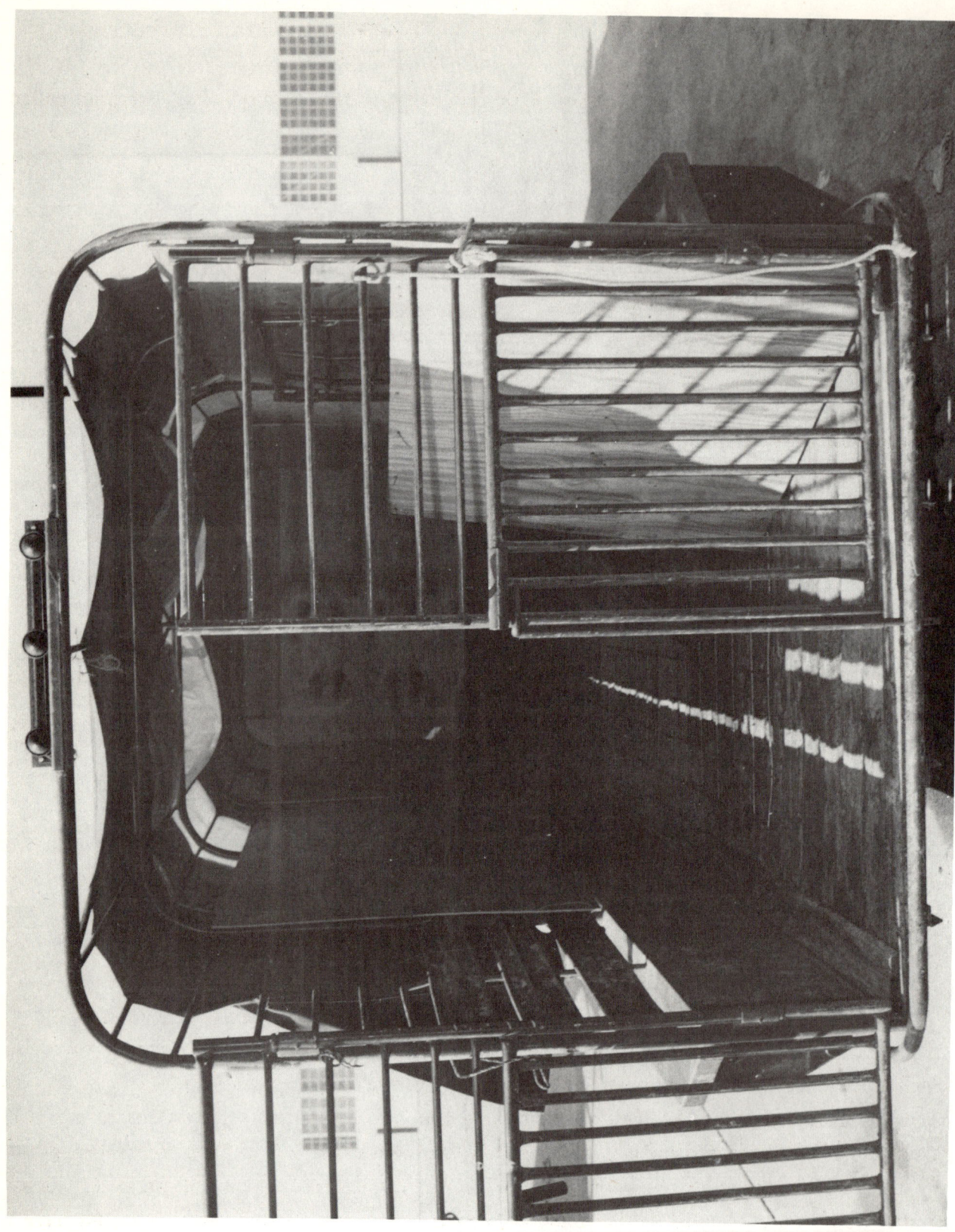

Figure 23: Rear view of second cattle trailer.

The modified plan required that most of the New Orleans agents climb onto the Compound's roof and enter the arms room and Koresh's room through two separate windows, while the balance of the New Orleans team secured the base area. The plan called for the New Orleans team to use "flashbangs"—diversionary devices that produce a flash and a bang but no fragments, and therefore do not cause injury—to enable it to safely enter the windows of rooms believed to be filled with weapons. The Dallas SRT was to enter the front door and secure the second and third floors and the tower—areas believed to contain the women and children's bedrooms. Half of the Houston SRT was to enter the front door and secure the first floor until it reached the trapdoor to the buried school bus; the other half was to circle around to the west edge of the Compound, secure the men in the pit area, and then proceed through the buried bus until it reached the other side of the trapdoor. After the premises had been secured and the residents taken outside, a proper search would be conducted. (See Figure 24.)

The plan called for deployment of at least two groups of forward observers armed with long-range rifles, who were to provide cover for the agents entering the Compound. In accordance with the ATF forward observer program, the Treasury Department's firearms policy, and the standard rules of engagement for federal law enforcement officers, the cover provided by the forward observers was limited to shooting in defense only (i.e., to protect the lives of agents and innocent third parties in imminent danger). Two forward observers and five other agents who would provide security for them and who would clear and secure vehicles parked nearby were to take positions near the hay barn, which was situated on low ground about a quarter of a mile behind the Compound; four forward observers were to set up in the undercover house. The hay barn team was to arrive at the barn approximately two hours before the raid and move into position as the cattle trailers entered the grounds; the team in the undercover house was to arrive the night before and set up surveillance the next morning.

The planners decided not to place forward observers on the east side of the Compound to provide cover for the New Orleans SRT members because of a concern that the terrain to the east did not provide the necessary cover. Although some planners favored placing such forward observers, the opinion of the planners concerned about the lack of cover to protect and conceal the observers from Compound occupants prevailed. As a result, the New Orleans team was required to achieve its objective without any covering support. A communications network was to link the various components of the raid, which in turn would be connected to the raid's command and control element, which would have its own radio channel. (See Figure 25.) The plan also called for another group of agents to

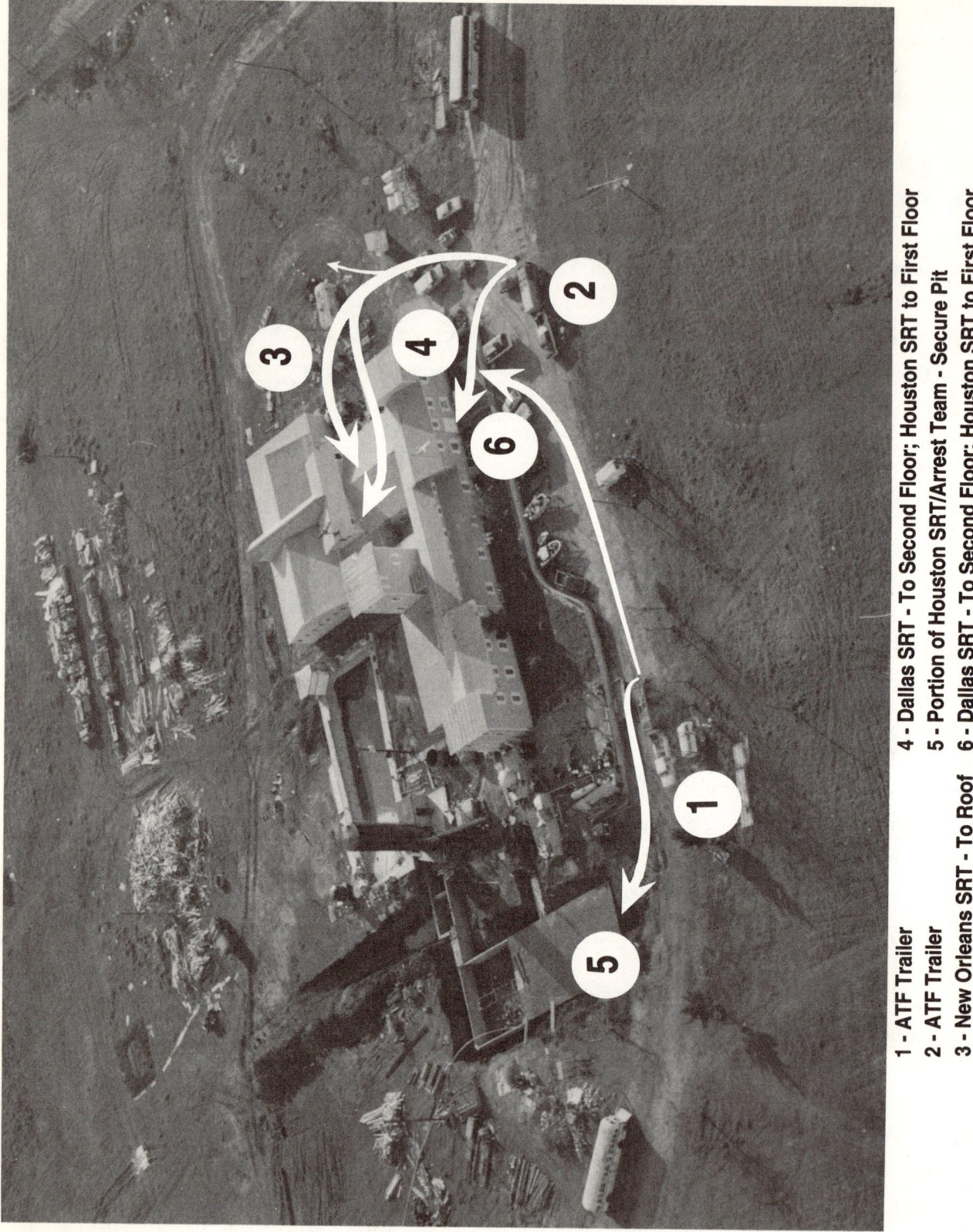

Figure 24: Photograph indicating planned deployment for SRTs.

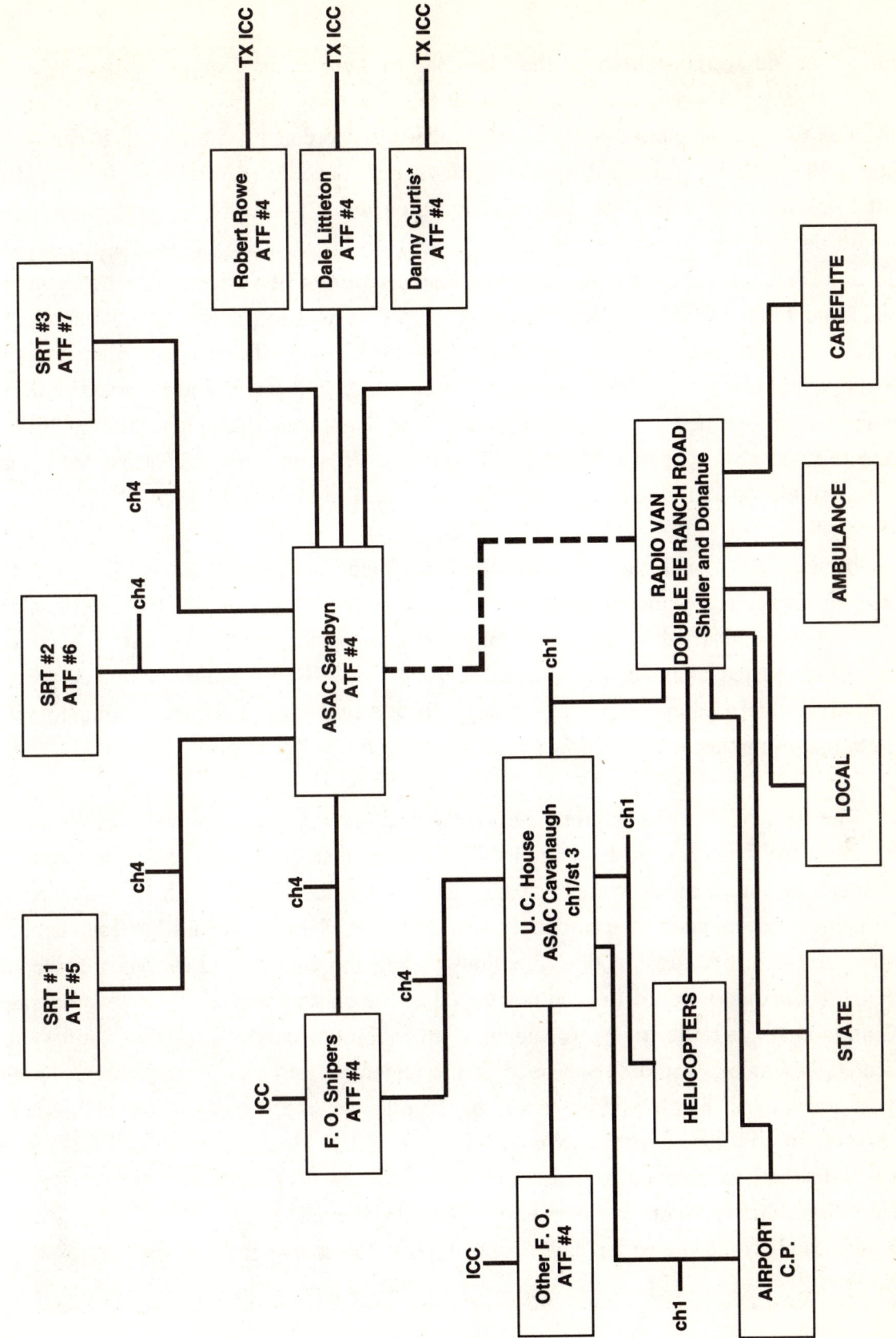

Figure 25: Diagram of communications network used for the raid.

61

execute a second search warrant at the Mag Bag as soon as the Compound was secured.

The tactical planners developed their plan in accordance with the ATF National Response Plan (NRP). The NRP, which Sarabyn had played a significant role in drafting, sought to define ATF objectives, policies, and procedures to ensure a coordinated response and rapid deployment of ATF resources to situations that exceeded the capabilities of a single field division. The NRP set forth the responsibilities of various ATF headquarters officials and field division leaders. One of its purposes was to permit ATF Washington officials to oversee operations and maintain communication with field commanders. On February 9, pursuant to the NRP, the planners formally requested, and received authority a week later from Hartnett, to activate three SRTs to handle the operation. The attempt to execute the warrants at the Compound was only the fifth time that ATF used more than one SRT in a single operation and the first time since ATF established the NRP.

In accordance with the NRP, the Waco raid plan designated certain field personnel to serve in particular command and control positions for the operation. Chojnacki, as SAC of the field division in which the operation was taking place, was, pursuant to NRP's directive, designated as incident commander. As Incident Commander, Chojnacki was charged with determining the overall strategy for the operation and for coordinating with the National Command Center in Washington.

The tactical plan for entering the Compound, as it evolved toward its final preraid form, called for Chojnacki to be stationed at the command post. Chojnacki then opted to be a passenger in one of the helicopters. Chojnacki designated Sarabyn, an SRT-trained ASAC, as the tactical coordinator in accordance with the NRP. Sarabyn would be responsible for directing and controlling all tactical functions during the operation. Pete Mastin, Deputy Incident Commander, would first be positioned at the staging area and then would ride to the Compound in a cattle trailer. Cavanaugh, an SRT-trained ASAC (Dallas) and Deputy Tactical Coordinator, would be stationed in the undercover house. From there, he could warn Chojnacki and Sarabyn if he or any of the other agents witnessed any changes at the Compound. In addition, once Sarabyn and Chojnacki left for the Compound, Cavanaugh would be in the best position to observe any activities at the Compound, particularly outward signs that residents were preparing for a raid, such as guns in the windows or barricades, and would thereafter have responsibility for aborting the raid if necessary. (See Figure 26.)

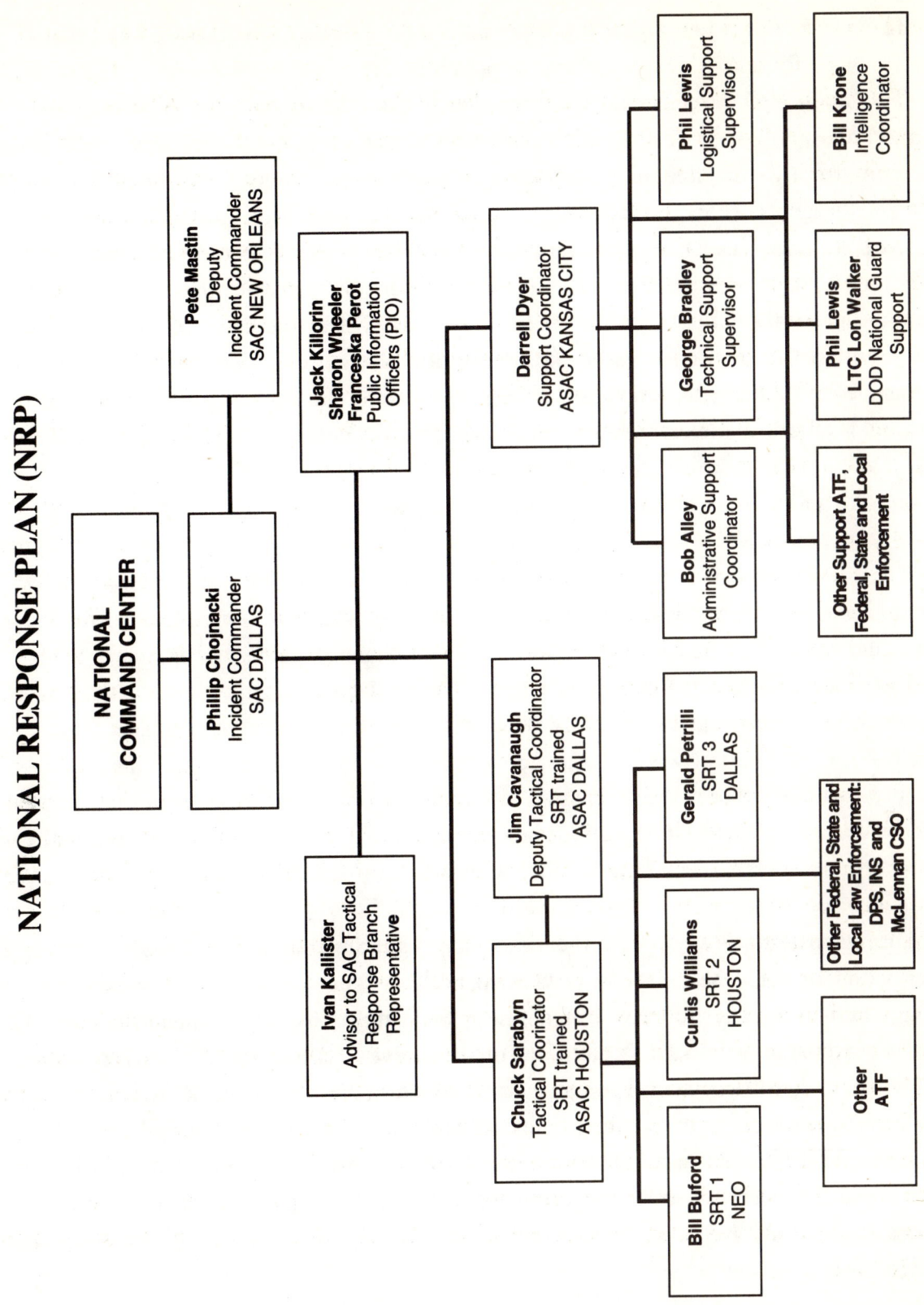

Figure 26: Organizational chart of National Response Plan structure and specific assignments for the Waco operation.

There was also a contingency plan in case the raid had to be aborted. The cattle trailers could easily take a detour at several points before reaching the road to the Compound. Even after turning onto the Compound road, the trailers could, for a short while, stop and allow the agents to disembark and retreat from the Compound. To provide concealment from the Compound's long-range weapons—particularly its .50-caliber guns—in case agents were forced to retreat from the Compound on flat and open terrain, ATF requested smoke canisters from military sources shortly before the raid. Because of the timing of the request, however, no smoke canisters were provided in time for the raid. But the planners determined that once the trailers had arrived near the front of the Compound, the raid could not be aborted because the terrain provided no concealment for the agents, and the driveway would not permit the trailers to turn around. At this point of no return, action would have to be taken, even if the Compound residents were not surprised.

Additional Intelligence Gathering, Training, and the Briefing of ATF Leadership

The formulation of a raid plan that rested on the assumption that the Branch Davidian men could be surprised in the construction pit, when they were away from their weapons, did not lead to any new direction in the intelligence gathering operation at the undercover house. Although the tactical planners recognized by early February that the plan hinged on the men being in the pit at 10:00 a.m., none of the undercover agents was informed that the operation would be based on this assumption. The development of the tactical plan, therefore, brought no change in the nature of the surveillance reports coming from the undercover house; if anything, the reports about the work in the pit became even vaguer and more sporadic until surveillance was officially terminated on February 17.

During the first few weeks in February, any lingering hopes that Koresh would leave the Compound or could be lured away were abandoned. The agents never saw him leave, and ATF's principal effort to draw Koresh away from the Compound failed when Joyce Sparks' supervisor at the Texas Department of Protective and Regulatory Services refused an ATF request that the agency summon Koresh to town for a meeting. A week before the raid, an attempt was made to obtain a state arrest warrant for Koresh's sexual activities with a young girl, which would have gained a basis for either the Texas Department of Protective and Regulatory Services or the District Attorney's Office to schedule a meeting with Koresh in town. The attempt fell short, however, when the girl was unwilling to testify about what had happened.

On February 11, Chojnacki, Sarabyn, and Aguilera flew to Washington and briefed Daniel Hartnett, ATF's Associate Director of Law Enforcement; Daniel Conroy, Deputy Associate Director of Law Enforcement; Andrew Vita, ATF's Chief of Firearms; David Troy, ATF's Chief of Intelligence; Richard Garner, ATF's Chief of Special Operations, and others about the investigation and the planned operation. The next day, the agents gave a similar briefing to ATF Director Stephen Higgins. Chojnacki and Sarabyn explained that Koresh would likely be at the Compound when any operation took place because he apparently rarely left the Compound. After reviewing the reasons for launching a raid rather than a siege—including their concerns about a mass suicide and Koresh's ability to withstand a siege for an extended period of time—Chojnacki and Sarabyn outlined their tactical plan's key aspects, including its focus on separating the men working outside in the pit from the weapons and the women and children.

After hearing the raid plan, ATF management raised several concerns about measures being taken to protect ATF agents and the women and children in the Compound. Higgins, for example, directed that particular care be taken with the diversionary flashbangs. When Hartnett questioned why the raid was scheduled for 10:00 a.m., rather than pre-dawn, when raids are generally begun, Chojnacki and Sarabyn explained how the plan depended on catching the men in the pit, when they were separated from their weapons. They also reviewed the provisions made for aborting the mission if necessary; Chojnacki and Sarabyn, as well as Mastin and Cavanaugh, would have authority to stop the mission at any time. With their concerns thus addressed, Higgins, Hartnett, and the rest of ATF top management approved the plan.

Shortly thereafter, Hartnett telephoned Chojnacki and expressed his concern that the men in the pit might sneak back into the Compound after the agents arrived. He directed that, rather than trying to secure the pit area from above, agents should enter the pit to secure the men inside. Hartnett also questioned the plan's abort options. But after receiving Chojnacki's assurance that the raid would only proceed if conditions were right, Hartnett again expressed his approval of the operation.

Part One

Section Three: ATF and the Media Prepare for the Raid

The *Waco Tribune-Herald*'s Investigation of David Koresh and Preparation of a Series for Publication

Even before ATF began its inquiry into firearms and explosives violations at the Branch Davidian Compound, a local newspaper, the *Waco Tribune-Herald,* had been investigating David Koresh and his followers. In spring 1992, Mark England, a *Tribune-Herald* reporter who had covered Koresh's 1988 trial for attempted murder, became intrigued by reports that Koresh proclaimed he was Jesus Christ and that there might be a mass suicide at the Branch Davidian Compound during Passover. With reporter Darlene McCormick, England gathered information and interviewed Koresh, former cult members, and the families of current cult members. By fall 1992, the reporters had information that children were being physically and sexually abused at the Compound. Having also learned that the Branch Davidians were using a buried school bus as a shooting range and that they were stockpiling large amounts of weapons and munitions, the reporters decided that law enforcement and social service agencies were not taking the situation seriously.

In October 1992, McCormick called Assistant U.S. Attorney Bill Johnston in Waco to ask what constitutes an illegal firearm. According to McCormick, Johnston informed her that the "Treasury guys" could tell her if any Branch Davidians had permits for automatic weapons. While Johnston did not give McCormick any specific information about the ATF investigation, she concluded that federal authorities were in fact investigating the Branch Davidians. After the call, Johnston notified ATF that the newspaper was working on a story.

By January 1993, England and McCormick had drafted a "Sinful Messiah" series of articles and submitted them to their editors. By early February, the galleys (used to detect and correct errors before a newspaper page is composed) went to Randall Preddy, the

Tribune-Herald's publisher, for his review. Because of its startling revelations of Branch Davidian lifestyles and its disclosure of dangerous weapons at the Compound, Preddy sent the galleys to his superiors at Cox Enterprises, the newspaper's parent company in Atlanta, for review. He also asked Cox's Vice President for Security, Charles Rochner, to assess the potential for violence against the *Tribune-Herald*'s plant and personnel and to recommend any necessary security procedures. Preddy and Rochner discussed the situation at the February Cox publishers meeting in Orlando, Florida, and Rochner agreed to visit Waco later in the month.

ATF Discussions About the *Tribune-Herald* Investigation and Contacting the Media

ATF first learned about media interest in the Compound when, in October 1992, Johnston told Aguilera that the *Tribune-Herald* was preparing a major story about Koresh. In December 1992, when Aguilera learned that Marc Breault, a former Branch Davidian, was supplying information to both law enforcement and the *Tribune-Herald*, Aguilera located Breault and asked him to stop dealing with the newspaper. That same month, Aguilera told his supervisor, Earl Dunagan, acting RAC of the Austin office, about the *Tribune-Herald*'s parallel investigation. Dunagan, in turn, suggested to ASAC Sarabyn, his supervisor in Houston, that ATF try to convince the *Tribune-Herald* to delay the story until after the ATF operation took place. At a meeting to discuss the investigation on December 4, SAC Chojnacki suggested meeting with the *Tribune-Herald* to request a delay in publication, but James Cavanaugh (then a Dallas ASAC and later Deputy Tactical Commander for the raid) opposed any such contact. By January 1993, however, an agreement was reached that a delay should be sought to ensure the safety of the undercover agents and the integrity of the investigation.

The February 1, 1993, Meeting With a *Tribune-Herald* Official

In mid-January, Barbara Elmore, the *Tribune-Herald*'s managing editor, contacted Assistant U.S. Attorney Johnston to assess the likelihood that the Branch Davidians would retaliate against the *Tribune-Herald*'s plant or personnel in the wake of the publication of the Koresh series. Johnston advised her of ATF concerns about publication of the articles and suggested a meeting.

On February 1, Sarabyn and Dunagan met with Elmore at the U.S. Attorney's Office and, citing their ongoing investigation, asked her to delay publication of the Davidian series. Johnston introduced the parties but did not participate in the meeting. The agents offered to give *Tribune-Herald* reporters "front-row seats" during the execution of the contemplated law enforcement action if the newspaper delayed publication of its series until after the raid. Elmore said that her publisher would have to make that decision and mentioned her concerns about the security of the *Tribune-Herald*'s personnel and building. At the conclusion of the meeting, Dunagan told Elmore that ATF planned to execute the search warrant on February 22 and that he would inform her if the date changed. Elmore recalls only that ATF told her that it might take some type of action concerning the cult in two to four weeks.

About two weeks later, Dunagan, with Sarabyn's approval, told Elmore that the raid had been postponed to March 1. According to Elmore, she told Dunagan that the *Tribune-Herald* had made no decisions about publication, but alerted other *Tribune-Herald* personnel of the date change. Dunagan believed the paper was cooperating with ATF's request to hold the story because Elmore had not told him anything to the contrary. Editors at the *Tribune-Herald*, on the other hand, have indicated that they felt no obligation to respond to ATF one way or the other; indeed, they report having been surprised that ATF agents did not contact other members of *Tribune-Herald* management after Elmore had told ATF she could not make the decision to delay publication of the articles.

Continued Discussions Between ATF and the *Tribune-Herald*

After these initial contacts, Chojnacki assumed sole responsibility for ATF communications with the *Tribune-Herald*. On February 9, Rochner informed Chojnacki that he would act as the *Tribune-Herald*'s liaison with ATF and that he was conducting a threat assessment for the *Tribune-Herald* in connection with its "Sinful Messiah" series. *Tribune-Herald* staff members, however, have said that they did not regard Rochner as the paper's liaison with ATF, but only as a security consultant to the paper. Because Rochner planned to be in Waco the week of February 22, Chojnacki agreed to meet with him. In the meantime, Chojnacki invited Rochner to observe raid training at Fort Hood on the 25th, later changing the invitation to the 26th or 27th.

To prepare for the meeting with the *Tribune-Herald*, Chojnacki sought advice from Jack Killorin, Chief of ATF's Public Affairs Branch. ATF's media policy does not require that headquarters personnel be notified of media involvement at the operational stages of an ATF action. It does, however, require such approval for media "ride-alongs" (ATF Order 1200.2B, January 20, 1988). Noting Koresh's messiah complex and his paranoia, they agreed that taking the press along on a raid could create an inflammatory situation.

Chojnacki said that he would offer *Tribune-Herald* key interviews and would recognize their hard work, but that he would not accept a demand that they be present at the raid or tell them the date or time of the raid. Killorin advised that ATF should not give the *Tribune-Herald* an exclusive story. He did not discuss this conversation with his supervisor, ATF Assistant Director of Congressional and Media Affairs James Pasco.

The *Tribune-Herald* Decision to Publish

By mid-February, reporters and editorial staff at the *Tribune-Herald* were eager to publish the "Sinful Messiah" series. Internal revisions and attorney libel review had been completed, and, at Rochner's direction, new security procedures were in place at the newspaper. Entrances to the building were locked, building passes were issued, and identifying decals had been removed from all *Tribune-Herald* vehicles. England and McCormick would leave Waco when the series appeared, and the homes of the *Tribune-Herald* executives would be protected. Only three hurdles remained before publication: Koresh was to be interviewed a final time so that his reaction could be included in the series; Rochner was to approve security procedures upon his arrival on February 24; and Chojnacki was scheduled to meet with *Tribune-Herald* editors on February 26. Preddy had told his staff that the series would not go forward until he had a face-to-face meeting with ATF officials.

On Friday, February 19, the *Tribune-Herald* editors took the first step toward publication and instructed England to interview Koresh. After contacting Koresh on Monday, February 22, for his reaction to the series, England left for Dallas on Wednesday, February 24, pursuant to the security plan. McCormick was already out of the country on vacation. On Wednesday morning, Rochner arrived in Waco and at Preddy's request, rescheduled the meeting with Chojnacki for that afternoon. Preddy recalls that before the meeting, Rochner mentioned that Chojnacki had invited him to observe ATF training at Fort Hood.

The February 24 Meeting With the *Tribune-Herald*

On February 24, Chojnacki, Rochner, and Preddy met with editor Robert Lott, City Editor Brian Blansett, and Managing Editor Barbara Elmore. Lott recalls that, at the time, he was committed to publication, absent clear and convincing evidence that the publication would cause harm. It is not clear, however, whether Chojnacki understood that this was to be the newspaper's standard for holding publication.

Chojnacki opened the meeting by thanking the *Tribune-Herald* editors for delaying the series, but the editors immediately made it clear that they had not held the series in deference to ATF—they had not been ready to run it for other reasons. Noting that he was concerned with the safety of ATF personnel as well as the safety of *Tribune-Herald* employees and facilities, Chojnacki begged the editors to hold off publication until after ATF had conducted its operation. Koresh appeared to be relaxed, Chojnacki explained, but publication of the series would agitate him and disrupt ATF's planned operation.

Chojnacki did not, however, give the paper any sense of when ATF's operation would take place or what it would entail. He noted that he had not yet obtained warrants and was not sure he would be able to get any; if he were unable to obtain such judicial authorization, he explained, he would have to "go home." While he told the editors that he could not "afford" a siege, Chojnacki refused to answer questions as to "what he had in mind" and "if he had an undercover." The most he would say was that a law enforcement action would likely take place "fairly soon." Asked if ATF planned to act within the next 7 to 14 days, Chojnacki declined to answer.

Chojnacki then asked the *Tribune-Herald* editors if their series would run in one to seven days. He recalls having received an affirmative answer. He asked the editors to give him some advance notice of the publication. He concluded by asking: "So, does that mean that you are willing to run this story even though we are asking you to keep it quiet for a few more days so that we can do what we have to do?" According to Chojnacki, Lott replied "The important thing to us is the public's right to have information that they need to know, and that's our job. We're not concerned about where it falls in or falls out in terms of your law enforcement case." Chojnacki then left the meeting and, as he told the Review, he was "hot."

All participants left the 30-minute meeting with the impression that the *Tribune-Herald* had not agreed to delay publication, and ATF had not revealed any specifics about its impending action. Elmore remembers the tone of the meeting as formal, but not antagonistic. Rochner recalls that Chojnacki appeared to be businesslike and that the meeting ended with an understanding that Preddy and the editors would discuss his request and that Rochner would get back to him. Chojnacki's impression of the meeting was that it was tense and did not end cordially. He had not expected to meet with all the *Tribune-Herald* editors and he was upset with the outcome of the meeting.

ATF and the Media Prepare for the Raid February 24-27

After the meeting with Chojnacki, the *Tribune-Herald* editors agreed that they had heard nothing to persuade them to delay publication. According to the those at the meeting, their chief concern was to inform the public about the Branch Davidians as soon as the security of the paper and its employees allowed. Preddy tentatively decided that the series would begin on Saturday, February 27. This day was chosen, according to *Tribune-Herald* management, to allow the newspaper to gauge Branch Davidian reaction during the two weekend days, when activity at the newspaper's office and plant was reduced. Preddy decided not to notify ATF of the decision to publish until after Rochner had answered all security questions.

Tribune-Herald officials have asserted that the March 1 ATF raid date was not a factor when they chose the publication date on Wednesday afternoon. Chojnacki's discussion of his difficulty securing warrants and his problems funding his operation made the March 1 date appear unlikely to the editors and publisher. In their view, his presentation was consistent with the *Tribune-Herald* editors' belief that local law enforcement had failed to take action for two years.

After the meeting on Wednesday, Tommy Witherspoon, the *Tribune-Herald* reporter who covered the courts, told City Editor Blansett that he had received a tip from a confidential informant that something "big" might happen at the Branch Davidian Compound between 9:00 and 10:00 a.m. next Monday, that the roads might be blocked, and that Witherspoon might want to be there when it happened. (The *Tribune-Herald* has told the Review that this confidential informant was not an ATF employee.) Without asking Witherspoon to verify the tip or making assignments, Blansett decided he would send a few reporters to the Compound area that Monday.

In the wake of his meeting with the newspaper, Chojnacki realized that it was unlikely that the newspaper would accommodate his request to delay its series. At the ATF command post, he and other ATF leaders concluded that the Koresh series would begin on Sunday, February 28, and Chojnacki told as much to the SRT leaders at Fort Hood. Chojnacki then asked Sarabyn whether it would be possible to move the raid date up two days to Saturday. Sarabyn said that such a change was impossible, but that the raid could be done a day earlier, on Sunday. Chojnacki set the raid for Sunday, alerted Hartnett and Conroy of the change in plans, and they concurred.

ATF Raid Preparations: February 24-26

Even as Chojnacki met with the *Tribune-Herald*, ATF's preparations were in full swing. On February 24, ATF's forward observers and SRTs began arriving at Fort Hood for three days of rigorous training. On Thursday, the first day of training, Sarabyn briefed the SRT leaders on the overall plan and set out each team's assignment. The team leaders then briefed their respective teams. In addition, Rodriguez told the assembled agents about the Compound. On Friday, the agents, coordinating with a Fort Bragg Army Special Forces unit, were able to use the Military Operations Urban Terrain (MOUT) site at Fort Hood, a mock setting for urban military exercises, and the firing ranges.

Each team trained on structures similar to areas of the Compound that it was assigned to secure. Some members of the Houston and the Dallas teams practiced entering the front door of a structure and securing the rooms and hallways inside. The New Orleans team practiced transporting ladders to the base of the structure and climbing up to secure the roof. In addition, the Special Forces personnel had constructed stand-alone window structures that permitted the New Orleans personnel to practice "break and rake" procedures, breaking a window and clearing the glass shards. Team members with prior emergency medical training also received trauma medical training, including the administration of intravenous transfusions, from the Special Forces medics. Meanwhile, the forward observers and agents who had been assigned AR-15s were given access to range facilities, where they qualified and zeroed their weapons to distances that would conform to their positions around the Compound.

Securing Search and Arrest Warrants

After Aguilera and Chojnacki briefed ATF officials, including Director Higgins and ADLE Hartnett, in Washington, D.C., on February 11 and 12, Chojnacki received approval to seek both an arrest warrant for Koresh and search warrants for the Compound and the Mag Bag. On February 25, Aguilera signed a sworn affidavit he had prepared with the assistance of Assistant U.S. Attorneys Bill Johnston and John Phinizy. On the same day, after reviewing the affidavit, Dennis Green, U.S. Magistrate-Judge for the U.S. District Court for the Western District of Texas, issued an arrest warrant for Koresh for violating federal firearms laws and a warrant to search both the Mag Bag and the Compound for evidence of that crime. Even though, to avoid disclosing the progress of the investigation, Aguilera had intentionally curtailed his contacts with firearms dealers who had sold weapons and components to Koresh, his affidavit's account of the documented flow of materials into the Compound gave some sense of the arsenal that Koresh had amassed in 1992. Listed in the affidavit were:

- 104 AR-15/M-16 upper-receiver groups with barrels
- 8,000 rounds of 9mm and .22-caliber ammunition
- 20 100-round-capacity drum magazines for AK-47 rifles
- 260 M-16/AR-15 magazines
- 30 M-14 magazines
- 2 M-16 E-2 kits
- 2 M-16 car kits
- 1 M-76 grenade launcher
- 200 M-31 practice rifle grenades
- 4 M-16 parts sets—Kits "A"
- 2 flare launchers
- 2 cases (approximately 50) inert practice grenades
- 40 to 50 pounds of black gunpowder
- 30 pounds of potassium nitrate
- 5 pounds of magnesium metal powder
- 1 pound of igniter cord
- 91 AR-15 receiver units
- 26 various calibers and brands of handguns and long guns
- 90 pounds of aluminum metal powder
- 30 to 40 cardboard tubes

Other Waco Media Learn About the Raid

While ATF agents were training at Fort Hood, reports of the impending raid were beginning to circulate among the Waco media. On Thursday, February 25, *Tribune-Herald* reporter Witherspoon told his friend Dan Mullony, who was a cameraman for television station KWTX, that something was going to happen at the Branch Davidian Compound on Monday. Mullony, in turn, alerted KWTX reporter John McLemore about the impending raid. Mullony attempted to confirm the tip. Darlene Helmstetter, his friend who was a dispatcher for American Medical Transport (AMT) ambulance service, told him that three ambulances had been put on standby for Monday at the request of law enforcement. On Friday, ATF advised AMT that the operation had been moved up and that ambulances should be at the Bellmead Civic Center rather than the airport. On Friday afternoon, at a wreck site, an AMT paramedic also told Mullony that something "big" was going to happen on Monday.

The Tribune-Herald Notifies ATF of its Decision to Publish on Saturday, and ATF Reacts

On Friday, February 26, publisher Preddy gave his final approval for the series to be published the next day. At about 3:30 p.m., Rochner gave this information to Chojnacki, advising him that a copy would be available at the *Tribune-Herald* loading dock at 12:15 a.m. on Saturday. Rochner says that he told Chojnacki that he would try to talk again with the newspaper editors and publisher if ATF had strong objections to publication. Chojnacki does not recall this offer. At Chojnacki's request, Rochner and Preddy reviewed the first story, and Rochner assured Chojnacki that it did not mention ATF.

That evening, Chojnacki advised other ATF supervisors, now gathered at Fort Hood, that the story would run the next morning. As a precaution, Chojnacki and Sarabyn decided they would send Rodriguez into the Compound on Saturday to gauge the effect of the article on conditions in the Compound.[19] Saturday was the Branch Davidian Sabbath, which usually entailed an all-day service in which Koresh preached to his followers. According to the revised plan, Rodriguez would enter the Compound at about 8:00 a.m. before the service began and look for signs that the article had caused Koresh to be on the alert for action by law enforcement or had otherwise caused a change in Compound routine.

ATF Notifies the Treasury Department's Office of Enforcement About the Raid

On Friday afternoon in Washington, ATF officials notified the Treasury Department's Office of Enforcement—which oversees ATF—of the impending raid. A one-page memorandum from ATF's liaison to that office went to Acting Deputy Assistant Secretary for Law Enforcement Michael D. Langan. The memo was later shared with John P. Simpson, who was acting as Assistant Secretary of the Treasury, and Ronald K. Noble, who had been designated to be the Assistant Secretary of the Treasury for Enforcement, but who, pending nomination and confirmation, was working as a part-time consultant to the office. After Langan, Stanley Morris, who had been detailed to the Office of Enforcement, Noble and others expressed grave reservations about the operation outlined in the memorandum, Simpson contacted ATF Director Higgins and, noting these

---

[19] The original raid plan had not provided for this undercover visit, or for the one on the day of the raid.

concerns, directed that the operation not go forward. Higgins spoke with Associate Director Hartnett, who was able to obtain additional information from Chojnacki that appeared to answer the Office of Enforcement's concerns. Higgins was thus able to assure Simpson and Noble that the raid plan recognized the dangers posed by Koresh's weaponry, and to assure them that though children were present at the Compound, the raid could be executed safely. Higgins noted that an undercover agent would be sent into the Compound before the raid to ensure that there had been no change in routine; he also assured them that the raid would be aborted if things did not look right. After these assurances were given, Simpson said he would permit the raid to go forward. (A fuller narrative of the Office of Enforcement's role in the operation appears at Part Two, Section Five of this Report.)

Sarabyn advised team leaders at a Friday afternoon meeting that Treasury officials had placed a "hold" on the raid. He suggested that this information be withheld from the agents until training was completed. After Simpson told Higgins that Treasury would not prevent the raid from proceeding, Higgins notified Hartnett, who gave Chojnacki the authority to make the decision to proceed. On Saturday, Chojnacki called Sarabyn to announce that Treasury had removed its "hold."

Saturday, February 27: Media Preparations

On Saturday, February 27, the first installment of the "Sinful Messiah" series appeared in the *Tribune-Herald*. The article described child abuse at the Compound, saying that Koresh encouraged the whipping of children as young as eight months and alleged that Koresh had fathered children with 15 women, many underage, living at the Compound. The article traced the 50-year history of the Branch Davidians and explained the importance of the Seven Seals from the *Book of Revelations* to Koresh and his followers. The newspaper also featured a sidebar entitled, "The Law Watches, But Has Done Little," and an editorial asking when the McLennan County sheriff and the district attorney would take action.[20]

The *Tribune-Herald* then shifted its focus away from its investigative series and prepared to cover the developing story of law enforcement activity at the Branch Davidian Compound. Tommy Witherspoon's confidential informant told Witherspoon on Saturday that the raid had been moved up 24 hours. As a result, early Saturday afternoon, Preddy, Lott, Blansett, and Rochner met and decided to send reporters to the Compound area on

---

[20] On Monday, March 1, the day after the ATF raid was repulsed, the *Tribune-Herald* published the remaining five parts of its "Sinful Messiah" series.

Sunday morning. Preddy encouraged them to consider the safety of the reporters, but left before specific plans for coverage were discussed. After the meeting, while returning to Waco from a drive to see the Branch Davidian Compound, Lott, Blansett, and Rochner saw a military helicopter headed toward the airport at Texas State Technical College (TSTC). Blansett, familiar with landing patterns at TSTC, believed that the helicopter was landing in an area not usually used by military aircraft. When the three drove to TSTC to investigate, they saw approximately 10 people, some in uniforms, greeting the helicopter pilot. Rochner thought that these individuals must be with ATF and that TSTC could be the staging area for the raid.

Blansett returned to his office about 4:30 p.m., developed story assignments, and directed reporters to meet at the *Tribune-Herald* office at 8:00 a.m. on Sunday. Because most reporters did not have Sunday assignments and he believed the updated tip about the raid to be reliable, Blansett assigned nine reporters to the story, triple the number he had contemplated on Wednesday. Blansett was interrupted by a call from Steve Schneider, one of Koresh's senior deputies. Schneider told Blansett that Koresh was upset by the first "Sinful Messiah" article and wanted an opportunity to tell the *Tribune-Herald* the "real story," the story of the Seven Seals and not, as Schneider put it, "seven days of lies." Promising to call Schneider back, Blansett called Mark England in Dallas and told him about the raid tip and Koresh's request for an interview. England left Dallas for Waco. Blansett next called Rochner, who suggested that England interview Koresh in a restaurant, so that Rochner and an off-duty police officer could be nearby. Rochner also asked if reporters wanted flak jackets for the raid, noting that he might be able to locate some. When England arrived in Waco, he told Blansett that he did not want to interview Koresh. Blansett never called Schneider back.

Rochner talked with Chojnacki twice that Saturday. First, he sought, unsuccessfully, to get Chojnacki's reaction to the story. That evening he also sought Chojnacki's counsel on Schneider's request that someone from the newspaper interview Koresh. They discussed sending reporters into the Compound on Saturday, which Chojnacki discouraged, explaining that he did not think it would be safe to enter the Compound.[21]

---

[21] Rochner recalls that he next proposed sending a reporter into the Compound on Sunday. According to Rochner, Chojnacki said, "Good luck, you will not be in our way if you go on Sunday." Rochner contends that this reinforced his view that no raid was planned for Sunday. Chojnacki does not recall making such a statement. In any event, the *Tribune-Herald* did not send reporters to the Compound on February 28 to interview Koresh; it sent reporters to cover a raid.

KWTX's preparations to cover the raid also moved forward. On Saturday morning, Mullony learned from Helmstetter, the AMT ambulance service dispatcher, that the ATF operation had been moved up a day. Helmstetter also told him that he should plan to be in town on Sunday. On Saturday afternoon, Mullony and Witherspoon acknowledged to each other that they knew the ATF operation was set to occur the next day. By Saturday evening, Mullony concluded that the raid would occur at about 9:00 a.m. Sunday based on standby times Helmstetter had given him. Helmstetter had also told Mullony that ATF had placed CareFlite, a Fort Worth helicopter medical transport service, on standby for Sunday. This fact led KWTX to believe the operation would be a major one.

That night, at the direction of KWTX News Director Rick Bradfield, Mullony asked Jim Peeler, another KWTX cameraman, and reporter McLemore to meet him and Bradfield early Sunday morning. Mullony was so concerned about what might happen the next day that he drafted his will. In contrast, McLemore, unconcerned, took his wife out to a local club. According to one witness, in a conversation at the bar, McLemore said ATF was going to conduct a big raid the following day. McLemore admits that he alluded to a big event but denies saying anything about ATF.

Saturday, February 27: ATF Preparations

Saturday was a hectic day for ATF as raid preparations continued. At the morning briefing, Sarabyn discussed the first installment of the "Sinful Messiah" series. He pointed to Koresh's picture, noting that the article did not mention an ongoing investigation, and explained to the agents that Rodriguez would be sent in Saturday and Sunday to gauge Koresh's reaction to the series.

The SRTs were joined by arrest team personnel for a rehearsal of the deployment from the cattle trailers into the Compound. The agents focused on exiting the trailers and getting to the Compound as quickly as possible. In an open field, Special Forces personnel had outlined the dimensions of the Compound on the ground with engineer tape and set up a front-door facade, thus allowing raid personnel to practice in a confined area similar to the Compound. In addition, the New Orleans and Houston SRTs practiced using "flashbangs"—distraction devices that, when detonated, produce a loud bang and a emit a bright flash—in one of the MOUT structures. The teams also simulated the arrival of the cattle trailers and the helicopter diversion.

Meanwhile, ancillary and support elements converged on Waco. Two marked ATF bomb-disposal trucks and National Guard support trucks, including a two-and-a-half ton military transport truck and a water truck, arrived at TSTC. After Fort Hood training, three National Guard helicopters also proceeded to TSTC. The Texas Department of Public Safety was prepared to set up roadblocks and the sheriff's department was prepared to provide other support functions. ATF reserved 153 rooms at three Waco hotels for the evening of the 28th. At 8:00 that evening Chojnacki and Sarabyn conducted a briefing at the Best Western Hotel for arrest and support teams, including National Guard members, explosives specialists, dog handlers, and laboratory technicians. Phillip Lewis, Support Coordinator, had arranged with local suppliers for such diverse items as the ambulance services, portable toilets, and the Bellmead Civic Center. On Saturday, he ordered doughnuts at a Waco grocery store, arranging to pick them up the next morning. He also arranged with the sheriff's department for coffee at the Bellmead Civic Center site the next morning.

Special Agent Sharon Wheeler, the ATF public information officer (PIO) assigned to the operation, prepared for the raid. Several weeks earlier, Chojnacki had asked that public information be handled by Killorin, but his request was denied because Pasco and Killorin determined that Killorin was needed in Washington on other matters. Wheeler was chosen because the Houston PIO was less experienced and New Orleans did not have a PIO.

Responding to direction from her SAC, Ted Royster, Wheeler contacted one Dallas television station for a weekend contact number. Then, following her press plan, she called two other Dallas television stations to obtain similar telephone numbers. While she indicated to all the stations that ATF might have something going on during the weekend, she did not describe the action or provide its timing, location, or any other information specific to the raid. She did not contact Waco television stations or newspapers, out of a concern that the raid's security might be threatened.[22]

Rodriguez entered the Branch Davidian Compound at 8:00 a.m. Saturday to join Koresh's worship service. Koresh preached about the "Sinful Messiah" article and told his followers that "they" were coming for him. He cautioned that, when this happened, his

---

[22] Despite earlier accounts to the contrary, Wheeler did not divulge any information about the raid in these contacts. The reporters she contacted were not able to determine what law enforcement action she was referring to, based on their conversation. Indeed, none of the stations she contacted were at the Compound until well after the firefight began.

followers should not get hysterical and should remember what he had told them to do; he did not specify at the time what those instructions were. Between noon and 5:00 p.m., Rodriguez met with Chojnacki at the TSTC command post. Chojnacki asked Rodriguez whether he had seen any guns or preparations to resist law enforcement. Rodriguez said he had not.

Rodriguez went back to the Compound for more services at 5:00 p.m., and stayed until about midnight. Upon his return to the undercover house, Cavanaugh and the forward observers who had arrived earlier that evening noted that Rodriguez was showing the strain of his assignment. Rodriguez called Sarabyn and reported that no changes inside the Compound were evident. Sarabyn instructed Rodriguez to return to the Compound Sunday morning for a final check on conditions and leave by 9:15. Rodriguez explained to Sarabyn that he was upset about this assignment because he was concerned that an unexpected return might arouse Koresh's suspicions. Rodriguez was also concerned about his ability to leave the Compound by 9:15 because Koresh exerted such control over the Compound and could be so intense in his personal interactions. Rodriguez was not confident that he would be able to leave by 9:15 without alarming Koresh. Nonetheless, he reluctantly agreed to return the next morning.

Part One

Section Four: The Assault On The Compound.
___

ATF Agents Assemble

On the morning of February 28, Cavanaugh and the forward observers watched the Compound from the undercover house for signs of unusual activity. They saw nothing out of the ordinary. A few men were walking about the grounds and some women were emptying waste buckets. The weather was overcast with traces of precipitation. The forward observer teams in the undercover house who, if necessary, were to provide cover fire for the raid teams, checked and prepared their equipment. Rodriguez was to enter the Compound at 8:00 a.m. Two undercover agents were available to support him. In addition, one of the undercover agents was assigned the task of taking forward observer and arrest support teams to a hay barn behind the Compound. Once the raid teams had left the staging area, the undercover agents also were to ensure that the residents of the neighboring house remained safely inside during the raid.

Meanwhile, at Fort Hood, the 76 agents assigned to the cattle trailers assembled at 5:00 a.m.[23] They traveled to the staging area, the Bellmead Civic Center, in an approximately 80-vehicle convoy with a cattle trailer at each end. Many of the vehicles bore the telltale signs of government vehicles—four-door, late-model, American-made vehicles with extra antennas. All the vehicles had their headlights on. Agents report that, once underway, the convoy stretched at least a mile.

The convoy arrived at the Bellmead Civic Center between 7:30 and 8:00 a.m. The civic center is adjacent to a residential neighborhood and is visible from the nearby intersection of Interstate 84 and Loop 340, 9.4 miles from the Compound. (See Figure 27.)

___

[23] With few exceptions, no definitive record exists of times for the events on February 28. Accordingly, except where otherwise noted, all times are approximations derived from witness recollections, logs, and other records.

An ATF agent wearing an ATF raid jacket and local police were in the street in front of the civic center directing the convoy into the parking lot. While waiting to be briefed, some of the agents went inside the center to have coffee and doughnuts; others milled about outside. A supervisor became concerned about the visibility of the agents, many of whom wore ATF insignia or were otherwise unmistakably law enforcement personnel. He ordered everyone to go inside and to remain in the civic center.

At 8:00 a.m., Sarabyn gave a short briefing at the civic center. He reviewed assignments with the various groups, discussed the recent *Tribune-Herald* article, and related the substance of Rodriguez's Saturday assessment of conditions in the Compound. He also distributed the most recent photographs of the Compound and took questions from team leaders. He told the assembled agents that Rodriguez was in the Compound and that there would be a final briefing after Rodriguez reported on conditions in the Compound. Sarabyn left the staging area for the command post to await Rodriguez's report. The agents gathered in small groups, talked, checked their equipment, and reviewed plans while awaiting Sarabyn's final briefing.

Activity at the command post at TSTC also began at dawn. Special Agent Lewis, in charge of logistics support, checked the telephone lines. The three National Guard helicopters, one UH-60 Blackhawk and two OH-58 Jet Rangers that had flown in the night before were parked on the tarmac.

Andy Vita, Chief of the Firearms Division, opened ATF's National Command Center in Washington, D.C., at 9:00 a.m. (EST). Richard Garner, Chief of the Special Operations Division; John Jensen, in charge of the National Communications Branch, and others designated by the National Response Plan, also were present. Director Stephen Higgins, Associate Director Daniel Hartnett, and Deputy Assistant Director Daniel Conroy were available by telephone.

The Media Sets Out To Cover The Raid

Even as ATF agents were gathering to embark on the raid, local reporters were deploying to cover the operation. At 7:00 a.m. at KWTX, Jim Peeler, John McLemore, and Dan Mullony received maps of the area and reviewed assignments with the station's news director, Rick Bradfield. Bradfield anticipated a major law enforcement operation because he had learned from Mullony's AMT Ambulance Service informant, Darlene Helmstetter, that CareFlight, a Fort Worth-based trauma flight company, was involved. Bradfield told the

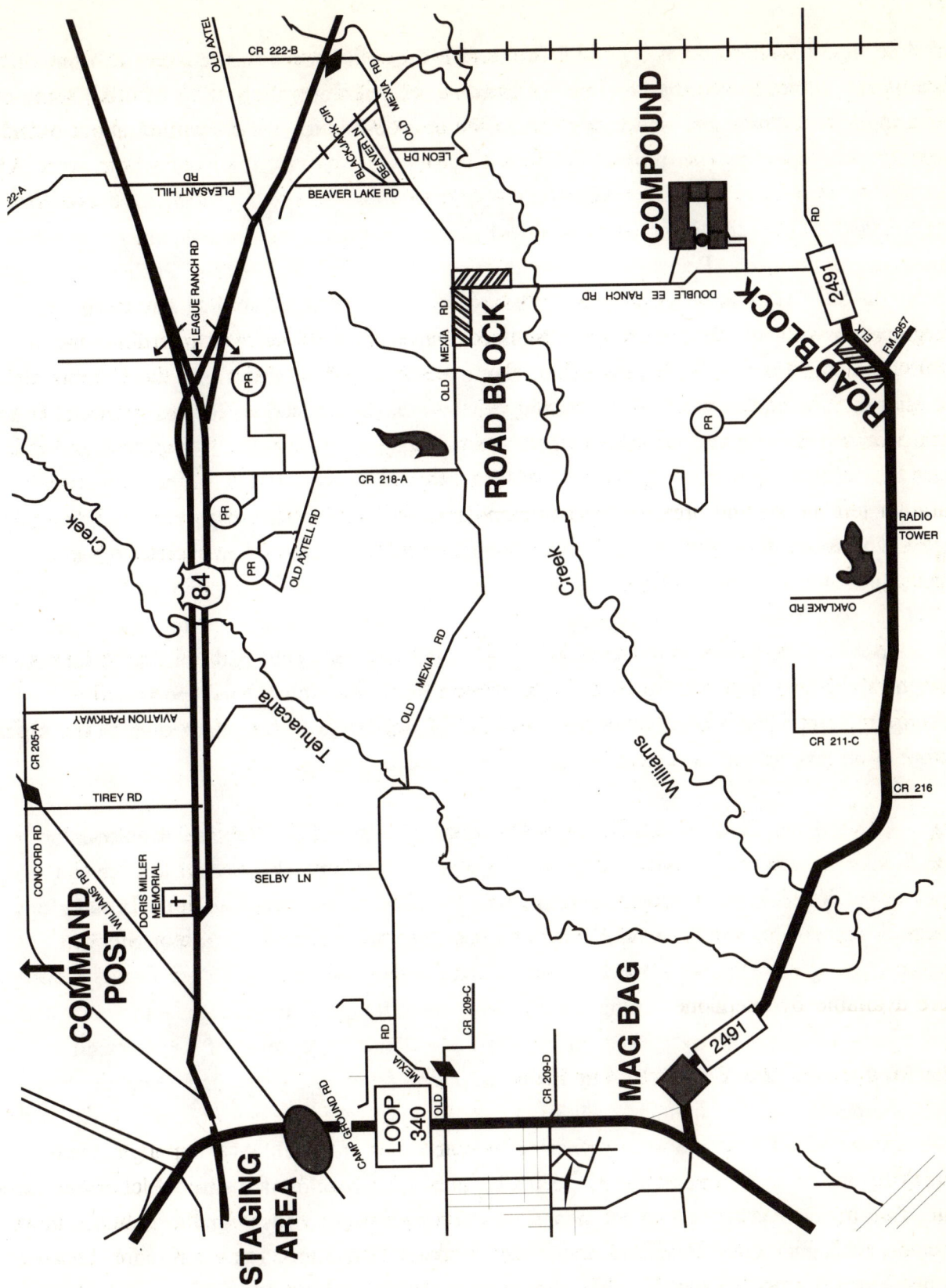

Figure 27: Map depicting staging area, Mag Bag, Compound, and road blocks.

Review that KWTX did not call ATF to confirm the raid because asking for information or permission is generally unproductive. (According to Bradfield, the policy of KWTX when covering law enforcement operations is to go to the news site, obey law enforcement orders, and respect private property.)

Peeler was sent to the intersection of Double E Ranch and Old Mexia roads where, according to Mullony, Peeler was to watch for and film raid helicopters. Peeler denies receiving any information concerning helicopters. Peeler thought his job was to film any prisoners brought out during the raid. Mullony and McLemore were sent to Farm Road 2491 (FR 2491) on the other side of the Compound's grounds. Bradfield, from the newsroom, communicated with his employees by cellular telephone. Radios were not used so that competitors could not overhear their conversation.

Prior to the raid, nine *Tribune-Herald* reporters were assigned to the developing story. The morning of the raid, some of them gathered at the newspaper's office before departing for the Compound in four cars, three heading for the Compound and the fourth to TSTC to watch for helicopter activity. The newspaper, concerned about the enormous cache of weapons at the Compound and Koresh's potential for violence, had gone to extraordinary lengths to ensure the safety of its plant and personnel. In contrast, the reporters were not given any safety instructions about covering the raid, nor were they instructed about possible affects their presence or actions might have on the raid.

As the reporters drove to the Compound they mistakenly expected to encounter roadblocks. In law enforcement operations however, a roadblock is usually not established until the action begins. In this case, establishing a roadblock more than two hours before the raid was to begin likely would have compromised the secrecy of the operation.

At about 7:30, after driving up and down the Double E Ranch Road in front of the Compound twice, Mullony parked on FR 2491 about one mile north of its intersection with Double E Ranch Road. By 8:30, other *Tribune-Herald* vehicles were patrolling the two roads bordering the Compound. At 9:30, Mark England asked a DPS officer parked on the side of the road if he could go by what he believed to be a roadblock. The officer told England that he could pass but that the road would later be closed. In the hour before the raid, five media vehicles could be seen driving or parked on roads near the Compound. The agents in the undercover house reported the increased traffic to Cavanaugh. The Review has been unable to verify whether Cavanaugh forwarded the information to the command post. (See Figure 28 and legend.)

But while other reporters were waiting for the raid to begin, KWTX cameraman Peeler became lost. At about 8:30, he used his cellular telephone to ask Bradfield and Mullony for directions. Despite getting directions, Peeler remained lost somewhere near the intersection of Old Mexia and Double E Ranch roads. There he encountered David Jones, a local letter carrier who was driving a yellow Buick with "U.S. Mail" painted on the door. Jones pulled up behind Peeler and asked him whether he was lost. Peeler, who was wearing a KWTX jacket, introduced himself as a cameraman with the station and asked for directions to "Rodenville," the name by which many Waco residents had referred to the Compound ever since it had been owned by the Roden family. Peeler did not know that Jones was one of Koresh's followers. Jones pointed to the Compound, which was in sight, and commented that he had read about the cult in the paper and thought they were weird. Peeler, deceived into believing that Jones was not affiliated with Koresh, warned Jones that some type of law enforcement action was about to take place at the Compound. He indicated that the action was likely to be a raid of some type and that there might be shooting.[24]

After the chance encounter with Peeler, Jones returned to his car and as he sped away toward the Compound, Peeler began to wonder whether Jones was affiliated with the cult. After this conversation, Peeler drove to a nearby store and called Bradfield, who told him to return to the intersection of Old Mexia and Double E Ranch roads, wait 30 minutes, and if nothing happened, go home. When Peeler returned to the intersection, DPS officers and ATF agents had set up a roadblock. Peeler was not allowed to pass, but he was told where he could set up his camera.

---

[24] There are conflicting reports about what Peeler actually told Jones. In a statement to the Texas Rangers, Koresh's attorneys stated that in one of their visits to the Compound during the standoff between the cult and the FBI, David Jones (now deceased) told them that Peeler warned him not to go near the Compound as there were going to be "60 to 70 TABC (Texas Alcohol Beverage Commission) guys in helicopters and a shoot-out would occur." Peeler has denied giving this much detail to Jones. However, he has admitted that on the morning of the 28th he believed that TABC was involved and had tuned his scanner to the TABC frequency. TABC was not involved in the action on the 28th and Peeler is the only witness interviewed by the Review who believed that TABC was involved. Peeler's admission lends credibility to the account provided by Koresh's attorneys.

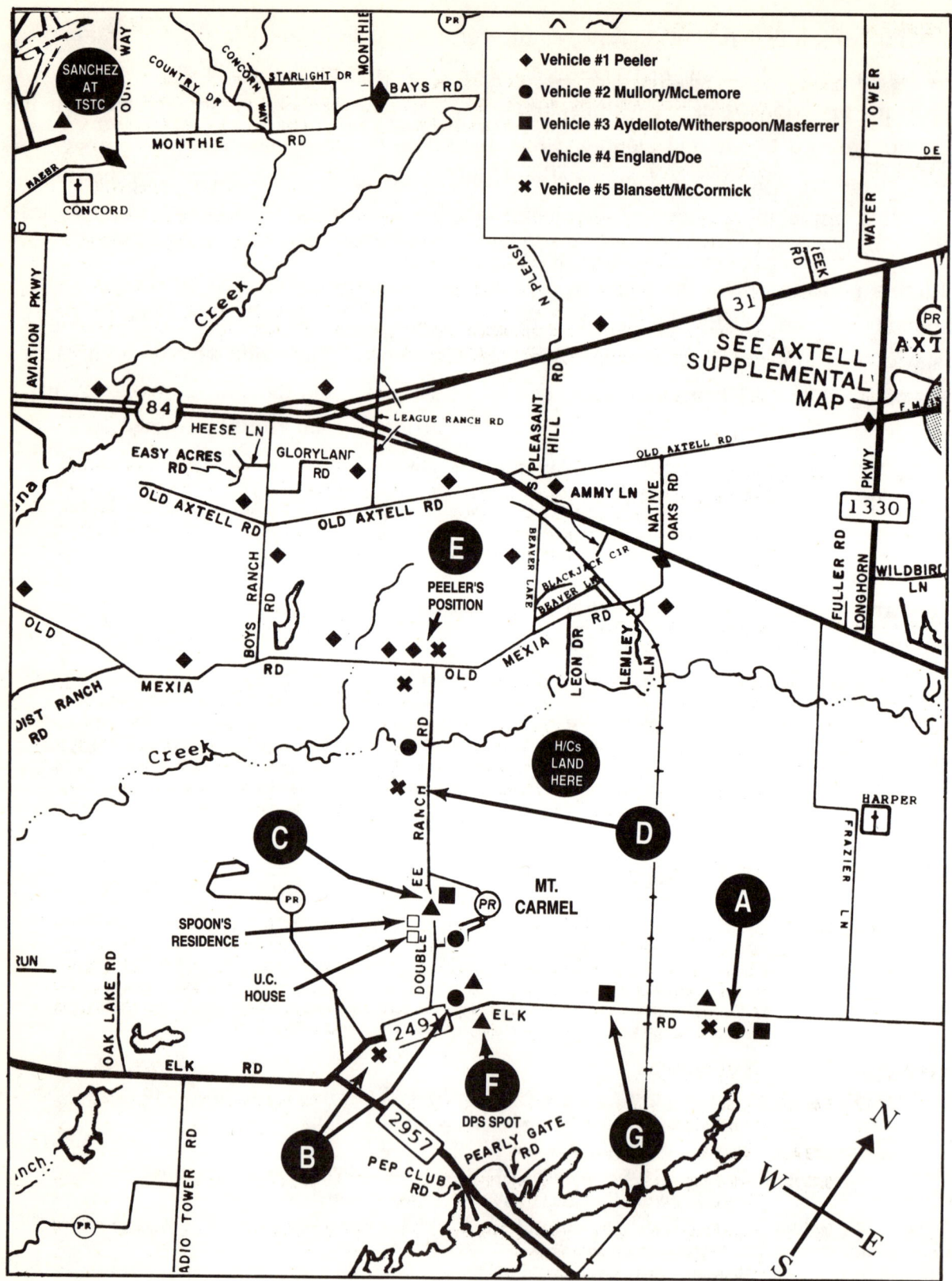

Figure 28: Location of Media Vehicles.

VEHICLE #1	**WHITE BLAZER**	**PEELER**

8:30 AM   Arrives the vicinity of Old Mexia Road and Hwy 84. Was lost, cellular telephone calls to Mullony or directions. Found way to Old Mexia Road and Double EE Road, parked on Old Mexia Road (Spot E), had conversation with Jones. Left area, returned following Trooper, parked at Spot E and videos the raid.

VEHICLE #2	**WHITE BRONCO II**	**MULLONY** **McLEMORE**

7:30 AM   Arrive 1.8 miles past Double EE Road on FR 2491 (Spot A). Received and made calls to Peeler giving directions and admonishing him not to talk to anyone. Talked to England, Doe, Aydelotte, Witherspoon, Masferrer and Blansett at various times while at Spot A.

9:15 - 9:30 AM   Received call from Peeler, said he saw helicopters, moved from Spot A and drove by DPS Trooper talking to England at Spot F. Turned down Double EE past Compound, on way to Old Mexia Road saw helicopters, turned around and proceeded past Compound to intersection of Double EE and FR 2491 (Spot B). Set up camera, saw cattle trailers, followed them down driveway to back of bus, videos raid.

VEHICLE #3	**SILVER HONDA ACCORD**	**AYDELOTTE** **WITHERSPOON** **MASFERRER**

8:30 AM   Arrive on FR 2491, drove past Double EE Road to a location in sight of the compound roof (Spot G). Remained for while, then moved further down FR 2491, met Mullony and McLemore at Spot A. Received cellular call from Sanchez, helicopters moving. Drove down Double EE Road past Compound driveway, parked. Witherspoon to Spoon House, Witherspoon returned to car, then drove down Double EE Road a short distance, stopped, backed up, saw cattle trailers turn down Compound driveway and remained at Spot C.

VEHICLE #4	**WHITE CAVALIER STN WGN**	**ENGLAND** **DOE**

8:45 AM   Arrive on FR 2491, drove past Blansett/McCormick parked near the intersection of Double E Road and FR 2491 (Spot B), continued to Spot A and are joined by Blansett, told to go to TSTC, to check on Sanchez, drove to TSTC. Met Sanchez, told helicopters are not moving. Returned to FR 2491, followed DPS Trooper to a small depression in road on FR 2491 (Spot F), left car to speak with Trooper. Trooper said road block not in force yet. Saw vehicles 2 and 3 drive by to Double EE Road. Followed to Spot B met Mullony/McLemore, remained there until they saw three helicopters, minutes later saw cattle trailers, followed Mullony/McLemore down Double EE Road to Compound driveway, parked beside Aydelotte's car at Spot C.

VEHICLE #5	**WHITE CAVALIER STN WGN**	**BLANSETT** **McCORMICK**

8:30 - 8:50 AM   Arrive Double EE Road, took Double EE Road past Compound to Old Mexia Road, turned around just before intersection Old Mexia and Double EE (Spot E). Return to intersection of FR 2491 and Double EE Road (Spot B), England/Doe pass (9:10 AM), followed England/Doe down 2491 to Spot A, told England to check Sanchez. Went back toward Double EE Road, turned down Double EE Road past Compound to Old Mexia, turned around before reaching intersection, and stopped at a ridge and depression (Spot D) and remained there until after shooting started, then moved to Spot E.

VEHICLE #6	**WHITE BRONCO II**	**SANCHEZ**

8:30 - 8:45 AM   Called by Blansett, while in route to Compound told to go to TSTC to check on helicopters. Parked 6 blocks from TSTC tower.

9:13 AM   Called Blansett, advised saw activity . . .

9:29 AM   Called Blansett, advised saw helicopters moving . . . decided to go to Compound, led DPS/ATF caravan (Mag Bag Search Team), used Loop 340 to FR 2491.

9:41 AM   Pulled over briefly, cattle trailers passed him, he tried to pass cattle trailers and called Blansett and told him ATF is coming in cattle trailers.
Sachez is pulled over by ATF on FR2491 . . .

Legend for Figure 28

Peeler's encounter with Jones was witnessed by one of the ATF undercover agents who was taking the forward observers and their arrest support teams to a hay barn behind the Compound. The undercover agent was dressed in casual clothes; the forward observers wore ATF battle dress utilities. When the undercover agent saw the two vehicles parked together on the road, he recognized Jones' postal vehicle. Jones was talking to the occupant of the second car, whom the agent did not recognize but suspected was a reporter. The agent, fearing that Jones might spot the uniformed agents in his car, told them to crouch down. Jones did not appear to look in the agents' direction and the undercover agent was satisfied that his group had not been seen. He drove to the hay barn, deposited the forward observers and arrest support team, and returned to the undercover house where he told Cavanaugh what he had seen. Cavanaugh claims to have relayed the information to the command post although no one there recalls receiving it.

Rodriguez Enters The Compound

At 8:00 a.m., not long before Peeler had his conversation with David Jones, Rodriguez went to the Compound one final time for the most critical phase of his undercover assignment, assessing whether the *Herald-Tribune* articles had incited Koresh and his followers to take up arms or otherwise increase their security measures. Koresh greeted the undercover agent and invited him to join a "Bible study" session with two of his followers. There were no signs of unusual activity.

While Koresh and Rodriguez were engaged in this Bible session, David Jones arrived at the Compound, fresh from his encounter with Peeler. He told his father, Perry Jones, what had happened. Perry Jones devised a pretext to draw Koresh away from Rodriguez.[25] He called to Koresh that he had a phone call. When Koresh ignored the request, Jones added that it was long distance from England.

Early interpretations of Jones' reference to England speculated that Jones was referring to Mark England, the co-author of the *Tribune-Herald* series whom Koresh had been trying to contact. This interpretation led to speculation that Mark England alerted Koresh to the impending raid. However, Koresh's attorneys have said that Jones told them that he was referring to the country. In any event, contrary to early accounts, there is no

---

[25] Cult members released from the Compound after the raid have stated that prior to the 28th, Koresh had suspected that Rodriguez was an undercover agent. One cult member stated that despite his suspicions, Koresh continued to meet with Rodriguez believing that he could nonetheless successfully recruit him.

evidence that Mark England placed a call to the Compound on the morning of February 28. Records provided by the *Tribune-Herald* of their telephone calls contain no record of a call to the Compound on the morning of February 28.

When Koresh left the room to take the fictitious call, David Jones described his conversation with Peeler. Upon Koresh's return, Rodriguez could see that he was extremely agitated, and although he tried to resume the Bible session, he could not talk and had trouble holding his Bible. Rodriguez grabbed the Bible from Koresh and asked him what was wrong. Rodriguez recalls that Koresh said something about, "the Kingdom of God," and proclaimed, "neither the ATF nor the National Guard will ever get me. They got me once and they'll never get me again." Koresh then walked to the window and looked out, saying, "They're coming, Robert, the time has come." He turned, looked at Rodriguez and repeated, "They're coming Robert, they're coming."

Rodriguez was shocked. As Koresh repeatedly looked out the window and said, "They're coming," Rodriguez wondered whether the raid was beginning even though he was still in the Compound. Needing an excuse to leave, Rodriguez told Koresh he had to meet someone for breakfast but Koresh did not respond. Other male cult members entered the room, effectively if not intentionally coming between Rodriguez and the door. Fearing that if he did not leave he would be trapped in the Compound, Rodriguez contemplated jumping through the window. He repeated that he had to leave for a breakfast appointment. Koresh approached him, and in a manner Rodriguez believed highly uncharacteristic, shook Rodriguez's hand and said, "Good luck, Robert." Rodriguez left the Compound, got into his truck and drove to the undercover house.

Rodriguez Reports

Agents in the undercover house recall that Rodriguez was visibly upset when he returned from the Compound. He complained that the windows of the undercover house were raised and that he could see a camera in one of them. Cavanaugh asked Rodriguez what had happened in the Compound. Rodriguez announced that Koresh was agitated and had said ATF and the National Guard were coming. Cavanaugh asked Rodriguez whether he had seen any guns, had heard anyone talking about guns, or had seen anyone hurrying around. Rodriguez responded in the negative to all three questions. Cavanaugh then told Rodriguez to report his observations to Sarabyn.

Rodriguez called Sarabyn at the command post and told him that Koresh was upset, that Koresh had said ATF and the National Guard were coming, and that as Rodriguez left Koresh was shaking and reading the Bible. Sarabyn asked Rodriguez a series of questions from a prepared list provided by the tactical planners: Did you see any weapons? Was there a call to arms? Did you see them make any preparations? Robert responded in the negative to each question. Then, Sarabyn asked what the people in the Compound were doing when Rodriguez left. Rodriguez answered that they were praying. Next, Sarabyn called Cavanaugh who reported that there was no observable activity in the Compound.

A special agent in the command post witnessed Sarabyn's part of the conversation with Rodriguez. After Sarabyn had hung up the phone, the agent stopped Sarabyn and asked what Rodriguez had said. Sarabyn responded that Rodriguez had been with Koresh when Koresh was called from the room to take an emergency telephone call. When Koresh returned to the room he said that ATF and the National Guard were in Waco and were coming. Sarabyn also stated that Rodriguez reported Koresh was nervous and dropped the Bible from which he was reading. The agent asked Sarabyn, "What are you going to do?" Sarabyn responded that Rodriguez had seen no firearms and that Koresh was reading the Bible when Rodriguez left. Sarabyn said he thought they could still execute the plan if they moved quickly.

Initial accounts by the participants in and witnesses to Rodriguez's conversations with Cavanaugh and Sarabyn differed significantly with respect to whether Rodriguez clearly communicated that Koresh knew the raid was imminent. Although there remains some variance with respect to Rodriguez's actual words, all key participants now agree that Rodriguez communicated, and they understood, that Koresh had said the ATF and National Guard were coming.

Now Sarabyn hurried out of the command post to the tarmac to confer with Royster and Chojnacki. The helicopters had already begun warming up. In order to hear over the noise of the rotors, the three supervisors moved to a fence bordering the tarmac, approximately 50 feet away. Although the noise still made conversation difficult, the three men huddled together so Sarabyn could pass on what he had learned. Sarabyn related that he had just spoken with Rodriguez who had said that Koresh knew ATF and the National Guard were coming but that, when Rodriguez had left, Koresh was reading the Bible and shaking. Sarabyn also stated, based on what Rodriguez had said, that Koresh was not ordering anyone in the Compound to do anything. Chojnacki asked Sarabyn whether Rodriguez had seen any guns. When Sarabyn responded that Rodriguez had not, Chojnacki asked Sarabyn what he thought should be done. Sarabyn expressed his belief that the raid could still be executed successfully if they hurried. Chojnacki responded, "Let's go." The conference lasted no more than three minutes. Sarabyn left immediately for the staging area.

Events began to reflect Sarabyn's perceived need for speed. News of Rodriguez's report spread rapidly among the ATF agents at the command post, creating an atmosphere of great urgency and commotion. Various agents were heard yelling that Koresh knew of the raid and that they needed to depart immediately. Royster hastened to the helicopters and told the agents there that Koresh knew of the raid and therefore it was beginning immediately. Royster then ran back to the command post, joined by Chojnacki who called the National Command Center and reported to Special Agent Jensen, responsible for the Center's communications, that the undercover agent was out of the Compound and that the raid was commencing. Chojnacki did not relate the substance of Rodriguez's report. Chojnacki then ran to and boarded his helicopter. A few minutes later, the helicopters departed. Shortly thereafter, Rodriguez arrived at the command post only to find that Sarabyn, Chojnacki and Royster had departed. Witnesses recount that Rodriguez became distraught, repeatedly asking how the raid could have gone forward when he had told them that Koresh knew they were coming.

The Raid Goes Forward

Sarabyn arrived at the staging area at 9:10 a.m. Witnesses report that he was excited and obviously in a hurry. Agents in the parking lot when Sarabyn arrived recall that he ran to them and told them that they had to hurry, making statements such as, "Get ready to go, they know we are coming," and "They know ATF and the National Guard are coming. We're going to hit them now."

Similarly, agents inside the civic center recall Sarabyn running in and calling for their attention. He announced, "Robert has just come out. Koresh knows that ATF and the National Guard are coming." Sarabyn told the agents they would proceed immediately. Sarabyn exhorted the agents to move quickly, repeatedly telling them to hurry, to get their gear because Koresh knew they were coming. There was no formal briefing, discussion or evaluation of Rodriguez's information. Several agents report having had qualms about going forward, especially since Koresh had mentioned the National Guard, yet they also felt questioning the decision would be inappropriate.

Within 15 minutes of Sarabyn's arrival at the staging area, the special response and the arrest teams boarded the trailers and left. According to agents in the trailers, although there was some lighthearted banter, the overall mood in the trailers was uncharacteristically somber. While some felt confident, others began to wonder why they were proceeding if Koresh knew they were on their way.

Sarabyn rode in the truck pulling the first cattle trailer. He maintained an open cellular phone contact with Cavanaugh throughout the trip to the Compound, keeping Cavanaugh posted as to the team's location and asking for reports on the level of activity at the Compound. Cavanaugh reported that he could not see any signs of activity in the Compound or on its grounds.

Activity In The Compound

According to some of the former cult members in the Compound at the time, preparations were being made in the Compound, although not detectable by Cavanaugh and the forward observers. Even as Rodriguez was departing, Perry Jones and the female members of the Compound had gathered in the chapel, thinking that they had been called for a church service. They had been waiting almost an hour when Koresh came in and ordered them back to their rooms. The older women and children went to the second floor and began to lay on the floor in the hallway, away from the outer walls of the Compound. Many of the cult members began to arm themselves, some with 9mm pistols, some with automatic and semiautomatic assault rifles, and others with both pistols and rifles. (See Figure 29.) Some donned bulletproof vests, others put on ammunition vests. (See Figure 30.) Ammunition was distributed. The Compound members assumed stations at the windows, waiting for the ATF agents to arrive.

The Media Covers The Approach Of The Raid Teams

According to *Tribune-Herald* cellular phone records, at 9:26 a.m., photojournalist Robert Sanchez called Blansett to advise him that several helicopters were leaving TSTC. Sanchez had earlier reported to his colleagues waiting near the Compound that he had seen agents at TSTC in camouflage fatigues loading duffle bags and gear into vehicles, and lining up to go. As Sanchez drove to the Compound he caught up to the two cattle trailers filled with uniformed agents. He relayed this information to his colleagues near the Compound. Agents in the second trailer reported that a vehicle was following them and two ATF agents in a chase car following the trailers stopped Sanchez. Sanchez again called his

Figure 29: Kalashnikov assault rifle, recovered from Schroeder's van which was parked in front of main Compound building (photograph taken after April 19, 1993).

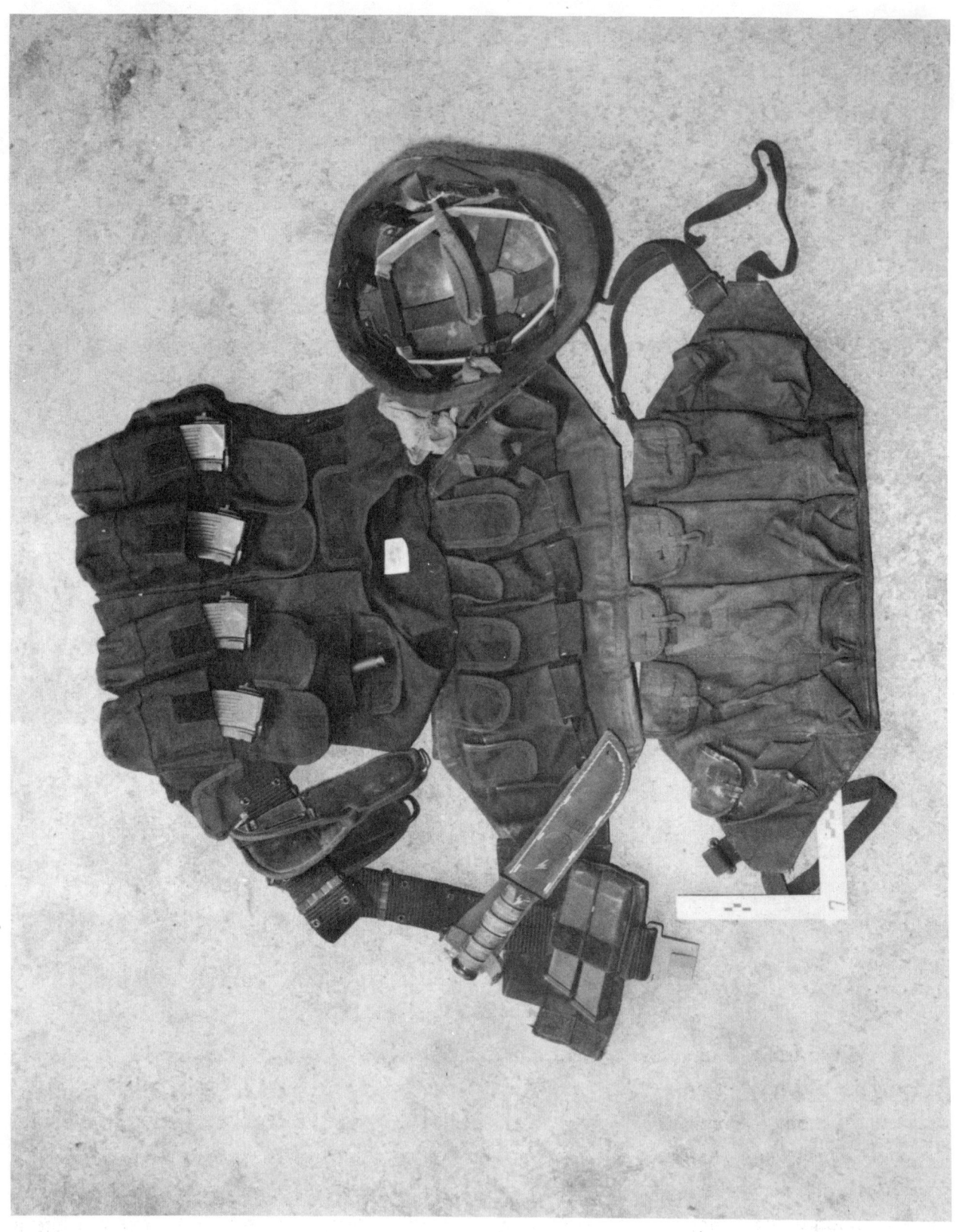

Figure 30: (From left) Load-bearing ammunition vests containing two 9mm magazines, four loaded AK-47 magazines, and a military helmet recovered from Schroeder's van after the 4/19/93 fire.

colleagues and advised them that he had been turned back and was unable to continue to the Compound.

Media personnel used radio and cellular telephones to communicate with one another and used scanners to monitor law enforcement frequencies during the hour before the raid. Several members of the press heard on scanners "no guns in the windows," and "it's a go" moments before ATF raid trucks entered the Compound's driveway.

Once Blansett relayed Sanchez's information, the reporters in the area moved closer to the Compound. *Tribune-Herald* reporters, Witherspoon, Aydelotte, and Masferrer drove to the house beside the undercover house to observe the raid from its front yard. Witherspoon knocked on the door to ask permission, but the agent safeguarding the residents inside declined to answer. As Witherspoon was knocking another agent approached. Believing the approaching agent to be a resident, Witherspoon said there was about to be a raid and asked whether he and his colleagues could observe it from the front yard. Without identifying himself, the agent ordered the reporters to leave the property. As the reporters were backing their car onto Double E Ranch Road, the trailers were turning into the Compound's driveway. The reporters parked their car on the road in front of the house next to the undercover house. Aydelotte was retrieving his camera from the trunk of his car, when a second car containing two more *Tribune-Herald* reporters pulled alongside. Aydelotte managed to shoot several frames before gunfire began striking the car, forcing all five reporters into a ditch alongside the road.

Meanwhile, KWTX's Mullony and McLemore turned onto Double E Ranch Road and followed the ATF cattle trailers up the Compound's driveway. McLemore pulled up behind a parked bus. As the trailers continued the short distance to the front of the Compound, Mullony set up his tripod. Seconds later gunfire erupted from the Compound.

The Helicopter Diversion

As the trailers approached the Compound from the Double E Ranch road, the helicopters had not yet arrived at their designated point, even though Cavanaugh repeatedly radioed for them to come in "low and fast." The helicopters approached the rear of the Compound at approximately the same time the trucks pulled along the front, which failed to create the intended diversion. When they were approximately 350 meters from the rear of the Compound, the helicopters were fired upon, forcing them to pull back. It was too late at this point for them to warn the trailers to abort.

Two of the helicopters were forced to land in a field to inspect for damage. Agents discovered that bullets had pierced the skins of each of the helicopters. The third helicopter, although also struck by gunfire, was able to remain airborne. It circled overhead to watch for additional attackers. Due to the damage, the two helicopter pilots initially decided not to attempt to fly them back to the command post. Chojnacki requested the third helicopter to land and take him back to the command post. While the pilots inspected the helicopters, agents climbed a small hill to determine how far they were from the Compound. From the hill they concluded that the group was still within range of hostile fire. They recommended to the helicopter pilots that if the helicopters could be flown, they should leave the area. The pilots decided that the helicopters were flightworthy and they returned to the command post without further incident.

The Raid Team Arrives

As the cattle trailers entered the driveway there was no sign of activity inside or outside the Compound. The approaching agents realized the absence of activity was a bad omen. When one agent noted over the radio, "There's no one outside," a second agent responded, "That's not good."

The trucks stopped in front of the Compound's main building as planned. Figure 31 shows their position. Agents with fire extinguishers for holding the Compound's dogs at bay were the first to exit the trailer. One agent opened the gate in the wall in front of the Compound, and another discharged a fire extinguisher at the dogs. Simultaneously, agents began exiting the second trailer. Koresh appeared at the front door and yelled, "What's going on?" The agents identified themselves, stated they had a warrant and yelled "freeze" and "get down." But Koresh slammed the door before the agents could reach it. Gunfire from inside the Compound burst through the door. The force of the gunfire was so great that the door bowed outward. The agent closest to the door was shot in the thumb before he could dive for cover into a pit near the door. Then gunfire erupted from virtually every window in the front of the Compound. The Dallas and Houston SRTs, which were approaching the front of the Compound and the pit area to the left, took the brunt of the initial barrage. Agents scrambled for cover. One of the first shots fired hit the engine block of the lead pickup truck. Consequently, neither the first, nor the second vehicle were able to leave.

As the Dallas and Houston teams attempted to get to the front of the Compound, the New Orleans team, which had been concealed in the second trailer, approached the east side

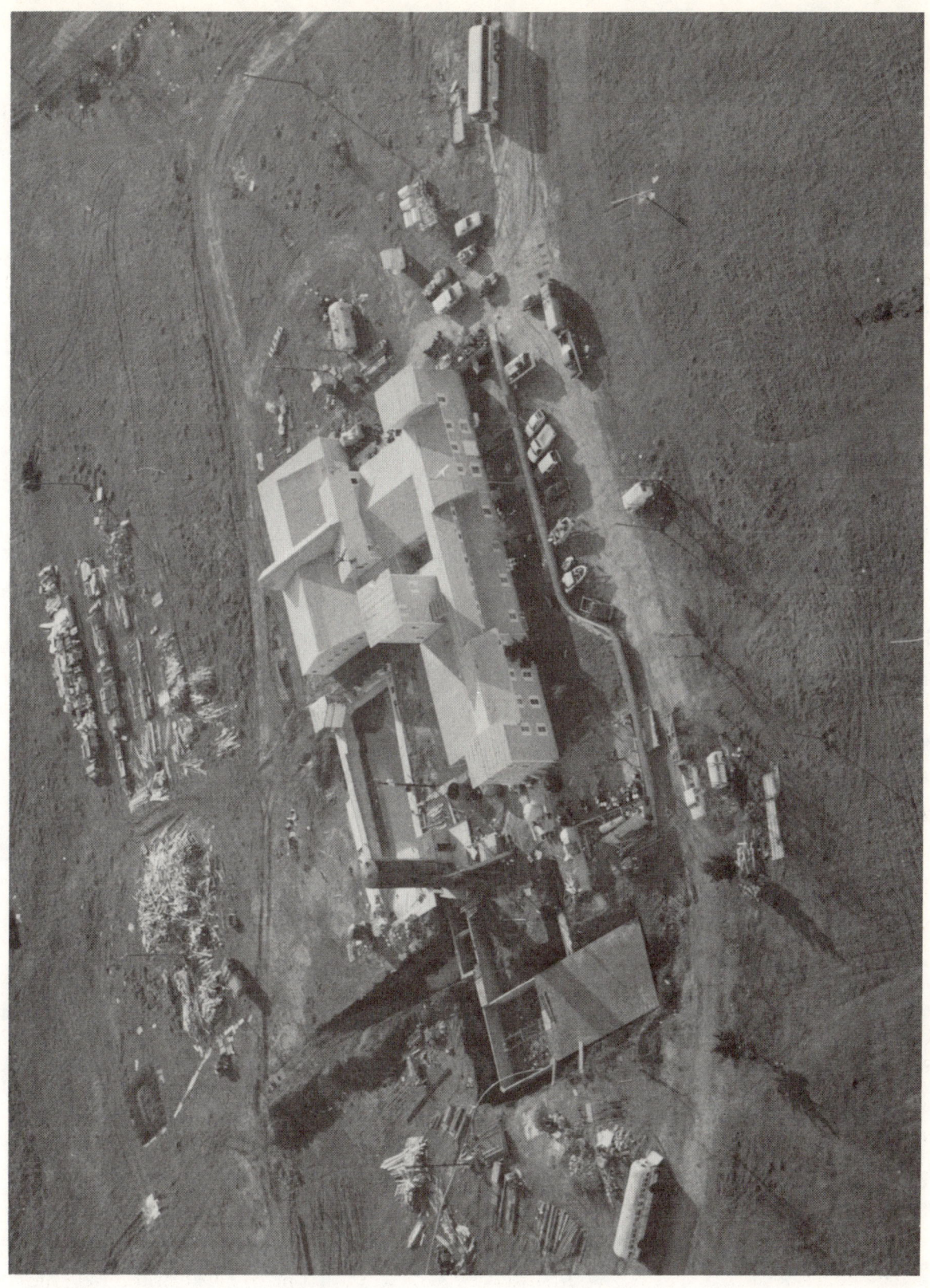

Figure 31: Photograph of Compound after 2/28/93 raid, which includes the ATF cattle trailers in the foreground.

of the Compound. As they left the trailer, the agents heard gunfire. At first, the agents thought it came from the dog teams. During training the agents had been told that they might hear the dog teams firing at the dogs if they were not able to subdue them with fire extinguishers. However, they quickly realized that the gunfire was coming from the Compound. While one agent provided cover from the ground, seven others approached the wall and climbed to the roof. Conway LeBleu, Todd McKeehan, Kenny King, and David Millen were to enter Koresh's bedroom on the west pitch of the roof, while Bill Buford, Keith Constantino and Glen Jordan were to enter the window on the east pitch of the roof. That window led to the room that ATF intelligence indicated contained the weapons. But soon after the agents reached the roof, they came under heavy gunfire. Special Agent Millen was able to retreat back to the east pitch of the roof where he stood guard outside the armory. Special Agent LeBleu and Special Agent McKeehan were killed.

Special Agent King was shot six times before managing to roll himself off the roof and into the courtyard behind the Compound. (See Figure 32.) As he lay trapped in the courtyard, too injured to move, King repeatedly called over his radio that he had been shot several times and was bleeding badly. Agents hearing King's pleas, tried to rescue him. New Orleans Field Division SAC, Pete Mastin, contacted Cavanaugh and asked whether the forward observers could suppress fire from the tower while agents on the ground attempted to rescue King. The forward observers directed rifle fire at the area of the tower from which shots had been directed at the agents. However, as the agents attempted to move toward the rear of the Compound, gunfire from other areas stopped them. Despite the agents' best efforts, the intensity of the gunfire made it impossible to rescue King until the final cease-fire, approximately an hour and a half later.

At the arms room, Agent Jordan managed to "break and rake" the window and Agent Buford threw a distraction device into the room. Buford, Constantino and Jordan entered. Inside, Agent Buford saw a person armed with an assault rifle backing out of a doorway in the far left corner of the room. That individual began firing into the room from the other side of the thin walls. The agents returned fire, but without automatic weapons, which are used to deliver a defensive spray of gunfire, they could not suppress the attacker's fire. The shots fired at the agents inside the room passed through the wall to where Special Agent Millen was positioned on the roof. Shots were also fired at Millen from the first floor up through the roof. He escaped the attacks by sliding down the ladder to the ground.

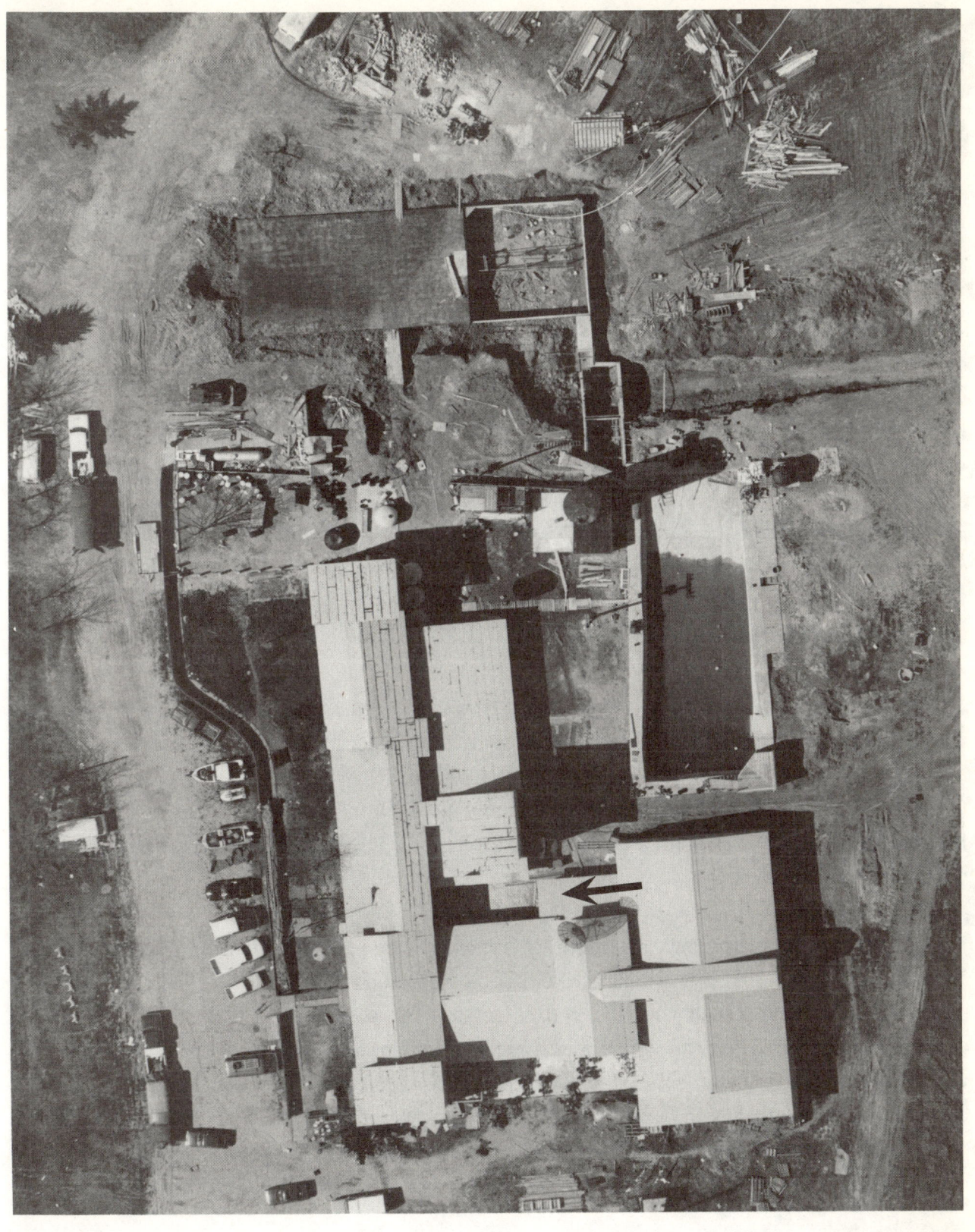

Figure 32: Arrow shows location of seriously wounded Kenny King after he rolled from the roof into the courtyard.

Inside the room, Buford was shot twice in the upper thigh. Agent Constantino provided cover for Buford and Jordan while they ran back for the window, dove out onto the pitched roof and then dropped to the ground. As Agents Chisolm and Bonaventure dragged Buford out of the line of fire, they were fired upon. A bullet creased Buford's nose. Agent Chisolm threw his body over Buford to protect him[26]. When the shooting stopped, Chisolm and Bonaventure pulled Buford to a safe position. Chisolm, the medic for his team, observed Buford's wounds and began administering an IV to him.

Immediately after Buford and Jordan were out of the arms room, the firing stopped. As Constantino was deciding whether to hold his position or make a run for the window, a cult member entered the room aiming an assault rifle at him. He fired two or three shots at Constantino. Constantino returned fire and the man fell. Constantino ran for the window, but as he was going through it, he struck his head, knocked off his helmet and dropped his weapon. Dazed, he rolled off the roof and fell to the ground, severely fracturing his hip and leg and causing extensive injury to both knees. As he lay on the ground, vulnerable to the cult's guns, he saw two agents who had taken cover near the wall of the Compound. Constantino put his hand out and Special Agents David Millen and Charles Smith dragged him out of the line of fire. (Contrary to some publicly disseminated accounts, none of the agents that entered the armory were killed.)

Special Agents Steven D. Willis and Robert J. Williams were killed during the ambush. Agent Willis, a member of the Houston raid support team, had taken cover behind a van parked near the right front corner of the Compound. Special Agent Williams, New Orleans SRT, was providing cover for his teammates mounting the roof. Intense gunfire forced him to seek cover behind a large metal object on the ground to the east side of the Compound.

Throughout the vicious firefight, ATF agents demonstrated extraordinary discipline and courage. Special Agents Bernadette Griffin, Jonathan Zimmer and Martin Roy were pinned down behind a shed when Special Agent Jordan, who had been wounded in the arms room, staggered over to where they were and collapsed on them. Special Agent Griffin discovered that Jordan's arm was bleeding profusely. She elevated his arm and compressed the wound with her hand until the cease-fire, 90 minutes later. Special Agent Chisolm, relinquishing his own protected location, came to their location and rendered

---

[26] There were many acts of sacrifice and heroism during the attack on the agents, only some of which can be recounted here.

medical aid. Special Agent Tim Gabourie, a medic with the Dallas SRT, who also repeatedly exposed himself to gunfire to treat several wounded agents, had one of his medical bags shot out of his hand by .50-caliber gunfire. He braved gunfire in an unsuccessful effort to reach Special Agent Willis who died during the battle.

In the face of insurmountable, unrelenting automatic and semiautomatic weapons fire from virtually every area of the Compound, the agents had no choice but to remain in their covered positions. The openness of the terrain made retreat impossible. They returned fire when possible, but conserved their ammunition. They also fired only when they saw an individual engage in a threatening action, such as pointing a weapon. Neither of these constraints applied to those in the Branch Davidian Compound who had a virtually limitless supply of ammunition (Several hundred thousand rounds of ammunition were later found in the Compound) and could fire at will. They even fired at the undercover house and at the reporters parked on the road in front of the Compound.

In addition to the agent fatalities, the cult's weapons inflicted vicious wounds on other agents. For example, one agent was shot in both legs by a shotgun. Another agent was shot in the left leg by one bullet while a second passed through his left leg and lodged in his right leg. There were many other serious wounds and related injuries which are listed in Figures 33 and 34.

In contrast to the extensive casualties inflicted upon the agents, there were few casualties among the cult members. (See Figure 35.) Autopsies revealed that two cult members were killed by agents in the entry teams returning fire. Autopsies of two other cult fatalities reveal that they were shot at close range: Perry Jones was killed by a shot in his mouth, a manner of death consistent with suicide; Peter Hipsman was wounded but was later killed by a cult member who shot him at close range in the back of his skull—an apparent mercy killing, although the autopsy revealed that his initial wound would not have been fatal. Koresh was wounded both in the pelvic area and in his wrist.

The Cease-Fire

According to McLennan County 911 records, Branch Davidian Wayne Martin called the Waco 911 emergency service at 9:48. His call was handled by Deputy Larry Lynch. Martin sounded very frightened and Lynch heard gunfire in the background. Deputy Lynch attempted to speak with Martin, but Martin did not respond and at 10:02, Martin hung up.

GUNSHOT RELATED DEATHS SUSTAINED BY ATF ON FEBRUARY 28, 1993

(according to CA-6 Forms submitted by ATF)

	Name	Team	Injury	Cause	Hospital where treated
1	Conway Lebleu	NO	Death	Gunshot	N/A*
2	Todd McKeehan	NO	Death	Gunshot	N/A*
3	Robert Williams	NO	Death	Gunshot	N/A*
4	Steven Willis	HOU	Death	Gunshot	N/A*

GUNSHOT AND SHRAPNEL RELATED INJURIES SUSTAINED BY ATF ON FEBRUARY 28, 1993

(according to CA-1 Forms submitted by ATF)

	Name	Team	Injury	Cause	Hospital
1	Clayton Alexander	NO	Two gunshot wounds - thigh in left leg; thigh in right leg	Gunshot	Providence
2	Roland Ballesteros	HOU	Gunshot wounds to the hand	Gunshot	Hillcrest
3	Bill Buford	NO	Gunshot wounds to both legs	Gunshot	Hillcrest
4	Samuel Cohen	DAL	Shrapnel fragments to lower right thigh	Shrapnel	Hillcrest
5	Eric Evers	HOU	Gunshot and shrapnel wounds to chest and shoulder area	Gunshot/Shrapnel	Hillcrest
6	Mark Handley	HOU	Shrapnel wounds in right leg	Shrapnel	Hillcrest
7	Walter Glen Jordan	NO	Gunshot wounds to both legs	Gunshot	Hillcrest
8	Kenneth King	NO	Gunshot wounds to arms, chest and legs	Gunshot	Providence
9	Mark Murray	DAL	Buck shot wounds to left shoulder	Gunshot	N/A*
10	Gary Orchowski	HOU	Shrapnel wound to the right hand	Shrapnel	Hillcrest
11	Joseph Patterson	DAL	Shrapnel wounds to right cheek	Shrapnel	N/A*
12	Gerald Petrilli	DAL	Shrapnel wounds to right hand, wrist, forearms and left upper arm	Shrapnel	Hillcrest
13	Clair Rayburn	HOU	Gunshot wound to the hand	Gunshot	Hillcrest
14	John Risenhoover	HOU	Gunshot wounds to both legs	Gunshot	Hillcrest
15	Robert Rowe	HOU	Shrapnel wounds to right hand; large abrasion on face	Shrapnel	N/A*
16	Michael Russell	DAL	Wound to back of left shoulder	Gunshot	N/A*
17	Larry Shiver	HOU	Multiple shrapnel wounds to left lower extremity, tissue loss to left medial calf, soft tissue injury to left thigh	Shrapnel	Hillcrest
18	Steven Steele	DAL	Shot in lower lip and left hand; injured lower back and left leg	Gunshot	Hillcrest
19	Robert White	DAL	Bullet wound to left shoulder, neck and bruise to right shin	Gunshot	N/A*
20	Curtis Williams	HOU	Bullet fragments and puncture wound to upper thigh of left leg	Gunshot	N/A*

*N/A means Not Applicable, treated by EMT at scene, or by private physician.

Figure 33

SERIOUS NON-GUNSHOT RELATED INJURIES SUSTAINED BY ATF ON FEBRUARY 28, 1993

(according to CA-1 Forms submitted by ATF)

	Name	Team	Injury	Cause	Hospital where treated
1	Keith Constantino	NO	Broken hip, extensive injuries to both knees and legs	Falling from roof	Hillcrest
2	Terry Lee Hicks	NO	Torn ligament between 3rd & 4th vertebra in neck; possible ruptured disk between 7th and 8th vertebra in neck; bruised or crushed nerve between 7th and 8th vertebra	Moving for cover	N/A*

OTHER NON-GUNSHOT RELATED INJURIES SUSTAINED BY ATF ON FEBRUARY 28, 1993

(according to CA-1 Forms submitted by ATF)

1	Wendel Frost	N/A	Ears subject to extreme noise levels causing possible hearing loss	Noise of two .308 highpowered rifles	N/A*
2	Felix Garcia	N/A	Severe irritation to left heel	ATF boots	N/A*
3	Steven Jensen	HOU	Severe back pain - lower back and right leg, muscle spasms	Carrying dead & wounded from scene	N/A*
4	Kenneth Latimer	HOU	Sprain/pull to right shoulder	Warrant execution	N/A*
5	Charles Meyer	N/A	Rib and back injury on left side	Diving for cover	N/A*
6	John Henry Williams	HOU	Two top front teeth chipped	Moving for cover	N/A

*N/A means Not Applicable, treated by EMT at scene, or by private physician.

Figure 34

BRANCH DAVIDIAN DEATHS ON FEBRUARY 28, 1993
CULT MEMBERS KILLED BY CULT MEMBERS

NAME	NUMBER OF WOUNDS	WEAPON DISTANCE TO WOUND (RANGE)	WEAPON CALIBER/ TYPE OF AMMUNITION	LOCATION OF WOUNDS/ CAUSE OF DEATH
WINSTON BLAKE	1	TWO TO THREE FT.	.223	CRANIOCEREBRAL TRAUMA
PETER HIPSMAN	4 (a)	ONE TO TWO FT.	9 MM. WINCHESTER SILVERTIP JACKETED HOLLOW POINT	(a) UPPER POSTERIOR NECK
	(b)	LESS THAN 1 INCH	9 MM. COPPER JACKETED SOFT POINT	(b) RT. PARIETAL SCALP
	(c)	MORE THAN 4 FT.	9 MM. COPPER JACKETED HOLLOW POINT	(c) LOWER LEFT ANTERIOR CHEST
	(d)	MORE THAN 4 FT.	UNKNOWN (NOT RECOVERED) PROBABLY BULLET (a)	(d) ENTRY TO POST- LATERAL ARM W/ EXIT OF ANTEROLATERAL ARM DEATH DUE TO (a) & (b) CRANIOCEREBRAL TRAUMA
PERRY JONES	1	WEAPON IN MOUTH	UNKNOWN (NOT RECOVERED)	CRANIOCEREBRAL TRAUMA- GUNSHOT WOUND TO MOUTH

CULT MEMBERS KILLED BY ATF

NAME	NUMBER OF WOUNDS	WEAPON DISTANCE TO WOUND (RANGE)	WEAPON CALIBER/ TYPE OF AMMUNITION	LOCATION OF WOUNDS/ CAUSE OF DEATH
PETER GENT	1	DISTANT	9 MM. HYDROSHOCK	PERFORATION OF AORTA GUNSHOT TO UPPER LF. CHEST
MICHAEL SCHROEDER	6 (a)	DISTANT	9 MM. HYDROSHOCK	(a) RT. ANTERIOR SHOULDER
	(b)	DISTANT	9 MM. HYDROSHOCK	(b) RT. LOWER FLANK
	(c)	DISTANT	9 MM. HYDROSHOCK	(c) LEFT THIGH
	(d)	DISTANT	9 MM. HYDROSHOCK	(d) RT. TEMPORAL SCALP
	(e)	DISTANT	UNKNOWN (NOT RECOVERED)	(e) RT. SUPRA-AURICULAR REGION - EXIT RT. POSTIOR AURICULAR SURFACE
	(f)	DISTANT	UNKNOWN (NOT RECOVERED)	(f) GRAZING GUNSHOT WOUND OF THE LEFT CHEST. DEATH DUE TO MULTIPLE GUNSHOT WOUNDS
JAYDEAN WENDELL	1	DISTANT	9 MM. HYDROSHOCK	CRANIOCEREBRAL TRAUMA- GUNSHOT WOUND TO HEAD

BRANCH DAVIDIAN INJURIES SUSTAINED ON FEBRUARY 28, 1993

NAME	NATURE OF INJURY
DAVID JONES	*GUNSHOT WOUND TO GLUTEUS MAXIMUS
DAVID KORESH	GUNSHOT WOUND TO PELVIC RIM AND LEFT WRIST
JUDY SCHNIEDER	*GUNSHOT WOUND TO INDEX FINGER
SCOTT SONOBE	*GUNSHOT WOUND TO LEG

*ALLEGED WOUNDS

Figure 35

Using the telephone number that appears on a screen when a call is placed to 911, Lynch called back to the Compound. An answering machine responded. Hoping that Martin, or someone in the Compound, could hear, Lynch yelled for Martin to pick up the phone. Martin responded and Lynch began attempting to arrange a cease-fire. Simultaneously, Lynch tried to contact ATF through Lieutenant Barber, who as the liaison between ATF and the sheriff's department, was at the command post. However, Barber had turned off his radio because he was planning to assist the bomb technicians in recovering and processing any explosives. Although Lynch was unable to raise ATF on his radio, a TSTC officer, Jim Stone, responded and said that he was able to contact ATF. Stone drove to the command post and reached SAC Chojnacki. Chojnacki used Stone's radio to speak with Deputy Lynch.

Afraid that if Martin was told to hang up the telephone to allow ATF to contact him directly, contact might not be restored, ATF worked through Lynch. Thus, Martin was in contact with Deputy Lynch, who had to relay what Martin said to Chojnacki by way of Stone's radio. Lynch told Martin to cease firing while simultaneously arranging for ATF agents at the Compound to do the same and pull back.

At 10:34, Martin advised Deputy Lynch that someone else in the Compound wanted to speak to Lynch. At 10:35 Koresh called Lynch. Lynch was then in contact with Martin on one telephone line, David Koresh on another, and ATF by radio, as he attempted to arrange a cease-fire. The negotiations were unproductive, stymied by the unwieldy communications and confusion in the Compound.

In the undercover house, Cavanaugh eventually decided that the sheriff's department was not making sufficient progress toward achieving a cease-fire, but he did not have the telephone number for any phone in the Compound. He yelled across to the agents in the neighboring house, who yelled back that the number was on the refrigerator. Cavanaugh found the number and dialed the Compound. The phone rang repeatedly but no one answered. Cavanaugh radioed to the agents on the Compound grounds to yell into the Compound for someone to answer the phone. Then, Branch Davidian Steve Schneider answered the telephone. Cavanaugh identified himself and told Schneider that he wanted to discuss the situation. Through the telephone Cavanaugh could hear yelling, screaming and crying in the Compound. Intermittent gunfire between agents and those in the Compound punctuated the tense standoff. Schneider was frantic and hostile. It took Cavanaugh several minutes to calm him. When Cavanaugh began to discuss arranging a cease-fire, Schneider was receptive because individuals in the Compound had also been wounded. But even after

Schneider and Cavanaugh had agreed to call a cease-fire, it took several minutes to achieve one. Schneider for his part had to walk throughout the Compound to tell people inside to stop shooting. Cavanaugh, who had no direct radio link to each agent, had to advise the team leaders of the cease-fire and the team leaders in turn had to communicate with their agents. The cease-fire was negotiated for a period of time before the shooting finally stopped.

The cease-fire agreement did not address how the agents would leave. Cavanaugh told Schneider that ATF wanted to retrieve its dead and wounded agents. Schneider demanded that the agents withdraw unconditionally. Cavanaugh insisted that the agents would leave only if they could retrieve their wounded and dead. Schneider who remained excitable and irrational insisted that the agents leave immediately. Cavanaugh assured Schneider that the agents would retreat, but vowed not without their fallen comrades. Retrieval of King, who had fallen in the rear courtyard, was a particularly difficult point of negotiation. Initially, Schneider would not allow agents to go to the courtyard for King. Cavanaugh was able to discuss with Schneider King's precise location, even arranging for Schneider to have someone in the Compound look in the Courtyard to verify that an agent was there. Eventually, Schneider agreed to let agents retrieve King.

Cavanaugh instructed the agents to raise their hands, not to make any sudden movements and begin leaving the grounds. At approximately 11:34, SAC Mastin approached Agents Griffin, Bonaventure and Chisolm to assist them in retrieving King from the rear courtyard. The four of them proceeded slowly, with their hands raised, around the east wall of the Compound to reach the rear courtyard. When they reached the courtyard area, they began searching for King. Suddenly, one of the Branch Davidians aimed a rifle at Griffin and yelled racial slurs at her. Griffin decided that if she was going to be shot, she would rather it be while attempting to assist one of her fellow agents. She turned and walked toward King. The cult member did not shoot.

King was too seriously injured to be carried without a stretcher, so the agents placed him on a ladder. They brought him out to the front of the Compound and put him in an ambulance that Special Agents Aguilera and Dunagan had driven to the Compound with Special Agents Rodriguez and Salas riding in the back to provide assistance: The AMT driver was not present because ATF could not guarantee his safety.

By this time, most of the agents able to walk had gathered near a large bus to the right of the Compound. At 11:46 Cavanaugh was able to persuade Schneider to allow ATF to retrieve the remaining dead and wounded agents. The cease-fire left the agents at a significant tactical disadvantage. The agents were not covered, while the cult members were shielded inside the Compound's main building with vantage points on floors above the ground. While many agents were almost out of ammunition, the Branch Davidians were well supplied, which became clear when the Compound was searched after the April 19 fire. Under the threat of Branch Davidian gunfire the agents withdrew, some with holstered weapons, some with their shields raised, some with their hands in the air, and some with their backs to the Compound. The dead agents and those unable to walk were placed in any available vehicle: the ambulance; a pickup truck that had been parked in front of the undercover house; and a KWTX reporter's Ford Bronco. The six agents in the undercover house, rearranged the furniture into a defensive configuration and the forward observers monitored the retreat, prepared to return fire if necessary. The agents stayed in the undercover house until later that afternoon, when they received support from the Texas Department of Public Safety SWAT team who took positions at the nearby roadblock. At roughly the same time, ATF agents who had taken positions in a building near the undercover house were also able to withdraw safely. During the ceasefire, some agents had moved from the hay barn closer to the Compound. From this relatively safe, high ground, they had an excellent view of the Compound. But soon they were ordered back to the hay barn, where they had no such vantage point.

Because no one had designated a rallying point at which agents would take defensive positions or had ordered a sequential withdrawal that might have permitted some agents to cover the movements of others, the retreat continued until the agents reached the roadblock at the intersection of Double E Road and FM 2491. There, arrangements were made for bus transportation, first to a nearby social club, the Pep Club, and then back to the staging area. It was approximately 1:00 when the withdrawal negotiations were completed. Once the agents had left the Compound grounds, Cavanaugh agreed with Schneider that no agents would come on the property and no one inside would attempt to leave. Cavanaugh told Schneider that he would call again at 2:00 p.m. Cavanaugh then arranged for the residents of the neighboring house to be taken to a hotel, and he went to the command post.

Part One
Section Five: Post-raid Events

Aftermath of the Shoot-Out on February 28

Once Cavanaugh and Schneider had negotiated the cease-fire, ATF was confronted with a number of demanding and urgent tasks. First, and foremost, ATF needed to give prompt medical attention to the agents who had been wounded in the gunfight. Second, as described in the preceding section, ATF agents needed to withdraw safely from their vulnerable positions around the Compound. Third, ATF had to establish and maintain a secure perimeter around the Compound to prevent the escape of any adult cult members—all of whom were suspects in the murder of four ATF agents and the attempted murder of federal agents—and to prevent cult members outside the Compound from rendering assistance. Fourth, residents of the Compound who had not resisted, especially the children, needed to be evacuated. Finally, ATF had to provide the public with a prompt and accurate outline of the events at the Compound, while making clear to both the general public and those inside the Compound that ATF was in control of a difficult and challenging situation.

Events in the aftermath of the cease-fire demonstrated that ATF lacked the planning, training, and resources to accomplish all of these tasks satisfactorily. Nonetheless, through the courage and tenacity of its agents and local law enforcement personnel, ATF managed to make substantial progress toward achieving several critical post-raid objectives.

The Evacuation of Wounded Agents

Before the raid on the Branch Davidian Compound, planners arranged for a private ambulance to stand by at a roadblock near the Compound during the operation and for a CareFlite helicopter to be available at the command post, which was five minutes' flying time away from the Compound, for medical evacuations. Soon after the operation began, it became clear that these resources were not enough to help all of the wounded agents. Even before the shooting was over, ATF agents called for more ambulances and an additional CareFlite helicopter. The additional evacuation vehicles soon reached the roadblock where the retreating agents had gathered. First, three additional ambulances and an additional CareFlite helicopter arrived. During the next fifteen minutes, emergency medical care was administered to the ATF agents most seriously wounded. Those who needed immediate additional attention were then taken by either ambulance or helicopter to one of the two hospitals in Waco equipped to treat persons with gunshot wounds. By 12:25 p.m., the helicopters were airborne, and by 12:35, they had landed at Providence Hospital in Waco. After one of the hospitals received death threats against the wounded agents, ATF sent agents to the Providence and Hillcrest hospitals to provide security for the wounded agents and to obtain accurate information about the extent of ATF losses.

The Media and the Shoot-Out

Tensions ran high between ATF and the media during the shoot-out and cease-fire. Many agents were angry with media personnel who had been in the midst of the shoot-out, distracting agents while they were under fire and whom agents had almost shot accidentally, fearing they were cult members. When the cease-fire was established, the five *Tribune-Herald* reporters who had been pinned in the ditch on Double E Road retreated quickly toward FM 2491. An ambulance driver, concerned that three of the media representatives might be Branch Davidians, ducked behind his ambulance and pointed the suspects out to an ATF agent.

Mullony, who had filmed portions of the shoot-out from the front of the Compound, walked along the Compound driveway after the cease-fire and filmed the agents as they walked to the roadblock. Once he reached the roadblock at FM 2491, ATF agents and local law enforcement authorities verbally and physically assaulted Mullony as he filmed the agents' dead colleagues lying on the ground. Witherspoon, who had spent the shoot-out huddled in the ditch, was scolded by a sheriff's department employee for being at the scene.

The Failure to Maintain the Perimeter

During the course of the afternoon, ATF withdrew from its positions, and aside from the roadblocks it maintained, relinquished much of its control over the perimeter of the Compound. At one of these roadblocks, an alert ATF agent and local law enforcement officer prevented cult member Donald Bunds from returning to the Compound within an hour after the firefight. Because Bunds was driving a car with an expired registration, he was arrested and taken to McLennan County jail.

The failure to maintain the perimeter other than the roadblocks was due in part to a communication failure. After learning that Koresh had threatened to use women and children as shields in order to bring wounded cult members to the hospital, Hartnett ordered that Koresh be permitted to leave the Compound if he made good on this threat. In Waco, however, this order was either received erroneously or transformed by command post supervisors as a directive to abandon perimeter positions and to permit Koresh and his followers to leave. Numerous agents in the field, receiving these instructions, were greatly demoralized because these instructions would permit people who had murdered other agents to escape.

The withdrawal of the agents from the hay barn, combined with ATF's failure to guard the rear of the barn from attack by cult members outside the Compound, resulted in a sequence of events that almost produced additional ATF casualties. While most of the agents had been deployed to execute the warrants at the Compound, a smaller group was sent to execute a search warrant at the Mag Bag. The plan called for the group to arrive at the Mag Bag shortly after the Compound had been secured. However, while en route to the Mag Bag, the group was told of the firefight and ordered to return to the command post. This left the Mag Bag unsecured, even though Aguilera's investigation had revealed regular communication between cult members in the Mag Bag and those in the Compound. Shortly thereafter, three armed cult members who had been inside the Mag Bag drove to a house near the Compound and walked from there toward the rear of the Compound.

Meanwhile, during the afternoon, one of the agents stationed near the hay barn spotted a Branch Davidian moving away from the Compound toward an adjacent property. Because the agents had been instructed to avoid confrontations and to permit persons who did not pose an immediate threat to leave the Compound, the agents allowed him to leave. Shortly thereafter, agents withdrawing from positions around the hay barn, led by ASAC Darrell Dyer, encountered in the woods the three Branch Davidians who had left the Mag Bag. When the agents identified themselves as federal agents, the cult members opened fire. After a prolonged exchange of gunfire, one of the three cult members surrendered. He was carrying a .22-caliber weapon and 100 rounds of ammunition. A second cult member, Michael Dean Schroeder, was killed by the agents; he had a loaded Glock 9mm semiautomatic pistol and two ammunition magazines—one empty and one full. The third Branch Davidian, Woodrow Kendrick, escaped, but was captured later.

When ASAC Dyer first saw the Branch Davidians in the woods, he informed the command post that he and the other agents were in contact with suspected cult members. By that time, a National Guard Armored Personnel Carrier (APC) had arrived at the forward command post, that ATF had established near one of the roadblocks after the cease-fire. Sarabyn asked the National Guard commander to send the APC to the rear of the Compound to support Dyer and his fellow agents. Cavanaugh, however, who was still engaged in negotiations with the Branch Davidians, feared that the appearance of an APC near the Compound might disrupt negotiations. In addition, the supervisors were concerned that the APC could be pierced by long-range .50-caliber fire. As a result, the APC was kept near the forward command post for the duration of the conflict. The agents made their way back to the roadblock where they were taken by car to the command post. Throughout this exchange of gunfire in the woods, Cavanaugh continued his negotiations with Koresh and other cult members.

With the withdrawal of these agents, ATF temporarily stopped efforts to prevent cult members from leaving the Compound. To the limited extent the perimeter around the Compound was controlled, that was accomplished principally through the efforts of local law enforcement personnel and SWAT teams, including the Austin Police Department, Texas Department of Public Safety, Waco Police Department, Killeen Police Department, McLennan County Sheriff's Department, and the U.S. Marshals Service. These officers refused to follow ATF directives to abandon the perimeter that would have allowed cult members to leave the Compound. However, local law enforcement were able to control only the roads to the Compound; other routes went unguarded. Colonel Charlie A. Beckwith, U.S.A., Ret., on assignment for *Soldier of Fortune* magazine, claims that he managed to advance on foot to within less than a mile of the Compound without being challenged.

A Siege Develops and ATF Obtains Assistance from the FBI

Chaos at the Command Post

After the shoot-out, the situation at the command post became chaotic. Nonetheless, throughout the afternoon, individual agents identified urgent tasks both at the command post and elsewhere and completed them. Cavanaugh negotiated with the Compound; Dyer provided support to agents at the rear of the Compound; Robert White, an assistant SRT leader (Dallas), began organizing agents to establish a perimeter; Phillip Lewis regularly updated the National Command Center in Washington, D.C., and various agents handled tasks related to the wounded, including providing security, contacting relatives, and insuring all received proper medical attention. With no one coordinating these diverse individual efforts, however, the logistical situation in Waco deteriorated rapidly. Many ATF agents, after returning from the shoot-out at the Compound, milled around the command post during the late afternoon and evening hours, awaiting orders. Others were told by supervisors not to return until early the next morning. In contrast, many of the agents who stood guard at the roadblocks and provided security at the hospitals for the wounded agents remained at their posts for lengthy shifts, some exceeding 24 hours. Many of the agents in the field were not adequately supplied with food, warm clothing, and other necessities.

Initial Relief

Based on conversations with agents at the command post, ATF management at the National Command Center determined that additional SRTs should be brought to Waco immediately to provide relief. Within a few hours of the firefight, three additional SRTs from Miami, St. Louis, and Detroit were requested by Washington ATF officials to report to Waco. They arrived over the course of the next 24 hours and, after being briefed by the tactical commanders, were rapidly pressed into service around the Compound. They relieved their fellow ATF agents as well as those local law enforcement personnel who had stood vigilant through the night.

The Decision to Bring in the FBI HRT

Shortly after the shoot-out, Chojnacki spoke with Hartnett, who was in Washington, D.C., and recommended that the FBI Hostage Rescue Team (HRT), which had experience with both prolonged standoffs and hostage negotiations, be brought to Waco to handle what had become a siege situation. At roughly the same time, FBI Director William Sessions learned of the shoot-out, contacted ATF Director Stephen Higgins and offered his condolences and his agency's assistance. After Hartnett arrived at the National Command Center and was fully briefed, he determined that the FBI HRT should be sent to Waco.

Soon after the cease-fire, Hartnett contacted Douglas Gow, FBI Associate Deputy Director of Investigations, and formally requested FBI assistance. Gow, in turn, contacted FBI SAC Jeffrey Jamar (San Antonio) and briefed him on the situation. At roughly the same time, FBI Special Agent James Fossum (Waco) was informed of the crisis by both AUSA Phinizy and another local FBI agent. After speaking with Jamar, Fossum drove to the ATF command post. Shortly after he arrived, Chojnacki told him the ATF would welcome whatever assistance the FBI could provide.

Meanwhile, the Office of the Assistant Secretary for Enforcement at the Treasury Department, particularly Ronald Noble, had contacts with both high-ranking FBI officials and ATF leadership. Noble, who had been informed of the firefight and the losses incurred by ATF while en route by train from Washington, D.C. to New York, sought advice and assistance from FBI Assistant Director Larry Potts and Deputy Director Floyd Clark.[27] Shortly after Hartnett requested the HRT, Noble and Clark discussed the possibility of dispatching the HRT to Waco in one of their conversations. Clark informed him that a request for the HRT had already been made by ATF and that the HRT was on its way to the Compound to evaluate the situation.

Jeffrey Jamar (San Antonio), as the SAC of the affected district, was given command of the FBI operation. He arrived in Waco at about 5:30 p.m. and together with Fossum and several other local FBI agents, immediately began to establish a command post and assess the situation. The balance of the HRT members began arriving on March 1.

After further discussions with FBI, ATF and Treasury officials, Noble spoke with ATF Director Higgins and ADLE Hartnett early March 1. Noble advised them that if the FBI determined that the HRT was needed for the long term, the FBI should have operational command to resolve the standoff. There were several reasons for this advice. First, the FBI HRT traditionally has control over operations in which it participates, and ATF was not in a position to assert such control. Second, the FBI was in a better position to stabilize the situation than ATF. The ATF had already absorbed heavy losses and if further hostilities occurred might be accused of seeking revenge. Noble also wanted to preclude any turf battles that might arise if the effort were jointly managed. At the FBI, Potts and Clark, as well as Gerson from Justice, agreed that were the HRT fully deployed, its leaders must have command and control of the operation.

---

[27] Due to the World Trade Center bombing, Potts, Clark, and Acting Attorney General Stuart Gerson were at the FBI command center in Washington, D.C., on the day of the raid.

Hartnett and Conroy Arrive at the Command Post

Hartnett, who had arrived in the National Command Center shortly after noon (EST) on the day of the raid, ordered Dan Conroy to leave immediately for Waco. Hartnett remained at the National Command Center until Director Higgins arrived at roughly 3:00 p.m. After Hartnett had briefed him, Higgins directed Hartnett to proceed to Waco. Hartnett, accompanied by several members of the FBI HRT advance team, including Dick Rogers, the HRT supervisor, traveled to Waco on an FBI airplane.

At approximately 6:30 p.m., Dyer returned to the command post and informed Assistant U.S. Attorney Johnston and the supervisors about the shoot-out near the hay barn. By that time, after hours of negotiation with cult members, Cavanaugh had managed to reach an agreement with Koresh who allowed the release of several children in exchange for ATF arranging to have a particular passage of scripture broadcast repeatedly on a local radio station. Cavanaugh was assisted by two negotiators from the Texas Department of Public Safety. Cavanaugh continued to play a leading role in these negotiations for several days, although the FBI took charge of them during the afternoon of March 1.

When Dyer returned, Cavanaugh directed him to assemble a group of agents to receive the children that would soon be released from the Compound. Dyer, Rodriguez and several others went to the Compound and received six children over the course of the evening. The children were immediately placed in the custody of the Texas Department of Protective and Regulatory Services.

Conroy arrived in Waco at approximately 8:30 p.m. and found the command post still in a state of disarray. Several of the commanding officers were trying to restore order and were striving to deal with the most pressing tasks. Cavanaugh was continuing to negotiate with the cult members; Sarabyn was coordinating the recovery of the children through contacts with Dyer and others, and Royster was trying to handle the large influx of ATF agents and the state and local law enforcement officers who were volunteering for service. Royster was also seeking night-vision equipment, lenses, Light Armored Vehicles, and Bradley Fighting Vehicles from the National Guard. Other agents were trying to deal with the media. In fact, the raid became an international story within hours after the shooting ended. According to the *Tribune-Herald*, by mid-afternoon the day of the raid, 60 newspaper reporters and camera crews from at least 17 television stations and the Cable News Network had deluged the police barricades near the Compound. More than 50 reporters attended the ATF press conference at the Waco Convention Center Sunday afternoon where SAC Royster read a statement from Director Higgins. A similar crowd attended Sharon Wheeler's short briefing and announcement that a press conference would be held at 10:30 the following morning. Despite ATF and FBI attempts to provide daily news briefings, the media complained that they were not getting enough information. Neither ATF, the local media, nor the town of Waco was prepared for the intense media coverage following the raid.

A few hours later, when Hartnett arrived at the command post at about 11:00 p.m., he found over 100 local law enforcement personnel and ATF agents, many still wearing bloodstained clothes from the raid. After Conroy briefed him, Hartnett took control of the operation, requiring the original operation commanders to report directly to him and Conroy. He then cleared the main area of all non-ATF people and told most of the ATF agents to report back the next morning.

Together with Conroy and Chojnacki, Hartnett established a new ATF command structure. Ivan Kalister, Program Manager for Tactical Response Branch, Washington, D.C., and Sarabyn were made responsible for establishing the SRT people on the perimeter of the Compound and for providing security for the hospitalized agents. Cavanaugh and the FBI were to conduct the negotiations with the Compound. Royster was given responsibility for the overall criminal investigation of Koresh and the other cult members. Once the Texas Rangers opened a formal homicide investigation, he became the liaison with the Texas Rangers. David Troy, Chief, Intelligence Division, Washington, D.C.; Dave Benton, Chief, Planning and Analysis Division, Washington, D.C., and Bill Wood, SAC, Cleveland Division, were the shooting review team, charged with interviewing all participants in the shoot-out. RAC Phillip Lewis, San Antonio, and Program Manager, Firearms Division, Dick Curd, Washington, D.C., were put in charge of managing all logistics, including lodging and vehicles. ATF Public Information Officers Wheeler and Perot were told to continue functioning as the public information officers.

These agents reported to Conroy and Hartnett until the FBI HRT took control of their respective aspects of the operation. Many supervisory and field agents believed the Hartnett and Conroy takeover exacerbated the problem of poor communication between the operation's leadership and the field agents. In addition, because Hartnett and Conroy often met privately, most agents, including the raid leaders, felt they were inappropriately being denied access to the decisionmaking process.

Hartnett instructed the ATF agents to take control of the roadblocks by midnight and to establish a full perimeter around the Compound at dawn. By early morning on March 1, with the assistance of both local law enforcement and the relieving SRTs, ATF had resumed its watch on most of the roads leading into and out of the Compound. From their posts, law enforcement officials could observe much of the Compound. In the days immediately following the raid, aside from the person seen near the hay barn escaping from the Compound, law enforcement officials did not see any other cult members leave the Compound.

Starting soon after the shooting ended ATF also attempted to provide support and counseling for the raid participants. Members of ATF peer support groups, which provide confidential support for agents who have experienced traumatic incidents, met with numerous raid participants. These support groups consist of agents who have been through earlier traumatic incidents and who are trained to provide peer support. In addition, professional counseling from experts in handling participants in violent incidents was available for those agents who elected to avail themselves of those services. Although many agents did use those services, other agents who could have benefitted from such services chose not to. Some of those who did not seek counseling apparently feared that if they did, they would be stigmatized as weak or troubled. Numerous agents also provided support and care for their hospitalized colleagues.

At approximately 10:00 a.m. on March 1, Hartnett and Jamar conducted a meeting with those ATF agents who were not posted around the Compound. This was the first post-raid meeting attended by most of the ATF agents who had participated in the raid. Hartnett announced that the FBI HRT was going to take over the operation because of its special expertise in hostage and siege negotiations. Hartnett expressed his concern that further ATF involvement in violence at the Compound might lead to accusations that ATF was seeking revenge. The agents were angered by Hartnett's remarks. He did not comment upon the four agent fatalities or the bravery exhibited the day of the raid. The agents resented the implication that they were not capable of handling the current situation. Next, Hartnett introduced Jamar who also failed to mention the slain agents and the valiant actions of ATF agents. Moreover, as Jamar explained the rationale for the FBI takeover, the agents felt he overemphasized FBI capabilities and, by inference, ATF shortcomings. Many of the agents, including several of ATF's top management team, were disappointed and angered by Jamar's remarks.

The next day, March 2, the HRT took control of the inner perimeter from ATF agents, who by then had supplanted local law enforcement officials. In turn, the ATF agents took the positions on the outer perimeter previously held by local law enforcement. Many ATF agents resented the way some of the HRT agents acted when taking over the perimeter, and they were especially troubled by what they perceived as the FBI's lack of interest in debriefing them. Although a few verbal exchanges took place between certain agents, the transition between ATF commanders and HRT supervisors was reasonably smooth, with ATF briefing the HRT leaders about Koresh and the situation at the Compound. A few days after the takeover, Hartnett sent the Dallas, Houston, and New Orleans ATF agents home. The remaining ATF agents assumed positions in an outer perimeter outside the HRT and provided support for the operation. Transfer to the FBI of control of the inner perimeter effectively ended ATF's authority over and responsibility for the standoff.

Part Two
Section One: The Propriety of Investigating Koresh and Other Cult Members and Seeking to Enforce Federal Firearms Laws

ATF Properly Initiated an Investigation of Koresh

Since ATF's repulsed effort to search the Branch Davidian Compound, some members of the public and the media have questioned the propriety of ATF's decision to initiate an investigation of Koresh and his followers. Questions have been raised as to whether the cult members were justifiably suspected of violating any applicable federal laws. Others have conceded that Koresh was violating the law but have suggested that the violations should have been ignored:

> What were the Davidians doing to provoke [the raid]? Probably they were converting semiautomatic rifles to full auto. That is certainly a crime; even possessing the capability to convert them is a crime. But down here in the Fifty-Caliber Belt this particular crime is usually treated about as seriously as spitting on the sidewalk (Larry McMurtry, "Return to Waco," *The New Republic,* June 7, 1993, page 16).

Some also have expressed concern about whether ATF was motivated inappropriately to focus a federal firearms investigation of Koresh because of its concerns about his alleged sexual abuse of children and his polygamy. Others have asked whether ATF selected Koresh improperly for investigation because of his nontraditional religious beliefs and practices. One columnist, for instance, asked shortly after the Compound burned to the ground:

> Who, exactly, were the Davidians bothering? The administration says they were hoarding guns. How un-American and how un-Texan. May we expect the administration to lay siege now to the National Rifle Association? The Davidians were also said to be abusing children. A graver charge, but not a

charge that [warrants the ATF's or the FBI's actions]. (Leon Wieseltier, "The True Fire," *The New Republic,* May 17, 1993, page 25).

A Washington, D.C., newspaper columnist raised similar concerns a few weeks before the Compound burned:

No government official has yet explained what crime was being committed by the dimwits of something called the Branch Davidians ... [W]hat provoked this show of force from the crack troops of the Bureau of Alcohol, Tobacco, and Firearms? Was someone caught smoking in a restricted area? Were the faithful of the Rev. David Koresh distilling ardent spirits in an illegal still for one of his holy rites? Was there an illicit drug on the premise or did someone have a shotgun that ran afoul of government standards? ... If Americans cannot live the life of the rugged—albeit somewhat loony—individualist in the vast reaches of the great West, where can they live normal American lives? (R. Emmett Tyrell, Jr., "Crystals in the Waco Crucible," *The Washington Times,* April 4, 1993, page B1).

These criticisms are not supported by the evidence. A review of the investigation makes it clear that the ATF inquiry into the activities of Koresh and his followers was consistent with the agency's congressional mandate to enforce federal laws regulating the possession and manufacture of automatic weapons and explosive devices. Indeed, ATF would have been remiss if it had permitted considerations of religious freedom to insulate the Branch Davidians from such an investigation.

At the outset, it should be emphasized that ATF focused on the Branch Davidians only after it was asked to do so by local law enforcement authorities who had been scrutinizing the conduct of cult members. Since the Roden shoot-out in 1987 and the return of a substantial cache of weapons and ammunition to the cult, the sheriff's department had watched Koresh add to his arsenal and had heard reports of other behavior on the Compound that generated concern, including the construction of an underground firing range and bunker and a tight cluster of ramshackle buildings that was beginning to resemble a fortress. Although neighbors feared cult members and complained about gunfire at the Compound, the local investigation developed slowly.

In late May 1992, however, the sheriff's department received concrete evidence from UPS that Koresh was receiving substantial shipments of weapons components. In addition, the sheriff's department received reliable reports that Koresh was purchasing large quantities of semiautomatic rifles from local arms dealers. Recognizing that the investigation of a large-scale firearms case involving a close-knit group such as the Branch Davidians would be a substantial undertaking, the sheriff's department sought the assistance of ATF, which has expertise in firearms investigations, as well as a tradition of working closely with local law enforcement agencies.

Even after ATF assistance was sought, ATF agents did not formally open an investigation until making a preliminary determination that federal crimes were being committed. Special Agent Aguilera debriefed local officials and then searched national firearms registries. When Aguilera learned that neither Koresh nor his followers were registered owners of any lawful machineguns, but nevertheless were receiving shipments of machinegun parts and paying for them with large quantities of cash, he reasonably grew suspicious that they were engaged in the illegal manufacture of machineguns. Upon learning that Koresh had received a shipment of materials used to manufacture explosives, specifically grenades, Aguilera formally opened an ATF case in early June 1992.

While some have suggested that ATF targeted Koresh because of his religious beliefs and life-style, the Review has found no evidence of any such motivation. Indeed, ATF recognized early the delicacy of an investigation of such an unorthodox community. Aguilera's supervisors appropriately classified the case as "sensitive," thus ensuring greater supervisory scrutiny of a case that was perceived at the outset to have the potential for raising thorny religious issues as well as difficult safety issues, particularly regarding the women and children living at the Compound.

Whatever controversy there might be about the types of weapons American citizens should be permitted to maintain, federal laws draw a definite line at fully automatic guns and explosive devices such as grenades, which are thought to be more suited for battlefield use than any other purpose.[28] That a private individual has access to a single unlawful machinegun must be cause for federal concern. Where a group is found to be stockpiling

---

[28] The history of the original 1934 legislation that taxed machineguns, where the House Ways and Means Committee report of the bill stated, "There is no reason why anyone except a law officer should have a machinegun or sawed-off shotgun" (Committee on House Ways and Means, "Taxation and Regulation of Firearms," Report 1780, 73rd Congress, May 28, 1934, page 1), and the 1986 legislation banning the manufacture of machineguns, where Sen. Edward Kennedy (D-Massachusetts) emphasized during floor debate that machineguns had become a far more serious law enforcement problem (*Congressional Record,* May 6, 1986, page S5362), underscores the rationale for restricting possession of such weapons.

many such weapons and to be developing the capability to manufacture many more, ATF must pursue the case. And while the group's religious beliefs should not be cause for targeting it, neither should the beliefs insulate the group from federal scrutiny.

Evidence Developed by ATF's Investigation Warranted Application for and Issuance of Search and Arrest Warrants

Some media accounts have asked whether ATF's investigation unearthed sufficient evidence to support either the ATF application for an arrest warrant for Koresh and related search warrants or Magistrate-Judge Dennis Green's issuance of those warrants. According to *The Washington Times,* for example:

> One Washington lawyer, considered a weapons expert, said a review of the affidavit, written by ATF agent Davy Aguil[era], shows there was no probable cause to arrest Koresh or search the property. The lawyer, who asked not to be identified, said the ATF search appeared to be based on a desire "to punish Koresh for showing disrespect" to the ATF. (Jerry Seper, "Affidavit to Search Waco Site Criticized," *The Washington Times,* September 2, 1993, page 6).

See also James L. Pate, "Waco's Defective Warrants," *Soldier of Fortune,* August 1993, page 46, which states, "The original affidavit does not show probable cause. Probable cause did not exist." The evidence that ATF presented in support of the warrant applications, however, plainly showed there was probable cause—as that term is commonly understood[29]—that numerous federal criminal violations were being committed by Koresh and his followers.

---

[29] Although there is no precise, mathematical definition for what constitutes probable cause—the standard to be met by arrest and search warrant applications—the Supreme Court has explained that probable cause to obtain an arrest warrant exists when law enforcement authorities have knowledge of facts and circumstances sufficient in themselves to warrant a belief by a person of reasonable caution that an offense has been or is being committed by the person to be arrested. *Beck* v. *Ohio,* 379 U.S. 89, 91 (1964); *Brinegar* v. *United States,* 338 U.S. 160, 175-76 (1949). Probable cause to search exists where there is "a fair probability that contraband or evidence of a crime will be found in a particular place." *Illinois* v. *Gates,* 462 U.S. 213, 238 (1983). Probable cause can be based on any reliable evidence, including circumstantial evidence, hearsay from reliable sources, and information from anonymous informants as long as it is corroborated by other independent evidence. See Rule 41(c) of the Federal Rules of Criminal Procedure.

Aguilera faced two significant obstacles in his investigation. First, he had to overcome the largely antisocial, isolated routine of Compound residents. As a rule, residents never spoke to outsiders about Compound activities and harbored deep suspicions of law enforcement personnel. Second, Aguilera wisely sought to keep his investigation a secret from Koresh and his followers in order to ensure strategic and tactical flexibility in case search or arrest warrants needed to be served. Aguilera sharply circumscribed his inquiries about Koresh to third parties, including arms dealers and former cult members, for fear of alerting the Branch Davidians that they were under scrutiny.

Still, by late February 1993, Aguilera had amassed an impressive amount of evidence that Koresh was unlawfully possessing and manufacturing machineguns and explosive devices and that he was unlawfully storing substantial quantities of black powder. At the outset, Aguilera knew that Koresh was receiving shipments of M-16 parts and materials used to make explosives, among other firearms materials. Because neither Koresh nor any of his followers were registered owners of any M-16 machineguns, indeed, of any machineguns at all, Aguilera could fairly infer that Koresh was purchasing the M-16 parts to convert AR-15 semiautomatic rifles into machineguns illegally. His suspicions were confirmed when he learned that Henry McMahon had sold about 90 AR-15 lower receivers to Koresh and that McMahon tried unsuccessfully to conceal the bulk of those sales and then to mislead Aguilera about the identity of the purchaser. Aguilera also discovered that Koresh had purchased AR-15s and AR-15 upper receivers from several other sources.

Once stocked with AR-15 receivers and M-16 parts, Koresh needed only a metal lathe and milling machine to make more than 100 machineguns. Reports from a number of sources soon made it clear that Koresh possessed both machines at the Compound and that he had experienced operators, including a mechanical engineer, who were designing fully automatic weapons for Koresh and manufacturing them on the premises. Former cult members related how Koresh seemed to be obsessed with the manufacture of machineguns, especially ones of high caliber.[30] They reported that they had seen automatic weapons on the Compound and that a fully automatic AK-47 had been passed around during one of Koresh's "Bible study" sessions. These statements found corroboration in the reports from

---

[30] In fact, after the April 19 fire, law enforcement agents found a milling machine at the Compound with a gun barrel mounted on the machine. In the same room, they found trigger assemblies and other weapons parts.

neighbors of automatic gunfire erupting from the Compound and the construction of an underground firing range replete with objects riddled with bullet holes.[31]

Evaluations from ATF experts gave Aguilera reason to believe reports that Koresh was manufacturing illegal explosive devices at the Compound. Indeed, ATF's explosives expert determined that several items Koresh had received, including gunpowder and igniter cord, were themselves explosives requiring proper registration and storage—neither of which Koresh provided. The expert also determined that those items, together with the inert grenade shells Koresh had received by UPS, probably were being used to manufacture explosive grenades. Aguilera knew from interviews of former cult members that Koresh had often expressed a keen interest in making live grenades and that grenades had been seen at the Compound. Hence, he had probable cause to believe a search would uncover unlawfully manufactured and maintained explosives.[32]

The intelligence that Aguilera gathered from former cult members and others who had dealt with the Branch Davidians was corroborated further once Special Agent Rodriguez began to visit the Compound in his undercover capacity in late January. Koresh impressed the undercover agent with his technical knowledge of how rifles can be made fully automatic and with his familiarity with the laws regulating the conversion of weapons into machineguns.

By the conclusion of his investigation, Aguilera had more than enough reason to believe that materials and equipment used to make machineguns and explosive devices, as well as the weapons themselves, would be found on the Compound and that Koresh had violated federal laws regulating the possession and manufacture of machineguns and explosive materials and the storage of explosive materials. The ATF decision to seek warrants on the basis of this evidence was thus entirely proper, and it is not surprising that the U.S. Attorney's Office applied for those warrants, and the magistrate-judge promptly approved them.

---

[31] The two weapons experts consulted by the Review, William Davis, Jr., and Charles Fagg, confirm that Aguilera and the magistrate-judge had ample evidence to find probable cause to search the Compound for evidence of the manufacture of illegal machineguns. See Appendix B.

[32] Both explosives experts consulted by the Review, Paul Cooper and Joseph Kennedy, conclude that the evidence gathered by Aguilera amounted to probable cause to believe that illegal explosives were being manufactured. See Appendix B.

Some critics of ATF's enforcement actions have questioned why ATF felt compelled to take any action at all at the conclusion of Aguilera's investigation—even assuming there had been probable cause to believe federal violations had taken place. Any suggestion that Koresh should have been left to produce and stockpile machineguns and explosives, however, is without merit. The weapons and explosive violations disclosed by the investigation went to the heart of ATF's mission, as defined by duly enacted statutes, and fell squarely within the range of unlawful conduct the agency routinely investigates. Moreover, the information uncovered by Aguilera indicated that Koresh and his followers posed a far greater threat to society than might be posed by an individual who quietly keeps an illegal weapon or even a collection of such weapons. (See Appendix G.)

Of greatest concern to Aguilera was the evidence that Koresh had a propensity toward violence and intimidation. Indeed, Koresh's control of the Compound originated with his triumphant gunfight with Roden, which only was ended by armed deputies who "got the drop" on Koresh before he and his followers could "finish off" the pinned-down and defeated Roden. Furthermore, not only did armed guards receive UPS deliveries, but also they were reported to have been given standing orders by Koresh to shoot any "intruders." On one occasion, the guards opened fire on a newspaper delivery person. Koresh's pronouncements that his time was coming and, that when it did, the Los Angeles riots would pale in comparison also marked him as someone ready to use the machineguns and grenades he was stockpiling.

The veracity of Sparks' account of Koresh's statement about the coming of "his time" and the Los Angeles riots has been challenged by many media sources. Its inclusion in the federal affidavit used to obtain the warrant to search the Compound has been cited as the leading example of how the affidavit was riddled with errors. According to doubters, Sparks last visited Koresh *before* the Los Angeles riots took place; therefore, her recollection of Koresh's statement must have been faulty. Jerry Seper, who wrote "Affidavit to Search Waco Site Criticized," *The Washington Times*, September 2, 1993, page 6, for instance, reported the following:

> The affidavit ... purported to document a conversation Koresh had with an investigator from the Texas Department of [Protective and Regulatory Services]. It quoted the cult leader as making a threat of a fiery compound battle that would make the Los Angeles riots 'pale in comparison.' But Koresh met with Sparks on April 6, three weeks before the riots began.

The purported comment is an example of the affidavit's apparent errors, which have caused some critics to suggest it was designed to justify the disastrous assault by ATF rather than portray conditions inside the Compound accurately.

See also Daniel Wattenberg, "Gunning for Koresh," *The American Spectator*, August 1993, page 32, which reported the following:

[T]he affidavit is wrong. Koresh did *not* tell Sparks on her visit to the Compound that 'the riots in Los Angeles would pale in comparison' to his self-revelation in Waco. Unless the man really was a prophet, he could not have told her this. The Los Angeles riots broke out on April 29, 1992, more than three weeks after Sparks had last visited Koresh.

The ATF affidavit, which unfortunately discusses only two visits by Sparks to the Compound, one in late February 1992 and one on April 6, 1992, indeed has been the source of this understandable media bewilderment. The source of this confusion lies not in any lack of candor by Sparks, but in the failure of the ATF affidavit to make clear that Sparks' information was the product of more than two visits to the Compound.

The Waco Administrative Review has determined that Sparks, together with other investigators, visited the Compound on at least three occasions: February 27, 1992; April 6, 1992; *and* April 30, 1992. In addition, she spoke by telephone with Koresh on many occasions, both before and after the April 30 visit. The Los Angeles riots began April 29, 1992, shortly after a Simi Valley jury returned its verdict in the "Rodney King case." The riots were the subject of Ted Koppel's "Nightline" broadcast that evening and were front-page news across the nation the next day—April 30, 1992—the last day on which Sparks made a contemporaneous record for a visit with Koresh at the Compound. See Seth Mydans, "The Police Verdict: Los Angeles Policemen Acquitted in Taped Beating," *The New York Times,* April 30, 1992, page 1. See also Linda Deutsch, "Officers Cleared in Beating," *Waco Tribune-Herald,* April 30, 1992, page 1.

Obviously, the timing of Sparks' visit to the Compound relative to the riots powerfully corroborates her account; Koresh naturally would rely on such a recent event to help Sparks visualize what he planned for when "his time" came. In addition to Sparks' recollection of the April 30 encounter, her fellow investigators corroborate both the timing and the substance of Koresh's remarks—and the case file for the Compound documents the April 30 visit.

Perhaps most troubling, in light of his collection of weapons and his threatening rhetoric, was Koresh's apocalyptic theology and his renaming the Compound "Ranch Apocalypse." Although Koresh might simply have been preparing to defend himself against an apocalyptic onslaught, ATF justifiably feared that Koresh might soon have been inspired to turn his arsenal against the community of nonbelievers. In fact, the Review has learned that well before the ATF action on February 28, Koresh made plans for just such an event. He told his followers that soon they would go out into the world, turn their weapons on individual members of the public, and kill those who did not say they were believers. As he explained to his followers, "you can't die for God if you can't kill for God." Koresh later cancelled the planned action, telling his followers that it had been a test of their loyalty to him.[33]

The extraordinary discipline that Koresh imposed on his followers, which enabled him, for example, to obtain all of their assets and to establish exclusive sexual relationships with the Compound's female residents, while not itself cause for ATF intervention, made him far more threatening than a lone individual who had a liking for illegal weapons. The Compound became a rural fortress, often patrolled by armed guards, in which Koresh's word—or the word that Koresh purported to extrapolate from the Scriptures—was the only law. And the accounts by former cult members, including an abused child, that Koresh was sexually abusing minors made it clear that Koresh believed he was beyond society's laws. Were Koresh to decide to turn his weapons on society, he would have devotees to follow him, and they would be equipped with weapons that could inflict serious damage.

In the wake of the tragic consequences of the ATF raid on February 28, 1993, and the evidence discovered at the Compound after it burned down on April 19, 1993, it is no longer necessary to speculate on the threat that Koresh and his followers posed. On February 28, as an agent finished reciting ATF's judicial authorization to enter the Compound, the Branch Davidians responded with volleys of deadly fire, using the weapons they had been stockpiling for so long. Some of these weapons were found later in the ruins of the Compound after April 19, including well over 200 firearms, dozens of unlawful

---

[33] Further details with respect to the plans described in the text will likely be developed through the prosecutions pending in Waco.

machineguns, and numerous prohibited grenades and grenade components. (See Figures 36 through 39.[34])

In short, the ATF investigation of Koresh and his followers, although posing difficult investigatory challenges for ATF, was an appropriate response to a dangerous situation.[35] In light of the information presented by local authorities, it would have been irresponsible for ATF not to have initiated an investigation and similarly irresponsible for ATF not to have pursued Koresh once Aguilera's investigation showed there was probable cause to do so. ATF's willingness to rise to this difficult challenge can only be commended.

The question remains, however, whether ATF selected the appropriate enforcement option when it decided to forcibly execute search and arrest warrants at the Branch Davidian Compound. The following section of this Report analyzes the process that led to the decision to attempt a raid and the development of the raid plan itself. Additionally, the Treasury-Justice forward-looking review focuses on the broader questions surrounding law enforcement's interaction with nontraditional groups like the Branch Davidians.

---

[34] In late April, after the Compound was ravaged by fire, ATF firearms and explosives experts collected evidence of the firearms and other destructive devices Koresh and his followers had possessed. At that time, based on the materials recovered, the experts concluded that Koresh and his followers possessed 57 pistols, 6 revolvers, 12 shotguns, 101 rifles, more than 44 machineguns, more than 16 silencers, 6 flare launchers, 3 live grenades plus numerous components, and approximately 200,000 unused rounds of ammunition. FBI experts are rigorously analyzing the evidence found at the Compound to determine more precisely the weaponry that had been accumulated by Koresh and his followers. Because of the fire, this process has been time-consuming, and the experts have been unable to determine with any certainty the amount of explosive materials that had been stored at the Compound.

[35] Although, as a general matter, law enforcement agencies must recognize that their investigative efforts might lead targets to take dangerous defensive measures, the sequence of events here shows that the ATF investigation had no such effect. Koresh and his followers had been accumulating weapons well before the investigation—as far back as the Roden shoot-out. Although there was an increase in weapons purchases after local law enforcement—not ATF—trained near the Compound in spring 1992, purchases did not increase once Aguilera began his investigation in summer 1992. In fact, during the eight-month investigation, there were periods when Koresh and his followers did not purchase weapons components.

Figure 36: "Pineapple" type grenade casings recovered after April 19, 1993, fire.

Figure 37: Arms bunker, after April 19, 1993, fire, with arsenal of assorted assault weapons and parts.

Figure 38: Remains of an assault rifle, recovered after April 19, 1993, fire.

Figure 39: Remains of assault rifle, recovered after April 19, 1993, fire.

Part Two
Section Two: Analysis of the Tactical Planning Effort

Introduction

Any analysis of the plan for the February 28 raid and the planning process that preceded it must recognize that the plan was never actually followed on raid day. In particular, although the plan was entirely dependent on the element of surprise, Chojnacki, the Incident Commander, and Sarabyn, the Tactical Coordinator, went forward despite learning from Rodriguez, the undercover agent, that Koresh had learned something about the coming raid. Failing to recognize the importance of this information, the commanders ignored a critical pre-condition of the plan—the presence of the men in the pit, separated from the weapons—and thus left ATF agents highly vulnerable to attack by the Branch Davidians. See Murphy at B-106; Kolman at B-62; Sobocienski at B-132[36]. The analysis that follows, therefore, addresses a tactical plan that was never implemented.

Nevertheless, even if improvements in the tactical plan might not have averted the tragedy at the Branch Davidian Compound, an analysis of the planning process and the plan itself is still warranted. Most of the Review's tactical experts agree that the plan had a reasonable chance of success if all of the planners' major factual assumptions had been correct. See Murphy at B-104; Ishimoto Executive Summary; Sobocienski at B-131. If the men in the Compound could have been counted on to be working in the pit, separated from the weapons reportedly locked away in the "arms room," and if ATF agents could have driven up to the Compound without its residents knowing of the operation until it was too late to offer effective resistance, the warrants might well have been executed with a minimum of disruption and without loss of life. But the caveat here is crucial, for many of the planners' assumptions were just that—expectations based on too little information about the Branch Davidians.

---

[36]All page references in this section are to Appendix B.

The problems here rest as much in the planning process as in the plan itself. Not only were the planners, led by Sarabyn, too quick in concluding that a massive mid-morning raid was the best possible enforcement option, but they chose a plan whose window of opportunity might have been far smaller than they realized. The planners also failed to prepare for contingencies that would arise if that window were missed. Against a target as formidable as Koresh, such errors exposed ATF to grievous consequences.

Responsibility for these flaws cannot simply be placed at the feet of those who did the actual planning. Those charged with this mission devoted considerable time and energy to devising a safe and successful operation. They lacked, however, the training, experience, and institutional support that were demanded by the extraordinary operation they were planning, which was qualitatively, as well as quantitatively, different from the many smaller enforcement actions each had led successfully in the past. See Ishimoto at B-15; Paschall at B-109; Murphy at B-95; Kolman at B-63; Morrison at B-88. ATF's management never addressed these deficiencies by giving the planners a supportive structure to supplement their own experiences. In addition, ATF's upper management did not actively oversee the development of the tactical plan, even though it involved the mobilization of more than 100 agents—the largest law enforcement effort ever mounted by ATF and one of the largest in the history of civilian law enforcement. See Morrison at B-87.

The Decision to Execute the Warrants by "Raiding" the Compound Was Made Before Other Options Were Fully Exhausted

Before reviewing the development of the raid plan devised for the Branch Davidian Compound, this section begins by looking at the decision to have a "dynamic entry" as opposed to some other type of enforcement action. Based on the limited information available when ATF selected the raid option, the Review simply is not in a position to say conclusively whether ATF's decision to rely exclusively on a raid—instead of, for instance, a scheme to arrest Koresh while he was away from the Compound or to establish a perimeter around the Compound and negotiate—was well founded. However, the Review does not believe that the ATF planners were in a position to make such a judgment either, and they should have been. A massive raid against a heavily armed, disciplined, and well-positioned group will always, however cunningly planned, be a risky operation, especially when children and other innocent persons are present. If less risky alternatives that can achieve the same ends are possible, they ought to be pursued. ATF did not adequately pursue these options. The agency's failure to gather the information needed to assess the chances of such alternatives succeeding made its rejection of them, and its choice of the raid option, far too premature.

The Decision to Use Force When Executing the Warrants

The threshold issue presented to ATF was whether any force would be needed to execute the arrest warrant for Koresh and the search warrant for the Compound. Some have suggested that, having obtained such warrants, ATF should simply have asked Koresh to surrender himself and his weapons or asked him for free passage into the Compound so that ATF could conduct a search for unlawful firearms and explosives. Claiming that Koresh had surrendered previously to local law enforcement authorities after his shoot-out with George Roden in 1987, critics have argued that ATF's decision to use force made a violent confrontation inevitable and played into what they have characterized as Koresh's apocalyptic vision of a final battle between his army and law enforcement agents, whom he called the "Assyrians." The Review finds no basis for these criticisms and believes that the decision not to rely on Koresh's goodwill was entirely appropriate and rested on valid considerations.

There was, in fact, no evidence that Koresh was prepared to submit to law enforcement authorities or that he had done so in the past. His surrender in the Roden shoot-out occurred only after deputies of the McLennan County Sheriff's Department "got the drop" on him while he and his followers were busy training their weapons on Roden, who was pinned down behind a tree at the Compound. Based on the information developed during the course of Special Agent Aguilera's investigation—which showed Koresh's propensity toward violence, his use of armed guards, and his control of a massive arsenal of automatic and semiautomatic weapons—the ATF planners reasonably concluded that a polite request to search the Compound without readiness to use force would have been foolhardy and irresponsible. This conclusion could only have been confirmed once Special Agent Rodriguez began his contacts with Koresh and learned of the latter's disdain for the firearms laws and hatred for those charged with their enforcement. While concern about Koresh's apocalyptic vision should have suggested using an enforcement approach that afforded an opportunity to first ask for voluntary compliance and to avoid an initial, potentially provocative show of force, it was not a valid reason for ATF to forsake its law enforcement responsibilities.

Intelligence Failures and the Failure to Try to Arrest Koresh Off the Compound Followed by an Effort to Execute the Search Warrants

Having understandably decided not to rely solely on Koresh's voluntary compliance with the warrants, ATF tactical planners initially focused their attention on arresting Koresh while he was away from the Compound, either by luring him off or by waiting until he had left it on his own accord. Koresh's followers, the planners believed, had become so accustomed to relying on his leadership and guidance that they would be far less likely to resist ATF in any organized way if Koresh could be removed from the scene; this advantage would be significant whether ATF established a siege of the Compound or conducted a raid.

It is now impossible to know whether ATF's execution of the search warrant would have been aided by arresting Koresh while he was away from the Compound. Still, the planners' reasoning on this score makes sense, and their consideration of this option indicates an effort to minimize the risk to agents and Branch Davidians. That effort, however, was not sufficient, because it was abandoned prematurely, without adequate exploration of its feasibility.

As early as their first tactical planning meeting in December 1992, the planners concluded that Koresh virtually never left the Compound; therefore, they thought they would not be able to lure him away from it. And they remained convinced of this when the undercover house was established in early January 1993. The Review, however, has not been able to identify the basis for this early conclusion. For example, no written ATF report addresses the issue before this meeting, and aside from Joyce Sparks, who had only visited the Compound a few times and told Aguilera she thought Koresh did not leave often, the Review was unable to identify a reliable source for this common assumption among the planners. Certainly, there is no evidence that any of the tactical planners evaluated either the source or substance of the initial intelligence on this point.

The establishment of the undercover house should have given the planners an opportunity to test the validity of their assumption, by having the undercover agents monitor Koresh's comings and goings. But this did not happen. Although reports from the undercover house seemed to confirm the earlier "intelligence" because the agents indicated that they never saw Koresh leave the Compound, this information was unreliable.

The defects in the intelligence relating to Koresh's movements are particularly significant, because they are symptomatic of the problems that afflicted the undercover house operation. To be successful, an intelligence operation must be able to develop adequate and reliable information, disseminate that information to the appropriate supervisors, and ensure that those supervisors recognize the meaning and limitations of that information. See Murphy at B-100; Ishimoto at B-17; Kolman at B-58; Morrison at B-87, 89; Paschall at B-109, 111. The undercover house operation fell short in all three of these areas.

From the outset, the production capabilities of the agents in the undercover house were crippled by ATF's failure to give them a comprehensive idea of what the planners needed. The agents also lacked the supervision and feedback needed to ensure that they performed their mission. "The organization of the undercover house and its activities was marked by no clear chain of command or direction of their actions." See Ishimoto at B-17. Generalized surveillance often serves an important function, especially during the investigative stages of a case, when agents begin to explore the nature of a target's activities. But by the time the undercover house was established, ATF's tactical planners had a number of specific questions that they either wanted answered or were assuming already had been answered. Instead of being told what these questions were, the agents in the undercover house were told only to look for certain routines at the Compound. Without clear objectives, supervision, or feedback, morale and performance began to deteriorate soon after the operation began, and the vigilance of the agents suffered accordingly.

One result of this intelligence production breakdown was that the agents in the undercover house could not tell reliably whether Koresh ever left the Compound, and they never took the additional measures necessary to find out. With Sarabyn's approval, the agents discontinued around-the-clock surveillance. And even when they were watching the Compound, the agents could not identify the occupants of cars seen leaving the Compound on the road in front of it and could not see whether anybody left the Compound on foot or in vehicles using the road or trails behind the Compound. With limited night-vision capability, the agents were unable to determine who left at night. In addition, several agents did not know, and no agents were certain, what make of car Koresh drove. Although some of the agents learned at various stages in the undercover operation that Koresh reportedly drove a Chevrolet Camaro, a number of other cars at the Compound were registered in Koresh's name because cult members gave all their possessions to him. Koresh, therefore, presumably might have driven any of the cars.

Dissemination of information was also a problem, because no adequate provisions were made for providing the raw intelligence that the agents in the undercover house were able to obtain to the tactical planners. Supervisors did not direct undercover house agents to keep comprehensive surveillance logs throughout the operation, and no arrangements were made for the agents to give oral briefings to the tactical planners or to an intermediary.

Although many of the tactical planners thought that surveillance was being supplemented with regular debriefings of Rodriguez about his contacts with Koresh and other cult members, little useful intelligence about Koresh's movements was actually gleaned from the agent's relatively few contacts. (See Figure 40.) However, salient intelligence was obtained on February 17, late in the planning process, when Koresh offhandedly told Rodriguez that he rarely went to town because the people there did not like him. Aguilera noted this significant statement in his reports. Even though the statement supports the belief that Koresh did not leave the Compound often, it contradicts the planners' view that he never left, and should have alerted them that from time to time, Koresh did leave the Compound.

ATF's mishandling of the intelligence regarding whether Koresh ever left the Compound resulted, in part, from the lack of a system to process intelligence. Rather than flowing to a single accountable person responsible for collection and analysis, intelligence swirled among many persons—none of whom sufficiently questioned its reliability. Overall intelligence collection and planning was not centrally managed. See Ishimoto at B-17. Because it was not treated with sufficient rigor, intelligence may well have been interpreted to conform to planning needs. If a single person had been responsible for the production and dissemination of tactical planning intelligence, the problems at the undercover house might have never arisen. If they had occurred, they could have been corrected or at least brought to the planners' attention.

The limitations of the intelligence operation were compounded because the tactical planners did not recognize those limitations. As a result, they overvalued the significance of the information they did receive. Thus, although the undercover agents' knowledge of Koresh's movements was thin at best, the tactical planners believed that they had confirmation that Koresh *never* left the Compound. Moreover, having surveilled the Compound and its surroundings only a few months earlier, the planners should have recognized the inherent limitations of monitoring Koresh's movements from the undercover house, since the rear of the Compound could not be seen from there. At the very least, Sarabyn, who had visited the undercover house, must have understood that Koresh could

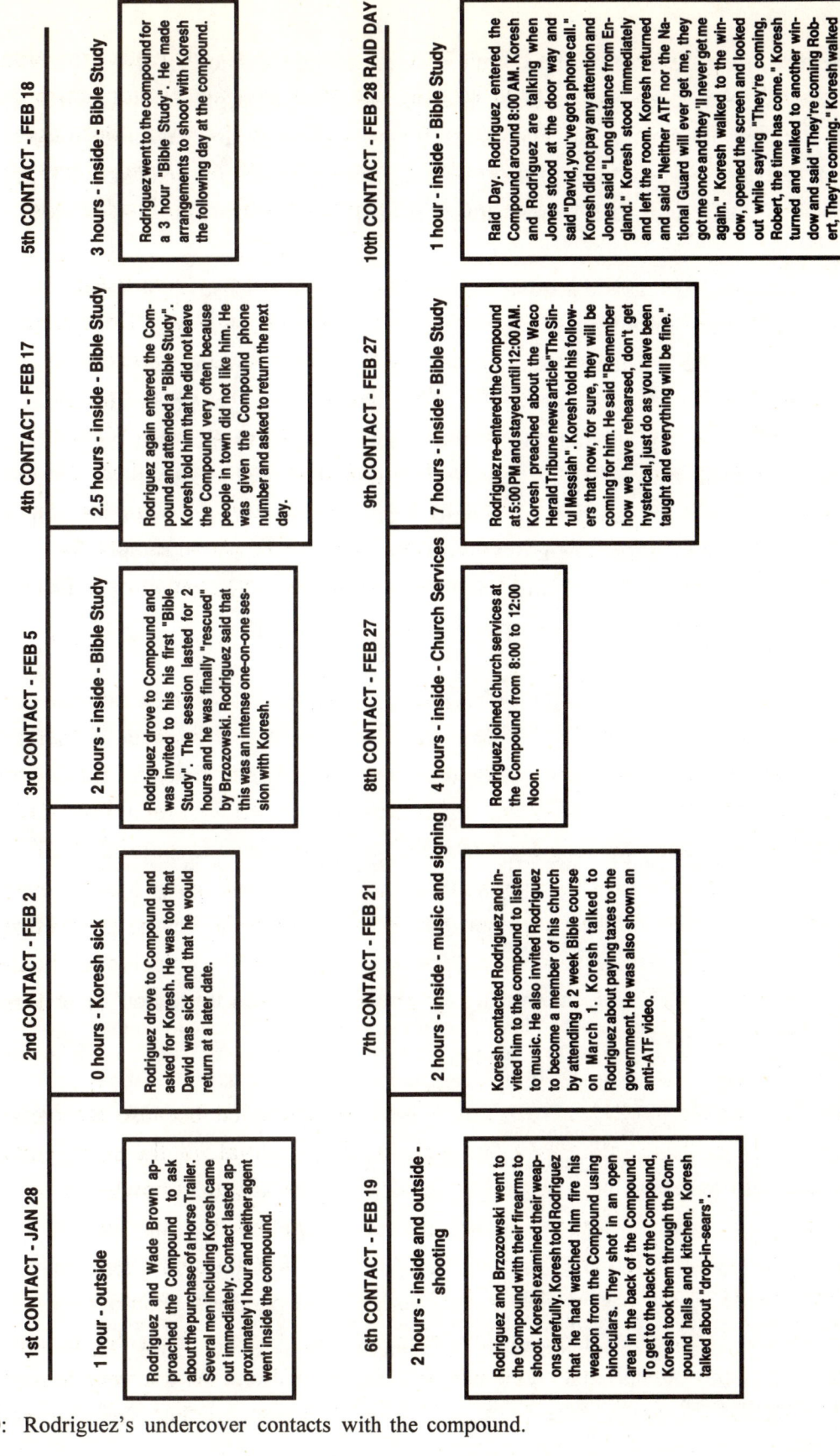

Figure 40: Rodriguez's undercover contacts with the compound.

have left undetected from the rear of the compound. As a consequence of their belief that Koresh never left, the planners devoted little effort to developing a plan to lure him off the Compound. By the end of January, after attempting unsuccessfully to convince Joyce Sparks' superior to allow Sparks to request a meeting with Koresh at her office[37], ATF largely abandoned any effort to lure Koresh away from the Compound.[38]

Had more attention been paid to determining whether Koresh ever left the Compound, ATF's planners might have learned that he did in fact leave the Compound on at least two occasions while the undercover house was in operation and on several other occasions in late 1992 and early January 1993.[39] This is not to say that he could have been intercepted on any of these trips or that ATF could have devised a plan that would have succeeded in luring Koresh away. But, given the planners' reasonable expectation that arresting Koresh away from the Compound would vastly reduce the risks attending any law enforcement action at that location, far more effort should have been made in this area. See Kolman at B-47, B-50. And ATF's failure to make such an effort must be attributed to management's failure to establish an effective intelligence operation.

---

[37] As she told Aguilera in late January, Sparks had met previously with Koresh in her office and at the Compound. However, Sparks told ATF that she had experienced difficulty in the past in scheduling such a meeting. According to Sparks, meetings took place at a time Koresh found convenient; on one occasion, he came to her office two days after the appointed date.

[38] In late February, after the raid had been scheduled for March 1, 1993, and the tactical planning was largely completed, ATF made one final effort to lure Koresh away from the Compound so that they could execute a search warrant. To seek evidence for a state arrest warrant for Koresh for sexual abuse and to seek a basis for state officials to meet with Koresh off the Compound, ATF asked Assistant District Attorney Beth Tobin to meet with a young girl who had resided at the Compound and allegedly had been the victim of sexual abuse. Tobin interviewed the girl on February 22, 1993, but because the girl was unwilling to testify about Koresh's conduct, there were neither grounds for an arrest warrant nor a reason to request a meeting with Koresh away from the Compound.

[39] In late January, Koresh visited a neighbor in the early evening at the house next to the undercover house. According to the neighbor, Koresh traveled there by motorcycle. On January 29, Koresh visited Performance Automotive Machine in Axtell, Texas, where he picked up parts for his Camaro. Although no entry exists in the undercover house's surveillance log for a Camaro leaving the Compound on January 29, the logs do record a Camaro leaving on January 28 and returning the same day. Moreover, between November 1992 and February 1993, at least six people recall seeing Koresh in town on separate occasions, and several sources have reported that Koresh traveled to Dallas with cult member Steve Schneider in November 1992.

A Siege With Koresh Present on the Compound

Regardless of whether Koresh could be arrested away from his followers, ATF still had to decide how it would execute the search warrant at the Compound. Initially, the tactical planners considered the siege option. In this scenario, agents would first ask those inside the Compound to honor the warrant. If access were denied, ATF would immediately establish a perimeter around the Compound and seal off its inhabitants until they relented and permitted the search to proceed. This approach would minimize the risk of a violent confrontation between ATF and the Branch Davidians and, even if violence erupted, would minimize the agents' exposure to gunfire from the Compound. These advantages led some planners to favor a siege over a dynamic entry plan even after they had surveyed the Compound and its surrounding area.

The planners ultimately rejected the siege option mainly because the intelligence obtained in January from former cult members highlighted the drawbacks of such an operation. Most significantly, several former cult members noted the distinct danger that Koresh would respond to a siege by leading his followers in a mass suicide. Even if no suicides ocurred, the costs of a siege would be high. With their own source of well water, a three-month supply of military rations, and experience with the rigors of a rudimentary lifestyle, the Branch Davidians, former cult members believed, could withstand a long and arduous standoff. The planners were also concerned that a siege would give Koresh and his followers time to destroy evidence of their violations of federal firearms and explosives laws. Several tactical planners expressed concern that Koresh would outlast the patience of the American public and that they might be directed to raid the Compound after a lengthy stalemate. They feared that such a raid, against a prepared and fortified foe, would be far more dangerous than a surprise raid.

In retrospect, many of the tactical planners' concerns about a siege were validated, especially the fear of mass suicide and the appraisal that Koresh had the discipline and resources to withstand a siege for a prolonged period. See Kolman at B-48-49 That the planners were proven correct, however, does not necessarily validate the process by which they reached their conclusions.

Several of the planners told the Review that they assumed, in substance, that when dealing with a cult, mass suicide is a serious risk. Interviews certainly provided an opportunity to assess former cult members' credibility, emotional state, and objectivity, and a basis for determining whether their suicide predictions were reasonable. Nonetheless, before allowing the specter of mass suicide to deter them from pursuing the siege option—which they considered less risky to all involved—the planners should have sought assistance from psychologists and other experts who were better equipped to evaluate the accounts of the former Branch Davidians. Consultation with such experts could also have improved ATF's overall understanding of Koresh and his followers, including the group dynamics among the cult members inside the Compound and their extraordinary belief systems. Such an understanding, in turn, might have broadened ATF's consideration of enforcement options other than a raid, and heightened their appreciation of the dangers of raiding a group that apparently shared an apocalyptic theology.[40]

There were many serious drawbacks to a siege, and ATF's tactical planners accurately perceived them. Because of these valid tactical concerns and perhaps because, like most law enforcement agencies, ATF had little experience with extended sieges, the tactical planners viewed a siege as a tough option. In the end, though, the chief reason the planners discarded the siege approach was their increasing optimism about the dynamic entry option. This optimism, unfortunately, was in large part based on faulty intelligence that made conditions seem much better for a raid than they really were. See Murphy at B-103; Morrison at B-87.

The Decision to Pursue a Raid Option and Develop a Raid Plan

The chief attraction of a raid scenario was that it offered the possibility of catching Koresh and his followers by surprise and avoided the risk of a protracted and costly standoff. The element of surprise seemed quite achievable to the planners, based on their flawed understanding of the daily routine in the Compound. If agents could sweep into the area at 10:00 a.m., they would find the Branch Davidian men working in the pit outside the Compound, without access to the weapons that Koresh kept under lock and key next to his bedroom. The men could be detained, the arsenal secured, and Koresh arrested. The assumptions on which this plan rested, however, relied on the same inadequately evaluated intelligence that led the planners to prematurely discount the possibility of Koresh ever leaving the Compound. As a result, the operation was far more vulnerable than its planners, especially Sarabyn, ever realized. And this vulnerability was increased by the failure of the

---

[40] In the future, either through the forward-looking review, which should include several behavioral science experts, or other means, the Review recommends that a national structure be developed to improve the access for law enforcement agencies to the assistance of experts in such fields as psychology, psychiatry, sociology, and theology when they are dealing with barricade or hostage situations or with suspects with nontraditional belief systems or thought processes that do not fit the profile of the standard criminal target.

planning process to produce a common understanding among the planners of what the operation's key assumptions were, and of the importance of surprise to the mission's success.

Had they appreciated the risks involved, the planners might have done far more to prepare for the possibility that ATF might not be able to surprise the Branch Davidians. As it was, they did virtually no contingency planning. See Murphy at B-104; Kolman at B-65, 36; Morrison at B-88; Ishimoto at B-15. And they failed to devise a structure that maximized the flow of intelligence to the key decisionmaker on raid day so that he could verify that Koresh was unaware of the impending raid before committing ATF agents to the front of the Compound.

Intelligence Failures

This section examines the plan's critical assumptions and the quality of the intelligence on which they rested.

The "Arms Room"

The tactical planners' conclusion that Koresh kept the weapons and explosives under lock and key in a room adjacent to his own was based almost exclusively on the statement of one former cult member, David Block.[41] Block's actual statements to ATF agents, however, were far less definitive than the planners treated them; he had simply indicated that Koresh maintained control over the weapons in the neighboring room and that his permission was needed to possess one. Although Sarabyn and the other planners could have contacted Block and other former cult members to clarify this matter and learn more about the circumstances under which Koresh distributed weapons, no such effort was made. Moreover, the planners failed to consider how Block's prior relations with Koresh, and his decision to break away from the Branch Davidians at the Compound, might have affected the reliability of his statements. Although the planners knew Block had met with a self-

---

[41] In early November 1992, during a telephone interview by Buford, another former cult member, Poia Vaega, noted in passing that her husband, also a former cult member, who was standing nearby during the interview, "had reason to believe that the guns were stored in the quarters that Vernon was sleeping in." Perhaps because this conversation occurred when Buford was primarily concerned with developing probable cause, he asked no further questions on the subject and made no effort to delve deeper into either Vaega's or her husband's knowledge of Koresh's practices with respect to the storage of the weapons. Unfortunately, when the tactical planners later intensified their efforts to craft a workable plan, none of them tried to contact Vaega or her husband to discuss the arms room.

described "deprogrammer," Rick Ross, they never had any substantive discussions with him concerning Block's objectivity about and perspective of Koresh and his followers. Nor did the planners pay appropriate attention to the fact that Block had left the Compound over six months earlier.

Even though the success of their plan might have turned on whether Block was right about the location and control of the Compound's weapons, ATF's planners simply began to treat the report that the arms were kept under lock and key in the arms room near Koresh's bedroom as established fact. When Sarabyn explained to Cavanaugh, who had not attended the late January meeting, why the planners had chosen to proceed with a raid rather than a siege, he noted that an important factor in the decision had been intelligence that the guns were kept under lock and key by Koresh. Sarabyn reported as fact his speculation that, because of an increasing paranoia, Koresh never distributed the guns for fear of a mutiny. Several other tactical planners inaccurately believed that Block's statement about the arms room was corroborated by several other former cult members.

Having fixed upon Block's statements about the storage routine for the weapons, the planners apparently ignored the rest of Block's information: that Koresh distributed AK-47s from time to time, that cult members would keep them under their beds on those occasions, and that Block was uncertain about whether they kept their guns loaded. They also discarded reports by other former cult members that they had seen weapons distributed around the Compound and that Koresh frequently conducted live-fire shooting practice. In particular, they did not pay sufficient attention to Block and Breault's assertions that they had left the cult in large part because of Koresh's insistence that they prepare to resist law enforcement authorities when the anticipated confrontation came. In fact, as law enforcement officials discovered after the Compound burned, powerful evidence indicates that arms were stored in other locations in the Compound in addition to the arms room.

No Guards or Sentries

At the outset of the planning process the tactical planners—based on the statements of former cult members, including Block and Breault, the UPS delivery person, the sheriff's department, and Texas National Guard overflights—anticipated that there would be armed guards or sentries at the Compound. After the agents in the undercover house saw no such guards, however, the tactical planners concluded that Koresh had stopped taking this precaution. Why he might have done so is something they did not sufficiently consider. If Koresh's control of weapons and refusal to leave the Compound stemmed from paranoia or fear of law enforcement, as the planners appeared to think they did, it would have been rather odd for him to suddenly stop posting sentries. The planners never considered that Koresh might simply have repositioned his guards inside the Compound where they would not have been seen by the undercover agents.

It appears that sentries were indeed concealed within the Compound during the weeks leading up to the raid. Mark Spoon, who lived next door to the undercover house, has related to the Review that, during this period, Koresh or one of his "Mighty Men" often would telephone him when an unfamiliar car drove up the road toward the Compound, and inquire about the car's occupants. To know a car had approached on the road, a vigilant cult member would have had to have been posted in the Compound's tower; such lookouts were in place on raid day.

The Men in the Pit

The same intelligence processing failures that led planners to be confident that Koresh never left the Compound led them to be unduly confident that all or most of the Compound's men could be found in the pit at 10:00 a.m., every morning, except on Saturday, their sabbath. Even though most dynamic entries are executed shortly before dawn—when most suspects are likely to be asleep and caught by surprise—the planners' confidence that the men would be in the pit led them to give up the predawn advantage in exchange for finding the men in the pit at 10:00 a.m.

The mother of a cult member, who had visited the Compound for two days in November 1992, had some recollections of the work routine there. But the principal source of the planners' information about the men in the pit was the surveillance conducted by the agents in the undercover house. However, neither the visitors' observations nor the reports of these agents supported the tactical planners' assumptions about a predictable routine.

Certainly, the surveillance logs maintained by the agents at the undercover house provided no basis for such a conclusion. See Ishimoto at B-19. For four days of the operation, there is no record that any surveillance was conducted and, for two other days, the only entry is the notation "no activity." Indeed, between January 11 and January 29—during which time the tactical plan was drawn up—on the majority of those days the logs do not refer to the men working in the pit. On several other days, the logs indicate that there was no activity when it was rainy, implying that no one had been in the pit. Over the life of the undercover house operation, from January 11 through February 17, the surveillance logs refer to the men working in the pit on only 14 out of the 36 days for which surveillance was maintained. Although the undercover house ceased 24-hour surveillance efforts on January 19 and terminated surveillance activities altogether on February 17, many tactical planners erroneously believed that tight surveillance continued until the day of the raid, compounding their overvaluation of the intelligence. In fact, several of the tactical planners first learned about the limited nature of the surveillance coverage only after being interviewed by the Review. Since Sarabyn approved the cessation of 24-hour surveillance, responsibility for the other planners' ignorance on this point must be shouldered by him.

Even though some log entries refer to the men in the pit, the logs only reported sporadically how many men had worked,[42] exactly when they began work,[43] whether the men worked in the rain, or the degree to which activity in the pit was actually visible from the undercover house. In fact, the agents never could have seen how many men were actually in the pit, because their reports of work there were based on their observations of traffic between the front of the Compound and the pit, people near the pit passing supplies down into the pit, and construction noises emanating from the Compound.[44] The absence of any view of the interior of the pit itself was significant because, as Sparks and others had informed ATF, Compound residents could enter and exit the pit through the buried bus, without ever having to walk above ground. And even if the agents had been able to look into the pit and count the men inside, they might not have known what proportion of the Compound's men were working, since they never knew how many men lived on the premises. While agents believed that approximately 75 people lived at the Compound, more than 125 people were there on February 28. On those days that the surveillance logs did indicate the number of men observed working in the pit, the number was never more than

---

[42] In response to questions from the Review, several agents estimated that the number of men in the pit varied from day to day—ranging from as few as four or five men to as many as a dozen or more.

[43] The undercover agents were aware that the men often started working in the pit later than 10:00 a.m., particularly after a late night of "Bible study," and the logs indicate that work in the pit sometimes began later than 10:00 a.m.; however, the tactical planners apparently never knew that. This lack of communication was serious, because the raid took place after a late-night Bible session that Rodriguez had attended. Hence, the raid commanders should have questioned whether on the day of the raid they could have expected the men to begin work in the pit as early as 10:00 a.m.

[44] Scale models of the Compound and the undercover house, as well as videos of the pit taken from the undercover house prior to the raid, show that a substantial portion of the area around the pit was obstructed from the agents' view by the four-foot-high fence in front of the Compound and the edge of the Compound structure itself.

13. Had the planners assessed the logs properly, they at least would have questioned their belief that almost all of the men residing at the Compound would be found in the pit.

Even though the surveillance logs were not the only source of intelligence from the undercover house, alternative avenues were not exploited sufficiently and hence did not compensate for the information lacking in writing. Oral communications were infrequent and informal. Aside from one occasion in mid-January when an undercover agent recalls speaking to Sarabyn about the routine of the men working in the pit, none of the agents in the undercover house recalls being debriefed by Sarabyn or any other tactical planner about the matter. Similarly, videos and photos of activities at the Compound were taken but never viewed by the raid planners.

Even though they were presented with insufficient information about the men in the pit, none of the tactical planners requested that particular attention be paid to this point. Instead, they assumed the existence of a predictable routine, based on the inadequate information they had, and then based their entire plan on that assumption. Indeed, the planners' misplaced confidence that virtually all the Compound's men could be found in the pit each morning might have caused their failure to take any measures to ensure that the presence of the men in the pit be confirmed before the raid went forward. No raid commander was charged on raid day with verifying this critical precondition for the operation's success. And when Cavanaugh, positioned in the undercover house on February 28, observed before the raid began that "all was quiet" at the Compound and did not see the men in the pit, he did not fully appreciate the enormous significance of this lack of activity. Certainly, Chojnacki and Sarabyn disregarded the importance of the condition, for they rushed to launch the raid before they expected the men to be in the pit.

The Discounting of Armed Resistance from Women in the Compound

The planners were able to base the raid plan on the presence of the men in the pit because they apparently assumed that the women would not use the weapons Koresh had stockpiled. Although the planners anticipated that one female cult member, a former police officer, might be armed with a handgun, they studiously ignored or discounted evidence that other women might also be prepared for armed resistance. The planners apparently gave little weight to Block's statement to Buford and Aguilera that Koresh issued rifles from time to time to at least five of the women. A photograph taken by undercover house agents in late January of a female aiming a rifle from the front door of the Compound was shown to Sarabyn, who did not share it with the other raid planners. Sarabyn apparently concluded that the rifle might be a BB gun and could not understand why the woman was aiming it. The picture, however, is of poor quality, and the type of rifle cannot be discerned. The failure to pursue this matter by enhancing the image or seeking more information from the undercover agents, is yet another example of how data inconsistent with the planners' assumptions often was shunted aside.

At one level, the intelligence failures that lessened the chances that ATF's tactical plan would succeed were management failures. The agents in the undercover house did not conduct effective surveillance or keep comprehensive records of what they did see and what they could not see. The planners did not alert the undercover house agents to their tactical intelligence needs or ask hard questions about the information they received. But it would be quite unfair simply to hold these individuals responsible for the breakdown here. The agents in the undercover house should have been supervised by someone attuned to the needs of the planners. And the planners, charged with engineering the biggest raid in ATF history, should not have been required to interpret raw intelligence. What was needed was a separate intelligence structure to ensure that usable, reliable information was funneled to the planners and that the planners knew the limitations of the data they received. See Ishimoto at B-17; Murphy at B-100; Kolman at B-59; Morrison at B-89. ATF's leadership at headquarters and in the Houston division must bear responsibility for allowing the operation to proceed without such a structure.

No Meaningful Contingency Planning

The same confidence that led ATF raid planners to discard intelligence inconsistent with the assumptions central to their plan might also have led them to do little to prepare for the possibility that conditions would not be right on raid day. See Kolman at B-14 and B-66. Perhaps they did not realize how fragile, because of its dependence on surprise, their plan really was. The absence of any contingency plan, other than to abort the raid before arrival at the front of the Compound, left the raid commanders with the stark choice between going forward or canceling an operation in which so much already had been invested. That failure also meant that when ATF agents encountered heavy gunfire upon their arrival at the Compound, most had little choice but to proceed with their mission, at great cost. See Morrison at B-88.

If there had been meaningful contingency planning for the possibility that ATF might lose the advantage of surprise before the cattle trailers arrived at the Compound, agents confronted with a forewarned target would still have been able to move into siege positions, securing a perimeter around the Compound. Compared with a surprise raid, a siege had marked disadvantages, all of which the planners recognized. Yet a siege was a preferable alternative when compared with a raid against a target that was ready and waiting. The planners should at least have explored using a siege as a recourse. The planners also did not prepare for the possibility that Koresh would try to break out of the Compound, alone or accompanied by his followers, if he learned about the raid. Indeed, there was not even a plan for postponing the raid, even though certain circumstances, such as a late-night Bible session or inclement weather, might cause the Compound's men to arrive at the pit later than 10:00 a.m. By failing to establish any alternatives to the raid plan, ATF's tactical planners contributed to the pressures on the raid commanders to go forward with the massive operation and to not let the training resources invested and the planning for the raid go for naught.

In addition, sufficient thought was not given to what ATF agents would do if they arrived in front of the Compound and were met with either an organized ambush or scattered pockets of armed resistance. If necessary, the cattle trailers could have made a detour before reaching the road leading to the Compound. But once the trailers went up the driveway and reached the front of the Compound, the agents reached a point of no return: The plan called for the agents to carry out their assignments, regardless of the resistance they encountered. Since the cattle trailers provided no protection[45] and the grounds in front of the Compound afforded only limited cover, the raid planners saw no better option.

If the tactical planners had given sufficient thought to the level of firepower that Koresh and his followers could bring to bear on agents massed in front of the Compound, they might have done more to ensure that the raid would not go forward without the advantage of surprise. The raid commanders sent Rodriguez into the Compound to check conditions only because of the publication of the first part of the "Sinful Messiah" series. The plan produced by the tactical planners did not call for such an effort. In addition, had the plan incorporated verification of conditions by an undercover agent, measures could have been taken to close the time gap between the undercover agent's departure from the Compound and the arrival of the trailers. They also would have prepared some scheme to help agents withdraw from their vulnerable positions if they became pinned down by hostile

---

[45] Because the cattle trailers were lined only with plywood and covered only with tarpaulins, the raid planners decided that the cattle trailers could not safely drive past the Compound in the event they met with resistance upon their arrival—to do so would permit Koresh and his followers to broadside the trailers with unanswered automatic weapons fire.

fire. One method of extracting the agents might have been to send in Bradley Fighting Vehicles, which could have been positioned a short distance from the Compound, concealed on flatbed trucks. In any event, a reserve force of agents could have been deployed nearby. To the extent that these precautions would have taxed or exceeded ATF's resources, the agency might have reached out for assistance from other law enforcement authorities or reconsidered whether to conduct the raid. Because the planners did not explore any of these contingency options, ATF did not have a plan or the capacity to extract any agents, including wounded agents, from their exposed positions in front of the Compound.

Having failed to prepare for an ambush, the planners also failed to prepare for a stand-off. Given their fears that Koresh might lead his followers in a mass suicide if surrounded by agents, it is unfortunate that the planners did not heed Deputy Tactical Coordinator James Cavanaugh's repeated requests that ATF have a contingency plan to negotiate with those inside the Compound. See Kolman B-51-52.[46] The raid commanders did not even arrange to have the telephone number for the Compound on the day of the raid. Cavanaugh was able to find the number written on a calendar in the undercover house after the shooting began. ATF was fortunate that Cavanaugh filled the planning gap and handled the crisis adeptly.[47]

Among other contingency issues the planners left unresolved was whether agents would still seek to execute the warrant at the Mag Bag if ATF agents were repulsed at the Compound or, alternatively, whether they would set up a perimeter around the Mag Bag to contain any cult members inside on raid day. In large part because this issue was not considered, ATF left the Mag Bag unsecured for a brief period on February 28, and three cult members ended up maneuvering around ATF's flank, endangering the lives of many agents and eventually engaging in a deadly shootout with a group of ATF agents. See Kolman at B-64.

---

[46] Although ATF has also been criticized for failing to notify the local sheriff's department and to warn them to monitor incoming 911 calls due to the raid, that criticism is misplaced. It is true that on the day of the raid, the 911 operator was not adequately prepared to field such calls or to serve as a conduit in the event negotiations were needed. ATF, however, did its part to cover this contingency when it alerted the sheriff's department that the raid would take place and had the sheriff's department personnel at ATF's command post.

[47] The planners' failure to prepare for negotiations with their targets might be attributed, at least in part, to the failure of the National Response Plan to make negotiators an integral part of the tactical command structure. This defect must be remedied.

The absence of any contingency planning cannot be attributed entirely to the planners' confidence that conditions would be favorable and that ATF's advantage of surprise would be decisive. It also reflected the planners' lack of experience in orchestrating operations of this magnitude. Only Buford had been involved in the planning of an enforcement action of comparable size, the CSA siege. This siege was a set-piece encounter where the need for fallback positions was less critical than it was for the dynamic entry contemplated at Waco. Indeed, the fact that the CSA siege was in large measure a success may have led the planners to discount the likelihood that the action against the Branch Davidians would go awry. In addition, this success confirmed what the other SRT leaders knew from their own experiences leading countless smaller operations: Things might not go as planned, but ATF could still successfully achieve its objectives.

The result of these diverse factors was a tactical plan that did not contemplate any meaningful contingencies. And the training for the raid followed the lead of the planning. The sessions at Fort Hood concentrated almost exclusively on preparing the agents to enter the Compound quickly and secure the residents expeditiously. Little time was spent training the agents to withdraw from the Compound in an orderly manner if necessary. In light of this planning and training focus, it is not surprising that the mind-set of ATF's commanders on raid day was to go forward with the raid unless the Branch Davidians were seen preparing to ambush.

Given law enforcement's limited experience in operations of this magnitude, the failure of the planners to consider that their operation might go awry and prepare for that eventuality is tragic, but somewhat understandable. In contrast, the failure of ATF's national leadership to ensure that some contingency planning was done is simply unacceptable. The headquarters officials briefed on the plan certainly knew that the raid planners lacked experience with operations of this size, and they should have recognized the risks involved in the raid. Yet it does not appear that anyone in ATF's leadership asked the obvious questions beginning with "What happens if ..." and then directed that further planning be done to address those concerns. Management cannot be expected to know all the details of a field operation, but its job is to ask these hard questions and carefully consider the answers. Had ATF's top managers considered the implications of a plan that could leave a large force of agents stranded in front of a Compound containing heavily armed fighters, and could leave the agents no alternative but to fight their way out, February 28 might have ended differently. See Morrison at B-86-87.

Command and Control Flaws in the Raid Plan

Other deficiencies in the planning effort that likely contributed to the pressures felt by the raid commanders on February 28 rest with the command and control structure established for the operation and with the selection, placement, and use of command personnel. Overall command of an operation of this magnitude must be placed in the hands of commanders who have access to the information on which decisions to proceed or abort must be based, who have an understanding of that information, and who have a perspective from which they can make measured judgments on how to proceed. Furthermore, because ATF's raid commanders placed themselves in locations where calm deliberation was difficult and because they lacked appropriate intelligence support, the likelihood that these commanders would make the right decisions on raid day was reduced. See Kolman at B-62-63; Morrison at B-88.

The General Command Structure

The raid on the Branch Davidian Compound was the first ATF operation conducted within the framework of the National Response Plan (NRP). ATF generated the NRP after a number of multiple-SRT mobilizations in order to establish consistent policies and procedures for such efforts. The NRP was finalized only shortly before the events near Waco. Although the plan barely addressed critical issues such as how a major operation should be planned, it did establish a command structure for such actions and specify how positions within that structure were to be filled.

The NRP described the two main command positions in an operation:

*(SAC)/ Incident Commander—"in charge and responsible for operational and administrative control of critical incident management resources," to "determine the overall strategy for responding to and/or resolving a critical incident or operation" and to prepare a written operations plan; and

*Tactical Coordinator—"[D]esignated by the SAC/Incident Commander to direct and control all tactical (operational) functions during a critical incident." "He/she will direct all SRTs assigned to the critical incident" and will "[s]upervise the development of specific tactics and procedures to support the SAC/Incident Commander's strategy for resolving the critical incident or completing the operation.

These tactics and procedures will be subject to the SAC/Incident Commander's approval."

Because Chojnacki was the SAC for the affected ATF field division, the NRP mandated that he serve as Incident Commander for the raid, regardless of whether he had adequate tactical training and experience for this particular mission. Chojnacki had more than 27 years of law enforcement experience at the time of the raid and had participated in and directed countless search and arrest warrant executions. Other senior agents with ATF, however, had more relevant training and far greater experience in substantial tactical operations. He in turn chose Sarabyn to be Tactical Coordinator, guided by the NRP requirement that this position be filled by "an ASAC who has completed SRT training." Because agents from both the New Orleans SRT and the Dallas SRT would be involved in the raid, Pete Mastin, the New Orleans SAC, and James Cavanaugh, the Dallas ASAC, were designated Deputy Incident Commander and Deputy Tactical Coordinator, respectively, consistent with the NRP.

Although credit must be given to ATF for establishing a framework like the NRP so that structural issues would not have to be reconsidered every time a major operation needed to be planned, the command structure dictated by the NRP set ATF's planning for the raid off on the wrong foot. By assigning personnel to critical command positions on the basis of rank—rather than ability, experience, training, or knowledge of the case— the NRP created a chain of command that did not ensure that each position was filled by the most qualified individual. See Kolman at B-65-66; Ishimoto at B-13. Sarabyn, who had led the tactical planning team, had supervised this investigation and had been instrumental in drafting the NRP, had to report to Chojnacki, who lacked this background, and consequently deferred to Sarabyn on many critical issues. This deference blurred lines of responsibility. In turn, Sarabyn was effectively in charge of the tactical planning for the operation despite his lack of any large-scale tactical planning experience. Sarabyn had attended SRT training, but only as an observer. In any event, that training was designed to teach SRT members to perform as a team, and it did not focus on developing tactical leadership skills or planning capabilities for larger operations. Sarabyn was selected as the Tactical Coordinator for the operation not because of his expertise, but because the NRP required the position to be filled by a person who had received SRT training and was an ASAC or a higher ranking official. These requirements limited the field of candidates and excluded persons of lesser rank who had significantly more experience. Likewise, Cavanaugh, who was chosen as Deputy Tactical Coordinator because of his position in the ATF hierarchy, also lacked the familiarity with the operation needed to be an effective commander. Meanwhile, Buford, the only participant in the raid who had directly relevant experience, was relegated to joint command of one of the SRTs.

Command and Control on Raid Day

The command and control plan established for the raid near Waco accentuated the NRP's structural deficiencies by failing to place commanders where they could make informed, considered decisions and maintain control over the day's events.

Chojnacki, although in charge of the entire operation, placed himself in a helicopter during the critical phases of the operation—the final 30 to 40 minutes before the cattle trailers arrived at the Compound and at the outset of the firefight. As a result, he could not effectively communicate with either the other raid commanders or the SRT team leaders during this entire period. See Ishimoto at B-14; Kolman at B-63; Sobocienski at B-130. Similarly, Sarabyn, who could best evaluate the significance of events at the Compound, could not see the Compound during his 17-minute trip from the staging area. By riding with the cattle trailers, Sarabyn severely limited his ability to receive and process information. See Ishimoto at B-14. Furthermore, when Sarabyn arrived at the Compound, he was pinned down and was unable to change the SRT instructions in light of the markedly changed circumstances. The ramifications of this leadership breakdown were substantial. Sarabyn, for example, never had an opportunity to communicate with the New Orleans team members when they took heavy fire while trying to secure the arms room. A commander in the undercover house would have known from hearing the extensive gunfire that weapons had already been distributed and that the New Orleans team's objective was significantly less vital. It may have been difficult under any circumstances to divert the New Orleans team members quickly to another task once they were committed. However, Sarabyn's poor vantage point, from which he could not see the New Orleans team, together with the lack of any preraid contingency planning, effectively precluded any such change in direction.

The only commander placed at a vantage point that allowed him to maintain the kind of perspective over an operation so critical to effective command and control was Cavanaugh. Cavanaugh was in the best position to make the final decision as to whether the raid should go forward. From his post at the undercover house, he was able to maintain open communication lines with diverse elements in the field, and he could himself keep an eye on the Compound to watch for any changes in conditions. This is indeed the place where the raid's overall commander should have been. See Ishimoto at B-14; Kolman at B-63; Morrison at B-88. However, Cavanaugh was not the overall commander. He was simply given responsibility for monitoring the Compound and aborting the raid if he saw signs that the Branch Davidians were laying an ambush. And, through no fault of his own, he was not well equipped to perform even this limited role properly. He was not particularly familiar with the normal routines of the Compound or the tactical details of the raid plan. In addition, Cavanaugh held a lower rank in ATF's hierarchy than Chojnacki, and lacking Sarabyn's status as a ASAC in Chojnacki's division, Cavanaugh could not be expected to be aggressive about calling the operation off if necessary.

Even had ATF deployed its raid commanders to positions more conducive to deliberate thought and an exchange of views, they would still have needed access to information on which to base their decisions, and aid in assessing that raw information. Pursuant to the NRP, an agent was designated to serve as the intelligence coordinator, but the sole reason for this designation seems to have been a desire to comply with the NRP. The designated agent was told nothing about the investigation or the tactical planning until he arrived in Houston for a briefing in mid-February. When he arrived in Waco, a few days before the raid, he was assigned the job of writing an operations plan, which kept him occupied until raid day. He was specifically told not to worry about intelligence matters, because they purportedly had already been dealt with. Indeed, in the days before the raid, he had difficulty contacting any of the raid commanders and never conferred with them about the intelligence operation. On February 28, the intelligence coordinator spent the crucial time immediately before the agents got underway driving from the command post to the staging area to signal the agents' departure, rather than being available to process intelligence information.

Had provision been made for a knowledgeable and involved intelligence coordinator, familiar with the conditions needed for the raid to succeed and charged with ascertaining whether they were present, he or she would have been able to brief the raid commanders on the significance of Rodriguez's report from the Compound. The coordinator might also have focused the raid commanders' attention on the reports from the forward observers in the undercover house, who saw no activity at the Compound and no men in the pit, but noted the presence of many media representatives roving near the Compound.

An intelligence coordinator might also have recognized that the forward observers assigned to the operation were a vastly underutilized intelligence resource. The purpose of ATF's new forward observer program was to put agents in the field before a mission to gather and provide raid commanders with current intelligence, and thereafter to give defensive coverage for those agents executing warrants. But forward observers were not meaningfully represented in the raid planning sessions, and the plan produced reflected their lack of participation. Even though forward observers recommended that enough teams be deployed to cover the Compound's entire perimeter, particularly the vulnerable position of the New Orleans team, the plan called for forward observers to be deployed to only two areas—one near the hay barn and the other at the undercover house. And the observers assigned to the hay barn moved from there to their position less than an hour before the arrival of the SRTs: too late for them to provide any meaningful intelligence to the raid commanders, too late for them to avoid crossing paths with cult member David Jones on the road, and too late for them to see cult members advance out of the Compound and occupy concealed positions from which they fired once the shoot-out began.

ATF's neglect of the use of the forward observers was not just an intelligence failure. See Morrison at B-90. The ATF plan also did not establish a common understanding among the raid commanders and the forward observers regarding the rules of engagement for the forward observers. As a result, there was no coordination between the forward observers and the agents in the SRTs. Although a forward observer did initially fire a shot at a clear threat in a window, this lack of coordination led to a delay of several minutes before the forward observers directed fire at the many other Branch Davidians who were shooting at the agents attempting to execute the warrants. See Ishimoto at B-14; Kolman at B-51.

The planning failures in the Waco raid stemmed in large part from an assumption on the part of ATF's leadership and those given specific planning responsibilities that an operation involving more than 100 agents against an extremely well-armed group of hostile cult members was just like any other enforcement action, only bigger. Lacking experience or training in raids like the one contemplated against the Branch Davidians, the planners assumed that what had worked for them in so many smaller operations would work again. The result of ATF's failure to support and guide this dedicated and well-intentioned group was a plan that rested on unreliable intelligence and that made the agents sent against the Branch Davidian Compound far more vulnerable to ambush than they realized. Therefore, the agents were unprepared to deal with the ambush when it occurred.

Part Two
Section Three: Media Impact on ATF's Branch Davidian Investigation
___

The media's interest in covering suspected criminal conduct and official responses to it will frequently be at odds with law enforcement's desire to have the advantage of surprise in its activities. However, the two sides generally accommodate each other partly out of necessity and partly out of each side's respect for the mission of the other. No such accommodation was reached at Waco. During their parallel investigations, both ATF and the media missed opportunities to take actions that might have averted the tragedy of February 28. Because the institutional tensions between law enforcement and the media are inevitable and perhaps necessary, this section underscores that there is more at stake than law enforcement's right to enforce federal criminal law and the media's right to get the story.

ATF's Efforts to Delay the Publication of the "Sinful Messiah" Series

Early in ATF's investigation of alleged criminal activity at the Branch Davidian Compound, Special Agent Davy Aguilera learned that the *Tribune-Herald* also was investigating Koresh. The two investigations continued on their separate courses for some time, with ATF trying to conceal the extent of its interest in the Branch Davidians. When Aguilera learned that former cult member Marc Breault was providing information to Mark England, a *Tribune-Herald* reporter, Aguilera asked Breault to stop speaking to the newspaper; it appears that Breault complied with this request. By January 1993, however, ATF's tactical planners began to fear that the *Tribune-Herald*'s publication of its series about Koresh would interfere with, or at least complicate, the agency's plans to execute warrants at the Compound. It was thus on February 1 that Chuck Sarabyn and Earl Dunagan met with Barbara Elmore, the *Tribune-Herald*'s managing editor, at the U.S. Attorney's Office[48] in Waco, and asked her to delay publication of the Davidian "Sinful Messiah" series until ATF could complete its operation. In the course of this meeting with

___

[48] Assistant U.S. Attorney Bill Johnston introduced the parties, but did not attend the meeting.

Elmore, and subsequent meetings with *Tribune-Herald* personnel, Sarabyn, Dunagan, and, later, Phillip Chojnacki, disclosed not only ATF's intent to take action against the Compound, but also the anticipated date of that action.

Nothing in the agency's formal guidelines at the time barred this kind of media contact or even addressed it.[49] The question remains, however, whether ATF exercised good judgment in initiating contact with the *Tribune-Herald*. Informed opinion differs on this point. Indeed, one of the tactical experts consulted by the Review wrote that ATF's efforts to obtain press cooperation violated basic principles of operational security. See Kolman at B-76. On balance, though, the Review believes that ATF made a reasonable judgment call in deciding to contact the *Tribune-Herald*. The danger that the *Tribune-Herald* would betray ATF's confidences might well have been outweighed by benefits to the agency if the newspaper's series could be delayed or, at the very least, if the publication dates were known. At the time ATF made its decision, the *Tribune-Herald* already had some knowledge of ATF's investigation and, in any event, ATF always retained the option to cancel or postpone the raid.

Given the resources the *Tribune-Herald* had committed to this investigation, ATF could hardly have requested the paper's forbearance in general terms. Nor could ATF reasonably ask the *Tribune-Herald* to withhold publication indefinitely. As a result, discussions between ATF and the paper were unlikely to be successful unless they reached some level of specificity.

Unfortunately, ATF did not adequately consider who should represent ATF in its negotiations or what strategy would best serve their desire to have the *Tribune-Herald* delay publication. ATF's media policy permits, and indeed encourages, local field offices to handle media issues without requiring headquarters involvement except when the national media are involved or ride-along requests for the media are concerned.

---

[49] ATF Order 1200.2B (January 20, 1988) sets out ATF's media guidelines. The order requires headquarters involvement when national media are involved, sets out the conditions under which media personnel can go along on ATF actions, and states that ATF employees will be responsible for releasing or not releasing information to the press. It also adopts a portion of the Department of Justice Media Guidelines, 28 CFR, Chapter 1, Part 50.2 (1986), for releasing information in criminal or civil matters. The ATF order does not address relations with the media during the investigative stage of an ATF operation.

Chojnacki's selection of Sarabyn and Dunagan to represent ATF, though consistent with ATF guidelines, exposes a structural defect in the guidelines. Although Sarabyn had taken ATF's general media relations course required for all supervisors, neither he nor Dunagan had any specialized expertise in media relations. Nor, for that matter, did Chojnacki. A field office should not be permitted to initiate contact with media about ongoing criminal investigations without formal participation or approval by ATF headquarters officials, particularly in an operation of the scope at issue here.

The point is not one of hierarchy, but of experience. During the course of his dealings with the newspaper, Chojnacki did seek advice, though only informally, from Jack Killorin, ATF's director of public affairs. But neither Killorin nor anyone else in the headquarters public affairs office was told that Sarabyn and Dunagan already had met with the newspaper or that Chojnacki had invited Cox officials to observe raid training. ATF headquarters might not have approved the raid if it had known that ATF had revealed possible raid dates to the *Tribune-Herald* early in the negotiations. Moreover, learning that the ATF Houston division had given up so much information without extracting anything in return, might have led headquarters to become involved in the negotiations.

Even though relations between the media and law enforcement can on occasion be adversarial, accommodation can bring important benefits to each side. A law enforcement agency's ability to inform the public about its achievements and to deter future offenders may depend upon the cooperation of the press. The media's ability to cover stories about criminal activity and to be protected adequately while covering such stories may depend on their having a working relationship with a law enforcement agency.[50] These working relationships develop over time and are often are based as much on personalities as on institutional needs. Here, there was no such relationship, no history of previous dealings between ATF and individual agents on the one hand and the *Tribune-Herald* and its parent organization on the other. ATF agents arrived in Waco and simply asked newspaper representatives to give up something of tremendous value to the paper—the opportunity to expose a local problem with independent, in-depth coverage. Were the paper to delay its series until after a raid had exposed the Compound's activities, the story would lose its exclusivity and its profitability. In exchange, the agents offered the paper security advice,

---

[50] Law enforcement is responsible for protecting bystanders during its operations. When the media becomes involved in an operation without giving notice to or getting consent from law enforcement, however, the media jeopardizes not only the success of the mission but also the safety of its personnel.

advice that any law enforcement agency would give freely if asked and a chance to watch raid training at Fort Hood, an event with minimal news value.

Had Chojnacki entrusted the press negotiations to those in ATF with more experience in media relations, an arrangement that would have been more suitable to ATF and the *Tribune-Herald* might have been made. ATF's representative in these negotiations might also have been more attuned to the kinds of arguments more likely to persuade the newspaper, arguments specifying the harms that could flow from publication of the "Sinful Messiah" series, instead of vague talk about how Koresh might become agitated.

And even if those responsible for press relations at ATF could not present better arguments to convince the *Tribune-Herald* to delay publication, they may have recognized the benefits of seeking assistance from local law enforcement officials in these negotiations, officials with whom the newspaper had a working relationship. Here, ATF's failure even to explore coordination with local officials increased its vulnerability to local conditions. The local U.S. Attorney's Office, which was instrumental in setting up the first meeting between ATF agents and *Tribune-Herald* representatives, might also have played a larger role in the negotiations.

Chojnacki's fervent pitch to the *Tribune-Herald* on February 24 gave the newspaper confused signals. ATF wanted the paper to delay publication of the "Sinful Messiah" series because publication might alert Koresh that some sort of enforcement action was imminent. But Chojnacki, seeking to conceal the precise timing of the raid, gave no indication that ATF would be definitely launching a raid or that if there was to be a raid, it would come soon. Chojnacki in fact suggested that ATF might have to "go home" if he could not get a warrant.[51]

If an ATF representative with more media relations experience and no critical role to play in the coming raid had been responsible for ATF's negotiations with the *Tribune-Herald*, ATF might have pressed its case beyond the February 24 meeting, perhaps with executives at Cox Enterprises. Chojnacki, however, was understandably preoccupied with his responsibilities as overall raid commander. When his presentation at that meeting failed, Chojnacki decided not to negotiate further with the newspaper.

---

[51] By suggesting that ATF might not be able to get a warrant, Chojnacki not only undercut his claim that publication would interfere with ATF's operation but also increased the *Tribune Herald*'s basis for writing that law enforcement had been ineffective in dealing with Koresh.

Media Activity Raid Day

Although the flaws in ATF's efforts to delay the *Tribune-Herald* series require attention if ATF is to be more effective in future negotiations with the media, it may be that no overtures, however skilled, would have convinced the newspaper to delay its series. What cannot be dismissed, however, is ATF's failure to consider how the emergence of the Branch Davidian Compound as a focus of media attention after publication of the first articles of the "Sinful Messiah" series could affect conditions in and around the Compound on raid day and to take precautions to minimize the possibility of media disruption.

By daybreak February 28, *Tribune-Herald* reporter Tommy Witherspoon's informant had alerted him to the timing of the raid. *Tribune-Herald* executives had seen helicopters landing at the Texas State Technical College airfield and had interpreted them correctly as a sign that an ATF raid was imminent. AMT ambulance dispatcher Darlene Helmstetter disclosed details about a pending law enforcement operation to her friend Dan Mullony, a cameraman at KWTX.

Based on what they deemed to be reliable information, KWTX and the *Tribune-Herald* decided to send a total of 11 of their personnel (three from KWTX and eight from the *Tribune-Herald*) to the Compound vicinity to cover the raid. The reporters arrived at the scene early and travelled up and down the roads around the Compound as they prepared to cover the story. One of their number, KWTX cameraman Peeler, became lost, and, in asking for directions, unwittingly tipped a cult member that a raid was imminent. Another group of reporters went to a house directly across from the Compound and asked for permission to watch ATF's enforcement action, without taking any precautions to ensure that these neighbors would not in turn alert Koresh to the impending raid. Many media personnel used cellular phones—unsecure communication devices whose signals are capable of easy, although illegal, interception.

The foregoing actions, which were taken by representatives of news organizations aware that Koresh and his followers were suspected of stockpiling weapons and manufacturing illegal firearms and explosives, belie the claim recently made by the Society of Professional Journalist's Waco Task Force that both KWTX and the *Tribune-Herald* "took precautions to prevent any alerting of the Davidians."[52] (Report at 6.) The extent of those precautions consisted only in using unmarked vehicles in the Compound's vicinity.

The Society of Professional Journalists' Waco Task Force makes another claim that bears mention here. According to its report, the Task Force "found no concrete evidence validating the accusations that journalists from the newspaper or the television station tipped off the Branch Davidians as to what was happening." (Report at 6.) In contrast to this claim, James Peeler has admitted to the Review that he told someone later identified as David Jones that a law enforcement action would soon take place at the Compound.[53] It is undisputed that Jones took this information and alerted Koresh. But however tragic the results of his carelessness may have been, Peeler should not be made the scapegoat for the fact that Koresh learned of the raid. Given the extent of other obvious media activity in the area, had Koresh not learned of the raid from Peeler, he might just as easily have been placed on guard by that other activity.

The prospect of substantial media activity in the area, and the dangers such activity could pose to the raid, should have been clear to ATF's raid commanders. They knew that ATF had been telling a newspaper for some time that a raid was imminent. And they knew that the appearance of the first installment of the "Sinful Messiah" series the day before had trumpeted the offenses going unprosecuted at the Branch Davidian Compound. Finally, they knew the paper was considering Koresh's request to send a reporter into the Compound Saturday or Sunday. From just this information, ATF should have foreseen the possibility that media personnel, or mere gawkers, would be in the vicinity of the Compound on February 28. Indeed, for all the agency knew, one of the *Tribune-Herald*'s rivals could have sent a reporter in to get Koresh's reaction to the "Sinful Messiah" series.

---

[52] The *Tribune-Herald*, in fact, had taken significant security precautions to protect its physical plant from possible retaliation by Koresh. It however took no meaningful steps to caution its reporters not to discuss the raid with people whom they did not know or to brief its reporters about the importance of not attracting any attention which might alert Koresh to the impending raid.

[53] Lee Hancock of the *Dallas Morning News* reported that Peeler spoke to a man in a car with U.S. Postal Service markings shortly before the raid but did not know he was a cult member. "TV cameraman admits his words tipped off cult by accident; He says he didn't know postal worker was member," *Dallas Morning News*, August 27, 1993. The recent report by the Society of Professional Journalists' Waco Task Force simply ignores the conflict between KWTX management's denial to the Task Force of responsibility for the leak to Koresh and KWTX cameraman Peeler's admission to Hancock and others, well before the Task Force report, that he had disclosed sensitive facts to a Branch Davidian.

As to the danger posed by such media activity, ATF should have recognized that Koresh's reported hostility to strangers could only have been increased, especially as to some media personnel, in the wake of the "Sinful Messiah" series. The presence of unwanted visitors on or near the Compound on February 28 might thus have triggered a hostile response that would interfere with the ATF raid whether or not ATF had the advantage of surprise. Increased activity around the Compound also could have impeded the ATF assault by forcing agents to take care that reporters did not become hostages or casualties.

ATF did set up roadblocks around the Compound shortly before the raid. Press vehicles, however, already had begun patrolling the area. Setting up roadblocks too early would have its own risks, because roadblocks could have tipped off the Branch Davidians that some sort of enforcement action was imminent. More importantly, even if ATF had opted not to use roadblocks, the agency could have been far more sensitive to press activity in the area by identifying possible press vehicles and keeping them under surveillance the morning of the raid.

Had ATF attempted to monitor media movements in the area, it might have prevented KWTX cameraman Peeler from ever speaking to cult member David Jones. At the very least, ATF would have recognized the significance of Jones racing to the Compound after his conversation with Peeler, thus reinforcing Rodriguez's report that Koresh had been tipped off.

Media activity in the vicinity of the Compound was not the immediate cause of the casualties suffered by ATF agents on February 28. These were inflicted by Koresh and his followers, and could have been avoided had ATF's raid commanders called off the operation once they recognized that they had lost the advantage of surprise. But the media's conduct posed a substantial danger not only to the security of ATF's operation but also to the lives of agents and civilians alike. While it is not the purpose of this report to suggest what the media might do to minimize such dangers in the future, the media should further examine its conduct near Waco on February 28.

Part Two
Section Four: The Flawed Decision to Go Forward With the Raid

On February 28, Koresh and his followers knew ATF agents were coming and decided to kill them. That the Branch Davidians, if forewarned, would try to lay such an ambush, however, should not have come as a surprise to those who planned the ATF operation. Indeed, the extraordinary danger posed by Koresh's arsenal and his propensity for violence were the reasons enforcement action was necessary. The issue addressed here is why ATF's raid-day decisionmakers proceeded with the raid, even though they should have realized—and indeed did realize—that they had lost the element of surprise, which was so critical to the raid plan.[54]

The decision to proceed was tragically wrong, not just in retrospect, but because of what the decisionmakers knew at the time. Surveillance certainly indicated that something was amiss. There was none of the usual activity outside the Compound, and agents had seen David Jones, a known cult member, speeding toward the Compound after his conversation with one of the many media personnel who had begun to congregate in the vicinity. And there was no need to speculate about what Jones might have told Koresh. Once Rodriguez was able to report back to the command post, the key decisionmakers had to know that Koresh had been tipped off that ATF was coming. Why, then, did no one at ATF call off the raid?

---

[54] "Raid-day decisionmakers" or "decisionmakers" refers in this section to those raid leaders who had the authority to call off the raid on Sunday morning. Chojnacki as incident commander, Mastin as deputy incident commander, Sarabyn as tactical coordinator, and Cavanaugh as the deputy tactical coordinator, had formal authority to abort the raid. And Royster, although he did not have a raid-specific title, apparently had the power to abort the raid by virtue of his position as SAC of the Dallas Division. As a practical matter, however, because this was a Houston Division case and Mastin and Royster were SACs from other divisions, they had an extremely circumscribed role in the decisionmaking process, and did not play critical roles in this area. Similarly, while Cavanaugh had clear authority to abort the raid based upon any new information obtained through the surveillance of the Compound after Sarabyn and the cattle trailers had left the staging area and headed for the Compound, Cavanaugh's status as an ASAC from another division might have led him to be reluctant to issue an abort order after Chojnacki and Sarabyn had given the go ahead.

The answer to this question lies in a complex set of factors that include the failure of the raid-day decisionmakers to adequately assess available information at the time of decision, the failure of those decisionmakers to appreciate the tactical significance of losing surprise close to an hour before the raid was to begin, serious deficiencies in the raid-day intelligence gathering and processing structure, and the placing of decisionmaking authority in the hands of individuals who lacked the requisite training and experience. In the end, this is less a story of wrong choices made than one of choices not made at all as the momentum of the massive operation—left unchecked by the raid commanders and ATF management—carried it inexorably forward, with speed substituted for reflection and inquiry.

ATF Decisionmakers Understood in Advance that the Raid Had Likely Been Compromised

Despite contrary public statements made by ATF officials in the days and weeks following the raid, it is now clear that the critical decisionmakers on February 28—Chojnacki, Sarabyn, and Cavanaugh—had sufficient information from Rodriguez to conclude that the raid had been compromised. They knew that Koresh had become upset and agitated after leaving to take a purported telephone call, proclaiming that neither the ATF nor the National Guard would ever get him, and commenting: "They're coming, Robert, the time has come. They're coming." Koresh's reference to the National Guard was particularly significant. Koresh had previously expressed hostility to ATF in Rodriguez's presence, and talked of ATF's coming to get him, but never before had he referred in this way to the National Guard. His reference to the Guard, which was indeed participating in the raid, was strong evidence that Koresh had specific information about the impending operation.[55] In addition, Rodriguez told Cavanaugh and others in the undercover house that "Koresh knows we're coming," and, according to Sarabyn, the first thing Rodriguez told him on the phone was "Chuck, they know we are coming."

The actions and statements of Sarabyn, Chojnacki, Royster and Cavanaugh, after hearing Rodriguez's report, strongly suggest that they not only had reason to believe, but in fact did believe, that the raid had been compromised. Their solution was to hurry up. After his telephone conversation with Rodriguez, Sarabyn related its substance to an agent in the

---

[55] Sarabyn has since noted that he found Koresh's reference to the National Guard to indicate a knowledge that "something was up." Chojnacki, however, recalls that he attached no significance to the reference because he works regularly with the National Guard.

command post. When asked what he planned to do, Sarabyn drew comfort from Rodriguez's having left Koresh reading the Bible, with no firearms in sight, and he opined that the agents could still execute the plan if they went quickly. Raid preparations immediately moved into high gear. Sarabyn, Chojnacki and Royster had a brief discussion on the tarmac, where Sarabyn related his conversation with Rodriguez and offered his thought that if they hurried they could still do the raid. After that conversation ended in agreement to go ahead with the operation, Chojnacki and Royster hurried into the command post. Chojnacki called the National Command Center in Washington to say the raid was going forward, and they both rushed back to the helicopters. Royster told various raid personnel "They know we're coming," and expressed the need to hurry. Sarabyn rushed to the staging area, several miles away, and, on arriving, repeatedly exhorted the agents there to hurry up and "get ready to go, they know we're coming." Cavanaugh, though he had no place to rush to, commented to others in the undercover house, "We better do this ASAP."

Sarabyn and Cavanaugh concede fearing the raid had been compromised before it began. Royster likewise acknowledges that he understood that ATF had lost the element of surprise. In contrast, Chojnacki maintains that Rodriguez's report did not lead him to this conclusion, since he felt that Koresh's statements, as relayed to him, were not materially different from what Koresh had been saying to Rodriguez all along. Chojnacki, like Sarabyn, however, appears to have interpreted Koresh's statements as significant enough to accelerate the raid's timetable and get agents to the Compound ahead of schedule.[56]

The Lack of a Control Agent

If any of the raid commanders, for whatever reason, found ambiguity in Rodriguez's report from the Compound, the fault lies not in Rodriguez's report—which was quite clear—but in ATF's failure to assign Rodriguez a control agent who could have obtained more details and, even more importantly, ensured that the undercover's information was understood.

---

[56] While Chojnacki does not recall running into the command post to call the National Command Center or running back out to the helicopters, he does not deny those acts. Moreover, he does recall wondering, as he sat in the helicopter, "We've got time, why are we were hurrying?" Although subjective levels of certainty are particularly hard to evaluate in retrospect, Chojnacki's thoughts and actions suggest that, at the very least, he believed Koresh's statements to Rodriguez revealed something that might well have a significant bearing on the raid.

The failure to give Rodriguez a control agent, not only on the day of the raid but also during the weeks before the raid, was an unusual departure from standard law enforcement practices. When an undercover agent makes repeated contacts with a target, particularly a target with a propensity toward violence and a powerful and influential personality, the agent must have substantial support. A control agent helps keep the undercover agent comfortable in that role, and attends to the undercover's needs, both physical and psychological. The control agent can also serve as a conduit for the undercover's information. Sarabyn, who was otherwise preoccupied and at a remote location, was certainly not the person to debrief Rodriguez, who was shaken by his experience in the Compound. This was a job that should have been handled in a face-to-face session with an otherwise unburdened control agent who knew Rodriguez well. Similarly, unlike Sarabyn, who focused his prepared questions on whether the cult members had openly exhibited weapons to Rodriguez or taken visible steps to resist law enforcement, a control agent could have patiently and objectively questioned Rodriguez about both the content and his impressions of his exchange with Koresh. More details on this score might have made the raid commanders recognize that ATF agents might face an ambush at the Compound.

Other Intelligence that Could Have Confirmed Rodriguez's Report that Koresh Knew ATF Was Coming

Even if Rodriguez's report did not convince the decisionmakers that the operation had been compromised, it should at least have led them to make further inquiries to determine whether Koresh's heated references to ATF, the National Guard, and their coming to get him were something more than an extraordinary coincidence. Such inquiries might well have caused them to abort the raid, since Koresh's behavior takes on a special significance when seen against the background of cult member David Jones' encounter with KWTX cameraman Jim Peeler. Although the agents in the undercover house did not know what Peeler told Jones, they did tell Cavanaugh that a known cult member had sped back to the Compound (while Rodriguez was still inside) after a conversation with someone they thought might be one of the many media personnel in the area. Cavanaugh believes that he, in turn, relayed this information to the command post.[57] Had anyone stopped to consider

---

[57] Although Cavanaugh recalls that he relayed all noteworthy surveillance information to the command post, and therefore assumes that he did so with the observation of the Peeler-Jones encounter, he cannot identify the person to whom he gave the information, and no one in the command post recalls having received it.

it, this information might well have shed critical light on the specificity of Koresh's assertions and made it even clearer that the raid had been compromised.

The failure to evaluate properly the intelligence from the undercover house should not be seen simply as a product of undue haste, however. It is not enough for raw surveillance information by forward observers to be relayed to operational commanders. There must be some system for gathering such pieces, putting them together, and ensuring that a meaningful evaluation gets presented to those who need it. As discussed above in the analysis of tactical planning, ATF's National Response Plan called for an intelligence coordinator, and an agent was assigned to that role. Unfortunately, through no fault of his own, that agent was given virtually no intelligence coordinating responsibilities, and had none at all on the day of the raid. Instead, surveillance was coordinated by Cavanaugh, who, unfamiliar with the day-to-day routines at the Compound, viewed his job as consisting largely of relaying information to the command post, rather than independently assessing it. Cavanaugh had no single contact at the command post, and no one had responsibility for gathering, integrating and assessing all the various intelligence inputs. While, at some level, Sarabyn undertook the intelligence evaluation role, there was no structure to ensure that he received all the raw intelligence data. Moreover, given the other responsibilities he had assumed, he could not possibly have performed that role adequately.

As a result of the flawed intelligence structure, while Cavanaugh, the other agents in the undercover house the morning of the raid, and possibly someone at the command post knew about the Peeler-Jones encounter, no one put it together with Rodriguez's report. Similarly, no one in the raid's command structure saw anything suspicious in the media activity all around the Compound that morning. As Cavanaugh later explained, everyone had become desensitized to the media's presence, assuming that reporters were just following up on or reacting to the publication of the first two "Sinful Messiah" articles. Raid commanders took comfort in the fact that substantial traffic had been reported in front of the Compound on Saturday as well. As it happens, however, at least some of the media personnel in the vicinity of the Compound on Saturday had come because they had been tipped off about the raid and wanted to look the premises over in anticipation of coverage the next day.

More attention to the acquisition and flow of raid-day intelligence, coupled with better technical support, might also have led agents to obtain what could have been the most concrete evidence that Koresh was planning an ambush. Because ATF suspected that cult members were using amateur radio equipment, the undercover house had been outfitted with a scanner for monitoring radio traffic. Given the range of frequencies on which the cult members might have been operating and the limitations of radio scanners, it is not particularly surprising that the agents in the undercover house were unable to pick up any traffic from the Compound, and that no efforts were made to use the scanner on the morning of the raid. More sophisticated, but widely available, monitoring equipment, however, would have greatly increased the chances of overhearing Compound radio traffic. And there appears to have been radio traffic inside the Compound that morning. Two area residents overheard radio communications among people they later believed to be Compound residents. The Compound residents described approaching ATF agents as looking like "a covey of quail," and one said "If I had a shotgun I could flush them out and kill every one of them." Shortly thereafter, the scanner picked up the sound of gunfire. Had ATF been monitoring that same conversation, even the decisionmakers undeterred by Rodriguez's report might have recognized the need to abort the raid.

Decisionmakers Failed to Realize Unacceptable Risk of Proceeding Without Surprise

The chief reason why Rodriguez's report did not lead ATF's decisionmakers to call off the operation, or even to make further inquiries into whether Koresh had indeed been tipped off, appears to be that they did not appreciate that surprise itself was absolutely critical to the operation's success. Sarabyn and Chojnacki recall that, for them, the determining issue was not whether Koresh would be surprised, but whether the Branch Davidians were arming themselves in anticipation of ATF's arrival. That this was indeed their concern is suggested by the questions that they asked Rodriguez upon his return to the undercover house on February 28. Although Rodriguez had been sent into the Compound to see if the Saturday and Sunday *Tribune-Herald* articles had led the Branch Davidians to take up arms or otherwise vary their routine, he emerged with information of far more direct importance to the ATF operation. But the decisionmakers stuck to the questions that had been prepared earlier, asking what Koresh was wearing, whether the Compound's gates were open, and whether anyone in the Compound was armed. On hearing that Rodriguez had seen no weapons in the Compound, the decisionmakers decided that they could still succeed so long as they hurried up the raid and got agents to the Compound before conditions changed. Should Koresh mobilize his followers while the agents were 1en route, Chojnacki and Sarabyn assumed that they would learn of the danger from the forward observers positioned in the undercover house with sights on the Compound, and could abort the raid if necessary.

Chojnacki's and Sarabyn's calculations apparently rested on two false premises: first, that Koresh would not mobilize his followers as soon as he learned that agents were coming; and, second, that if an ambush were prepared, signs of it would be visible to the forward observers more than 250 yards away.

This underestimation of Koresh's resolve was inconsistent with the intelligence that had been amassed during ATF's investigation. Those familiar with Koresh's stockpile of weapons, ammunition, and explosives, his increasing propensity toward intimidation and violent rhetoric, and his prior statements expressing extreme hostility to the ATF, could have predicted how Koresh might react to a tip that the ATF and the National Guard were coming. Former cult member David Block had told Aguilera that he had left the Branch Davidian because Koresh would always remind his followers that if they were to have a confrontation with the local or federal authorities, the group should be ready to fight and resist. In light of the information provided by Block, Koresh's statement to Rodriguez that "the time has come" was also a strong indication that something Koresh had planned for was about to happen.[58]

It is true that Chojnacki and Sarabyn lacked the firsthand or secondhand familiarity with Koresh that Rodriguez and Aguilera had, and therefore were less able to predict how Koresh would react to a tip about the raid. But they never turned to anyone for help. Instead, they asked Rodriguez only about whether he had seen defensive preparations, and they never made any inquiries of Aguilera or of the raid plan's other architects. Had they done so, they would have better understood how these new facts jeopardized a plan that depended entirely on the advantage of surprise. The Compound's structure, the firepower that Koresh had amassed inside, the loyalty and discipline of cult members, and the absence of cover in the surrounding terrain made a direct assault against forewarned assailants unacceptably risky.

Instead of seeking such counsel, the raid commanders thought they should hurry up. This, too, made no sense. If Koresh was not going to arm and deploy his followers, there was no need for haste. The raid commanders could follow the original plan and wait for the

---

[58] Indeed, the day before, when Koresh had preached about the "Sinful Messiah" article in Rodriguez's presence, he had cautioned his followers that when "they" came to get him, his followers would have to remember what he had told them to do. Unfortunately, the Saturday debriefing of Rodriguez was short and incomplete, and this information was not conveyed to the raid commanders. Had Rodriguez had a control agent, unburdened by responsibility for a massive law enforcement operation, the result might have been different.

Branch Davidian men to begin their work in the pit, away from their weapons. If the men did appear, the forward observers or ATF's fixed wing aircraft would be able to tell the raid commanders.[59] If, on the other hand, Koresh was going to resist the agents, any acceleration of the raid would again not help. It would still take at least 30 minutes from the time Sarabyn left the command post for the cattle trailers to get from the staging area to the Compound. This delay would give Koresh more than enough time to hand out weapons and deploy his followers in a Compound that appeared to be designed for just such defensive measures. And it was scarcely likely that anyone stationed outside the Compound would be able to tell that an ambush was being prepared. Cult members with access to machineguns and semiautomatic assault weapons should not have been expected to display their weapons out the window while they lie in wait.[60]

Perhaps one explanation for why the raid commanders underestimated the ability and resolve of Koresh and his followers might be that they overestimated ATF's ability to intimidate their target simply by arriving at the Compound in force. No decisionmaker has said that he acted in the belief that Koresh would back down in the face of ATF's show of force. Several ATF raid participants, on the other hand, have said they never thought the Branch Davidians would fire on scores of uniformed agents. Such statements betray an insensitivity to the volatility of the situation that ATF should have known it was entering. Given that a small segment of the population harbors extreme hostility both to ATF and the federal laws it is charged with enforcing, the agency must always be wary of violent responses from the targets of its investigations. And here, Koresh's pronouncements left no need to speculate about his hatred of the agency and the apocalyptic violence with which he would greet its agents.

The narrow answer to why the raid was not called off Sunday morning is that ATF decisionmakers failed to realize that surprise was critical to the operation's success and why it was so critical. Looking only for indications of defensive measures that were unlikely to be seen by the forward observers, the commanders never paused to reflect on the

---

[59] At about 9:00 Sunday morning, in order to conduct aerial surveillance of the raid, two ATF agents flew from TSTC in a twin engine airplane. Approximately 40 minutes later, they followed the two cattle trucks to the raid site at an altitude of 2500 feet. After the shooting started, they decreased their altitude to 1500 feet, to better identify and report the location of hostile firing positions, and pinpoint the location of injured agents. The plane could have been used to determine whether, despite Koresh's statements to Rodriguez, the Branch Davidian men would be following their perceived routine of working in the pit.

[60] While Koresh had posted sentries outside on other occasions, that certainly was no guarantee that he would respond to news of the impending ATF raid in the same way.

consequences of Koresh's having been tipped off. They hurried up when they should have slowed down. This narrow explanation, however, is incomplete, for it must be understood against the backdrop of the momentum inevitably generated in an action of the type contemplated by ATF, and the upper-level management decisions within ATF that exacerbated the pressure imposed by that momentum.

Handling the Momentum of the Raid

Most major law enforcement actions develop momentum as the moment of execution approaches, particularly raids that are viewed as high risk. Anxiety, fear, bravado, and the desire to accomplish the raid's objectives combine to put pressure on the raid participants to go forward. As the point of no return approaches, the pressure to go forward increases.

A raid of the scope, expense, and logistical complexity contemplated by the planners of the Waco operation can generate a momentum that, if unchecked, can be inexorable. By the time Rodriguez left the Compound on Sunday morning and reported to Sarabyn, all was poised to go forward. The eight-month investigation had generated probable cause to believe that Koresh and his followers had amassed an enormous stockpile of weapons, ammunition and explosives. Raid planning had been in the works since early December. Over 130 ATF agents were in or near Waco for the raid. Three ATF special response teams and three arrest support teams, comprising 76 highly motivated agents with a common mission, had been training and living together for three days at Fort Hood. Dozens of other ATF agents had been brought in to participate in and support the raid. The agents had been drawn from seven different ATF field divisions and 18 different cities, and could not be kept in the Waco area indefinitely. National Guard and emergency medical personnel and equipment were in place, as were members of other federal, state and local law enforcement agencies. ATF headquarters personnel were assembled at the National Command Center to receive up-to-the minute information about the raid. No one associated with the venture could have doubted the fantastic cost and effort it would take if the operation were aborted and put off for another time.

It is difficult to measure what effect the operation's built-in momentum may have had on the raid-day decision to go forward. Several ATF agents who participated in the raid have strongly suggested that the raid probably would have been aborted but for this pressure. At the very least, the pressure to go forward might well have played a critical role in the failure of the raid commanders to seek more information from Rodriguez, Aguilera, and raid planners about the significance of Rodriguez's report from the Compound. Decisions that now appear flawed may well not have been decisions at all, but simply steps taken along what seemed at the time to be a preordained road.

The point is not that momentum must be avoided in large-scale raids. Surely it is inevitable, and may even be beneficial to the success of an operation. Such pressures, however, should not be permitted to infect the decisionmaking of those charged with giving the go-ahead for what, at best, is a high-risk endeavor. Many law enforcement agencies provide training in crisis management to those supervisory personnel likely to face high-risk situations where alternatives must be weighed under extreme pressure.[61] ATF gave its supervisory agents no such specialized training.

The absence of such training was particularly unfortunate for the decisionmakers here. Neither Chojnacki nor Sarabyn had any experience remotely comparable to the raid attempted on February 28. The bulk of their experience was with typical street enforcement actions. Nor had they had any meaningful training in operations of this magnitude, or any relevant military tactical experience that might have compensated for that lack of training. As a result, they were ill-prepared for the command of a large-scale, high-risk assault on a large, heavily armed structure.

The pressures on Sarabyn were particularly great. Indeed, it is questionable whether any training could have prepared him for the many responsibilities that he took on. He served as the manager of the investigation, the manager of the tactical planning, and the de facto intelligence coordinator. He was also a principal liaison between the field agents involved in the raid and ATF headquarters, obliged to respond to high-level inquiries, prepare numerous reports on all aspects of the investigation and operation, and give briefings. Sarabyn's responsibilities continued to build as the investigation and tactical planning progressed. February 28 was to be the culmination of all of these efforts, and it would be understandable if Sarabyn was reluctant to postpone the long-awaited event and lacked the dispassion so critical to crisis management.[62]

---

[61] Typically, such training involves real-time exercises in which managers develop and enhance their skills in situation evaluation, resource assessment, team interaction, managing multiple demands, and near-, mid- and long-term planning. Many federal and state law enforcement agencies, as well as private industry, use such training.

[62] ATF management had at its disposal a number of senior agents with far greater relevant experience and training than either Chojnacki or Sarabyn, and who would not have had the same responsibilities that pressured Sarabyn.

The pressures on the raid's commanders could only have been increased by the absence of any meaningful contingency planning for the raid. When presented with Rodriguez's report, they considered but two choices: proceed with the raid as planned or call it off. A third alternative that is always available, delay, apparently was not considered. Had the raid planners prepared a more productive tactical alternative, such as deploying for a siege in the event surprise were lost, the pressure to proceed with the raid would have been substantially eased. A range of meaningful options, considered and practiced in advance and accounting for the real possibility that surprise might be lost, almost certainly would have improved the crisis decisionmaking process.

The final check on the pressures of momentum faced by those in the field can come through monitoring by headquarters personnel, far removed from the scene. But no meaningful monitoring occurred here. On February 28, pursuant to the National Response Plan, ATF headquarters activated the National Command Center in Washington to follow the progress of the raid. Staffed as it was with high-level managers who had extensive experience in field operations, the Command Center could have served as a valuable check on the decision to go forward with the raid. Had the Command Center been briefed on what Rodriguez had learned inside the Compound, the raid might well have been aborted. At the very least, Command Center personnel might have recognized that caution and careful thought, not speed, was the appropriate response to Rodriguez's information. Instead, when Chojnacki called the Command Center after being briefed by Sarabyn, he said only that the raid was going forward, and made no mention of Rodriguez's report. Moreover, the person he spoke to was neither a superior nor someone with particular knowledge of the operation. No questions were asked, no further information requested. As a result, the Command Center involved command in name only. In reality, it served as a front-row seat for what everyone anticipated would be a major, successful operation. In that capacity, the Command Center simply reminded the decisionmakers in the field that headquarters was watching, and it could only have added to the pressure to go forward with the operation for which all had waited so long.

Part Two
Section Five: Treasury Department Oversight

ATF Notifies Treasury of Impending Operation

As the planning for the raid on the Branch Davidian Compound entered its final stages, Associate Director (Law Enforcement) Daniel Hartnett, at the direction of ATF Director Stephen Higgins, asked Special Agent Christopher Cuyler, ATF's liaison to the Treasury Department, to brief the Assistant Secretary of the Treasury for Law Enforcement about the impending operation. Although ATF falls under the jurisdiction of the Assistant Secretary —as do the U.S. Secret Service, U.S. Customs Service, Financial Crimes Enforcement Network, and Federal Law Enforcement Training Center—no regulation then in force required ATF to seek approval from the Office of Enforcement for the execution of search or arrest warrants, even for an operation of this magnitude. Indeed, no regulation required ATF even to notify the Assistant Secretary that such an operation was about to be launched. Nonetheless, it had been ATF's practice to apprise the Assistant Secretary of significant events, especially those expected to generate substantial media attention.

Accordingly, on the afternoon of February 26, Cuyler prepared a one-page memorandum for Michael D. Langan, then Acting Deputy Assistant Secretary for Law Enforcement, alerting him that the Branch Davidian Compound would be raided on February 28 by SRTs from Houston, Dallas, and New Orleans, assisted by state, local, and military authorities. The memorandum noted that "approximately 75 people (men, women, and children)" were thought to be in the Compound, but it provided no details about the planned operation. However, the memorandum did assure: "A well-reasoned, comprehensive plan has been approved [that] allows for all contingencies." (See Appendix D.)

Shortly after preparing his memorandum, Cuyler gave a quick briefing to Ronald K. Noble, who had been designated by President Clinton, through the Secretary of the Treasury, to be Assistant Secretary of the Treasury for Law Enforcement. Pending his nomination and confirmation, Noble worked in the Office of Enforcement as a part-time consultant. He was authorized to give advice, but had no authority, operational or otherwise, over Treasury Department personnel. Because of his advisory status and because he was occupied with the bombing at the World Trade Center in New York City, which had occurred hours before,[63] Noble suggested that Cuyler brief Langan and John P. Simpson, Deputy Assistant Secretary (Regulatory, Tariff and Trade Enforcement), who was acting as Assistant Secretary for Enforcement.

At the briefing, Cuyler added little to the one-page memorandum, except to say that the operation had been moved up from Monday to Sunday in response to the anticipated publishing of the *Waco Tribune-Herald* series. Questions were raised among officials at the Office of Enforcement as to whether there were alternatives to an operation of such magnitude and they decided to discuss the matter further. Meanwhile, Langan alerted Philip Diehl, then counselor to Secretary of the Treasury Lloyd Bentsen, and Joshua Steiner, then special assistant to Deputy Secretary of the Treasury Roger Altman, to the fact that a raid was scheduled to take place the following Sunday near Waco. Steiner in turn informed Altman of the existence of the planned raid. Secretary Bentsen, who was in England, was not notified. When Simpson sought clarification about the purpose of the ATF briefing, Director Higgins explained that ATF merely wanted to keep the Office of Enforcement informed and was not seeking Simpson's authorization.

Friday afternoon, Noble had a discussion with Simpson, Langan, and Stanley Morris, the former Director of the U.S. Marshals Service, now working in the Office of Enforcement. Langan and Morris had serious reservations about the operation. Noble, who had been a Deputy Assistant Attorney General and Assistant U.S. Attorney at the Justice Department, agreed. He observed that Cuyler's memorandum had not addressed critical questions as to why so much force was needed to execute the warrants, what precise precautions were being taken to ensure the safety of ATF agents and those inside the Branch Davidian Compound, and why ATF believed it could achieve its mission without a shoot-out. Based on the information he had available at that time, Noble noted that if he were in Simpson's position, he would not let the raid go forward.

Simpson, Langan, Noble, and Morris also discussed the extent to which the Office of Enforcement should defer to the decision of a bureau within its jurisdiction to proceed

---

[63] The bombing, which occurred at 12:18 p.m. on February 26, heavily damaged Secret Service and Customs facilities, raising concerns within the Office of Enforcement over possible injuries to Secret Service and Customs personnel. ATF personnel were already playing a major role in the investigation of the blast.

with an operation about which the Office had reservations. Simpson decided that the Office was obliged to intervene and prevent the operation from going forward. Simpson called Higgins and directed that the raid be called off.

While Higgins offered no objection at the time, a half hour later he called Simpson and asked him to reconsider his order to call off the raid. First to Simpson alone, and then in a conference call with Noble and Simpson, Higgins explained that the warrants had to be executed forcefully because Koresh was not likely to surrender voluntarily and because ATF feared that Koresh and his followers might destroy evidence or commit mass suicide if given the opportunity. Higgins assured them that ATF was familiar with the routine in the Compound and that the raid had been scheduled for a time when the men would be separated from the women and children, who would be inside, and from the weapons, which were stored in an "arms room" under Koresh's control. Higgins stressed that the raid needed to go forward that Sunday because the *Tribune-Herald* series might alert Koresh that he was the subject of law enforcement scrutiny and lead him to alter his routine.

Higgins asserted that those directing the raid were instructed to cancel the operation if they learned that its secrecy had been compromised or if those in the Compound had departed from their established routine in any significant way. Higgins explained that an undercover agent would be sent into the Compound shortly before the raid to determine whether there had been any such changes in routine. At the conclusion of this three-way telephone call, Noble and Simpson said that they were satisfied that their concerns about the raid had been addressed. Simpson revoked his earlier direction that the raid not go forward.[64]

The next day, February 27, Higgins informed Simpson that the first *Tribune-Herald* article had appeared, but that it did not indicate that any law enforcement action was imminent. Higgins reiterated that an ATF undercover agent would be able to confirm the next day whether the investigation had been compromised, and he felt confident that the raid could proceed as scheduled. Simpson advised Noble of Higgins's call. The Office of Enforcement heard nothing more about the raid until late in the morning of February 28, when Higgins informed Simpson that the raid had been repulsed and agents had been killed and wounded.

---

[64] The Office of Enforcement was the highest office in the Department of the Treasury to permit ATF to proceed with its planned raid.

Discussion

Although the Office of Enforcement is formally charged with overseeing ATF, ATF gave Enforcement fewer than 48 hours' notice that it was about to embark on the biggest raid in its history. Moreover, the notice the agency did send was minimal, a one page memorandum giving little sense of the nature of the operation and its risks. The presentation seems to have been made more to enable the Treasury Department to field media inquiries after a successful raid was concluded than to allow it to rigorously review the raid plan; perhaps, it was simply intended to keep Treasury from hearing about the raid from the media first.

The procedure that ATF followed, however, was consistent with prior practice established by previous Assistant Secretaries and still in force in February 1993. Indeed, ATF was not required to give the Office of Enforcement any notice at all of the impending raid. Nor was there any system in place for the Office to make regular inquiries about significant ATF operations. ATF's Director and the Assistant Secretary for Enforcement met once a month. The Office of Enforcement relied on the discretion and good judgment of the Bureau's senior management for making day-in, day-out decisions, and gave the Bureau no reason to believe that any enforcement issue was to be identified for special scrutiny. Thus, the Office of Enforcement must itself bear some responsibility for ATF's failure to treat the operation differently and to give anything but minimal information about the impending raid on the Branch Davidian Compound.

When information about the raid was finally presented to it, the Office of Enforcement did seek to exercise some oversight authority. The raid would not have been permitted to proceed if Director Higgins had been unable to answer critical questions raised by the Office about the operation's necessity and its risks. Had the Waco raid commanders adhered to Director Higgins's assurance to Simpson and Noble that the raid would not go forward unless ATF had the advantage of surprise, the operation might have ended differently. The manner in which the Office of Enforcement was brought into this case, however, demands that some thought be given to the role the Office can and should play in ATF operations in the future.

Theoretically, the Office of Enforcement could choose to review the plans for every ATF operation and, indeed, for every Secret Service and Customs operation as well. To do so, however, would either turn the Office into a rubber-stamping operation or make enforcement activities by these agencies come to a grinding halt. In 1992 alone, ATF's more than 2,000 agents executed 10,134 federal warrants. In addition, they participated with state and local agencies in the service of 12,884 search warrants throughout the nation. Given the speed with which most enforcement activities occur and the degree of familiarity that is needed before an operation can be assessed, involvement by the Office of Enforcement in most ATF raids is impossible. For routine operations, the Office must rely on ATF leadership. Indeed, any micro-management in this regard would be inappropriate as well as inefficient, because those who plan these operations should feel and be responsible for them.

For certain significant enforcement operations, however, Treasury Department oversight is both realistic and appropriate. Where an extraordinarily large raid is being planned, the Office of Enforcement can provide a critical check on a process that tends to develop a momentum of its own. Even while leaving law enforcement agency planners considerable discretion over operational details, the Office can assess the risks being taken and bring its independent judgment to bear on sensitive issues, such as criminal activities by religious cults, that the agencies are not used to dealing with. Charged with enforcing criminal laws, law enforcement personnel will understandably have a tendency to look to enforcement solutions that may not always be appropriate. Civilian oversight can check this tendency, and ensure that agencies consider other approaches as well, if suitable. And where enforcement action is required, the Office of Enforcement can ensure that an agency consults and coordinates with other law enforcement agencies with special expertise.

It is difficult to craft precise rules and guidelines regarding when ATF should seek approval from the Office of Enforcement for an operation. The raid that later becomes the subject of congressional or media attention will not always seem worthy of special scrutiny before it happens. Moreover, each assistant secretary, as with any other manager, will doubtless have his or her own particular concerns. The most effective way to communicate those interests and clarify what "significant" means is not simply through formal rules, but also through a close working relationship between agency heads and the Office of Enforcement.

When presented with a law enforcement agency's plans for a significant operation, the Office of Enforcement must give due recognition to the expertise and experience of the agents who put the plans together. While the Office can bring a critical outside perspective to bear on sensitive issues, such as whether the public believes the level of force the agency plans to employ is justified by the violations targeted or whether adequate measures have been taken to protect agents and civilians, the Office must allow agents considerable leeway in deciding how those concerns should be addressed. At bottom, however, the Office must ensure that tactical objectives will be accomplished in a manner consistent with public expectations of fairness and proportionality and safety.

For the Office of Enforcement to play a constructive role in any operation, it must be brought into the picture while the operation is being planned. Otherwise, agents will see its review as just another last-minute bureaucratic hurdle to overcome. When Simpson and Noble expressed their concerns about the Waco plan on February 26 and put the operation on hold less than 48 hours before the raid was set to go, their intervention was unlikely to spark any meaningful ATF reassessment of the plan. By this time, there were pat answers about how the element of surprise could be preserved and how contingency plans had been prepared. With such reassurances given quickly, the raid could go forward. A broader and more precise definition of the Office's interests in this area is needed.

The tragedy near Waco exposed deficiencies in the way the Office of Enforcement oversees its bureaus' activities. The process of addressing these deficiencies is underway. First, the Office of Enforcement has established a Treasury Law Enforcement Council comprising the directors of the U.S. Secret Service, ATF, and Federal Law Enforcement Training Center, the Financial Crimes Enforcement Center, the Commissioner of Customs, and the Assistant Commissioner for the Criminal Investigative Division of the Internal Revenue Service. Its purpose is to provide Treasury law enforcement leaders a forum to discuss significant policy or operational matters with one another and with the Assistant Secretary for Enforcement. Working closely with the council, the Assistant Secretary for Enforcement has developed formal reporting requirements and crisis management procedures for the bureaus. Second, the Office of Enforcement has instituted weekly meetings with bureau heads to ensure that policy-level officials are provided with timely information to allow them to conduct meaningful oversight.

In the end, however, the Assistant Secretary for Enforcement must have confidence in the judgment of ATF leaders and be ready to allow them considerable discretion in selecting the means to accomplish a worthy objective. These leaders must in turn clarify the degree of discretion that field supervisors will be allowed and be able to respect the judgment of these field supervisors within their allotted spheres of expertise. With discretion, at every level of the agency must come accountability, because no level of oversight will prevent tragedy where—as here—a plan presented for Office of Enforcement review is based on assumptions and contains preconditions that are ignored by the agents charged with implementing them. Any individual whose judgment or integrity cannot be trusted by those who must rely on those qualities must be removed from a position of discretionary authority. The Assistant Secretary will work with ATF to ensure that these goals are met.

Part Two
Section Six: Operations Security

Among the many questions posed publicly after the raid failed were those concerning how the Branch Davidians could have known that ATF was coming. Many theories were circulated by the media and within the Waco community. Some theories suggested that a reporter had telephoned Koresh shortly before the raid. Others believed that the visibility of numerous agents in the Waco area before the raid had alerted local residents, particularly hotel employees, waitresses, and patrons of bars and restaurants.

The Review investigated the various theories that attempted to explain how Koresh was warned of the impending raid. The precise answer to how Koresh was alerted is now clear: KWTX cameraman Jim Peeler told David Jones that a raid was imminent, and Jones quickly passed that information to Koresh. Koresh's reaction to the news, as described by Rodriguez, strongly suggests that Jones' warning about the operation was the first to reach him. Contrary to some initial reports, Koresh was not consciously tipped off by a reporter. Similarly, reports that Koresh got wind of the raid due to careless ATF operations security practices are unfounded. Witnesses who thought they had seen ATF agents in Waco before the raid were actually recalling post-raid events during which ATF and other law enforcement were highly visible.

Although Koresh learned of the raid through the chance encounter between Peeler and Jones, not by ATF action, there were many other actions taken in the course of the investigation that could have alerted Koresh to ATF's investigation or the timing of its entry plan. Although many of these actions were needed to advance the investigation, some actions needlessly risked raising Koresh's suspicions. This was particularly dangerous because maintaining the element of surprise was vital to the plan's success. Although some criticisms of ATF's security practices were unfounded, a few of the salient actions are examined here so that ATF can improve the way it manages these inevitable risks in the future.

The Investigation

Although, in the course of their investigation, ATF agents pursued several avenues of inquiry that risked compromising the secrecy of the investigation, steps were taken to reduce the risk when possible and most of these risks were appropriately taken. During the compliance inspection of Henry McMahon, who was thought to be supplying Koresh with weapons and components, Special Agent Aguilera deliberately led McMahon to believe that the inspection was a routine administrative inquiry. In his interview of the Andrade family, Aguilera initially posed as a Texas businessman concerned about his relatives in the Compound. Aguilera did not reveal his true identity until he was satisfied that the family was trustworthy. When Aguilera and Special Agent Buford contacted several former cult members and the families of active cult members the agents identified themselves, but avoided releasing any details about the planned operation.

The Undercover Operation

The danger that Koresh would be alerted to possible enforcement actions against him vastly increased once ATF began its undercover operation. ATF appears to have given little attention to how cult members might have viewed the undercover house, even though the planners knew, or should have known, that the Branch Davidians were extremely suspicious of changes in their environment. The agents' cover was that they were Texas State Technical College (TSTC) students living in one of the houses that Gayle Peery, the owner, usually rented to his ranch hands.

Some efforts were taken to lend credibility to this cover. The agents obtained TSTC student identification cards and TSTC parking decals for their vehicles. Occasionally, some of the agents actually spent time at TSTC. A telephone was installed under one agent's undercover name, and the agents received mail at the house.

The routine at the house, however, could easily have undermined the agents' cover. Chosen for its view of the Compound, the house was small and only had two bedrooms. But it was occupied by eight agents, with four agents staying in it at one time, working two-man shifts. If the Branch Davidians had been keeping an eye on their new neighbors, this rotation would have been an odd, and suspicious, sight. Even if the constant changing of the house's occupants went unnoticed, the traffic created as agents came and went as well as the intermittent visits of technical operations officers and supervisors would have been difficult to miss.

Moreover, the agents selected to play the role of students did not fit the profile of TSTC students. Shortly after the agents moved in, Koresh visited the people in the house next to the undercover house and questioned them about the agents. In the course of the discussion, Koresh expressed doubt that the men were students because their cars were too new for most college students to afford and, according to Koresh, three of the four cars had no credit liens. (Koresh claimed to have found this out through an informant in the motor vehicles department.) In addition, Branch Davidians interviewed after the raid stated that Koresh had been suspicious of the men living across the road because they were too old to be students, their cars were too new, the men carried briefcases and the owner had previously refused to rent the house but then summarily rented it to these individuals. Cult members believed the men were law enforcement, but were not certain what agency they represented. And suspicions within the Compound could only have been heightened when the agents refused to allow cult member David Jones to enter the undercover house, despite his repeated efforts to do so.

The aspect of ATF's undercover operation that was carried out with the least regard for secrecy occurred on January 27, when a special agent posing as a UPS trainee accompanied the regular delivery person to the Compound. The UPS employee cautioned ATF that UPS requires its employees to keep their hair short and the agent's shoulder-length hair might raise suspicions. The UPS employee expressed concern that this irregularity presented a safety risk to both men. His warning was ignored.

The agent's conduct during the course of the delivery was even more suspicious than his appearance. The ATF agent instructed the UPS delivery person to drive his truck into the Mag Bag's driveway, go to the door, and ask to use the telephone and the bathroom. The delivery person told the agent that he always parked on the street and had never driven his truck into the driveway. More importantly, he also told the agent that in the course of making numerous deliveries during an 18-month period he had never entered the Mag Bag. The delivery person expressed his concern that the appearance of a second person coupled with such unprecedented actions was certain to arouse suspicions.

Upon arriving at the Mag Bag, they were greeted by Woodrow Kendrick and Michael Schroeder. The delivery person complied with the agents' instructions. He was permitted to make his phone call and the agent was allowed to use the bathroom, however Kendrick asked many questions about the new person.

Upon leaving the Mag Bag, while on the way to the Compound, the agent told the delivery person to follow the same procedure as before. He should drive the truck to the front of the Compound and once they were inside, ask to use the telephone and the agent would ask to use the bathroom. The delivery person responded that he never drove to the Compound but always left the delivery at the gate; he never entered the Compound. The agent also instructed the delivery person that while he was using the bathroom, the delivery person was to drive away, as if he had forgotten his trainee. The delivery person refused to comply with this part of the plan.

Upon arrival at the Compound, the two men were met by David Jones and Koresh, which was unusual because Koresh rarely, if ever, accepted deliveries. Before the delivery person could ask to use the telephone, the undercover agent asked to use the bathroom. Jones already had a roll of toilet paper in hand. He gave it to the agent and told him to use the outhouse. (There were no toilets inside the Compound.) When the agent left, Jones questioned the delivery person about the trainee. Attempting to change the subject, the delivery person tried to engage Koresh in small talk. Koresh told the delivery person, "I know we're being watched." He then returned to the Compound. This undercover effort was so transparent that Koresh complained to the local sheriff's department. He accused the department of trying to infiltrate the Compound.

ATF's failure to exercise more discretion in conducting its undercover probes of Koresh was not responsible for alerting the Branch Davidians that a raid was being planned for a particular day. It did, however, confirm Koresh's conviction that some law enforcement action against him was being contemplated and lent urgency to preparations in the Compound to resist such an action.

Pre-raid Logistics

ATF appears to have given sufficient attention to concerns about operations security as it made final preparations for the raid on the Compound. Beginning February 25, large numbers of agents began to converge at Fort Hood for training. Some agents billeted in barracks at Fort Hood; a few opted to stay in local motels. Support team personnel arrived in Waco on Saturday, February 27, and lodged at local motels. Agents at all locations demonstrated adequate concern for operations security, despite early news accounts to the contrary. Agents did not wear ATF clothing, discuss the operation in public areas, or conduct themselves in a manner that would draw undue attention. Although agents lodging at local motels used government credit cards, if asked, they explained that they were participating in a training course.

Wherever possible, ATF obtained support services from military and other law enforcement sources. When the agency had to deal with private contractors, it was appropriately circumspect. ATF told representatives of a private portable toilet company that their services were needed for a construction project. Company employees were instructed to have a truck at TSTC on Sunday morning where they would receive further directions. Arrangements for the ambulance service were made with similar care. ATF dealt exclusively with the manager and assistant manager, who were told only that the company's services would be needed on February 28 and warned not to discuss this information with anyone else. The ambulance company, which had worked previously with the local sheriff's office, was considered trustworthy.

In hindsight, ATF's use of a private ambulance service did have tragic consequences. A dispatcher for the local ambulance service told Dan Mallony, a KWTX cameraman, about the timing of the raid. This tip started a chain of events that resulted in Koresh being warned about the impending raid. Peeler was directed to go to the Compound area, and ended up discussing the raid with cult member David Jones, who approached Peeler because he appeared lost. Naturally, Jones took this information to Koresh. ATF cannot be faulted for the decision to give the ambulance service information about the pending operation, however. Even though the risk of spreading knowledge about the raid might have been reduced if ATF had used an ambulance service from another city, the benefit gained would have been offset by using a company whose drivers might not know the local roads and hospitals.

The Raid

Three operations security problems stand out in reports about the day of the raid: the convoy was too conspicuous, the forward observers might easily have been seen during their deployment, and the raid commanders' communications were not secure.

Many agents expressed concern about the convoy in which they traveled from Fort Hood to the Bellmead staging area early on February 28. Once the cattle trailers and vehicles assembled for the 100-mile trip, the result was an 80-vehicle caravan, headlights on, with a cattle trailer at each end. This spectacle did not necessarily announce that law enforcement action was imminent, but it did suggest that something highly unusual was happening. Certainly, had thought been given to the convoy's visibility, steps could have been taken to avoid to the problem.

In addition, more thought should have been given to when to deploy six forward observers to the hay barn behind the Compound. Because the distinctly dressed observers deployed at 8:00 a.m., without the cover of darkness, they might have been seen by Branch Davidians and reporters who were traveling the roads.

Finally, Sarabyn and Cavanaugh's use of nonsecure cellular telephones to speak to each other as they traveled to the Compound in cattle trailers from the staging area violated basic operations security practices and was contrary to the communication plan. An antenna on the Compound indicated that the cult members might have had scanners that could have received the cellular telephone transmissions if tuned to the proper frequencies.

Conclusion

Operations security works best in tandem with intelligence. While an effective intelligence operation ensures that decision makers get reliable information about an adversary, effective operations security denies the adversary access to the same sort of information. It is thus not surprising that the operations security problems in the ATF operation mirrored the intelligence failures. Particularly when a raid is so dependent on surprise, operations security cannot be simply a matter of individuals thinking about the consequences of their own actions. Constant attention must be devoted to how the agency's activities might look to a target or his or her allies.

ATF never entrusted any particular individual with this responsibility, and, as was the case with the intelligence gathering effort, the tactical planners and raid commanders were too overwhelmed with other matters to pay sufficient attention to operations security. Consequently, on the morning of February 28, raid commanders underestimated the risk that the raid could be compromised other than by the Saturday and Sunday newspaper articles.

Even though Rodriguez returned from the Compound with information indicating Koresh had been alerted to the raid, those evaluating the information continued to focus on their earlier expectations, that after reading the articles, Koresh would distribute weapons and post sentries. If operations security concerns had been assessed properly, the agents would have treated the newspaper articles as just one of many possible threats. Having done so, they might have had a broader perspective from which to assess the significance of Rodriguez's information. This experience shows that operations security is crucial to the success of large-scale tactical operations.

Part Two
Section Seven: ATF Post-raid Dissemination of Misleading Information About the Raid and the Raid Plan

Following a tragedy of this magnitude, it was inevitable that the law enforcement community, the Executive Branch, Congress and concerned private citizens would demand an accounting of these events.

In the wake of the tragedy on February 28, the raid commanders, who made the decision to proceed with the raid despite the clear evidence that Koresh had been forewarned, and their superiors in the ATF hierarchy endeavored to answer the call for explanations. But critical aspects of the information that they provided—to superiors, to investigators, and to the public—were misleading or plain wrong. It was not that they lacked access to the relevant facts. Rather, raid commanders Chojnacki and Sarabyn appear to have engaged in a concerted effort to conceal their errors in judgment. And ATF's management, perhaps out of a misplaced desire to protect the agency from criticism, offered accounts based on Chojnacki and Sarabyn's statements, disregarding clear evidence that those statements were false.

ATF Management's Misleading Post-raid Statements

In the aftermath of the Waco raid, perhaps the most frequently asked questions were: Had Koresh been tipped off that ATF was coming? And, if Koresh indeed was forewarned, did ATF commanders know this before they launched the raid? Certainly the news media representatives pouring into Waco sought answers for these questions from official and unofficial ATF spokespeople. The answers would also be significant for those looking toward a criminal prosecution of Koresh and his followers, since evidence that the Compound's residents had deliberately planned an ambush after getting tipped off would blunt any claims that they had merely acted in self-defense against unknown assailants. And ATF's leadership sought answers, that they might respond to media and official inquiries, and that they could work to prevent future tragedies.

ATF's top management appropriately set about to determine whether surprise had been lost, and how. They established a "shooting review" team, and that team systematically looked for answers. Even before a complete picture of the Waco tragedy had emerged, however, Associate Director for Law Enforcement Daniel Hartnett and Deputy Associate Director for Law Enforcement Edward Daniel Conroy, together with Intelligence Division Chief David Troy—who became ATF's principal spokesman about the incident—soon began to make false or misleading public statements about the raid. Moreover, Director Stephen Higgins, relying on their reports from Waco, unknowingly made similar misstatements. To some extent, these misstatements were the product of inaccurate, untruthful or misleading information from Sarabyn and Chojnacki about what they had learned from Rodriguez before deciding to go forward with the raid. In making his initial public statements, Hartnett appears to have consciously avoided confronting the truth and, at the very least, displayed a serious lack of judgment.

As top ATF officials began to receive additional information from line agents and other sources indicating that the raid commanders had proceeded with full knowledge that they had lost the element of surprise, those officials must have realized, had they not already known, that their earlier public statements were either misleading or flatly false. Yet they stuck to their original story, thereby misleading the public and undermining the integrity of their agency.

What follows is a brief summary of the relevant events as they unfolded after February 28.

The Shooting Review Team

On March 1, 1993, consistent with ATF policy, Hartnett and Conroy established a shooting review team to probe the circumstances of the firefight at the Branch Davidian Compound. The team consisted of ATF's Intelligence Division Chief David Troy, Bill Wood, Special Agent in Charge of ATF's Cleveland Field Office, and Dave Benton, the agency's Chief of Planning and Analysis. Troy was placed in command of the review; Benton was not able to participate in aspects of the inquiry, due to other duties. Between March 1 and 3, Troy and Wood interviewed the key participants in the decision to go forward with the raid. During this process, Troy took notes, and he and Wood kept ADLE Hartnett and DADLE Conroy apprised of what the review was being told. At the end of each day, Troy turned over his interview notes to Hartnett.

Shooting Review Team's Interview of Rodriguez

The team's first interview was with Robert Rodriguez, the undercover agent, who related what had happened in the Compound during his visit the morning of the raid.

In his interview with the shooting review team, Rodriguez said that he had been in the foyer with Koresh and others and that the Compound had appeared to be "normal." Koresh was preaching and reading from the Bible. Then Koresh was called from the room to take what was said to be an emergency telephone call. When he returned, he was visibly shaking and very nervous, and he repeatedly looked out the window and dropped the Bible he was carrying. He looked at Rodriguez and said, among other things, "He who kills me kills the Kingdom of God and that includes ATF and the National Guard." Rodriguez also recalled that Koresh said he "could only die once," and, upon looking out the window said, "They are coming for me but they can't kill me."

Rodriguez told the team that, upon hearing Koresh's proclamations, he said he had to leave. In response, Koresh walked up to Rodriguez, shook his hand and said, "Good luck, see you later," and told him to be careful. Rodriguez reported that Koresh had never done or said anything like that before. As a result, Rodriguez felt that he had been "burned," that is, he believed that his undercover identity had been revealed.

Rodriguez then told the team about how he had reported back to his superiors. Upon entering the undercover house, he told Cavanaugh what had happened at the Compound, then called Sarabyn and repeated his account. He specifically recalled informing both Cavanaugh and Sarabyn that Koresh had said ATF and the National Guard were coming. In response to Sarabyn's specific questions, Rodriguez had reported having seen no weapons or signs of preparations to resist a raid while he was at the Compound.

Shooting Review Team's interview of Mastin

After interviewing Rodriguez, Troy and Wood interviewed SAC Mastin, whose account of Sarabyn's actions and statements corroborated Rodriguez's claim to have informed Sarabyn that Koresh knew that "ATF and the National Guard" were coming. According to Mastin—and as the over sixty ATF agents who heard Sarabyn on the day of the raid have since recounted—when Sarabyn arrived at the staging area, he had "a sense of urgency about him." He told the agents, "Let's load up and go." Mastin candidly told the team that although Sarabyn had said "Koresh knows we are coming," he followed Sarabyn's lead and moved to get the trailers loaded and ready.

Shooting Review Team's Report to Hartnett and Conroy

Upon hearing Rodriguez's and Mastin's accounts of events, Troy was at a loss to explain why ATF proceeded with the raid and he doubted the wisdom of the decision to go forward. Troy and the shooting review team promptly let Hartnett and Conroy know what Rodriguez and Mastin had related. After being briefed, Hartnett was upset and expressed chagrin that Mastin had not tried to stop the raid or even questioned the decision to go forward after hearing what Sarabyn had said. Thus, as early as the day after the raid, Troy, Conroy and Hartnett were on notice that ATF's raid commanders might well have proceeded with the raid despite knowing that they had lost the element of surprise.

Shooting Review Team's Interview of Sarabyn

When the shooting review team interviewed ASAC Sarabyn the next day, March 2, he was unable to provide a detailed account of most of his critical conversation with Rodriguez, claiming that Rodriguez "was not real descriptive as to the ATF-National Guard statement," and that Rodriguez had said words to the effect that Howell (Koresh) must know something was going on but nothing explicit that Sarabyn could recall. However, Sarabyn clearly remembered that Rodriguez had said that he had not seen any guns or armed guards. Sarabyn also recalled very little about his conversation with Chojnacki on the tarmac at the command post, when the decision to go forward with the raid had been made. Furthermore, in contrast to Mastin's clear recollection, Sarabyn did not recall making any statements at the staging area to the effect that Koresh knew that ATF was coming.

Shooting Review Team's Interview of Cavanaugh

On March 3, the team briefly interviewed ASAC Cavanaugh, who reported that Rodriguez had returned to the undercover house extremely upset and reported that Koresh had said that ATF and the National Guard were coming to get him and that Koresh had said "our time has come." Cavanaugh had instructed Rodriguez to advise Sarabyn of what had occurred at the Compound.

Shooting Review Team's Interview of Porter

The team next interviewed one of the forward observers in the undercover house, Herman Porter, because they had heard that Porter was upset that the raid had gone forward even though the commanders knew that Koresh had been tipped. When interviewed, Porter was candid and distressed. He said that he had heard Rodriguez's report to Cavanaugh—which he confirmed had been accurately recounted by Rodriguez to the team—and had been shocked that the raid had not been canceled. Indeed, Porter recalled that after hearing Rodriguez's account of what had happened in the Compound, he had been so certain the raid would be canceled he began putting his gear away.

Shooting Review Team's Interview of Chojnacki

When interviewed by the team, SAC Chojnacki could not recall anything specific that Sarabyn had told him about Koresh's statement regarding ATF and the National Guard. However, he was sure that Sarabyn had said that there were no guns or sentries; this information, Chojnacki claimed, had formed the basis for his decision to go forward with the raid.

After the interviews, the shooting review team was concerned because Sarabyn's urgency and his statements at the staging area about Koresh's knowledge that ATF and the National Guard were coming were inconsistent with his lack of any recollection that Rodriguez had told him that Koresh had been tipped about the raid. As a result, the team was prepared to conduct additional interviews. However, after being told by Hartnett that the local U.S. Attorney's office had directed ATF to stop the shooting review because it was needlessly duplicating the pending leak and murder investigations, the team concluded its efforts.

Hartnett, Conroy and Troy knew surprise was lost

By the conclusion of these interviews, Hartnett, Conroy and Troy were thus confronted with two conflicting versions of the events immediately preceding the decision to go forward with the raid. On one hand was Rodriguez's vivid account of Koresh's extraordinary behavior at the Compound and of his own reports to Cavanaugh and Sarabyn, reports that left little doubt that Koresh had been tipped off. Rodriguez's account was internally consistent and completely corroborated by Mastin.[65] On the other side were Sarabyn and Chojnacki's statements. Not only did these raid commanders—who, given the magnitude of the tragedy at the Compound, obviously had a strong motive to conceal their own misjudgments—display a selective memory about critical facts, but also, what they "remembered" made little sense. Sarabyn's claim that Rodriguez had not informed him that Koresh had been alerted to the raid contradicted reports from agents at the command center of Sarabyn's announcements that Koresh knew ATF was coming. And Rodriguez's account offered the only plausible explanation for the sense of extreme urgency that gripped Sarabyn after receiving Rodriguez's telephone call.

ATF's Media Statements After the Shooting Review

The story ATF top management told the American people bore little resemblance to what had been told to the shooting review team, and had been relayed to Conroy and Hartnett. Uncritically accepting Sarabyn and Chojnacki's account, and disregarding the far more persuasive, and rapidly growing, evidence that the their account was false, ATF's top managers uniformly said, in substance, that ATF's raid commanders had not known that the element of surprise had been lost before they made the decision to go forward.

On March 3, 1993, three days after the raid, and the day the shooting review was terminated, Hartnett was asked during one of the press conferences held near Waco: "When the undercover agent [Rodriguez] heard this phone call [in the Compound on the day of the raid], did he realize at the time that this was a tip?" He responded that "[h]e did not realize this was a tip at the time." (CNN, March 3, 1993). Expanding on this line, Hartnett explained:

---

[65] This Review, relying in large part on the work of the Texas Rangers, has gathered substantial evidence that now further corroborates Rodriguez's and Mastin's account. In addition to the over sixty agents who witnessed Sarabyn's behavior at the staging area, Phil Lewis, who was seated next to Sarabyn while Sarabyn had the critical conversation with Rodriguez, overheard Sarabyn's end of the conversation and saw his reactions. After the call was finished, Lewis asked what Rodriguez had said. Sarabyn told him that Rodriguez had related that, while he was in the Compound, Koresh had received a telephone call which he took out of the room, and that when Koresh had returned, among other things, he had nervously announced that ATF and the National Guard were in Waco and "that they were coming." According to Lewis, upon hearing this, he grabbed Sarabyn and asked what was he going to do; Sarabyn told him that he thought that they could still do the raid if they went quickly and he rushed out the door. Lewis's account confirms what both Mastin and Rodriguez recollect happened.

Despite his initial blanket denials, Sarabyn has eventually admitted the essential accuracy of Rodriguez's account. According to one of Sarabyn's later statements to the Review, the first words Rodriguez had said to him were "Chuck, they know."

[T]here was an ATF agent in the Compound shortly before the execution of the warrant. When he left the compound everything was normal—children were outside, people were going about their business. While he was there, a phone call was received by [Koresh], and he began reading scriptures. There was more to it than that, but that was about what occurred. Id.

Similarly, according to an article in the *Los Angeles Times* the next day:

On the morning of the raid, Hartnett said, the undercover ATF agent reported that "everything was normal" at the compound....But the agent left the compound just "as a phone call received" at the facility tipped off the sect members. The agent did not realize at the time that the raid had been compromised. ("Agents Prepare for a Long Cult Siege," *Los Angeles Times* at 1.)

Three days later, relying on what he had been told by Hartnett and Conroy, Higgins appeared on "Face the Nation," and flatly denied a report that ATF had known about Koresh's receiving a telephone tip about the raid:

Q. There has been some suggestion that perhaps your agents knew beforehand that the security had been compromised, that they were aware that Mr. Koresh had received some sort of phone call. Can you just give us your side of that?

A. Without being too specific, let me say as I did earlier, this plan was based on the element of surprise. It had to be done quickly, and it had to be a surprise. We would not send our agents into a situation where we didn't think we had the element of surprise....

Q. But your bottom line is that you absolutely did not believe the security had been compromised when the agents went into the compound?

A. Absolutely not, because as you can see, we walked into an ambush, and there's no way that our people, from the team members to the leadership, would have allowed that to happen had they known it.

When he made these remarks, Higgins apparently had not been informed about Rodriguez's and Mastin's statements.[66]

The Texas Rangers' Reports

Hartnett and Conroy's hierarchical management style, which discouraged rank and file agents from speaking to them directly, effectively insulated them from hearing from the agents with contrary accounts.[67] While Chojnacki, Sarabyn, Royster, and Cavanaugh had access to Hartnett, we have been unable to find a single rank and file agent who spoke to Hartnett about whether the raid commanders had known the raid had been compromised. But management style cannot explain Hartnett and Conroy's failure to change their public statements in the face of yet more evidence that Rodriguez's account was correct.

Within days after the raid, as part of the State's homicide investigation of the February 28 ambush, two Texas Rangers, David M. Maxwell and Coy Smith, interviewed Rodriguez and other ATF agents, including several of the agents who had been positioned in the undercover house when Rodriguez returned from his encounter with Koresh. Rodriguez's account was strikingly consistent with the statement he had recently given ATF's shooting review team. In addition, several of the forward observers informed the Rangers that, while they had not heard Rodriguez's telephone conversation with Sarabyn, they had heard Rodriguez clearly tell Cavanaugh that Koresh had returned from a "telephone call" visibly shaking and agitated and that he had been "tipped" that both the ATF and the National Guard were coming.

---

[66] In addition to their public statements, on March 10, 1993, Higgins, Hartnett and other ATF officials testified before a Special Executive Session of the Subcommittee on Treasury, Postal Service and General Government of the House Appropriations Committee, convened for the purpose of reviewing ATF's actions in raiding the Compound. In deference to Congress' oversight role, and the closed nature of such a session, the Review has not interviewed those Members of Congress who attended the session and has made only limited inquiries of others about what was discussed during that session. There is nevertheless reason to believe that Hartnett failed to disclose Rodriguez's account to Congress and did not inform the Committee of the possibility that ATF's raid commanders had gone forward with the raid despite being aware that the element of surprise had been lost. The ATF leaders took a similar line the next day when they briefed Secretary Bentsen and his staff.

[67] As both the Texas Rangers and the Review discovered, many of the agents present at the staging area on the day of the raid were talking among themselves in the days following the raid about why the raid went forward despite the raid commanders' awareness that Koresh knew they were coming.

During the evening of March 3, shortly after their first interview of Rodriguez, the Rangers briefed Hartnett and Conroy about their interviews, noting that they had found Rodriguez to be a credible witness. Although Hartnett had already been briefed by Troy as to the shooting review team interviews, the Rangers recall that he seemed surprised to learn that Rodriguez positively recalled informing Sarabyn that the raid had been compromised. The next day, after speaking with Rodriguez again, and hearing the same account supplemented by minor additional details,[68] the Rangers reiterated their view of Rodriguez's credibility to Hartnett and Conroy. But Hartnett's and other ATF top managers' public statements supporting the raid commanders continued.[69]

The Rangers interviewed Sarabyn and Chojnacki on March 25 and 26 respectively, and thereafter told both Hartnett and Conroy that Sarabyn's and Chojnacki's accounts made little sense and were inconsistent with the weight of the evidence; and that they found the two men lacked credibility. Sarabyn now had claimed to have specifically asked Rodriguez if Koresh knew that ATF and the National Guard "were coming" and was told "no." The Rangers noted that Sarabyn's story could not be squared with his later announcements at the staging area that the agents should hurry up because Koresh knew they were coming. The Rangers also told Hartnett and Conroy that Sarabyn was evasive during his interview and had unfairly accused Rodriguez of changing his story.

Chojnacki had also claimed to have been unaware that Koresh had been tipped, but the Rangers stressed to Hartnett and Conroy that Chojnacki's claim was contradicted by his decision to join Sarabyn in rushing forward with the raid. Indeed, when pressed by the Rangers, Chojnacki could not offer a coherent explanation for why speed had been necessary. Like Sarabyn, Chojnacki had tried to blame Rodriguez for the flawed decision to go forward, saying, somewhat incoherently to the Rangers:

> It's very disturbing to me that if Robert [Rodriguez], and I'm not trying to cast blame on anybody, because that I, I thought we had built in enough safeguards to cover ah a cowboy, you know, who would go under any costs or of any of those

---

[68] Specifically, Rodriguez recalled that Koresh had been ushered out of the room by a "telephone call" from "England." Apparently, Rodriguez's additional recollections, which did not change the gist of his statement, may have become the basis for Hartnett's and Conroy's erroneous belief that he was "changing his story."

[69] In mid-March, the Rangers also provided Hartnett with Rodriguez's sworn March 16, 1993 statement, which also was consistent with his earlier oral statements.

kinds of terms. Anything or one person would, would be willing to, ah, ah, put us in a risky situation, riskier than our typical work, and ah, his role was so key in this thing and was the key to the whole thing. And I can't believe that at the most critical time if he felt absolutely sure that that was the case that that couldn't be communicated, ah...or that we couldn't recognize that he was attempting to communicate....

At the conclusion of their briefing, the Rangers told Hartnett and Conroy that the morale of the rank and file ATF agents was suffering because they did not believe Chojnacki and Sarabyn's stories, yet the two were still high in the chain of command near Waco. The Rangers suggested to Hartnett and Conroy that morale might improve were Sarabyn and Chojnacki removed from their positions in the chain of command. Their advice was not followed.

The Late March and Early April ATF Statements

Although Director Higgins had begun to hear bits and pieces of information belying ATF's public statements about not having knowingly lost the element of surprise, Hartnett and Conroy failed to keep Higgins informed about the mounting weight of evidence that Sarabyn and Chojnacki's account was false. Higgins's own public statements thus deepened ATF's commitment to a story which was fast losing its credibility.

The occasion for these statements to the media came when, in the face of the agency's misleading public stance, agents "leaked" a competing story to the press. A March 28, 1993 *New York Times* front page headline proclaimed: "U.S. Agents Say Fatal Flaws Doomed Raid on Waco Cult." The article stated:

> Contradicting the official version of events, four of the agents involved in the raid and in a review of its aftermath said that supervisors had realized even before they began their assault that they had lost any element of surprise but went ahead anyway.

The article initiated a barrage of ATF denials.

On March 29, 1993, on NBC's Today Show, Higgins, still unaware of Rodriguez's account of what had happened, engaged in the following exchange:

Q. Let's talk about one of the other charges, and that is that you have, in fact, said that cult members were tipped off, and now there are reports that bureau supervisors knew that the element of surprise had been lost and yet decided to go ahead with the raid anyway. Is that correct?

A. This was a plan which depended on the element of surprise. We would not have executed the plan if our supervisors felt like we had lost that element. So my position has been and continues to be we did not believe that we had lost that element of surprise.

In the next few days, Higgins heard from many agents who challenged the agency's public stance on the element of surprise issue. These contacts prompted him to request a copy of Rodriguez's statement to the Rangers with respect to the raid day events. Hartnett gave the statement to Higgins during the first few days of April. According to one of his top assistants, Higgins, usually a reserved person, exclaimed on reading the account: "What would Koresh have to do, paint himself up with war paint and shoot up the undercover house before we would have known enough to call off the raid?"

Troy also made a number of similar public statements during late March and early April. But, in contrast to Higgins, he was fully aware of the conflicting accounts of what had happened on raid day, and should have realized Higgins, Hartnett and others had overstated the agency's position in early March. As a result, many of his statements in late March and early April appear to have been carefully tailored to confirm that ATF did not realize that it had lost "the element of surprise" while artfully recasting the concept to accommodate the eventual release of Rodriguez's account of raid day events. On CBS's "Street Stories" program, on April 1, Troy stated:

There is no way that we would have executed the raid if the people running the operation would have realized that the element of surprise was lost. That would have been obviously a suicidal mission. We were not aware at that point in time, and did not become aware that the element of surprise was lost until they opened fire on us.

In response to reports that unnamed agents at the staging area had claimed that one of the raid supervisors had run around yelling that "we need to go" and "they know we're coming," Troy protested:

> If the supervisory staff...was aware and convinced that the element of surprise was lost, there's no way we were going to go driving in there and execute a warrant because the element of surprise was a key factor.

The next day, Troy began to recast the issue when he told the *Washington Post*:

> We felt that there wasn't compelling evidence that Koresh knew that a raid was planned for that day. Had agents known that the element of surprise was lost, the raid would have been halted.

"Koresh Described as 'Nervous' After Call Before ATF Assault," *Washington Post*, April 2, 1993 at A3.

His remarks signalled a shift toward portraying the raid plan as requiring "compelling evidence" that Koresh had been tipped before the raid could be halted, rather than confirmation that conditions were right before the commanders would go forward.[70] See also *Houston Chronicle*, "ATF Knew Koresh Tipped Off, Sources Say," April 2, 1993 at 1 ("Troy...said at a news briefing Sunday that agents did not know Koresh had been warned when they ordered the raid to proceed."). Similarly, on April 2, Troy appeared on ABC's "Good Morning America" and stated:

> At this point in time our position is this. We know exactly what statements were made by our undercover agent to our tactical commanders when he came out of the compound Sunday morning.... [W]e know exactly what statements were made by our commanders when they were at the staging area prior to departing for that raid.... [T]he important thing that was said, that we feel, is the undercover agent saw absolutely no preparation for any kind of battle plan, <u>there were no firearms displayed by anyone...we did not feel that they were gearing up, getting ready for any kind of offensive activity</u>.

(Emphasis added). In so doing, Troy held to the position that ATF had not known it had lost the element of surprise, but again subtly tried to redefine the concept of losing "the element of surprise," this time, to require outward signs of an ambush being prepared. By implication, therefore, according to Troy, so long as no weapons were visible, Rodriguez's

---

[70] At the same time, top ATF officials sharply attacked what they called "disgruntled agents" for "taking out of context" Sarabyn's statements at the staging area in their remarks to the media. Id.

information was not sufficient grounds to stop the raid. In keeping with this theme, on April 3, 1993, Troy told the *Dallas Morning News*: "We were not looking at a situation where we had a shrinking window of opportunity. We didn't say, 'this thing is turning bad, so let's go in before it does.'" Troy further reconstructed the concept of the element of surprise on May 3, 1993, when he told *Time* magazine that "[t]he element of surprise does not mean they don't know you're coming. Only that they can't take control." By then, Troy had diluted the concept of surprise into a functionally meaningless term.

The Significance Of ATF's Misleading Statements

There may be occasions when pressing operational considerations—or legal constraints—prevent law enforcement officials from being less than completely candid in their public utterances. This was not one of them. And a desire to shield one's agency from public criticism cannot justify false or misleading pronouncements on matters of clear public concern. Hartnett, Conroy, and Troy permitted public statements to be put forward that were either most likely false or definitely false. Troy admitted to the Review that he wrongfully misled the press and the public. Troy provided two explanations for his actions. First, that he was trying to provide information to the press corps. Second, that he was acting at the direction of Hartnett, whose management style discouraged subordinates from challenging his instructions. Neither explanation is acceptable. Hartnett and Conroy, in contrast, were not subject to instructions to make misleading statements, and never gave their superior, Higgins, an opportunity to learn the truth.

The extent of Director Higgins's knowledge places him in a different category, since he was not aware of the falsity of Sarabyn and Chojnacki's account when he adopted that account in his public statements. However, Higgins must accept responsibility for continuing to take public positions on the issue when repeated questions from the media and information readily available to him should have made it clear that he was on shaky ground. Higgins never adequately questioned his subordinates to determine the facts until early April.

An oft-stated justification offered by top ATF management officials for their misleading statements, and their failure to inform the public about Rodriguez's and the other agents' conflicting accounts, is that they were prohibited from doing so. Various ATF officials have claimed that at various times that the local United States Attorney's office, the Texas Rangers, and officials in Treasury prohibited them from speaking to the public or the media on the subject of the loss of the element of surprise. And the Review has found, in fact, that representatives of both the Texas Rangers and the local United States Attorney's Office <u>asked</u> Hartnett, Conroy and Troy to refrain from commenting in specific terms about the loss of the element of surprise because of concern about how such statements might affect ongoing investigations and likely future prosecutions. Similar requests came from the Treasury Department. Over time, as ATF kept mischaracterizing the raid commanders' knowledge, these requests were sharpened and put more forcefully—and indeed, by early April, particularly with respect to Treasury's concerns, ripened into an effort to convince ATF to make no further statements on the subject. Still, since ATF officials obviously ignored these requests, and spoke regularly about this subject to the media, the requests offer no justification for making statements known to be misleading or false.

In addition to misleading the public, the statements by Conroy, Hartnett and Troy also had the effect of wrongfully pointing the finger at Rodriguez as being responsible for the failed raid. If the raid commanders were not informed that Koresh had been tipped, then the necessary corollary was that Rodriguez likely had failed to tell them what they needed to know. He was to blame. Moreover, despite the consistency of Rodriguez's recollection of what happened immediately before the raid, persistent rumors circulated that he was changing his story. As Rodriguez appropriately protested:

> They're saying that [I've changed my story about what I saw in the compound and what I told raid commanders.] That's not true. Every time I told my story, I said it the same way—every time. The Rangers know that too. There's no reason for me to go and make up stories.

"ATF Agent Says He Saw Disaster Loom," *Dallas Morning News*, May 13, 1993 at 8A. ATF's top managers should have acted swiftly to quash those rumors; they did not.

Sarabyn and Chojnacki lied to their superiors and investigators about what Rodriguez had reported. Their consistent attempts to place blame on a junior agent were one of the most disturbing aspects of the conduct of senior ATF officials. The recollections of Sarabyn and Chojnacki have diverged considerably since the immediate aftermath of the raid. After being confronted with the collective contrary recollections of dozens of line agents, Sarabyn finally admitted the accuracy of Rodriguez's account. In contrast, despite the weight of contrary evidence, Chojnacki steadfastly has contended that Sarabyn neither said nor did anything that alerted Royster and him that Koresh had been tipped.[71]

The Alteration of ATF's Written Raid Plan

In addition to making misleading statements to their superiors and investigators about the basis for their decision to proceed with the raid, Chojnacki and Sarabyn altered documentary evidence, misleading those probing their operational judgments.

The Drafting of the Raid Plan

ATF's National Response Plan required that a written plan "for managing the critical incident or major ATF operation" be produced prior to the initiation of the operation. But the plan did not have to be distributed. The point of the requirement appears to have been limited to ensuring that multiple SRT activations were predicated only upon a well considered, reasoned and thorough raid plan.

Although the raid on the Branch Davidian Compound had originally been set for March 1, 1993, no one had even started to draft the mandatory documentation of the raid plan by February 23, 1993, when ASAC Darrell Dyer (Kansas City) arrived in Waco and was assigned to be the Support Coordinator for the operation. Dyer's past military service led him to assume that there was a detailed written raid plan, but, when he asked the raid planners for a copy he was advised that none existed. Thereafter, Dyer and agent William Krone took it upon themselves to produce one, even though they started with little knowledge about the work of the tactical planners. In a flurry of activity, the two conducted interviews, gathered information and eventually were able to generate a written raid plan. Due to the tight timetable, the plan did not meet Dyer's standards in terms of quality, and from his perspective was still a "work in progress." Nevertheless, the two of them had essentially finished a written raid plan the day before the raid. The plan, however, remained

---

[71] Royster, a witness to the conversation in which the decision to go forward was made by Chojnacki and Sarabyn, initially was not even sure that he was present for the critical conversation, but has since recalled, among other things, that Sarabyn reported that Rodriguez had told him that Koresh "knew they were coming." According to Royster, Sarabyn urged that if they "hurried up," they could still do the raid. Royster has informed the Review that he felt considerable pressure from Hartnett in the aftermath of the failed raid to tell the line agents that the raid commanders did not know they had lost the element of surprise. In late March, Royster told the agents he supervised that ATF did not know it had lost the element of surprise, despite not being certain that such a statement was accurate.

on Krone's desk; it was never distributed to any agents, or relied upon by any of the planners. (See generally Appendix C - Original Raid Plan, dated February 25, 1993.)

The Alteration of the Raid Plan

After the failed raid, authorities began to ask ATF officials for the raid plan. The Texas Rangers were the first to ask ATF's Houston Office for the raid plan. When Dyer was told of the request, he realized that the written plan had never been put in a satisfactory form. He advised Chojnacki and Sarabyn, and the three decided to revise the plan to make it more thorough and complete. Nowhere on the new version of the plan they crafted was there any indication that this was not the original document, or any identification of what had been added. The only hint that the plan had been modified was a handwritten notation in the margin of one page that did not indicate when and how the notation was made. Moreover, Chojnacki—the agent responsible for producing it for the Texas Rangers—never advised them that there was an original raid plan that differed substantially from the plan produced. Indeed, when the Review asked ATF for all documents relating to ATF's investigation of the Branch Davidians, initially only the altered raid plan was received, without any indication that it was anything other than a document prepared prior to the raid. In fact, the document received reflects yet another revision, since the handwritten margin note in the Ranger's copy was now incorporated into the typewritten text. At no time did any ATF official inform the Review that the plan submitted was not the original raid plan.

The alterations indicate not an attempt to create a plan that existed in the minds of the tactical planners and raid commanders on February 28. Rather, they suggest a self-serving effort to clarify the assumptions on which the planners had relied and enhance the reader's sense of their professionalism. For example, to rebut criticism that ATF should have arrested Koresh when he ventured away from the Compound, the following language was added to the altered raid plan: "The subject has not left the Compound in months and has made statements that he does not plan to leave." (Appendix C - Altered Raid Plan, dated March 22, 1993.)[72] A second alteration sought to buttress ATF's initiation of the raid at 10:00 a.m. instead of the standard pre-dawn timing which law enforcement organizations customarily use to gain surprise:

---

[72] As already noted, the added statement is false because Koresh had left the Compound during the months preceding the raid. However, no evidence was found that Chojnacki or Sarabyn knew it to be false at the time the alteration was made.

The women, men and firearms are kept in different areas in the structure. Usually at approximately 10:00 am in the morning, the majority of the males and Howell should be in the underground area. SRT teams have been divided to handle the areas listed above. (Appendix C - Altered Raid Plan, dated March 22, 1993.)

Inquiries into the Alteration of the Raid Plan

The readiness of Chojnacki, Sarabyn, and Dyer to revise an official document that would likely be of great significance in any official inquiry into the raid without making clear what they had done is extremely troubling and itself reflects a lack of judgment. This conduct, however, does not necessarily reveal an intent to deceive. And, in the case of Dyer, there does not appear to have been any such intent. The behavior of Chojnacki and Sarabyn when the alteration was investigated does not lead to the same conclusion.

After the Review had obtained a copy of the original raid plan from a different source, and compared it to the revised document that ATF had produced, Dyer, Sarabyn and Chojnacki, the only three people who could have been involved in changing the document, were questioned. When asked about the alterations, Chojnacki denied knowing that the raid plan had been altered in any fashion except the handwritten comment in the margin of one page of one of the altered versions. (See Appendix C - Altered Raid Plan, dated March 11, 1993.) Similarly, Sarabyn claimed that he had directed only that the date of the raid be changed from March 1 to February 28. Chojnacki and Sarabyn also denied knowing that other changes had been made, how they had been made, and who directed that they be made. Neither Chojnacki's nor Sarabyn's denial is credible.

When questioned about the alteration of the raid plan, Dyer recalled that it had been changed following the Texas Rangers' request because the original document had been incomplete, inaccurate in certain respects and had not fully articulated the reasoning behind the plan. He had advised Chojnacki and Sarabyn of these shortcomings, and the three decided to change the original plan in a manner that would "upgrade" it. Dyer candidly admitted to the Review that he had made certain changes to the plan. He said that, at the time, he had not thought he was doing anything wrong, but was simply "correcting" the original document. When questioned about the importance of identifying the altered plan as amended, Dyer agreed that it was a serious error in judgment not to properly label the altered document. In fact, he candidly stated it was a "stupid" mistake.

When advised by the Review that Chojnacki and Sarabyn had denied making any changes except the handwritten marginal comments Chojnacki had affixed to one of the already altered versions of the plan and Sarabyn's change of the raid date, Dyer seemed shocked. Obviously, as Dyer realized, when taken together, Chojnacki's and Sarabyn's denials amounted to a joint accusation that Dyer had directed or made all of the other changes.

The Review credits Dyer's account of events and believes that both Sarabyn and Chojnacki falsely denied participating in the alteration of the original raid plan. The assessments are reinforced by Dyer's relative lack of knowledge about the facts that were changed in the raid plan. Certain changes that were made went beyond Dyer's knowledge of the raid plan and the factual assumptions upon which it was built. Everything he knew came from someone else; he created nothing; he decided nothing. And, of course, as the only one of the three who was not intimately involved in planning the failed raid, he lacked motivation to lie about making changes to the plan. Sarabyn and Chojnacki's false statements with regard to altering the raid plan document is consistent with their failure to tell the truth about raid day events. And their readiness to blame Dyer indirectly is equally consistent with their efforts to do the same to Robert Rodriguez.

Part Two
Section Eight: National Guard Support

Introduction

During the investigation of the Branch Davidians and the subsequent raid on the Compound, ATF obtained assistance from the military, including the Texas National Guard. This support included the provision of training facilities and equipment, aerial reconnaissance missions, the use of helicopters during the raid, and advice concerning ATF's medical and communications plans. In the wake of the raid's outcome, specific questions were raised about the representations made by ATF in its effort to obtain the use of the helicopters which had been provided by the National Guard. This section responds to those questions.

ATF's Initial Contact with the Military

While investigating Koresh for violations of federal firearms laws in November 1992, ATF believed it required military assistance. ATF, therefore, approached the U.S. military and Texas National Guard for support. In early December, at ATF's request, the Department of Defense liaison to ATF briefed ATF officials about military support available for the Branch Davidian operation. During this briefing, the Department of Defense representative told ATF officials that ATF could obtain military assistance without having to reimburse the Department of Defense if the investigation was related to narcotics enforcement, i.e. had a "drug nexus." An ATF agent then met with officials of the Texas National Guard Counterdrug Support Program to determine what assistance the Texas National Guard could provide. During the meeting, the Guard and individuals representing the state of Texas reiterated the fact that nonreimbursable military support could be made available to ATF if the case had a drug nexus.[73]

After these meetings, ATF officials investigated whether there was any drug activity at the Compound. The ATF case agent learned from an informant that parts of an illegal methamphetamine laboratory had been at the Compound when Koresh took control of the premises, and that the McLennan County Sheriff's Department had planned to collect this equipment. The informant, however, did not know whether such parts were ever collected. Upon inquiring at the sheriff's department, the agent found no records indicating that these parts had been collected by or turned over to the sheriff, raising the possibility that the illegal equipment might still have been at the Compound.

ATF acquired additional information that suggested there was drug activity at the Compound. An ATF agent who was acting in an undercover capacity during the investigation reported that Koresh had told him that the Compound would be a great place for a methamphetamine laboratory because of its location. Furthermore, information obtained from informants and a search of the criminal records of the Branch Davidians revealed that one cult member living at the Compound had a prior conviction for possession of amphetamines and a controlled substance, and that 10 other individuals associated with the Compound had previously been identified as having some involvement in illegal narcotics activity. The drug involvement of the 10 individuals varied; some had been arrested for alleged drug violations while others had been investigated for suspected drug activity.

After ATF had gathered this information, ATF officials informed representatives of the U.S. military and the Texas National Guard on numerous occasions about possible drug activity at the Compound. On February 4, 1993, ATF officials met with representatives of both groups to discuss the Branch Davidian operation. At this meeting, the military representatives were accurately informed of the results of ATF's investigation into the existence of a drug nexus. This briefing satisfied the representatives that a sufficient drug nexus existed to justify military assistance on a nonreimbursable basis.

---

[73] Under 10 U.S.C. § 371 et seq. and 32 U.S.C. § 112, the Secretary of Defense is authorized to provide military support to law enforcement agencies engaged in counterdrug operations. The Secretary of Defense is authorized to pay for the support pursuant to Section 1004 of P.L. 101-510, Section 1088 of P.L. 102-190, and Section 1041 of P.L. 102-484.

ATF's Specific Requests for National Guard Support

On December 14 and 18, 1992, an ATF official wrote to the Texas National Guard Counterdrug Support Program requesting that the Guard take and interpret aerial reconnaissance photographs of the Compound. The National Guard subsequently conducted a total of six flights over the Compound and Mag Bag from January 6 through February 25, 1993. During the flights, the Guard used infrared scanning devices, which identified "hot spots"—heat sources—inside and outside the Compound. A Texas National Guard airman then provided ATF with an unofficial interpretation of the reconnaissance videotapes that suggested a hot spot inside the Compound was consistent with characteristics of a methamphetamine lab. ATF, however, never obtained an official interpretation of the videotapes.

In addition to the reconnaissance flights, the Texas National Guard supplied three helicopters and pilots for training exercises on February 27, and for the raid the following day. Prior to February 27, ATF officials told representatives of the Guard that the helicopters would be used as an airborne command platform and to transport ATF personnel and evidence on the day of the raid. During the training exercises, however, ATF officials informed the National Guard pilots that on the day of the raid, the helicopters were to arrive at the rear of the Compound shortly before the raid teams to draw the attention of the Branch Davidians away from the agents arriving in the cattle trailers. On raid day, however, the helicopter pilots encountered unexpected gunfire from the Compound as soon as their aircraft came within range, and they were forced to abort their mission.[74]

Analysis

ATF did not mislead U.S. military or Texas National Guard officials in obtaining their assistance on a nonreimbursable basis. ATF conducted a legitimate inquiry into whether a drug nexus existed in the investigation after military representatives told ATF officials about the possibility of nonreimbursable assistance. ATF officials were aware that they could have obtained military support for the operation even if no drugs were involved in their investigation. However, in the absence of a drug nexus, ATF was told by both the U.S. military and the National Guard that the assistance would be reimbursable.

---

[74] ATF should have notified the National Guard earlier than February 27 that its pilots might be exposed to dangerous gunfire. In any event, the helicopters could not serve effectively as an airborne command platform while being used simultaneously as a diversion on the day of the raid.

Once ATF gathered information about a possible drug nexus at the Compound, it presented this information to the U.S. military and the Texas National Guard. Representatives of these groups evaluated the information and found that it was sufficient to warrant assistance on a nonreimbursable basis. Because there is no formal standard by which the military defines a drug nexus in a law enforcement investigation, a substantive review of this decision cannot be conducted.

Nonetheless, the Review finds that the standards for nonreimbursable military support raise questions about the appropriate scrutiny that should be given when considering the issue of a drug nexus. The lack of a formal standard by which the military defines a drug nexus in a law enforcement investigation raised questions regarding the nonreimbursable assistance provided to ATF. It would be appropriate therefore that federal law enforcement, the U.S. military and National Guard develop more precisely defined criteria for determining when a drug nexus is sufficient to justify nonreimbursable military assistance.

CONCLUSION

On February 28, 1993, near Waco, Texas, a major law enforcement operation failed. The Bureau of Alcohol, Tobacco and Firearms tried to carry out a flawed raid plan based on one critical element, the element of surprise. Despite knowing in advance that the element of surprise was lost, the raid commanders made the decision to go forward. This decision was brutally exploited by Koresh and his followers. Despite the courageous efforts of ATF agents, four agents were murdered and twenty others were wounded. The vivid and painful conclusion of the operation focussed national attention on these events and on ATF. The Review was a response to that public concern.

This review of ATF's investigation of Koresh, ATF's attempt to plan and to execute search and arrest warrants at the Compound, and its efforts to "manage" the aftermath of the raid, provides a rare opportunity to identify what went wrong, to understand the mistakes that were made, and to learn from this experience to make future operations wiser and safer. Although a few in ATF's management saw the Review as an effort to be resisted, the line agents, throughout the process, have been partners with the Review team. They have been cooperative and committed to finding the truth as an essential effort to advancing the professionalism of their agency.

In the course of its examination, the Review identified significant failures on the part of a few individuals. But more importantly, it uncovered serious, systemic defects in ATF's ability to plan for and to conduct a large scale, tactical operation in the context of the difficult circumstances confronted near Waco. These shortcomings, however, should not minimize the difficult challenge such a situation presents to all law enforcement.

ATF should not be judged by the events of February 28 alone. There is strength, experience and professionalism throughout the agency, and this Review identifies no problems that cannot be corrected. ATF's leadership can take steps to repair the agency's bruised morale and sharpen and refocus its skills on those unique capabilities which have contributed to its pride and its effectiveness in the past. However, to do so the leadership must be committed to positive change and reform.

The Review has greatly benefited from the wisdom and experience of the three distinguished independent reviewers and the six renowned tactical experts. In addition to the contributions they have made to the Review itself, all nine have drawn generously on their substantial expertise to make concrete, forward-looking recommendations to improve ATF's future performance. Treasury's Office of Enforcement, working in partnership with ATF's leadership, must embark upon a process of evaluating these recommendations.

Specific recommendations will be provided separately to ATF's leadership in such areas as improving oversight of major operations through early notification; clarifying the rules regarding media contacts; developing effective supervisory training programs; improving the agency's capacity to perform intelligence operations and to integrate them with the overall tactical operation; and reexamining the uses of Special Response Teams.

ATF's leadership has much to accomplish; they also have much to build upon. Despite the flaws exposed by the events outside Waco, the agency is made up of dedicated, committed and experienced professionals, who have regularly demonstrated sound judgment and remarkable courage in enforcing the law. ATF has a history of success in conducting complex investigations and executing dangerous and challenging law enforcement missions. That fine tradition, together with the line agents' commitment to the truth, and their courage and determination has enabled ATF to provide our country with a safer and more secure nation under law.

ACKNOWLEDGMENTS

At the outset, the Review and I want to extend our appreciation for the support we have received from Secretary Bentsen, who provided the Review with everything necessary to accomplish its mission of finding out what happened near Waco and why. Perhaps more importantly, the Secretary set the tone for the Review through his commitment to uncovering the truth and his insistence that the Review accomplish its work both quickly and thoroughly. At critical stages, the Secretary provided essential advice and counsel to the Review.

This Report reflects a great deal of effort by an exceptionally talented group of people. Although it is impossible to acknowledge properly all the contributions that were made, a few require special mention.

The seventeen agents and two specialists that conducted the investigation were drawn from all of the law enforcement bureaus of the Treasury aside from the Bureau of Alcohol, Tobacco and Firearms, including the Internal Revenue Service ("IRS"), the United States Customs Service, the United States Secret Service, the Financial Crimes Enforcement Network ("FinCEN") and the Federal Law Enforcement Training Center ("FLETC"). Their integrity and commitment to finding out what happened should give the American public confidence in federal law enforcement. To articulate the contributions of each of the individuals listed below would dwarf the contents of this report. I can conceive of no greater compliment than to say: There is no project too complex, no level of trust too great, and no expectation of commitment too high for this fine group of public servants. Specifically, Secret Service gave the Review: Robert B. Blossman, Colleen B. Callahan, Rafael A. Gonzales, Paul D. Irving, Frederick R. Klare, Joseph A. Masonis, Lewis H. McClam and Dick M. Suekawa. The Customs Service provided: Robert L. Cockrell, John J. Devaney, Robert M. Gattison, Susan G. Rowley, Thomas R. Smith and Robert K. Tevens. The IRS contributed Mary C. Balberchak, Kenneth L. Buck and James Rice.

The agents generated a tremendous number of interview reports and collected thousands of documents, and related items. Organizing, reviewing and analyzing this wealth of material in the short period of time allotted for the review would not have been possible but for the expertise and unflagging efforts of the Review's computer specialist, John H. Battle, who came from FLETC, and its intelligence research specialist, Ina W.E. Boston.

Assistant Project Director Lewis C. Merletti, Deputy Assistant Director, U.S. Secret Service, brought to the Review leadership skills developed over 19 years with the Secret Service and limitless good humor that is his, naturally. His talent and energy set a standard of excellence for the entire investigative effort.

The Review also was truly fortunate to have a team of dedicated lawyers that provided direction and focus to the investigation. It was the steady hand of Project Director H. Geoffrey Moulton, Jr., an experienced former federal prosecutor, that guided this project. He possesses the breadth of experience, legal and practical, essential to conducting an investigation that had little precedent. The Review and I are indebted to Moulton for his sage counsel, integrity and uncompromising dedication to making this project a success. Assistant Project Director David L. Douglass, a former federal prosecutor, brought seasoned judgment and ready familiarity with a breadth of legal issues. His perceptiveness, organizational skills and calming influence over me proved invaluable.

The Review also benefited from the efforts of other former federal prosecutors. Andrew E. Tomback, who was detailed to the Review from the Interagency Council on the Homeless, contributed legal expertise, sharp analytical writing abilities and a knack for synthesizing facts quickly. Professor Daniel C. Richman, Fordham Law School, conscientiously edited the report and provided cohesiveness to the Review's written product. The report's readability owes much to Richman's facility with the written word. The Review also received substantial support from Sarah Elizabeth Jones and Billy S. Bradley of Treasury's Office of the General Counsel, both of whom contributed abundant legal expertise and law enforcement knowledge. They provided the experience and knowledge of Treasury procedures, formal and informal, necessary for a team drawn primarily from outside the Department. Kenneth Thompson, a former student of mine at the New York University School of Law, received permission to conclude his clerkship early in order to contribute an intellectual rigor and seriousness of purpose beyond my highest expectations.

In addition to the agents and the attorneys, the Review received stellar support from a number of others. Jennell L. Jenkins, Lead Document Control Assistant, offered creativity and grace under pressure that was greatly appreciated. The logistics of conducting a lengthy investigation were accomplished by the diligent efforts of the Review's support staff, including: Mary Steinbacher, who handled correspondence, and secretaries, Vanessa L. Bolden and Deborah Jenkins. The meticulous professionalism of the principal copy editors, Beth A. Rosenfeld and Adele H. Mujal, improved the product immeasurably. Finally, Alison Kindler combined superb computer skills and incredible dedication to bring our product to conclusion.

Aside from the "team" itself, the Review was greatly strengthened by many independent persons. The Review's investigation and its final report benefited significantly from the scrutiny and guidance provided by its three independent reviewers, Edwin O. Guthman, Henry S. Ruth, Jr. and Chief Willie Williams. Each of the reviewers brought tremendous integrity, objectivity and knowledge to the Review. Their rigorous questioning of the Review's agents and attorneys and their probing examination of the Review's reasoning and findings ensured that the Review asked and answered the tough questions. Their efforts substantially strengthened the accuracy and reliability of the final report. Likewise, the Review thanks the Treasury's Office of Inspector General for thoroughly monitoring the Review's investigation and ensuring that the Review pursued all leads.

Similarly, the six tactical experts helped guide the Review's tactical investigation and informed its analysis of ATF's tactical planning. The tactical experts' analyses of the raid plan and ATF's planning process greatly aided the Review team. The questions they asked and the experience they brought to bear helped the Review both identify the key issues and gain a proper understanding of them. Likewise, the weapons and explosives experts assisted the Review's evaluation of whether ATF had a sound basis cause to search the Branch Davidian Compound.

The Review thanks all of the experts and reviewers for contributing their time and energy. Their willingness to provide such fine service without pay is a testament to their commitment to helping American law enforcement. Their reports are in the Appendix.

The Review also wishes to acknowledge the support and assistance of the following agencies: The Texas Department of Public Safety, especially the Texas Rangers; the Department of Justice, specifically the United States Attorney's Office for the Western District of Texas and the Federal Bureau of Investigation; the McLennan County Sheriff's Department; the Waco Police Department; and the Tarrant County Office of the Chief Medical Examiner.

The Review and I also wish to thank the employees of the Department of the Treasury for their support and encouragement, especially the employees of the Office of Enforcement, for their willingness to shoulder an extra burden while the Review was in progress.

Finally, I thank the agents of ATF. From the beginning, they answered the Review's questions candidly. Throughout the process they have supported our work. These agents were the most powerful advocates for telling the true story. It is our hope that this report supports their courageous efforts to provide quality law enforcement.

Ronald K. Noble
Assistant Secretary for the Treasury (Enforcement)

Appendices

Appendix A

Independent Reviewer
Chief Willie Williams' Report

September 22, 1993

The Honorable Lloyd Bentsen
Secretary of the Treasury
U.S. Department of the Treasury
1500 Pennsylvania Avenue, N.W.
Washington, D.C. 20220

Dear Mr. Secretary:

I am pleased to submit my comments as an independent reviewer of the Waco Administrative Review. I have found that the investigative team which you assembled is of the highest quality and integrity. These men and women have worked tirelessly to uncover the facts surrounding the events which led up to and included the raid on David Koresh's residence near Waco, Texas, on the 28th of February 1993.

I arranged my thoughts focusing first on the propriety to investigate Mr. Koresh, and second on the facts surrounding the probable cause to seek a Search Warrant and Arrest Warrant. I then moved to the tactical operation on the 28th of February. My comments address the serious issues of managerial oversight by both the Treasury Department and the Bureau of Alcohol, Tobacco and Firearms. Training is discussed as I conclude my comments by offering several insights which I believe will help both the Bureau of Alcohol, Tobacco and Firearms and the Treasury Department continue to serve this country in the manner we have come to expect.

It has been a pleasure to assist you in this very important undertaking.

Very truly yours,

WILLIE L. WILLIAMS
Chief of Police
Los Angeles, California

Enclosure

Report for the Waco Administrative Review

Independent Reviewer Report

1. My first comments go the brave men and women of the Bureau of Alcohol, Tobacco and Firearms (A.T.F.) who were involved in the service of the Search Warrant at the Branch Davidian compound in Waco, Texas. These federal officers had a difficult task to accomplish if everything in the plan had worked as designed. The plan unraveled and the raiding party was ambushed and assaulted with the type of firepower that no municipal or federal law enforcement agency had ever before experienced.

   The men and women in the A.T.F. SRTs, when faced with overwhelming gunfire, still made every attempt to meet and complete their objective. Several acts of bravery saved lives and prevented further serious injury to members of the warrant service teams. All of these agents should be commended for their actions.

2. The Special Investigative Team

   The team of investigators assembled by the Treasury Department are, in my opinion, among the most experienced and knowledgeable that one could ask to conduct such a critical review. I am pleased to report that the investigative review was conducted with the highest degree of honesty and integrity.

   Mr. Ronald K. Noble, Assistant Secretary (Enforcement) is to be complimented for his leadership of this review. Mr. Noble has been quite candid and insisted that no stone be left unturned in the quest for what occurred in the planning, execution, and recovery after the A.T.F. raid in Waco, Texas.

3. Appropriateness of the investigation of David Koresh

   The investigative report is correct when it asserts that A.T.F. had probable cause to investigate David Koresh for his purchases of huge amounts of weapons parts, firearms and ammunition. The purchase of many of these parts was done for an illegal purpose -- that is to assemble prohibited weapons. It was appropriate to conduct a full investigation when it became apparent that David Koresh had also unlawfully purchased AR-15 lower receivers which could be used to convert semi-automatic rifles into fully automatic weapons similar to M-16 machine guns. This type of information, coupled with other intelligence, was more than enough to justify the opening of an investigative case on David Koresh who resided with others known as the Branch Davidians.

4. Justification to seek Search Warrants and Arrest Warrants

The evidence which the A.T.F. investigators accumulated to justify seeking either arrest warrants or search warrants was more than sufficient by January/February 1993.

It was known that Koresh had received M-16 parts which could be used to convert AR-15 semi-automatic rifles into fully automatic weapons. It had also been verified that Koresh had purchased AR-15 weapons. When A.T.F. investigators learned that an arms dealer had intentionally lied to them and tried to hide the purchase of AR-15 lower receivers by Koresh, this further strengthened the evidence that Koresh was unlawfully possessing and manufacturing machine guns or converted fully automatic weapons.

Investigators also had evidence that Koresh had in his possession gunpowder and other ignition items which, when coupled with the grenade shells he purchased, gave him the ingredients to manufacture live grenades.

The A.T.F. investigators consulted with the U.S. Attorney's office during the investigation and did in fact secure a Search Warrant for the Branch Davidian Compound from a Magistrate Judge.

5. The Tactical Operation of February 28th, 1993

The tactical operation planned by A.T.F. personnel was designed with several key assumptions being present to ensure a reasonable chance of success. These critical success factors include the following.

   A. Surprise arrival of the A.T.F. SRTs and the inability of the persons in Koresh's compound to have time to react to the these events. This was a key critical success factor.

   B. Finding most of the men outside and working in the pit area north of the compound.

   C. The quick and successful entry of the compound by designated SRTs and the separation of persons inside from weapons in the upstairs arms room.

   D. Seizing the arms room by surprise entry from outside while the residents were being detained both outside in the pit area and on the first floor of the compound.

An examination of the planning for the operation indicates that there is no copy of the entire raid plan available. It is apparent that the planners had the raid plan in their heads but never reduced it to writing. This omission led to a series of later failures by all personnel involved in the planned operation to have an opportunity to review a completed plan and question the assumptions. This lack of a completed written plan also ensured that all those agents who should have had a clear understanding of what was expected of them and others did not. This is made very clear when you examine the type of information and direction given to the agents in the undercover house.

The fact of not having a clear written plan which listed the critical success factors almost ensured from the start, that when these success factors began to unravel, no one would grasp the significance of the unfolding events.

When examined in totality some reviewers agree that the plan was not well thought-out. The reasons include: no provision for contingencies; a less than adequate command and control of the SRTs and their support units; the failure to design an intelligence system which gathered all pieces of data and provided an analysis of this information; the failure of adequate oversight from senior A.T.F. management and the Office of the Assistant Secretary of Treasury for Enforcement; and insufficient reserve personnel available or enough first aid and medical support on site.

After reviewing interviews conducted with A.T.F. personnel who planned the raid on February 28th, and all of those who had support or other roles in the planning, it is my belief that the planners never thought about, nor planned for a partial or full failure of the operation. This, in my opinion, is one of the greatest failures of management in A.T.F.

6. Management Oversight - Structural Deficiencies

The management oversight responsibilities between the Treasury Department and A.T.F. must be re-examined. At the time of the Waco raid on February 28th, 1993, there was no written policy delineating areas of responsibility that for example, required A.T.F. to notify anyone in the Treasury Department that A.T.F. was planning, or about to implement a raid such as the one planned and executed on February 28th. There was no policy that required the notification of the Treasury Department when an investigation of the magnitude of this one was contemplated or had already begun.

The lack of active oversight by the Office of the Assistant Secretary for Enforcement, Treasury Department, was one reason that there was no early notification by A.T.F. of the Waco raid. The fact that this was the same policy for several years only magnifies the problem. The investigative report correctly points out that had oversight taken place, many questions which needed to be asked may have come up much earlier.

The investigative report correctly states that had the Office of Enforcement been involved in the early planning stages, its intervention might have led the planners to reevaluate the faulty factual assumptions on which they had relied. This failure contributed to a condition where little or no analysis of intelligence information was made by those at A.T.F. headquarters or at the Treasury Department.

The understanding of the importance of intelligence and the operational decisions which were being built around these assumptions was inadequate at nearly every level of ATF's management from the command personnel in Texas who planned and executed the raid, to personnel at the National Command Center to the leadership at A.T.F. Headquarters. Moreover, because such matters were outside the scope of the Office of Enforcement's defined responsibilities, the office did not have an adequate opportunity to rigorously scrutinize these matters.

7. Training Issues

This report points out several areas where training is needed in areas such as command and control decision-making. Training is needed at all levels on the importance of understanding what is meant by intelligence gathering, how to analyze it and most importantly how to build a tactical operation around the facts and assumptions based on an investigation and the intelligence gathered. It is very apparent that senior managers in A.T.F. need advanced training in Media Relations. This investigation shows that the A.T.F. leaders in Texas never successfully managed the growing interest by the media in both the Branch Davidians and the escalating activities by A.T.F. personnel in and around Waco, Texas.

Training is required to ensure that all members of A.T.F., particularly field supervisors, have the requisite skills necessary to plan and execute an investigation and operation such as the raid on the compound of David Koresh.

I will not go into detail about all of the other training issues, but they include command and control skills for SRT operations and particularly the SRT team leaders. Training must include how to set up an undercover operation and what is expected of the undercover operatives. In this case, the agents in the undercover house were never given a clear mission. The agents in the undercover house as an example, were never told of the raid planners' assumption that the men in the compound would be outside when the raid began.

CONCLUDING COMMENTS:

I was asked to be an independent reviewer of the work product of the Waco Administrative Review Team's report to the Secretary of Treasury.

The investigation team conducted an exhaustive and thorough review of the events which led up to the raid on February 28th. The investigative team's report also offers clear and factual analysis of the events as they unfolded and what caused the plan to disintegrate as the first SRT personnel alighted from the cattle trailers.

The investigative report appropriately identifies improper planning and offers guidance to help ensure that A.T.F. does not repeat the same errors in the future.

I would recommend that upon review of the investigative report and each of the Independent Reviewers' Reports, that the following should be undertaken.

1. New procedures must be put in place to ensure appropriate oversight by the Department of Treasury with each of its subordinate agencies.

2. The Director of A.T.F. and the other senior managers in headquarters must take a more active role in oversight of field operations, especially when they are potentially of the magnitude of the David Koresh investigation.

3. A.T.F. must examine its goals and objectives and determine what type of enforcement role it is going to require its agents to fulfill. Once that role is determined then it is the responsibility of both A.T.F. and the Treasury Department to ensure that the employees receive the training necessary to meet the objectives of the organization.

Appendix B

Expert Reports

Appendix B

Tacitcal Operations Experts

(alphabetically by author)

Wade Y. Ishimoto

John A. Kolman

George Morrison

John J. Murphy

Rod Paschall

Robert A. Sobocienski

AN INDEPENDENT ASSESSMENT OF THE

BUREAU OF ALCOHOL, TOBACCO & FIREARMS

RAID OF THE BRANCH DAVIDIAN COMPOUND IN WACO, TEXAS

PREPARED BY:
Wade Y. Ishimoto, Consultant

FOR THE U.S. DEPARTMENT OF TREASURY

August 16, 1993

TABLE OF CONTENTS

Executive Summary B-9

I. Introduction B-11

II. Command and Control B-11

III. Intelligence B-17

IV. Operations Security B-21

V. Training and Exercises B-22

VI. Support Operations B-23

VII. Weaponry, Armament, and Other Equipment B-27

VIII. Concluding Remarks B-28

EXECUTIVE SUMMARY

This Executive Summary is prepared in response to the major concerns raised during my tenure on the Department of Treasury's Waco Review team. My remarks represent independent analysis, and that analysis is found in the body of this report. The body of the report also addresses a number of potential improvements which are not discussed in this Executive Summary.

I.   The Bureau of Alcohol, Tobacco, and Firearms (ATF) raid plan, *as conceived*, had a reasonable chance of success.

II.   The critical success factors for the raid plan were not necessarily recognized nor understood by the leaders of the ATF operation because of inexperience or lack of training. The leaders I refer to extend from the Special Response Team (SRT) Leaders all the way to the ATF Director. These critical success factors were:

   a. Surprise consisting specifically of:

   (1) Insufficient advance warning of the impending raid to allow cult members to arm and deploy.

   (2) The Branch Davidians not understanding the significance of the trucks/cattle trailers until these vehicles were at least at the intersection of the compound road and Double EE Ranch Road which would have provided about 30 to 45 seconds of advance warning. The Branch Davidians would have found it difficult to arm and deploy themselves in the manner witnessed during the actual execution of the search and arrest warrants.

   b. Isolation of the majority of the cult's weapons and ammunition from cult members through seizure of the arms room located next to Vernon Howell's living quarters.

   c. Successful entry by the ATF SRTs through the front door of the compound which was critical to separating cult members from the bulk of their weapons in the arms room.

   d. Finding the men in the compound working in the outdoor (excavated pit or underground) area to the North of the compound.

III. The reason for the raid's failure is directly attributable to the fact that the critical success factors defined in II. above were, at best, only partially achieved. The fact that the cult members were armed and deployed as ATF deployed from their cattle trailers is particularly relevant.

IV.   When viewed in totality, the raid plan was not well conceived regardless of my opinion that it had a reasonable chance of success. The plan did not provide for contingencies, lacked depth, and did not provide adequate command and control of support and tactical forces. My assessment is that the SRTs possessed the minimal amount of training and experience to meet the raid's objectives. However, in an operation of this magnitude, the SRTs require equally well-trained and experienced command, control, and support personnel. These personnel lacked a requisite amount of training and experience.

V. Other factors that contributed to the subsequent loss of life and failure to complete the mission include:

    a. A complex command, control, and communications mechanism.

    b. Less than adequate training in a number of different areas.

    c. An intelligence system which was weak.

    d. A lack of well-developed Operations Security (OPSEC) policy and procedures.

    e. Equipment limitations.

    f. Task organization that principally centered on SRT actions.

    g. A lack of reserve forces.

    h. A plan that was not developed in-depth to include contingency actions.

These and other factors pertinent to future success are discussed in the main body of this report.

VI. Key Recommendations and Findings:

    a. ATF will require a future and continuing SRT capability as long as that organization continues to have an enforcement versus compliance-only mission.

    b. Improvements are required in policy and procedural guidance pertinent to high risk operations requiring the use of ATF SRTs. This guidance must include command and control matters, technical support (communications and surveillance), investigative techniques to include electronic monitoring, intelligence in support of tactical operations, reorganization of SRTs to include Forward Observers, media relations, OPSEC, use of the military, equipment to include armament, and training.

    c. The key to success in raid operations, no matter how large or small, always resides in the field and with field personnel. The actions of ATF Headquarters personnel on February 28, 1993, did not significantly contribute to the success or failure of the mission. The proper role for ATF Headquarters is one of planning oversight, plan approval, and resource allocation *prior* to execution of the operation. All parties must strenuously avoid trying to run a field operation from a headquarters location with subsequent micro-management and loss of decisive action and decision-making in the field.

I. INTRODUCTION

The missions of the Bureau of Alcohol, Tobacco, and Firearms (ATF) bring the men and women of this agency face-to-face with a wide variety of criminal adversaries. The very nature of the laws they must enforce in the firearms and explosives arena virtually ensures that ATF agents are subject to life-threatening situations in a high percentage of their operations. They are also subject to a great deal of public criticism from special interest groups who are particularly vociferous over ATF enforcement of firearms statutes.

During the last decade and a half, ATF's mission has expanded to meet greater criminal sophistication in the use of explosives and firearms. Explosive attacks have always been a favored tactic of those who wish to terrorize the public; and the use of automatic weapons has also become much more prevalent in the execution of crimes.

I respect the difficulty of the ATF mission along with the dedication and bravery of their personnel. The death of four agents and the wounding of sixteen in one action is unprecedented in American law enforcement. After-the-fact criticism and "Monday-morning quarterbacking" are very easy traps to fall into and made preparation of this report difficult.

However, my review of the Branch Davidian event detects a very definite need to provide ATF personnel with additional tools to allow them to better deal with situations like they faced in Waco, Texas. These tools include more defined policy in some areas, the need for written procedural references, training, and some equipment. I attempt to avoid individual criticism as that is a matter best left to Department of Treasury personnel. Unfortunately, my analysis also discovers some questionable individual performance; and I would be remiss not to discuss these possible shortcomings.

II. COMMAND AND CONTROL

A. ATF Headquarters

1. **Concerns over the role of ATF Headquarters in commanding and controlling large raid operations** are expressed by members of Congress, Treasury officials, and by ATF personnel at all levels. These concerns evolve around possible poor performance and future roles for ATF headquarters personnel.

   a. I believe the **overall performance of ATF Headquarters** in command and control of the Waco raid was **adequate except in the area of providing pre-raid support to the field.** The headquarters role included plan review and approval, provision of oversight (e.g., asking of questions pertinent to the investigation and need for a raid, and involvement of the Special Operations Division), and provision of support.

   b. There are **two matters** which I believe are **worthy of further inquiry**. The first is **whether the raid could have been conducted earlier** in February and the second concerns procedures to obtain **military support**.

- With respect to the possibility of conducting the raid earlier in February, there are reports that the Houston office proposed conducting the raid a week before February 28, 1993. This meeting was supposedly postponed because some key Headquarters personnel were unavailable. This implies that the raid could have occurred prior to publication of the Waco Tribune article and any subsequent rise in awareness or paranoia by the Branch Davidians. This is speculation but is worthy of additional inquiry to **determine whether there is a need to improve ATF policy and procedures with respect to approval of an operation.**

- Based on my review, I am **not confident that ATF Headquarters understands and has appropriate policy to obtain military support for large-scale operations.** The ATF Military Liaison Officer appears to be assigned from the Office of the Department of Defense (DOD) Coordinator for Drug Enforcement Policy and Support. Interviews indicate that statements were made by the Military Liaison Officer that narcotics-related activity was needed to justify military support. If true, those statements are contrary to existing DOD policy which permits support to law enforcement on a reimbursable basis. The alleged Branch Davidian narcotics activity was tenuous, at best, and subjected ATF to intense scrutiny by Congress. In addition, the Special Operations Branch Chief does not appear to understand how military support is obtained. This is unacceptable since the Military Liaison Officer works for the Branch Chief and proper oversight cannot occur unless the Branch Chief has a better understanding of this matter. Finally, field personnel also appear to only understand how to obtain military support through narcotics-related activity.

    c. **Other headquarters shortfalls** include a policy which limits the firepower available to the field; limited ability to provide intelligence support; a lack of understanding of electronic surveillance operations; and not providing additional technical support to the field.

    d. **Over-reaction to the proper role of ATF Headquarters in command and control of future operations must be avoided.** Studious attempts must be made to avoid micro-management and the accompanying deleterious effect it will have on decisive action and decision-making in the field. The key to success in raid operations resides in the field and with field personnel. I believe that the proper role for ATF Headquarters is planning oversight, plan approval and resource allocation prior to the conduct of an operation.

    e. **Recommendations:**

- Existing ATF policy and procedures should be reviewed to ensure that streamlined plan approval with appropriate oversight will occur in the future.

- Military support policy should be fully documented and either included or referred to in the National Response Plan for ATF.

- The policy on electronic surveillance should be reviewed and consideration given to improving ATF capabilities to include possible augmentation of field personnel from headquarters. (Note: The FBI has had a long-standing plan and capability to augment their Field Divisions during crisis situations.)

- The ATF National Response Plan should be modified to better define the role of ATF Headquarters and their field organizations.

2. The **National Response Plan (NRP)** provides a basis for planning any future operation of the magnitude encountered in Waco.

   a. A very necessary first step towards a mature planning process was taken with the creation of the NRP. As in any initial endeavor, the NRP can be improved.

   b. The NRP, as currently written, is a combination of a Headquarters policy document along with providing a variety of procedural guidance. Some of the procedural guidance is quite detailed (e.g., the logistical support officer being responsible for obtaining water) while some of it does not address important concepts. For example, there is no conceptual guidance concerning command post operation and selection of a command post location.

   c. **Recommendations:**

   - The NRP should be reviewed and modified in light of the Waco incident.

   - The military model of a stand-alone policy document (e.g., a Department of Army Regulation) with separate implementation and procedural guidance (e.g., Field Manuals) should be considered versus one all-encompassing document.

   - Implementation and procedural guidance should be expanded and training in the NRP conducted for anyone that is an ATF supervisor.

B. Field Command, Control, and Planning

1. The Command, Control, and Communications mechanism for the raid was complex, and a comprehensive understanding of roles and missions for the organization was not evident.

   a. At the individual SRT level (e.g., Houston) command, control, and communications was established in an adequate manner except for two matters. First, it is not evident that a chain of command within the individual SRTs was established to provide for leadership succession in the event that the leader became disabled. Secondly, the Forward Observers did not appear to be in direct support of a specific team and the teams could not directly communicate with the Forward Observers. The Forward Observers provide a means of both information/intelligence and "heavy" fire support (i.e., rifles) which may be used as an essential element of a raid or to assist in contingency situations.

      b.   The chain of command and specific role for the Forward Observers was not clear. The interviews of the Forward Observers reflect this observation and the fact that they had different understandings of their rules of engagement and to whom they were responsive. The military would describe the Forward Observer role on the raid as being in General Support of the operation versus Direct Support (e.g., directed to support a specific SRT). Both concepts have their merits, but a direct support role is generally favored for raid operations. The net result on the Waco raid was that the Forward Observers were not positioned advantageously (i.e., to provide adequate coverage of the compound in a timely manner) and could have been used more effectively in an information gathering role (e.g., determining whether compound members were deployed or working in the pit area).

      c.   The focus on command and control was on the SRTs. I believe that the same statement applies to planning matters. The coordination of other agencies appeared to be in the hands of one individual, Phil Lewis, at the Texas State Technical College (TSTC) Command Post (CP). He performed admirably, but the system and process should provide for better coordination of activities with outside agencies and more than one individual from ATF tasked with this responsibility.

      d.   The TSTC CP did not function well. The Incident Commander was airborne and was therefore less able to command and control activities. There did not appear to be an adequate means of providing status information to other agencies from the CP, much less to ATF personnel. Roles and missions were not adequately stated to these staff members. These observations reflect the need for policy and procedural guidance along with training of personnel.

      e.   The equivalent of a Tactical Operations Center (TOC) was not established. Whereas field CPs normally concentrate on interagency coordination and overall command and control, a TOC focuses on the tactical aspects of the operation. In a TOC, Forward Observer information may be consolidated and analyzed, reserve forces deployed and coordinated (these were not available at Waco except from outside agencies), negotiations with suspects conducted (this was a happenstance), and other matters directly important to the success of the tactical mission coordinated and controlled. The TOC needs to be staffed with personnel who have defined roles and responsibilities. The Tactical Coordinator may choose to operate from a TOC or, as was the case at Waco, forward with the SRTs. The Undercover (U/C) house was suitable as a TOC and had some TOC type functions under ASAC Cavanaugh, but in reality did not contain the staffing nor the planning of a true TOC. One of the advantages of commanding from a TOC was evident when Cavanaugh became the person most able to coordinate tactical activities versus ASAC Sarabyn who was pinned down in a firefight. The Tactical Coordinator unfortunately chose a position where he was at the forward edge of the battle and less able to command and control the SRTs...I believe this illustrates the need for better procedural guidance and training versus individual negligence on the part of Sarabyn.

f. The plan was developed principally by SRT personnel whose focus was primarily in actions at the compound. My observation is that they could have benefitted from trained staff planning assistance. This is especially true in intelligence support which is addressed later in this report.

g. ATF personnel (possibly due to inexperience coupled with policy and procedural guidance gaps) sought advice, guidance, and assistance from persons and agencies who were not the best qualified to provide such help. This comment is particularly pointed at the manner in which military support was obtained. For example, there are reports that ATF went to Operation Alliance (a counter-narcotics related organizational grouping) to request military support. The ATF Headquarters Military Liaison Officer could have gone through the Department of Defense (DOD) Director of Military Support (DOMS) organization to obtain more complete military support. In another example, ATF appeared to be ill-advised by a member of the Texas Governor's staff to use the Texas National Guard for various operations with a strong implication that such support could be provided for free if there were a narcotics relationship...tenuous at best. A third example is the use of a Special Forces Communications NCO to design and "approve" the communications network. Additional observations on military support are found in other sections of this report.

2. Inexperience in crisis management and operational planning skills for a large scale operation such as Waco was clearly evident in the planning and execution of the raid. The lack of a written operations order is one indication of this inexperience. Other examples include:

a. The lack of in-depth planning for contingencies as witnessed by the lack of an alternative means of entry should the first fail; and an "Oh shit" plan consisting of running away from the compound rather than using supporting fire and maneuver or the use of armored vehicles to provide cover and to recover personnel.

b. The briefings that I observed on videotape (one at Fort Hood and one in Waco) are reflective of this inexperience. The briefings rambled instead of focusing on key issues and presenting information succinctly.

c. The lack of a functional staff (no matter how reduced in size) at a TOC location or in the CP are also indicative of inexperience, the need for more training, and the need for additional procedural guidance on command and control matters.

d. The lack of depth in the communications plan, undercover house operation, the medical plan, and media plan are also indicative of inexperience.

e. The failure to conduct the Mag Bag raid resulted in a fire fight and additional actions to apprehend suspects. These actions would not have been necessary if the plan to raid the Mag Bag had been executed as planned.

3. The number of courses of action and tactical options available to ATF were limited because of limitations on equipment, training, experience, and policy along with the presence of presumably innocent children and females.

 a. Equipment considerations are discussed elsewhere in this report and include the paucity of night vision equipment, technical surveillance equipment, and restrictions on weaponry. The decision to follow the advice of a member of the Texas Governor's staff may have caused problems with ATF not receiving better helicopter capability and armored vehicles. Going through the military's DOMS mechanism for military support rather than Operation Alliance and Joint Task Force (JTF) 6 might have made a difference in ATF getting smoke generating devices, armored vehicles, and other assistance.

 b. Training and experience gaps are reflected throughout this report. The training gaps can be remedied and, if done properly, can make up for the lack of experience. Training is addressed in greater detail elsewhere in this report.

 c. Policy limitations which impacted on the operation included restrictions on weaponry, restrictions on chemical agents and distraction devices, uncertainty over electronic surveillance issues, and failure of policy to address the provision of military support through the DOMS organization.

4. The raid plan lacked depth and did not provide for adequate consideration of contingencies. Improvement in these matters can be attained through additional training and the development of doctrinal guidance (e.g., reference manuals and checklists on SRT operations).

5. There are feelings that the ATF Incident Commander and other key leaders in the ATF chain should be limited to those from SRT ranks. My belief is that will not prove adequate. This belief is based on a general need for additional training in crisis management procedures and operational planning which are not well-developed at any level within ATF. I do agree that SACs and ASACs should at least attend the SRT courses as observers to enhance their knowledge and that they should also receive additional training on crisis management and planning.

6. **Recommendations:** The observations listed above are reflective of ATF's relative lack of experience in command and control of operations of the magnitude seen in Waco. Policy needs to be established, procedural guidance provided in writing, and strenuous training provided to personnel at all levels who may become involved in these kinds of operations in the future. If ATF or the Department of Treasury cannot provide the resources to pursue doctrinal development and training, then serious consideration must be given to limiting the scope of ATF tactical operations.

III. INTELLIGENCE

A. Organization

1. The ATF organization to provide intelligence support during the investigative and operational (raid) phases was not effective.

    a. Intelligence analytical support did not effectively bridge the gap between the investigative support mission and tactical support. Analysis appeared to be a function of different individuals (e.g., the Case Agent, RAC Buford, ASAC Sarabyn, etc.) rather than a function of a defined system and process. There was no clear focal point where all intelligence flowed and was fully analyzed and subsequently delivered to the tactical planners.

    b. There were numerous instances of assumptions being made on the basis of incomplete, dated, or overstated information which adversely influenced operational planning. For example:

    - The number of people in the compound was estimated at 75, a 25% error. The surveillance logs and interviews of former cult members did not substantiate the 75 person figure. Therefore, I question how those numbers were derived.

    - The U/C Agent had about eight limited visits into the compound. Yet there were those that felt he had continuing access and gave more credence to his information than was true.

    - Information on the physical structure of the compound was a composite of a few visits by the U/Cs and information from unvetted sources that was a year old in some cases.

    c. A number of incorrect assumptions could have been put into proper perspective if there were trained, experienced personnel working within a defined organizational structure to conduct in-depth intelligence analysis.

2. The existing intelligence structure does not tie all-source intelligence (e.g., technical surveillance, U/Cs, Forward Observers, aerial photography) together in a systematic fashion. Overall intelligence collection and planning is not centrally managed. Analysis occurs in pockets rather than through a capable, defined organizational structure; and dissemination of intelligence (the product of recording, evaluation, and interpretation...i.e., analysis of information) versus raw information is not consistent with proven techniques used by other organizations.

3. The organization of the U/C house and its activities was marked by no clear chain of command or direction of their actions. The rapid establishment of the U/C operation is commendable, but poor organization neutralized what could have been a major source of intelligence and confirmation that the Branch Davidians were waiting in ambush.

B.   **Intelligence Operations**

1.   **General Comments:**   The remainder of this section is organized into a discussion of typical intelligence operations disciplines: Intelligence Liaison activities; Human Intelligence operations (to include undercover activities); Imagery Intelligence (including aerial intelligence collection, photographic and video collection); and Electronic Intelligence.

2.   **Intelligence Liaison:**

a.   It appears that ATF worked closely with McClennan County law enforcement officials to obtain intelligence about the Branch Davidian organization, its operations, and its physical facilities (i.e., the Mag Bag and the Mount Carmel compound). This interface was, in my opinion, highly useful in the investigative and tactical planning phases of the operation. Unfortunately, there was limited information available from this source. Also to its credit, ATF exploited information and sources available from the Texas Human Resources Department and the Texas Department of Public Safety. With the latter organization, it is not clear whether all aspects of information and intelligence were explored...i.e., Criminal Intelligence, Narcotics, Texas Rangers.

b.   Various interviews indicate that ATF attempted to obtain information available from Interpol, Immigration and Naturalization Service, and the El Paso Intelligence Center (through Operation Alliance). I found only one approach to the Federal Bureau of Investigation, no attempts to obtain information from the Customs Service, and none through the Department of State and Central Intelligence Agency. Since there were foreign nationals in the compound, inquiries should have been made of these agencies whether intelligence was available or not. I sense, but cannot substantiate, that interagency rivalry coupled with inexperience may have led to this incomplete search for information.

c.   **Recommendation:**   ATF should review its policy and procedures to obtain intelligence from other agencies and provide guidance to their field organizations and headquarters personnel on that matter.

3.   **Human Intelligence:**

a.   My previous discussion of the lack of central control of intelligence planning and collection also applies to ATF's human intelligence operations. Central control of policy should be established at ATF headquarters along with national Intelligence Community interfaces. However, the field organization must be able to control intelligence operations in support of tactical operations.

b.   There were several successes in human intelligence operations to include information obtained from United Parcel Service personnel, the use of a U/C to obtain physical information about the Mag Bag and one trip into the Mount Carmel compound, the recruitment of the Double EE Ranch owner, and the information gleaned from former cult members by the Case Agent, RAC Buford, and others.

c. The interview of the former cult members posed a difficult problem in terms of determining their reliability and accuracy of information. Again, a system was not in place to pool information coming from these sources, to fully analyze it, and to disseminate the resulting intelligence in a useful way to tactical and support personnel.

d. The U/C house operation was an excellent idea which did not pay high dividends because of a lack of organization, proper tasking, and supervision of their activities. The logs which I reviewed were incomplete and do not substantiate many of the assumptions which were made on activity in the compound. For example, the tactical planners were adamant that a "routine" was evident in the compound with the males working outside at 10:00 AM onwards...logs from the U/C house do not corroborate this assumption. At best, the U/C house operation resulted in limited information about the physical structure, incomplete observation of activities, and information about a few of the personnel inside the compound. The U/C house operation was capable, in my opinion, of providing much more intelligence. One of the supposed goals of the U/C house was to obtain additional information on probable cause for a search or arrest warrant...it is not evident to me that this occurred.

e. The Forward Observers were not effectively used and a TOC was not in place to exploit information coming from the Forward Observers. The lack of effectiveness in this event refers to gaps in tasking, limited deployment around the compound, lateness of deployment, and the provision of extremely limited amounts of collection devices to the Forward Observers.

f. **Recommendations:**

Without access to all ATF policy, procedural guidance, and training information for intelligence, I am not able to make detailed recommendations on improvement of human intelligence operations. I therefore recommend that ATF or an outside organization conduct a more in-depth review of intelligence operations to determine whether there is need for changes/additions to policy, procedure, and training.

4. **Imagery Intelligence:**

a. In-house ATF capabilities to collect and process imagery intelligence appear extremely limited. There are references to **a** (i.e., only one) 35mm camera in the U/C house, a pole camera which did not work very well and was positioned poorly (both physically and in terms of how permission was obtained to install it), poor intelligence analysis and posting of information from the U/C house photographic operations, and little or no use of night vision equipment with video or photographic capability.

b. ATF capability to collect aerial imagery intelligence appears to be very limited. ATF turned to both Customs and the Texas National Guard for support in these areas. I do not find strong evidence that the ability to plan and collect imagery intelligence using aerial platforms was well planned or directed by ATF. The offer by a member of the Texas Governor's Office to overfly the compound and to use relatively unsophisticated Forward Looking Infrared

Radar (FLIR) to obtain information does not give me a great deal of confidence in the knowledge of system capabilities by either ATF personnel or the person who offered that advice to ATF.

    c.   I do not believe shortcomings in imagery intelligence had a direct bearing on the failure of the raid. However, these shortcomings in knowledge, planning, and equipment capabilities do not bode well in the future if ATF must engage in raid operations against adversaries of similar or greater levels of sophistication as the Branch Davidians.

    d.   **Recommendations:**

- ATF should improve their ability to manage the collection, processing, and dissemination of imagery intelligence; increase their knowledge of existing capabilities available from other Federal agencies; and develop methods to obtain proper support from those agencies.

- ATF should also review their in-house capabilities and determine whether there were performance problems with cameras and video equipment (rectifiable through training), or policy and procedural gaps, or gaps caused by inadequate equipment.

5.   **Electronic Intelligence:**

    a.   Electronic intelligence operations suffered because of poor management and equipment limitations. In hindsight, increased electronic intelligence capability (e.g., Title III installation on telephones or listening devices within the compound) might have provided information on whether the raid was compromised.

    b.   There are a number of conflicting statements from ATF personnel concerning why a full Title III installation (much less a Pen Register) was never pursued. This indicates misunderstanding on the part of ATF personnel. A current ATF Order provides adequate guidance for Title III surveillance, but senior ATF personnel did not appear to understand this. In addition, there are conflicting statements on whether a scanner in the U/C house was operating or whether U/C personnel knew how to use the equipment.

    c.   **Recommendation:**

- ATF should review its electronic intelligence equipment, policy, procedures, and training for inadequacies. Reduced electronic intelligence capability affects their ability to conduct very sophisticated operations in a world where criminal adversaries have demonstrated increased counterintelligence capabilities.

IV. OPERATIONS SECURITY (OPSEC)

A. Policy and Procedural Guidance:

1. It is not clear to me that ATF has published OPSEC policy and procedural guidance, or provided appropriate OPSEC training to its personnel.

2. **Recommendation:** Review and provide such guidance with accompanying training at all levels of the organization.

B. OPSEC Planning and Execution:

1. OPSEC operations are not easy to plan nor execute. There are always trade-offs in an open society and in an environment where it is difficult for ATF to divert personnel from on-going cases and other missions. The key ingredient to OPSEC success is to systematically plan, understand the risks involved, and then decide on actions based on the risk. Proper planning and execution of OPSEC measures requires appropriate policy, documented procedural guidance, and training. I did not find these ingredients for OPSEC success within ATF's Waco operation.

2. There were numerous chances for compromise of the operation through inadvertent disclosure. These include the Command Post opening days before the operation began and its location in a semi-secured area; the selection of the U/C house and the manner in which U/C operations were conducted; the pole camera operation; the training at Fort Hood; the need to involve other agencies, etc. ATF attempted to strike a reasonable balance between security and OPSEC measures, but it did not appear that OPSEC was centrally planned nor managed. OPSEC and other security practices appeared to occur as a happenstance and as a result of individual intuition rather than being deliberately planned and orchestrated.

3. Current resource allocation does not allow ATF to be self-sufficient and in total control of all operations subject to security and OPSEC measures. The United States military establishment comes close to self-sufficiency only in a combat environment, but Federal law enforcement agencies do not have that advantage. These comments should **not** be construed to be in support of self-sufficiency. I mention this phenomena only to illustrate that there will always be risks for compromise even when the operation may be totally self-contained. These risks must be managed, and some risks must be taken on any operation.

On the assumption that ATF will examine and strengthen their security and OPSEC policy, procedures and training, ATF should include measures to deal with the risks posed by a number of activities to include: Was an open-stance with the media was in the best interests of ATF? Would bus transportation have been better versus the car convoy on the morning of the 28th? Was backstopping of the U/Cs enrolled as TSTC students sufficient?

4. **Recommendation:** ATF should develop additional policy and procedural guidance and provide different levels of training to all personnel on security and OPSEC measures

applicable to various operations. Different levels of training refer to the fact that at the entry level, personnel should be provided with reasons and basic methodology while at the journeyman and above level the emphasis should be on planning for security and OPSEC.

V. TRAINING AND EXERCISES

A. General Comments:

1. I identify numerous potential training needs throughout this report. ATF has identified their training needs and instituted considerable training already. However, in the vein of continuous improvement and in the wake of deficiencies identified in my review, there is a need to expand those training efforts. I also suggest that ATF expand their efforts to determine "best-in-class" processes to achieve specific training goals. For example, mention was made of using a one to two week seminar by a private organization to achieve executive level training in crisis management. I submit that this would **not** be an example of a best-in-class process. Those areas which I identify as definitely needing training improvement include:

- Advanced SRT training
- Forward Observer training
- Intelligence Operations (management, analysis, intelligence in support of tactical operations)
- Command and Control

3. There are other areas which may require additional training but where I am not clear as to whether they represent performance problems or the need for more training. These include:

- Intelligence Analysis and Operations during the Investigative Phase.
- U/C Operations.
- Technical Support Operations.
- Media Relations.

B. Improved Sophistication of Training Management:

1. Overall, the Lesson Plans and training design which I reviewed do NOT reflect a high level of sophistication in training management. For example, most SRT lesson plans do not use performance-oriented, measurable objectives. Improvements are needed in what is to be learned and how it is to be measured to ensure that the learning has occurred.

2. Significant gaps exist in the completeness of all training. For example, the proposed Forward Observer Course syllabus only devotes two hours towards observation and recording skills and no time towards establishment of a command and control mechanism and TOC for the Forward Observers.

3. SRT Basic training does **NOT** result in a skilled team member, team leader, or in any other particular skill. The SRT course appears to be delivered as an overview of most skills found on a Special Response Team. The current training could be viewed as being barely adequate for small-scale operations; however, if ATF is to continue with the mission of tackling adversarial groups which require the use of multiple SRTs, more sophisticated training is required to help ensure success. At a very minimum, additional training is required in command and control skills for SRT operations.

To also improve, ATF should carefully review the usefulness of specific instructional blocks to their course objectives. For example, the SRT Course includes time for physical training. Rhetorically, should physical training be a pre-requisite for attendance and the time better spent on practical exercises designed to reinforce entry team skills and techniques? Physical fitness in a realist situation could be demonstrated in these exercises.

4. Very importantly, it was suggested that crisis management skills could be learned by attending an IACP seminar on crisis management. This is absolutely the wrong approach. ATF must develop its own in-house training for these important skills and teach current ATF policy and procedures, thereby making the training specific to ATF's needs. This type of training must also include extensive practical exercises to further the learning and retention of those skills that are taught. "Best-in-class" benchmarking would show that the U.S. Army presents command and control skills during Basic Officer Training, Advanced Officer Training, Command and General Staff College, and the Army War College. I do not have the exact time spent on command and control matters in those four courses, but a rudimentary estimate would be that the training is months long.

C. **Exercises:**

1. Individual and small group training activities must be expanded to include periodic exercises to hone and evaluate preparedness. This is missing from the training program within ATF.

2. Exercises should studiously avoid becoming a vehicle to learn new skills. Instead, exercises should be used to evaluate and verify preparedness to conduct specific missions. The learning of new skills is most conducive to other training endeavors.

VI. **SUPPORT OPERATIONS**

A. **Military Support:**

1. It appears that there are several performance related problems associated with ATF's acquisition of military support. The ATF Headquarters Military Liaison Officer was quoted as saying there needed to be drug activity to justify military support. This is simply not true. Perhaps he meant that drug activity was needed to justify non-reimbursable military support, but that is an exceedingly poor reason (i.e., non-reimbursement) to seek military support of law enforcement for ATF.

An ATF Headquarters manager to whom the Military Liaison Officer reports stated that he was not aware of how military support was obtained and that he trusted the Military Liaison Officer to do what was right. I do not accept that as good management practice because the manner in which military support may be obtained by Federal law enforcement agencies is not complicated and should be known by all ATF Supervisors.

    2.   The reliance on Operation Alliance as a main source of obtaining military support is also a poor practice since the focus is on narcotics related activity. When such activity does not exist or when information must be stretched to provide such a connection, ATF is subjected with either not obtaining military support or being in danger of civil or criminal liability if information is fabricated or does not provide good probable cause.

    3.   One person from the Texas Governor's office appeared to favor the use of National Guard assets versus active duty military support. Through innuendo, there are appearances that he also hinted at the need for narcotics relationship so that the support could be provided for free. I do not feel that this attitude served ATF very well. For example, better imagery intelligence support could have been obtained from other Federal law enforcement organizations or active military forces; armored vehicle support would have been more readily available; smoke grenades might have been obtained if regular Fort Hood forces were used versus Special Forces advisors; and the use of U.S. Customs Service helicopters would have provided better capabilities than those supplied by the National Guard.

  B.   **Air Operations:**

The decision not to use U.S. Customs helicopters ostensibly stemmed from a concern over OPSEC. I am of the opinion that it was due more to interagency rivalry rather than OPSEC. The use of Customs helicopters and crews offer several advantages to include communications capabilities not found on the National Guard helicopters and the ability to fire from the helicopters.

  C.   **Communications:**

    1.   There are many conflicting statements concerning the adequacy of communications and communications support during the operation. At the very least, planning for communications shows a need for improvement. Communications planning should help to ensure continuity of command and control and is therefore closely linked to the adequacy of training and procedural guidance on command and control. Simply stated, if one cannot or will not communicate, then command and control will not exist. For example, the Tactical Coordinator appeared to be out of the command and control loop once the raid ran into difficulty. I was not able to determine what the cause for this was.

2. There are a large number of examples which point towards performance problems, planning problems, potential training shortfalls, and a few possibilities of inadequate equipment. They include:

- Linkages to local law enforcement and other supporting organizations were not outlined well in terms of net control and communications responsibility or redundant communications links between ATF and these organizations.

- There appears to be confusion concerning who was to operate the open-line with ATF Headquarters and what their duties were.

- The Forward Observers were not able to communicate directly with the Tactical Coordinator nor the SRT Leaders.

- The Incident Commander was not effectively communicating from the helicopters to the Tactical Coordinator nor to any other segment of the ATF operation. This was especially true when the helicopter he was on had to land once it received fire from the ground.

- Cavanaugh in the U/C House was not provided with sufficient communications personnel support to allow him to control all the activities (e.g., crisis negotiations, control of the Forward Observers, control of the deployed SRTs) which fell on his shoulders when the raid ran into difficulty.

- The Forward Observers and other ATF personnel on the back side of the compound ran into communications problems.

D. **Medical:**

1. Overall medical planning and preparations were excellent. The Special Forces personnel appeared to provide excellent assistance in planning and helping ATF personnel prepare and rehearse for medical emergencies. One gap in the plan appears to be that mass casualty situations were not anticipated with no plans in place to handle such a contingency. The contracted medical services could have been easily overwhelmed if the Branch Davidians had attempted mass suicide. When faced with a well-armed or potentially suicidal group, medical planning should consider mass casualty situations.

2. Improvement opportunities for ATF exist in developing policy and procedures to ensure that appropriate planning support is obtained or to develop an in-house capability for medical planning.

E. **Media:**

1. ATF's problems with the media potentially began with the interview of Mark Breault who was already in contact with the media; were exacerbated with the meetings and

discussions with the media prior to the raid; were compounded by the media being suspected of compromising the raid on February 28th; and were further fueled by media relations in the aftermath of the raid.

    2.   I find **four potential areas for improvement** of ATF's media relations:

- ATF personnel can benefit from **strengthened media policy, publication of procedural guides for media relations, and additional training**. Many media situations are judgemental calls (e.g., Chojnacki deciding to meet the media in Waco), so additional training based on coherent policy is a key to help ATF personnel understand the potential risks and benefits of dealing with the media.

- ATF ASACs and above should be prepared to accept **press conference responsibilities** or to ensure that the ATF spokesperson is physically and emotionally prepared. I refer specifically to the poor judgement shown by the use of Special Agent Wheeler as the spokesperson in the aftermath of the raid's failure when she had not slept for a reported 36 hours.

- ATF Headquarters should be prepared to **augment field personnel** on major operations which have the potential to attract major media attention.

- The Department of Treasury, in conjunction with Justice and the Congress, **examine** the potential of enacting **legislation** to provide criminal penalties for willful and negligent acts contributing to the loss of life on law enforcement or national security operations.

F.   **Coordination of Other Agencies:**

    1.   There are numerous indicators that ATF's preparations to coordinate their actions with other agencies were less than optimal. They include:

- The lack of a written operations order which would have provided specific instructions to ATF personnel to coordinate the activities of other agencies while providing overall guidance to those agencies.

- The failure to rapidly transfer the 911 call from the Branch Davidian compound to ATF control from McClennan County.

- The inordinate length of time required to get military armored vehicles on-scene.

- The lack of instructions on pursuit of suspects that could have fled the compound.

    2.   The appearances are that ATF personnel require additional training and procedural guidance to plan large-scale operations which require close coordination with a varieity of non-ATF organizations.

VII. WEAPONRY, ARMAMENT, and OTHER EQUIPMENT:

A. Automatic Weapons:

1. The ATF SRT leaders do not feel that automatic weapons capability is a necessity. I recommend that ATF review their current policy and consider the use of automatic weapons situationally...if the adversary has full auto weapons, then ATF should have the capability to overcome these. The use of automatic weapons by a criminal adversary could be overcome through ways other than using comparable weapons (e.g., better tactics, use of vehicles for entry, explosive entry). The difficulty in such a strategy is that ATF personnel will have to be much better trained to overcome a firepower deficiency.

B. Rifles (Assault and Forward Observer):

1. There is a definite need for ATF to review their decision to limit the use of rifles. Sub-machine or machine pistol type weapons simply do not have the range nor the accuracy inherent with longer barreled weapons such as AR-15s or other assault rifles. One ATF report refers to accuracy of the MP5 weapon out to 300 meters, but that ignores the fact that rural and some urban operations may require longer shots. In addition, the ability to penetrate some materials and to incapacitate a human is better with rifle rounds such as the 5.56mm and 7.62mm than with 9mm ammunition. In addition, 7.62mm weapons should also be considered since they can prove highly useful on vehicle stops and road blocks...not to mention longer range forward observer shots.

2. A number of SRT members raised questions over the availability of rifles to support their operations. They question the ATF Headquarters proclamation that AR-15s will be phased out. Since these personnel are the ones tasked with mission execution, it is my belief that they should have a greater say in what weaponry they are allowed to use.

C. Suppressed Weapons:

1. ATF personnel have not mentioned the potential need for suppressed weaponry on extremely high-risk operations. Suppressed weapons are useful in a variety of situations and provide a means of providing a critical edge to SRT-type units. There are a number of military and law enforcement organizations which possess such weapons and have proved their ability to use them discriminately. ATF should consider their need for such weapons if they are to continue with missions similar to the one they faced in Waco.

D. Chemical Munitions:

1. ATF is limited by their own policy on the use of smoke and disabling chemical agents. Again, these capabilities are found in a number of law enforcement and military organizations tasked with SRT type activities and have been used discriminately by these organizations for years. The ability to use chemical munitions can provide a needed advantage to

SRTs and can be used to lessen the chances of loss of life. For these reasons, ATF should reconsider their policy on the use of chemical munitions.

    E.   **Distraction devices:**

        1.   The use of distraction devices such as the commonly referred to "Flash Bang" are limited by ATF policy. The policy requires that ATF personnel use a "peek and throw" philosophy on ALL operations. Such a policy is extremely limiting and can result in additional danger to ATF personnel.

        2.   ATF policy should be modified to allow the use of distraction devices other than through a "peek and throw" technique. The policy and any accompanying procedural guidance should specify situations in which exclusions from the "peek and throw" method are permissible. In addition, all SRTs within ATF should receive training on the use of distraction devices.

    F.   **Vehicles**.

        1.   Armored vehicles would have been highly useful in Waco for a variety of operations ranging from use in recovering wounded, protecting personnel during retrograde movement, use in entry, etc. The fact that armored vehicles were not available appears to be a significant planning oversight.

        2.   ATF should qualify a number of their personnel on the use and operation of specified armored vehicles to include use of on-board weapons systems such as machine-guns and smoke generators. The procedures to obtain military support for these types of vehicles should be reviewed and solidified to ensure their availability for operations similar to Waco in the future.

VIII.   **CONCLUDING REMARKS:** Throughout my report and analysis of information there has been a continuing theme of:

- The need for policy review and modification
- Providing additional procedural guidance beyond policy documents to ATF personnel
- A very definite need for improved training in a number of areas

Perhaps these sound overly redundant. I submit that it is only through sound policy, supported by additional reference (i.e., procedural) materials, and thorough training that the tragedy which befell ATF at Waco can be prevented in the future. These focus on system fixes rather than individual actions along with the development of processes which provide a sound foundation for operational actions.

CURRICULUM VITAE FOR
Wade Y. Ishimoto

Education
M.A., Human Resources Development, Webster University
B.A., Asian Studies, University of Hawaii

Professional Schooling
U.S. Army Special Forces Operations and Intelligence Course
U.S. Army Counterintelligence Agent's Course
U.S. Army Special Warfare Center Instructor Training Course
Numerous courses relating to intelligence, security, and special operations

Current Occupation
Technical Manager, Sandia National Laboratories, Albuquerque, NM

Instructional Experience
University of New Mexico, Division of Continuing Education and Community Services, 1985-Present
U.S. Air Force Special Operations School, 1987-Present
U.S. Department of Energy Nuclear Emergency Search Team courses, 1985-present
California Department of Justice Terrorism Course, 1984-1986
Delta Force Operator's Training Course, 1977-1982
University of Santa Clara, 1975-1977
U.S. Army J.F. Kennedy Special Warfare Center, 1973-1975
Mobile Training Team special operations assignments to foreign, allied military and law enforcement organizations
Numerous instructional engagements with law enforcement organizations to include the Calgary Police Service, Royal Canadian Mounted Police, Canada Security & Intelligence Service, Los Angeles Police and Sheriff's Departments, Texas Narcotics Officers Association, and the National Tactical Officer's Association, 1962-present

Pertinent Experience
Nuclear Emergency Search Team (NEST) 1978-Present; founder of the NEST Training Management Working Group; project leader to reorganize and restructure the organization in 1989; Exercise Director of several Interagency (FBI, DOD, DOE, FEMA, local law enforcement) terrorist-related national exercises; planner or participant in other NEST exercises; developed a Key Leader Training Course.

Nuclear Security Systems Directorate 1985-1992, led numerous projects related to high-threat security situations including a Defense Nuclear Agency funded Insider Study, a Recapture and Recovery of Nuclear Weapons Study involving overseas and domestic situations, documentation of R&D requirements to support the TSWG for terrorist incidents; and

Curriculum Vitae for Wade Y. Ishimoto (continued)

Pertinent Experience (continued)

participation on a U.S. Physical Protection Bi-Lateral Team to Korea and Japan. Also performed liaison functions to various military special operations organizations and the FBI's Hostage Rescue Team. Designed and implemented the construction of a new Emergency Operations Center for Sandia National Laboratories and revamped their emergency operations program.

Security and Intelligence Specialist, U.S. Department of Energy, 1984-85, Key member of a Tiger Team assigned to revamp emergency operations within the Albuquerque Operations Office complex which included over 40,000 employees at six locations from Florida to New Mexico. Inspection staff duties. Organized mobile training teams for special response team training.

Vice-President for Operations, SAS of Texas, 1982-1984; led a White House directed examination of security preparations for the 1984 Summer Olympic Games in Los Angeles with over 2/3 of the recommendations being adopted; led security projects in support of the Nuclear Regulatory Commission, other governmental agencies, and private concerns.

Delta Force, 1977-1982; Intelligence Officer leading the effort to automate terrorist information in a interagency data base; Team Leader on the 1980 attempt to rescue 53 American hostages in Tehran; participant in several real-life counterterrorist operations; liaison and consulting duties to the FBI, Secret Service, Navy SEALS, overseas counterterrorist forces, and other special operations units.

Other pertinent experience includes Special Forces assignments in the U.S., Korea, Japan, Taiwan, the Philippines, and Vietnam (three tours) including training duties, exercise development, and combat operations; Counterintelligence and Human Intelligence collection duties in Korea, Hawaii, and the continental U.S.; and Military Police and investigative duties.

A Selective Analysis

of

Operation Trojan Horse

Conducted by

the Bureau of Alcohol, Tobacco and Firearms

Conducted by

John A. Kolman, Captain (L.A.S.D. retired)

for the Staff

of the

Waco Administrative Review

United States Department of the Treasury

TABLE OF CONTENTS

    Page

EXECUTIVE SUMMARY B-35

Chapter   Page

1. THE PROBLEM AND DEFINITIONS OF
   TERMS USED B-39
   INTRODUCTION B-39
       The BATF Special Response Team Program —
           An Historical Overview B-39
       A Synopsis of Operation Trojan Horse B-40
   THE PROBLEM B-44
       Statement of the Problem B-44
       Limitations of the Project B-44
   RESEARCH METHODS B-44
   DEFINITIONS OF TERMS USED B-45
       OPSEC B-45
       TEMS B-45
       Dynamic Entry B-45
       T.S.T.C./T.S.T.I. B-45

2. ANALYSIS B-46
   PLANNING AND PREPARATION B-46
       Tactical Alternatives B-46

Chapter   Page

    Tactics and Related Matters B-50
    Logistics B-53
    Emergency Medical Service B-54

Communications	B-56
Intelligence Function	B-57
Briefing	B-60
Training/Rehearsal	B-61
COMMAND AND CONTROL	B-63
Decisions Impacting the Operation	B-63
Organization and Structure	B-66
OPERATIONS SECURITY	B-70
MEDIA INVOLVEMENT	B-73

3. CONCLUSIONS AND RECOMMENDATIONS B-76
    CONCLUSIONS B-76
    RECOMMENDATIONS B-77

    REFERENCES B-80

EXECUTIVE SUMMARY

The attempted service of search/arrest warrants by agents of the Bureau of Alcohol, Tobacco and Firearms (BATF) on February 28, 1993, at the Branch Davidian Compound near Waco, Texas, was, in all probability, unprecedented within American law enforcement. Although many agencies (Federal, state and local) have conducted countless major high-risk warrant operations involving heavily armed multiple suspects, within the experience of the evaluator, none have rivaled the weaponry and fervent opposition which confronted the brave men and women of the BATF during Operation Trojan Horse. Certainly none have resulted in the tragic loss and wounding of so many law enforcement officers.

The purpose of objectively analyzing this or any other tactical incident is not to castigate or condemn, but rather to learn from what occurred with a view toward future improvement. The loss of Steven Willis, Robert Williams, Conway LeBleu, and Todd McKeehan, and the wounding of numerous other dedicated agents, make it essential that an objective evaluation be conducted.

The purpose of this project was: (1) to conduct a selective analysis of the planning, preparation, and subsequent attempted service of search/arrest warrants on February 28, 1993, by BATF personnel at the Branch Davidian Compound, (2) to develop conclusions based upon the analysis of BATF efforts in this regard, and (3) to make recommendations related to possible future operational improvements.

This project relied upon an extensive review of numerous documents, reports, videotapes, and training curricula provided by Waco Administrative Review staff; personal monitoring of Congressional hearings on June 9 and 10, 1993; personal interviews of selected BATF personnel; a review of the limited literature available in this subject area; personal observation of the areas surrounding the Branch Davidian Compound, as well as the Command Post, undercover residence, and Staging Areas; personal knowledge of contemporary policy, procedure and training within the tactical community; and extensive personal experience within the field of law enforcement tactical operations.

The results of this analysis are believed to support the following conclusions:

1. BATF personnel involved in planning Operation Trojan Horse were dedicated, experienced law enforcement professionals.
2. Much time and effort was expended in planning and preparing for Operation Trojan Horse.
3. Planners relied upon and trusted intelligence information which, in many cases, lacked corroboration.
4. A lack of knowledge existed on the part of both command and operational personnel concerning the proper utilization and deployment of countersniper (Forward Observer Team) personnel.
5. Insufficient attention was directed by command personnel to the Operations Security (OPSEC) process.
6. There was an apparent lack of supervision over the intelligence gathering mechanism in terms of direction, coordination, corroboration, dissemination and control.
7. Though well intentioned, contacts initiated by command personnel with the **Waco Tribune-Herald** violated basic principles of operations security.
8. No media contacts should have been initiated by BATF before the operation's conclusion.
9. Command personnel lacked experience and training in directing major tactical operations.
10. The Incident Commander should have been located at the designated command post to facilitate communication and control.
11. Once information had been received and corroborated that the operation had been compromised through the loss of surprise, command personnel should have aborted the mission.
12. There was no planned alternative course of action to be taken if the mission was aborted.
13. Following the negotiation of a cease fire to remove and evacuate the dead and wounded, perimeter positions should not have been abandoned until relief

personnel had assumed them.

14. Had the operation not been compromised, there was a high probability that the tactical plan would have succeeded.

15. Sufficient oversight was exercised by BATF Headquarters during all phases of Operation Trojan Horse.

16. Numerous acts of heroism were displayed by the men and women of the BATF during, and subsequent to, the extensive firefight with the Branch Davidians.

These conclusions, and others of less significance, contained within the body of the full report, constitute justification for considering the following recommendations.

1. Assign personnel to command positions (Incident Commander, Tactical Coordinator, Deputy Tactical Coordinator) based upon qualifications — not rank or position.

2. Develop and provide tactical crisis management training for those assigned to these positions.

3. Explore the feasibility of selecting and training an on-call cadre of personnel with proven decision-making and leadership ability to assume the roles of Incident Commander and Tactical Coordinator.

4. Ensure that all command and supervisory personnel understand their joint responsibility to abort an operation if circumstances justify doing so.

5. Increase the training time of Division Special Response Teams to a minimum of twice a month.

6. Explore the feasibility of establishing regional, full-time Special Response Teams for deployment during major operations.

7. Review and modify, as necessary, the criteria for selecting Special Response Team members.

8. Review and modify, as necessary, the curriculum of Special Response Team training.

9. Establish a Tactical Emergency Medical Support (TEMS) program and formally assign EMS-trained personnel to each Special Response Team.

10. Develop and implement a hostage negotiation program as an integral part of Special Response Team operations.

11. Evaluate existing Special Response Team equipment based on contemporary standards within the tactical community (to include chemical agents).

12. Review the organization, structure, and functions of the Technology and Tactical Issues Committee to ensure the timely evaluation and approval of tactical equipment and procedures.

13. Conduct meetings, at least annually, of Federal special operations team leaders and command personnel (BATF, FBI, Marshals, Customs) to discuss past tactical analyses and contemporary procedures. Emphasize necessity for interagency cooperation and training.

14. Ensure familiarity with guidelines related to requesting and utilizing air support.

15. Review and modify, as necessary, OPSEC training for all command and operational personnel.

16. Review and modify the media notification process.

17. Review and modify the BATF National Response Plan.

18. Pursue legislation enabling electronic surveillance and monitoring under circumstances such as existed at the Branch Davidian Compound.

19. Empanel a committee comprised of representatives from affected BATF entities to review these and other recommendations made by the Tactical Advisory Expert Panel.

In spite of extensive planning and preparation by well-intentioned, experienced agents, success was not achieved at the Branch Davidian Compound. It eluded them, not because of a lack of ability or resources, but rather deficiencies in policy and procedure, which were exposed by the magnitude of the situation.

Prior operations conducted by BATF Special Response Teams (433 in the past two years) apparently failed to reveal these deficiencies, due to their varying circumstances, as well as the reduced size of many of the operations.

Chapter 1

THE PROBLEM AND DEFINITIONS OF TERMS USED

INTRODUCTION

The BATF Special Response Team Program — An Historical Overview

In recent years, the Bureau of Alcohol, Tobacco and Firearms (BATF) responsibility to enforce Federal firearms, explosives, and arson statutes has met with increasing resistance from those individuals and groups involved in these activities (10). Because of the nature of these laws, almost every arrest or search warrant executed by the BATF involves armed suspects.

Accordingly, in 1989, after reviewing the Bureau's capabilities and limitations in managing these incidents, each of the twenty-two Field Divisions were authorized to form what were then called high-risk entry control teams. These teams, comprised of specially selected volunteers, initially made use of available state and local training resources within their particular areas. However, in 1991, a decision was made to develop a centralized training program in order to ensure uniformity and the ability of agents to meet required physical fitness standards. Ultimately, Fort McClellan, Alabama, home of the U.S. Armys military police, chemical, and special response team training schools, was selected as the site of the basic two-week BATF Special Response Team (SRT) training program. Each Field Divisions team is now required to attend this rigorous course.

The live-in program, consists of approximately 130 hours of training over a 10-day period, and places heavy emphasis on promoting teamwork. Subject areas vary from building entry and tactics to firearms training, trauma aid, operational planning, and physical conditioning. A high instructor-to-student ratio of one per two is maintained during training to enhance the learning process and enable appropriate performance evaluation (9:38). Instructors are selected based upon their background and experience. Over one half of the instructional cadre have past pertinent military experience, and one third are former members of law enforcement tactical units.

Following successful completion of the basic program at Fort McClellan, each team is required to train a minimum of 24 hours each quarter. Much of this training is conducted in conjunction with area state and local SWAT teams. Special Response Team members are equipped with the best tactical safety equipment available, including body armor, ballistic shields, firearms, and communications equipment.

Since their inception, the Special Response Teams have actively proven their worth. During the past two fiscal years, BATF SRTs were activated 433 times to resolve cases determined to be the most dangerous (10). These activations varied from assisting at the scene of the 1992 riots in Los Angeles, to providing assistance in capturing murder suspects in Idaho that same year.

Significantly, until Operation Trojan Horse on February 28, 1993, only one SRT member had been injured by gunfire (10).

A Synopsis of Operation Trojan Horse

The Bureau of Alcohol, Tobacco and Firearms officially became aware of the Branch Davidians and David Koresh on June 4, 1992. This awareness resulted from a referral by the McLennan County Sheriff to the Austin ATF Office. Additional referrals of complaint were received from a Congressman, the U.S. Attorneys Office, and the media. These complaints basically addressed allegations of sexual abuse by David Koresh, as well as firearms violations. Concern was also expressed over why nothing had been done by the authorities to alleviate the problem. As a result of this information, a case agent was assigned, and an extensive investigation initiated to determine if violations of laws enforceable by BATF were occurring. Information related to probable cause was later presented to the Assistant U.S. Attorney, who expressed the belief that there was sufficient information for a search warrant based upon the purchase of firearms and items necessary to convert them to fire in full automatic mode.

The continuing investigation next placed emphasis on linking Koreshs purchases of chemicals with the manufacture of explosive devices. Because of the sensitive nature of the investigation, activities were closely monitored by BATF Headquarters. In anticipation of obtaining search and arrest warrants, operational planning commenced in December, 1992. Numerous planning meetings were conducted, and after extensive discussion, focused on utilizing three Special Response Teams with support personnel to effect service of the warrants.

Although many options were explored by planners (i.e., siege [contain and call out], luring Koresh away from the Compound, doing nothing, etc.), for reasons that will be addressed later in this report, a dynamic raid of the Compound, using helicopters as a diversion, was agreed upon. As a result of intelligence gathered from the continuing investigation, which included undercover operations at and in the vicinity of the Compound, and selected interviews of disillusioned former cult members, a plan was finalized and approved.

The plan called for the raid to be initiated at approximately 1000 hours on a date to be specified. This time was selected because, according to intelligence sources, following Bible study, the men of the Compound would be outside working on a construction project and separated from their weapons, which were kept in a storeroom on the second floor of the Compound adjacent to Koreshs living quarters. Women and children would reportedly be studying the Bible or involved with chores. Containment (cover) personnel would be responsible for isolating and securing the men at the construction site, or anyone outside the structure. One SRT team would secure men on the first floor, and another would isolate and secure women and children on the second floor and clear the towers. Lastly, a third team would secure the second floor weapons room and arrest David Koresh.

It was recognized early on that it would be difficult to approach the Compound undetected because of the terrain and remoteness of the area. Therefore, planners opted to use two pickup trucks and cattle trailers to transport the raid force to the Compound. These vehicles were known to be very common to the area, and consequently would not cause alarm or suspicion if driven in the vicinity of the Branch Davidian Compound. Surprise and speed of execution were believed critical to achieve success. As the raid force arrived at the front of the Compound, three Texas National Guard helicopters would arrive shortly before, some distance to the northwest. The presence of helicopters would hopefully attract the attention of the men working at the rear of the Compound and mask the arrival of the raid force. Once the Branch Davidians and the Compound were secure, support personnel would handle arrestees and search for and process evidence. A search warrant for a second location associated with the Compound, referred to as the "Mag Bag", was to be served simultaneously. This location was a screening point for UPS deliveries destined for the Compound, and was manned by cult members. Undoubtedly, it also functioned as an early warning system for the Compound.

The operational plan provided for the assignment of ATF Emergency Medical Services (EMS) personnel to each Special Response Team. Medivac helicopters would be on standby at the Command Post, and an ambulance and crew would be staged at a roadblock position. Unfortunately, it would not be possible for civilian EMS personnel and ambulances to accompany the raid force to the Compound because of the potential hazard, as well as the fact that their presence would alert the Compound to the impending warrant service. Contingency plans provided for the mission to be aborted at any time after the raid force left the Staging Area, but prior to the vehicles turning into the Compound. The abort decision would be based upon continuous surveillance of the location from an undercover site.

In late 1992, BATF became aware of local media interest in the Branch Davidians and David Koresh. Specifically, the Waco Tribune-Herald was preparing a series of articles on the cult and its leader. Concerned that any article of this nature might cause Koresh to become more alert and paranoid about possible law enforcement action against him, and prompt an increase of curious onlookers in the area, an ATF representative contacted the paper in an effort to delay publication of the series until after March 1, 1993. These and subsequent negotiations with the newspaper concerning this issue were fruitless. BATF representatives were told that the series would begin as soon as it was complete. Eventually, they were advised on February 26, 1993, that the first article in the series would be released on February 27, two days before BATF planned to serve the warrants. At this point, support personnel and equipment had already arrived in the Waco area, and Special Response Teams, along with selected support personnel, were rehearsing and training for the operation at Fort Hood, Texas. Consequently, it was decided to advance the scheduled date of execution by one day to February 28, 1993. The final decision would be kept in abeyance until David Koresh's reaction to the first article could be assessed through undercover contacts. These contacts revealed nothing untoward at the Compound as a result of the article. It was decided that prior to the raid on February 28, one last undercover contact would be made. In the meantime, support elements and Special Response Team personnel had responded from Fort Hood to a staging area at Bellmead, a Waco suburb, to await the final command to proceed with the operation.

On the morning of February 28, 1993, an undercover contact was made with David Koresh. During the conversation, Koresh was interrupted by a cult member and advised that England is on the phone. Note: Mark England was one of the reporters who wrote the first article. When he returned, according to the undercover agent, Koresh was very nervous, quoted the Bible, and remarked to the effect that "the ATF and National Guard are coming for me. Theyll never get me. The undercover agent left the Compound as soon as he could without arousing suspicion, and provided this information personally to the Deputy Tactical Coordinator, and by telephone to the Tactical Coordinator. The Tactical Coordinator personally related the information to the Incident Commander, and after consultation with him, it was decided the operation could still be carried out successfully (even though compromised) if done quickly, before Koresh could distribute weapons and prepare his defenses.

Accordingly, the Tactical Coordinator went to the Staging Area and ordered personnel to obtain their equipment, load on the cattle trailers, and respond to the Compound to effect service of the warrants. The Tactical Coordinator was in communication with the Deputy Tactical Coordinator throughout the 8-mile drive from the Staging Area to the Compound, and was given periodic situation reports from the undercover surveillance location. Nothing unusual was reported. In fact, no activity at all was noted in the vicinity of the Compound. Apparently not recognizing the significance of the no activity report (the men were supposed to be working at the construction site), the convoy continued toward the Compound. While enroute, the convoy passed two vehicles, one of which displayed a Waco Tribune-Herald sign on the door. These vehicles followed the convoy, unchallenged, almost to the Compound. Other media vehicles, perhaps the same, had been noted on the road in front of the Compound earlier in the morning by surveillance personnel. However, they were believed to be a reaction to the first newspaper article, and not viewed as a threat to the warrant service operation.

After passing the final checkpoint (and last opportunity to abort), the convoy turned into the Compound and parked in front of the main structure (**approximately forty minutes after the undercover agent had reported Koresh knew they were coming**). As the cattle trailers were being unloaded, the front door opened slightly and a man (believed to be Koresh) was seen standing in the doorway. The door was quickly shut and gunfire was immediately initiated through the closed door directed at the approaching agents. The helicopters arrived simultaneous with the raid force, and were almost immediately taken under fire, causing all three to land and subsequently withdraw. Only the Special Response Team assigned to secure the arms room was able to reach their objective, and although they were able to enter the arms room through a second-story window, were forced to exit because of intense gunfire directed at them. Other SRT and support personnel were forced to seek cover behind whatever was available. Cult members utilized both semi- and fully automatic weapons, as well as fragmentation grenades, against the raid force.

During the ensuing firefight, four agents were killed and at least fifteen wounded. Because of the continuing heavy gunfire, it was impossible to remove the dead and wounded. A few wounded agents were tended to by assigned EMS personnel, but others lay untreated. After approximately an hour, a negotiated cease fire was arranged by telephone through the efforts of the Deputy Tactical Coordinator and a lieutenant from the McLennan County Sheriff's Department.

As a result of the cease fire, ambulances and other vehicles were utilized to evacuate the dead and wounded. The most seriously wounded were evacuated by helicopter once safe landing zones could be established.

Orders were subsequently given, presumably by the Incident Commander, to abandon the Compound entirely. A few agents remained of their own volition to maintain loose containment, but eventually, they too were ordered to leave. Because of the severity of the situation at the Compound, the search warrant for the "Mag Bag" was not served. Later, three men left this location and while attempting to return to the Compound, engaged departing BATF agents in a gun battle. One was killed, another surrendered, and the third fled but was later captured. Fortunately, a number of local

SWAT teams arrived and assumed containment positions around the Compound.

As a result of a decision made at high levels of BATF management, control of the operation was relinquished to the Federal Bureau of Investigation on March 2, 1993. Selected BATF agents remained in support roles until the siege ended on April 19, 1993.

THE PROBLEM

Statement of the Problem

The purpose of this project was: (1) to conduct a selective analysis of the planning, preparation, and subsequent attempted service of search/arrest warrants on February 28, 1993, by BATF personnel at the Branch Davidian Compound, (2) to develop conclusions based upon the analysis of BATF efforts in this regard, and (3) to make recommendations related to possible future operational improvements.

Limitations of the Project

In accordance with the charter given the evaluator, this project will explore only the actions of BATF personnel leading up to, and including, the attempted service of search/arrest warrants at the Branch Davidian Compound. It will not address actions of the Federal Bureau of Investigation, which assumed control of the operation on March 2, 1993.

For simplicity, the non-gender-based pronoun "he" is used in place of "he/she" throughout this document, and no inference should be drawn as to gender.

RESEARCH METHODS

This project utilized the following data collection methods:

1. A review of documents, reports, videotapes, and training curricula provided by Waco Administrative Review staff.

2. Personal monitoring of Congressional hearings on June 9 and 10, 1993, regarding the operation.

3. Personal interviews of selected BATF personnel.

4. A review of available literature related to the subject area.

5. Personal observation of the geographical area surrounding the Branch Davidian Compound, as well as the Command Post, undercover residence, and Staging Area.

6. Personal knowledge of contemporary policy, procedure, and training within the tactical community.

7. Extensive personal experience within the field of law enforcement tactical operations.

DEFINITIONS OF TERMS USED

OPSEC

An acronym for Operations Security. Developed by the military during the Vietnam War, OPSEC is a process by which specific programs or operations are viewed from an adversarial perspective to identify possible vulnerabilities.

TEMS

An acronym for Tactical Emergency Medical Support. TEMS involves the integration of emergency medical services with SWAT/tactical units. Tactically trained, commissioned or non-commissioned paramedics/Emergency Medical Technicians, directly provide EMS at the scene of tactical operations. They may be supplemented by an on-scene physician(s) operating in either an active or advisory capacity.

Dynamic Entry

A type of entry which is sudden, vigorous, and unexpected.

T.S.T.C./T.S.T.I.

The Texas State Technical College (T.S.T.C.), or Texas State Technical Institute (T.S.T.I.). Both terms are used interchangeably in this report.

B.A.T.F./A.T.F.

The Bureau of Alcohol, Tobacco and Firearms (B.A.T.F.), or Alcohol, Tobacco and Firearms (A.T.F.). Both terms are used interchangeably in this report.

Chapter 2

ANALYSIS

The attempted service of search/arrest warrants by agents of the Bureau of Alcohol, Tobacco and Firearms on February 28, 1993, at the Branch Davidian Compound near Waco, Texas, was in all probability unprecedented within American law enforcement.

However, although unprecedented, the BATF operation can be examined objectively by comparing various phases of the operation with contemporary law enforcement/military concepts, principles, and practices. By approaching the analysis in this manner, it is possible to reveal both positive aspects as well as areas of deficiency. It is important to note that the purpose of conducting this analysis is not to castigate or condemn, but rather to learn from what occurred with a view toward future improvement.

PLANNING AND PREPARATION

Preparing and implementing a comprehensive plan is one of the most important factors in achieving operational success. In order to ensure that nothing is left to chance, and all foreseeable problems are considered, it is imperative that a definite course of action be followed (1:143).

There is no doubt in the mind of the evaluator that those involved in preparing for Operation Trojan Horse fully appreciated the importance of their efforts in achieving operational success. Although there were others who provided assistance, the Special Response Team Leaders from Dallas, Houston, and New Orleans became the principal planners. Over the ensuing weeks, in addition to their other duties, they sought out and utilized all sources of information and assistance known to be available to them. After considering and evaluating information thus obtained, and relying upon their individual and collective experience, both within and outside of law enforcement, they formulated a plan of operation which they believed would afford the highest probability of success.

Tactical Alternatives

During the course of preparing for Operation Trojan Horse, planners discussed and refined a number of tactical alternatives, or options For reasons to be discussed subsequently, circumstances prompted them to select a dynamic warrant service, or raid, as the most viable of available options. The following alternatives were considered by planners:

Take No Enforcement Action

This alternative was quickly determined to be unacceptable. Numerous complaints had been received concerning firearms violations by the Branch Davidians, and the violent takeover of leadership by David Koresh from George Roden in 1987, along with alleged threats against former cult members, demonstrated a high propensity for violence. The BATF simply did not want to risk the added possibility that cult members would turn their weapons against members of the community.

Additionally, the alleged physical and sexual abuse of children at the Compound, combined with complaints of inaction and lack of concern by local and outside law enforcement agencies, left little, if any, doubt that the problems had to be addressed.

Arrest David Koresh Away From the Compound

Planners recognized early on that it would be advantageous to arrest David Koresh away from the Compound because of the weaponry believed to be maintained there, and the obvious control he exercised over the cult members.

If cooperative after his arrest, Koresh would be asked to call the Compound and encourage his followers to comply with instructions of the authorities. In the event Koresh refused, the Compound would be notified by authorities of his arrest, and cult members instructed not to resist the lawful service of the search warrant. Failure of the cult members to comply would result in containment (siege) of the Compound until compliance was achieved.

Plans to lure Koresh from the Compound using the ruse that the Texas Division of Children's Protective Services wanted to discuss allegations of child abuse at the Compound with him failed when a supervisor at the agency refused to approve the request. This avenue apparently was not pursued further.

Other ruses were discussed and rejected. Additional ideas (follow Koresh to town and arrest him, etc.) were also rejected when information was received from the undercover site (a residence in view of the Compound) that Koresh had not left the Compound in the past two months, and there was nothing to indicate he would do so in the immediate future. This information was based upon the belief that the undercover location was being operated around the clock, and would have been able to determine if, and when, Koresh left the Compound. Unfortunately, this was an honest, but false, assumption on the part of planners and others, who should have been able to rely upon information provided by undercover agents.

Contain and Call Out (Siege/Negotiate)

This alternative had been utilized successfully in the past by the BATF — most notably in Arkansas during a 1985 joint operation with the FBI to effect service of search warrants at a heavily fortified compound. Armed members of a right-wing group known as the Covenant of the Sword and Arm of the Lord (CSA), occupied the compound, and surrendered after three days of negotiations.

Although there were similarities in the two cases, information received through interviews of disgruntled former cult members and other sources made it apparent that this alternative would be extremely risky at the Branch Davidian Compound for the following reasons:

- There was a great risk of mass suicide.

- The physical and sexual abuse of children could continue.

- The evidence necessary to prosecute Koresh for firearms violations was capable of being destroyed.

- There was reportedly enough food stored on the Compound to sustain cult members for at least three months. Water was also available in quantity.

- The Compound could continue to be barricaded and fortified.

- The operation could involve a lengthy commitment in terms of personnel and logistics.

- The resources of local agencies could be strained, and neighboring areas disrupted.

- The lack of sufficient and adequate cover would make it extremely difficult to effectively contain the Compound without the use of heavily armored vehicles.

Dynamic Entry (Raid)

The very nature of a dynamic entry necessitates the existence of three elements in order to achieve success: (1) surprise, (2) speed of implementation, and (3) diversion. BATF planners were well aware of the significance and importance of these elements, as evidenced by their inclusion not only in the tactical plan, but also the rehearsal and training segments conducted at Fort Hood.

Experience has shown, and it is generally conceded, that while diversion is not always critical to the success of every dynamic operation, surprise and speed are absolutely essential. Certainly, if surprise is lost, the likelihood of achieving success is reduced greatly, because it is difficult to overcome its compromise through speed and diversion. By incorporating all three elements into their dynamic scheme, planners ensured a high probability of success, and enhanced the safety of participating agents as well as cult members.

Undercover observations, interviews of former cult members, and patterning of cult activities confirmed the selection of this tactical alternative. For example, it was determined that:

- Weapons were stored in a second-floor room at the east side of the Compound.

- Following Bible study, male followers left the Compound structure to work on an outside construction project at the west side of the Compound, thus separating them from the arms room.

- Women and children were separated from the men.

- No armed guards accompanied the men, and it was likely very few, if any, persons on the Compound would be armed.

The successful implementation of the dynamic entry option would prevent mass suicide, alleviate the continued physical and sexual abuse of the children, and enable cult members held against their wishes to leave. In addition, it would facilitate the arrest of David Koresh and the recovery of evidence.

One of the controversial areas confronted by planners in "selling" this tactical alternative was the selection of when the warrants would be served. Generally speaking, the most advantageous time of service would be during the hours of darkness or early dawn, when occupants are more likely to be asleep. However, in the case of the Branch Davidians, intelligence information reflected that several of Koresh's most trusted followers, the "Mighty Men", slept with assault rifles under their mattresses. This potential threat, along with the estimated number of cult members believed to be in the Compound (75), the fact that the men would be close to the arms room, and the size of the complex, prompted planners to reject service during the hours of darkness. Instead, the decision was made to effect service at 1000 hours, because, as previously noted, patterning reflected that by then the men would be busy at the construction site at the opposite end of the Compound from the arms room, and the women and children would be separated from the men, performing their chores elsewhere.

As mentioned before, planners realized from the outset that the safest and most effective alternative available to them was to arrest David Koresh away from the Compound. However, relying upon misleading intelligence, and rejection of other suggested means of enticing Koresh from the Compound, they abandoned what was believed to be the best tactical option. In fairness to the planners, it should be pointed out that, with the exception of a few interviews and observations made while surreptitiously visiting the areas surrounding the Compound, they had no direct link with intelligence providers. Consequently, they were forced to accept intelligence which was often considered inconsistent and untimely.

Lacking the ability to arrest Koresh away from the Compound, and based upon the information provided them, planners logically selected the dynamic entry (raid) option.

Tactics and Related Matters

Having adopted the strategy of using a dynamic approach to effect service of the warrants, planners next established the duties and responsibilities of each SRT and cover team. These functions have been addressed previously, but briefly stated, the New Orleans SRT team was given the assignment of surmounting the roof, securing the arms room, and arresting David Koresh if he was encountered. A segment of the same team was to maintain a holding position at the warehouse until they were joined by others to clear that area. The Dallas SRT team was to enter the front door, go to the second floor, clear it, the towers, and chapel, and secure women and children. The Houston Team was to enter the front door, clear the first floor, the kitchen, dining area, an underground tunnel (a buried school bus), and secure all men encountered. Each SRT team was supported by an exterior cover team. Forward Observer Teams (countersniper) were to provide long-range cover and support for the SRT and cover teams. This would be the first time members of the newly adopted program were deployed on an actual operation. Because so many agents would be entering the interior of the Compound, the value of the Forward Observer Teams was probably underestimated. Their primary responsibility was to provide long-range cover during the approach to the Compound. Planners recommended two, two-person Forward Observer Teams be deployed inside the undercover residence, which would also act as a forward command post. Also, one, two-person team would deploy at the rear of the Compound, along with five BATF members who were to clear a series of vehicles and trailers once the raid had commenced. Planners had hoped to deploy a fourth team east of the Compound, but it was felt that the cover and concealment were too sparse to prevent their detection.

While it is conceded that planners were appreciative of the benefit of deploying the new teams, there is little question that realization of their full potential was not possible under the described deployment. The desired fourth team could have been deployed through the assistance of a cooperative rancher from whom the undercover site was obtained. He had offered to place large, tightly rolled hay bales (rolls) strategically around his property, which bordered the Compound, to act as surveillance posts. These bales could have been placed weeks in advance so they would not have caused the Davidians to become suspicious. Their protective value could have been tested beforehand by undercover personnel firing into them to determine the best configuration in which to arrange the bales. The rancher's offer was noted, but not accepted.

Deployment of the Forward Observer Teams also created concern. Although the two teams at the undercover site arrived the evening before, they did not deploy until two hours prior to the raid. The team at the rear of the Compound was not deployed until moments before the raid. One of the most important roles performed by a position of this type is to surveill the objective continuously, well before the operation begins (2:352). Had this team been deployed the night before, the possibility exists that valuable intelligence information might have been obtained through their observations.

Both managers and supervisors are often unfamiliar with the role of countersniper teams and their deployment. However, in the case of the BATF, it is submitted that this unfamiliarity was complicated by the newness of the program. Operation Trojan Horse was literally a "test by fire" for the program, and its members proved their worth. In the future, problems can be reduced by assigning a trained and experienced coordinator (supervisor) to the program. The coordinator, or his designate, would represent Forward Observer Teams at all applicable planning sessions, and respond in a supervisorial capacity during deployment. This simple modification will increase the likelihood that the teams are utilized to their full potential. Also, it should result in a better understanding of their capabilities and limitations.

Tactical contingencies were considered by planners, including aborting the operation at various stages if a compromise occurred. However, as will be addressed under *Command and Control*, planners had no control over those with assigned authority to abort the mission. One of the problems with the abort plan was that there was no alternative course of action available to decision makers once an abort had been declared. For example, and as provided for in the plan, if a compromise occurred while enroute to the Compound, the raid force would be ordered to continue past the Compound and not carry through with the dynamic warrant service. Had this occurred, what were they to do? Return to the Staging Area? Respond to the Command Post? Apparently, no provisions were made for this contingency, and if they were, there is no evidence of their knowledge by decision makers. Of course, it could be presumed that decision makers should know their options in a situation like this. However, one of the purposes of planning is to eliminate as many presumptions as possible by providing direction and guidance.

Once the firefight broke out at the Compound, agents found themselves without an effective means of withdrawal. Although the use of Bradley Fighting Vehicles was discussed by planners as a necessity if the siege alternative was implemented, once the dynamic entry option was adopted, their use was de-emphasized. Given the suspected weaponry of the Branch Davidians, it would have been advisable to have had at least three of these armored vehicles standing by at the Command Post.

Another problem with the contingency plan arose because there was a lack of definite guidance with regard to negotiations. Loose reference was made to the use of local agency negotiators, but it appears clear that no one foresaw the necessity to utilize them. Unfortunately, the need arose quickly and tragically. Luckily, the Deputy Tactical Coordinator had received negotiations training in the past. After David Koresh had called 911 and communicated with a Sheriff's Department lieutenant, the Deputy Tactical Coordinator made telephone contact with another cult member and negotiated a cease fire to evacuate dead and wounded agents. In defense of the planners, it is difficult to provide for a negotiations function where none exists. This is an area which must be addressed in the future. The experience of the evaluator has been that protracted operations involving tactics and negotiations are best managed when negotiators are an integral part of the tactical team or unit, and under the same tactical command and control. It has been said that perhaps the most critical element of decision making is timing (3:69). There are sometimes occasions during the course of tactical operations when a resolution can be achieved as a result of a sudden change in circumstances. The tactical commander must make what can be a difficult decision at this point. If he must also consult with a separate negotiation command prior to implementing the resolution, the opportunity may pass and never present itself again.

Regardless of the negotiations concept utilized, it is absolutely essential that tactical, command, and negotiations personnel work together toward the successful resolution of the incident. Negotiations and tactics are successful if they assist in any way to achieve a positive outcome (4).

While planners did not select Command Post and Staging Area sites, some had an opportunity to view them during a visit to the Waco area in December, 1992. Understandably, their interests were more concentrated on surveilling the Compound and evaluating tactical options than assessing the location of support sites. Nevertheless, the selection of these sites can often adversely affect an operation, and for this reason, planners should participate in choosing them.

The selection of the Texas State Technical Institute (College) Airport facility as the principal Command Post was logical, based upon necessary requirements. However, interviews of some participants reflected concern over the location of the Staging Area because of its proximity to a traveled highway, and the fact that arriving vehicles and personnel were easily observable. Having viewed the Staging Area during an independent post-operation visit, the evaluator shared this concern. Although the location was certainly adequate to meet space and comfort requirements, its location adjacent to a traveled road, and on an almost direct route to the Compound (albeit 8 miles distant), makes its selection questionable. This point is particularly critical when it is considered that an estimated 50-100 vehicles were utilized to transport the raid force from Fort Hood. Had buses been utilized, it might have been possible to use an area adjacent to the Command Post at T.S.T.I. as a staging area. This would probably have been more conducive to operations security. Buses could have been obtained commercially, or through military sources.

One way to reduce potential problems with the selection of sites such as these is to prepare, and faithfully utilize a printed checklist or form detailing specific requirements for the site and emphasizing operations security concerns. This is always important, but especially when someone other than the planners are making the selections

Logistics

Logistical support of a large-scale operation requires a concerted and cooperative effort on the part of planners and those obtaining and providing the requested assistance. In addition to existing individual and team SRT equipment, the tactical strategy selected will also determine what support and supplemental equipment and personnel will be required. Assigning this important, and often critical, responsibility to a specific individual will ensure that logistical requirements are met in a timely manner. In the case of Operation Trojan Horse, a Support Coordinator was assigned in accordance with the BATF National Response Plan, which was implemented for the first time as a result of the investigation.

Because of the geographical distances separating the Support Coordinator and individual planners, a request was made asking them to submit a list of desired equipment. These lists were then consolidated, and most of the items were obtained or borrowed from one source or another. Post-operation interviews with the SRT team leaders reflected that they had received all critical equipment they had requested, with the exception of smoke grenades, which were apparently unavailable from military sources. Under the circumstances, smoke grenades might have been of benefit in concealing the withdrawal or movement of the raid force. A controversy developed later concerning the availability of additional AR-15 semi-automatic rifles, but according to the Support Coordinator, all that were requested were received, and if more had been requested, they, too, would have been provided. In retrospect, there is no question that more could have been utilized.

With reference to helicopters, it had been the understanding of planners that necessary aviation assets would be provided by U.S. Customs Service. However, the decision was made at a later date to utilize Texas National Guard assets. This assistance was obtained with the cooperation of the Department of Defense liaison officer to the BATF in Washington, D.C. Whether the decision to utilize National Guard assets was based upon politics, rivalry, or practicality is a moot point. In either case, the National Guard ultimately committed to providing aviation assistance, armored vehicles on a standby basis, and other support equipment.

Fortunately, full-scale, multi-agency activities, approaching the size of Operation Trojan Horse, are still rare within law enforcement. Nonetheless, agencies must be prepared should they be confronted by circumstances of this nature requiring their attention. Logistical support of any operation, and particularly one of great magnitude, can have a marked affect on its outcome. Therefore, the assigned coordinator must be especially familiar with his role, as well as various sources of logistical assistance.

One approach to ensuring future uniformity and directed action in obtaining logistical support for an operation is to prepare and provide to each BATF Field Division Office a logistical manual. This manual, which would be provided to the Logistical Coordinator at the time of his assignment to the position, would contain a full description and statement of duties and responsibilities, along with logistical sources, procedures, and points of contact. The National Response Plan provides some direction in this regard, and that information could easily be expanded into a more helpful format, as described above.

Emergency Medical Services

One of the areas for which the BATF was most criticized by those with little or no knowledge of Operation Trojan Horse was an alleged failure to provide Emergency Medical Services (EMS). Research for this report revealed that these allegations were patently false. Unfortunately, television coverage of the evacuation of dead and wounded agents, and the withdrawal of others, prompted these allegations because there was no attempt made to explain why ambulances and EMS providers were not immediately at the scene when the need arose.

In actuality, not only were ground ambulance and paramedics requested and pre-staged, but so too, was a civilian medivac helicopter. National Guard helicopters would be used if additional airborne medivac service was required. Because of the open terrain and the need for operations security, EMS assets could not be staged in view of the Compound, and for obvious reasons, civilian EMS personnel could not accompany the raid force to the location. Instead, an EMT-trained and -equipped agent was assigned to each team. Other medical assets would be brought in from their staging areas if they were required. Ultimately, circumstances strained medical resources to the maximum. It is unlikely, as a practical matter, that enough resources could have been staged in advance to handle the unforeseeable number of casualties that occurred. As a matter of fact, the remoteness of the area and the weaponry possessed by cult members, prompted extra effort to be exerted in preparing a comprehensive medical plan. Assisting in this effort was an Army Special Forces complement, which also provided instruction on trauma care to members of the raid force at Fort Hood. This instruction proved of value during the operation.

In addition to providing instruction, Army medics also suggested that members of the SRT teams print their blood types on their neck and legs with a marker. This questionable suggestion was accepted and implemented. Although this practice might have application in the military environment, in the evaluator's opinion, it has no place within law enforcement operations. Not only does this practice have an adverse psychological effect on team members, and heighten their anxiety, but civilian emergency medical facilities are unlikely to accept a patient's assertion of having a particular blood type. For reasons of both accuracy and liability, a patient's blood would be typed regardless of their claimed knowledge of blood type.

Because of the almost total dependence of the BATF on outside sources of EMS to support their tactical operations, it would prove of benefit to organize an internal program within each Special Response Team.

Within the contemporary law enforcement tactical community, this concept is known by the acronym TEMS (Tactical Emergency Medical Support). A few agencies have staffed full-time SWAT-trained police paramedics within their tactical units for many years, but most are unable to afford this luxury. Instead, some agencies have discovered that there are a number of alternative means of integrating this life-saving service, albeit on an on-call basis. These alternatives include:

- Paramedic or EMT-trained agency personnel

- Fire department paramedics or EMTs

- Private hospital/ambulance paramedics or EMTs

- Private physicians

Outside EMS services may be obtained by contract or through a volunteer program. Regardless of which is selected, the consensus of those experienced in the field is that all EMS personnel be required to complete basic tactical response team, as well as periodic in-service, training. A few agencies require EMS personnel to meet their tactical response team selection criteria to ensure acceptable physical condition, as well as acceptance by team members.

Integration of EMS capabilities within an agency or team should not be considered a substitute for existing civilian EMS providers, but rather a supplement. Unlike their civilian counterparts, tactical paramedics and EMT personnel are trained to operate in life-threatening situations that may involve an armed adversary (7:56). Not only can these specially trained personnel provide almost immediate basic and advanced life support care on scene, and occasionally under fire, but they are also a valuable tactical planning resource. Planning for a tactical mission should obviously include concern for medical care, whether or not an agency maintains an in-house EMS program. It should be apparent that when the level of care and medical capability increase, potential risk and liability factors diminish (8:55).

The application of TEMS to BATF operations is obvious. There are undoubtedly a sizable number of special agents within the service who are trained and certified former paramedics or Emergency Medical Technicians (EMT). Those personnel whose certifications have expired could be retested and certified. Their ranks could be supplemented by civilian EMS volunteers within the various BATF divisions. Activation procedures could be aligned with those of Special Response Teams, as outlined within the National Response Plan.

Guidance in developing a program of this nature is available from a number of law enforcement and related sources.

Communications

A reliable and effective communications system is, of course, a critical factor in resolving any major tactical incident. The communications plan for Operation Trojan Horse was developed jointly by representatives of the BATF and a Special Forces unit of the U.S. Army. Although some criticism has been directed at the communications plan, team leaders who were interviewed believed the system addressed operational needs and worked well.

The communications system consisted of secure radios and telephones, as well as cellular telephones. Additional equipment was located inside the Command Post at T.S.T.I. and the Forward Command Post at the undercover residence.

Basically, the communications net utilized a separate command channel, a channel for each of the three SRT teams and cover teams, and another for the helicopters and other support entities. Each SRT team member carried a secure handheld radio, and could communicate with other members of the same SRT and cover teams, as well as his team leader. In order to communicate with another team or other entities, he had to switch to the appropriate channel.

Team leaders carried two handheld radios with an earpiece in each ear, and could communicate on one radio with his SRT and cover teams, and to other team leaders and tactical command personnel on the other. The Deputy Tactical Coordinator at the Forward Command Post (undercover residence) acted as a relay point for communications to the helicopters, the Command Post at T.S.T.I., and all support entities, either directly or through a radio van which was staged for maximum communications capability.

Minor complaints from SRT personnel referred to the awkwardness of changing channels on their radios and, of course, the team leaders adjusting and manipulating two radios. While the BATF radios were secure, local agency communications were not. This undoubtedly explains the assertion by some area residents that they were able to monitor the operation on their scanners.

Although it would have been of future value to tape record all channels utilized during the operation, the radio van only had the capability of recording the command channel, and this was apparently done.

Intelligence Function

One of the recognized basic principles of intelligence is that tactical operations and intelligence are interdependent. Intelligence does not exist for its own sake, but to assist in executing operational missions (5:8).

Like any large-scale operation, planning for the service of search and arrest warrants at the Branch Davidian Compound relied heavily on intelligence sources. These sources included:

- Interviews of selected former cult members
- Other law enforcement agencies
- Undercover contacts
- Undercover surveillance
- Aerial photographs
- Criminal records checks
- Court documents
- Information from neighbors

In order to obtain the most pertinent information, planners prepared a list of thirty-eight questions to ask of former cult members. Responses were compared to confirm or refute information provided. The results of these interviews proved very beneficial, when supplemented by other sources, in developing the operational plan. Information from other sources was provided intermittently to planners through reports and documents screened by the assigned case agent and the Tactical Coordinator. Although an Intelligence Coordinator was assigned to the operation, as prescribed by the National Response Plan, this assignment was made during the latter stages of planning. Through no fault of the person assigned, he had little opportunity to contribute to the intelligence effort.

As the planning phase progressed, the most current information was provided by undercover personnel residing at a house across the road from the Compound. The undercover operation commenced on January 11, 1993, on a twenty-four-hour basis, with eight undercover agents assigned. According to those agents interviewed, initial instructions regarding their mission were minimal, and no supervisor was assigned to the house to oversee the operation. For this reason, undercover agents decided among themselves what information should be gathered and what work schedules should be followed. Agents rotated shifts, with four on-duty and four off. Periodic logs of activity were kept, and efforts were directed toward confirming or refuting information provided by former cult members. Logs and reports were forwarded to the case agent for review and dissemination. Surveillance of the Compound continued on a twenty-four-hour basis for two weeks, during which time David Koresh was never seen leaving the Compound. At the end of two weeks, undercover personnel decided on their own that there was nothing occurring at night to warrant surveillance. Accordingly, they agreed to watch the location only during the hours of daylight. It is important to note that tactical planners believed the undercover operation was being conducted twenty-four-hours a day, and relied upon information provided them on that basis.

Shifts and assignments were established and changed by the agents on a regular basis, and lacking any supervision or direction, it is to their credit that surveillance was conducted with any regularity at all.

Undercover agents were provided with 35mm cameras, lenses, and a video camera. Unfortunately, no one was familiar with the equipment, and the quality of the photographs taken reflected this lack of expertise. Complaints about the quality of the photos, which were developed primarily in Austin for security reasons, were not accompanied by suggestions for improvement. Requests for additional equipment, i.e., night vision equipment to replace an inoperable set provided initially, and technical support in other areas, proved fruitless. A "pole" camera placed on the property of a local resident was of negligible value, and had to be removed at the insistence of the property owner. No assistance or direction was forthcoming, and undercover agents began to feel isolated and neglected. As a result, surveillance became more and more sporadic.

After several weeks, and apparently in response to concerns about the undercover house, a superior from the Houston office visited the agents. Complaints were aired and a number of changes made. However, with the exception of placing increased emphasis on infiltrating the Compound, as directed by BATF Headquarters, these changes had little influence on the surveillance. Finally, a supervisor was assigned to oversee undercover activities. He seldom came to the undercover house, however, and basically became a point of contact and drop-off point for exposed film and reports at either the Command Post or an undercover safe house in Waco.

According to agents, cult members occasionally visited them. During the first visit, they inquired who the agents were and why they were staying at the house. Agents did not believe cult members were suspicious of them or their cover stories. The undercover agent who had met with David Koresh on several occasions inside the Compound shared this belief.

Two weeks prior to the raid, four of the undercover agents were removed, because of their assignment as part of the raid force. The four remaining agents sporadically surveilled the Compound through the day of the raid.

As mentioned earlier, intelligence and tactical operations are interrelated. The importance of this relationship in terms of operational success cannot be overemphasized. Establishment of the undercover surveillance operation to confirm information obtained from other sources certainly reflects concern for this relationship. Be that as it may, establishing an undercover operation without providing definite direction regarding objectives and expectations, and supervision to ensure acceptable compliance, demonstrates a lack of appreciation and understanding of the intelligence function. Undercover agents had every right to expect oversight guidance and feedback related to the usefulness of their efforts. When it wasn't received, their response in making decisions on their own was understandable, and should have been foreseen.

Any item of equipment provided should have been accompanied by instruction on its care and utilization. To expect acceptable results without ensuring agents are capable of operating the equipment is absurd.

Supervision of the undercover operation should have been an integral part of the assignment from its inception, and assurance given that whatever support was required by the agents would be provided as expeditiously as possible.

This seeming lack of understanding of the intelligence function can perhaps best be addressed in the future through in-service training at all levels likely to be involved in a full-scale tactical operation. Future operational planning might also make better use of divisional Intelligence Research Specialists (IRS), and their training modified to emphasize the interrelationship of intelligence and tactical operations. One of the intelligence-related issues disclosed during Congressional hearings on June 9-10, 1993, involved the use of electronic surveillance and listening devices. Those who testified from the BATF expressed doubt that approval would have been granted for such intrusions at the Compound. Whether or not this is true is for others to determine, but it goes without saying that such devices could have easily confirmed the raid on February 28 had been compromised. There is no doubt that additional information of potential tactical, as well as evidentiary value, could also have been obtained. Hopefully, as a result of both the Congressional inquiry and that conducted by the Waco Administrative Review, enabling legislation will be pursued (if indeed none exists) to prevent this problem from occurring in the future.

Briefing

One of the most important, but often neglected, elements of a successful warrant service is a comprehensive briefing. If conducted properly, a briefing can develop confidence in both the planners and the operation (1:147). Because of the extreme magnitude of Operation Trojan Horse, the duration of the investigation that preceded it, and the number of agents involved from different geographical areas, the task of making everyone aware of their duties and responsibilities was enormous. For the most part, the

Tactical Coordinator assumed this responsibility. Prior to the date of implementation, briefings were held for different entities at several locations, including Waco and Fort Hood.

Operational personnel (SRT and direct support) attended a number of briefings in conjunction with the rehearsal and training sessions at Fort Hood. Tactical briefings of SRT team members included visual aids, such as ground/aerial photographs, diagrams, and maps. Briefings were also conducted for support personnel at Fort Hood. It would appear from statements made that most of those who participated believed the briefings adequately addressed their questions and concerns.

Nonetheless, forward observers took exception to this belief. They reportedly received no specific direction regarding their mission, and were not invited to attend any briefings other than that held for support personnel. When two forward observers attempted to attend a meeting of SRT teams, they were told it wouldn't be necessary. A meeting which was supposed to take place between forward observers and SRT team leaders did not occur. Forward observers learned of the planned tactical deployment of the SRT teams by observing the rehearsal training, which they found helpful. Whether this unfortunate situation was an oversight or the result of unfamiliarity with the program is unknown, but it was certainly preventable.

One method of making certain that *all* participants are aware of their role and what is expected of them is to conduct a mandatory general briefing. This briefing should not replace separate specialized briefings, but rather supplement them by ensuring that everyone from a particular entity involved is aware of the general role and relationship of others in carrying out the operation. It was reported by one participant that there were many briefings conducted at Fort Hood, and if a person's concerns weren't addressed at one briefing, they would surely be discussed at another. Again, a comprehensive follow-up general briefing might have reduced the number of briefings required.

A printed briefing checklist or format can also be of benefit when the size of an operation requires conducting multiple briefings.

The importance of a comprehensive briefing in achieving operational success cannot be stressed too strongly. No matter how well an operation is planned, it is essential that participants be properly briefed regarding their role in its implementation.

Training/Rehearsal

The relationship between quality training and successful performance has been well established. From all indications, the training and rehearsal conducted over a three-day period at Fort Hood was well planned, relevant to the tasks required, and prepared those involved for the assignments they were to perform.

Fort Hood, Texas, was selected for training and rehearsal purposes because of the excellent quality of training sites and ranges there, as well as the security a military base would provide.

Personnel arrived at the base at staggered times and dates, but the majority were present for training on February 26 and 27. During briefing sessions, they were cautioned about operations security and admonished not to wear any law enforcement-identifiable articles of clothing when off the post. This was necessary because they were billeted on the post, but allowed to eat off post.

Much of the SRT training was conducted at the Military Operations in Urban Terrain (MOUT) site, which contained structures similar to those expected to be encountered. Following briefing, SRT teams practiced entry techniques, and later, each team rehearsed their particular roles in executing the plan. Loading and unloading of the cattle trailers were also rehearsed. Glass was inserted in window frames to enable team members who would be breaking windows to practice proper technique, and teams which would be deploying flash/sound diversionary devices (flashbangs) rehearsed proper deployment. Special Forces personnel at the site assisted in duplicating the floor plans of Compound buildings with marking tape to facilitate movement and deployment exercises, and generally assisted in creating as realistic an environment as possible.

Once support elements arrived, the entire raid force rehearsed loading and unloading the trailers and deploying to their assigned areas. Reportedly, after repetitive training, the raid force was able to exit the trailers in eight seconds. The truck/trailers were also driven the same distance as the Staging Area to the Compound to determine necessary driving time.

SRT team members who would be ascending ladders to the second-story roof practiced deploying and climbing them until their Team Leader was satisfied with timing and proficiency. Later, SRT team members test-fired their weapons. Forward observers zeroed their rifles for the distances within which they would be working, and agents who would be carrying AR-15 rifles were required to fire a qualification course.

The time spent at Fort Hood also provided an opportunity for the Tactical Coordinator and Team Leaders to review and refine the tactical plan. The general consensus of those participating in the training and rehearsal at Fort Hood was that it was very helpful, and adequately prepared them for the anticipated warrant service. SRT team leaders believed their teams were well prepared, and expressed some concern that they were overtrained.

COMMAND AND CONTROL

The term command describes the exercise of complete authority to direct the actions of others. It also describes those factors necessary to manage a crisis situation. Control is often confused with command, and while closely related, the two are considered inseparable by the military (11:12). It is not unusual for a person to be in command and not be in control. Conversely, it is possible for a person to be in control but not in command, due to the fact that it is not possible for a person in command to control every aspect of the tactical organization he directs This description is especially appropriate, because the issue of command and control is perhaps the most significant area of concern in evaluating the outcome of Operation Trojan Horse.

Decisions Impacting the Operation

While there were other problems of significance which occurred prior to the date of implementation (discussed elsewhere), they are eclipsed by the command decisions which were made, and not made, on the day of the operation. From the outset, it should be noted that nothing has been provided the evaluator which would reflect that command personnel performed unprofessionally, or with the intention of purposely hampering the safe conduct of the operation.

There is no doubt that command personnel were well-intentioned, dedicated professionals, and performed their duties and responsibilities within the limits of their capacity. However, research for this project revealed that they were not prepared, in terms of knowledge and experience, for the assignments they were called upon to perform. Once under way, the magnitude and size of the operation simply overwhelmed them, in spite of their extensive efforts to "make everything work".

Although other areas could be addressed here, the main emphasis will be placed upon decisions and actions which directly, rather than indirectly, affected the outcome of the operation.

- o When word was received from the undercover agent that David Koresh had received a telephone call, and apparently as a result of the call, announced he knew the ATF and National Guard were coming for him, the operation should have at least been delayed or postponed by the Incident Commander, because any chance of surprise had been lost.

- o The decision to proceed with haste based upon the belief that surprise wasn't necessary was ill advised. To have stood any chance of success without surprise, the raid force would have to have been positioned at the Compound ready to proceed the minute Koresh was alerted to the raid.

○ The fact that continuing surveillance revealed no activity outside the Compound prior to, and during, the movement of the raid force from the Staging Area should have been viewed as significant, since the separation of the men from the arms room was critical to the safe conduct of the raid. The operation should have been aborted by the Tactical Coordinator while enroute to the Compound, if not before.

○ The observation of two press vehicles in close proximity to the Compound while the raid force was enroute, when combined with the report of inactivity outside the Compound, should have confirmed the obvious. The operation had been compromised, and the raid should have been aborted by the Tactical Coordinator.

○ The Deputy Tactical Coordinator should have questioned the initial decision to proceed with the operation, based upon his personal interview of the undercover agent, the inactivity outside the Compound, and his observation of press vehicles on the farm road in front of the Compound. Following the decision to proceed, since he had abort authority, the Deputy Tactical Coordinator should have encouraged the Tactical Coordinator to abort the mission while the raid force was enroute to the Compound.

○ The fact that the described observations were all reported by the Deputy Tactical Coordinator to the Command Post at T.S.T.I. did not relieve him from the responsibility of questioning what should have been viewed as an inappropriate and hasty decision.

○ SRT Team Leaders should have questioned the Tactical Coordinator's orders to proceed with the raid, based upon his announcement that the Davidians knew they were coming. The Team Leaders, above all others, knew the importance of surprise in safely carrying out their mission.

○ The Incident and Deputy Incident Commanders should have remained at the T.S.T.I. Command Post, as provided in the operational plan. They should not have accompanied the helicopters. By so doing, they seriously reduced their decision-making ability at a critical time, and effectively eliminated their access by subordinate supervisors. The fact that the command helicopter was struck by gunfire from the Compound and forced to land in an adjacent field, confirms this point.

o   The Tactical Coordinator should have been located inside the Forward Command Post. Because he was probably the most knowledgeable of the entire operation, his ability to recognize significant activities at the Compound and act upon them could have been invaluable. In addition, this location would have removed him from the additional pressures created by accompanying the raid force.

o   The Deputy Tactical Coodinator should have been assigned to accompany the raid force. This would have placed a high level of supervision with the raid force and, in conjunction with the Tactical Coordinator, facilitated any decisions that may have been required while enroute or following their arrival at the Compound.

o   The decision to abandon the Compound once dead and wounded agents had been evacuated was unprecedented within the evaluator's experience. Doing so caused confusion, frustration, and embarrassment to agents involved, and created the risk that cult members might escape into the City of Waco and elsewhere, endangering the lives of those with whom they came in contact. At the very least, forward observer positions should have been maintained and reinforced, perhaps with an APC which had been provided by the National Guard, to contain the situation until additional armored vehicles could be brought in to further strengthen the positions.

o   The Tactical Coordinator assumed more responsibility throughout the operation than could reasonably be managed. Although some areas were delegated to others, it seems apparent in retrospect that he was overburdened with details that should have been the responsibility of others.

o   The decision not to effect service of the search warrant at the "Mag Bag" posed a potential threat to personnel manning the roadblock at the intersection of Loop 340 and Farm Road 2491. It is fortunate that the armed occupants chose to make an attempt to join fellow cult members at the Compound, rather than engage roadblock personnel in a gunfight. As related elsewhere, one of the three was killed after engaging special agents elsewhere while enroute to the Compound, and two were taken into custody.

Since the subsequent end of the siege at the Branch Davidian Compound on April 19, 1993, it has often, and understandably, been asked, why, considering everything that happened prior to the attempted service of warrants at the Compound, would anyone even entertain thoughts of proceeding with the operation? Certainly, all command level personnel wanted the operation to succeed. Then why did they fail to recognize what now seems so obvious? A few possible explanations include the following:

- The scope and magnitude of the operation were unprecedented and overwhelming.

- The collective lack of experience in crisis management and tactical operations made the decision-making process more difficult.

- The large accumulation of manpower and resources created an instinctive reluctance to cancel, postpone or abort the operation.

- The lack of another planned alternative if the raid was aborted, i.e., contain and negotiate, caused a built-in reluctance to cancel the operation.

- The belief that something had to be done to resolve the continuing situation at the Compound.

Whether any or all of these explanations played a role in the decision to proceed may never be known. However, regardless of their well-intentioned reasoning, it can be said that decision makers took a calculated risk which did not succeed.

Finally, it must be recognized that what now appears obvious may not have been so apparent under the pressures of command.

Organization and Structure

When conducting an operational analysis, it is always easiest to identify a deficiency and attribute it to an individual. Unfortunately, doing so fails to address why the deficiency existed in the first place. In the case of Operation Trojan Horse, it is suggested that the root cause lies within the organization itself, specifically the manner in which command personnel are assigned to tactical operations.

As prescribed by the BATF National Response Plan, whenever a sector (comprised of three or more SRTs) is activated for an operation, certain organizational requirements are mandated. Specifically, the Special Agent In Charge (SAC) of the division within which the incident occurs is designated the Incident Commander. Other SACs of divisions within the sector are required to provide SRT and other support, and one SAC is designated the Deputy Incident Commander.

The position of Tactical Coordinator is designated by the Incident Commander, and he is required to have completed SRT training. The Tactical Coordinator is assisted by a designated Deputy Tactical Coordinator, who must also be SRT trained. In addition, a Support Coordinator is designated by the Incident Commander, and he in turn is authorized to designate subordinate positions to assist him; i.e., Intelligence Coordinator, Logistical Support Supervisor, etc. The basic duties and responsibilities of each of the positions described above, as well as those of Headquarters superior and subordinate personnel, are contained within the National Response Plan.

This organizational (Command and Control) concept is similar in many respects to that utilized by the majority of civilian law enforcement agencies, and, it is submitted, responsible for a myriad of problems which have and continue to adversely affect tactical operations. If most law enforcement officers at an operational level were to be asked what consistently caused the greatest difficulty or failure of a tactical operation in which they were involved, the overwhelming response would be decisions made, or not made, by command personnel. This unfortunate impediment to success in tactical operations is not necessarily prompted by an organizational concept. Some organizational structures are better than others, and it should be recognized that the BATF model is better than most, though ponderous in some areas.

Rather, the problem is caused by personnel who are assigned to critical command positions by policies that direct the designation because of rank, and not ability. Assigning command personnel in this manner presumes that all persons of the rank required to fill the position are equally knowledgeable, experienced, and capable. This unfortunate, and often destructive, assumption is made almost universally within the organizational structure of American law enforcement. There is no intention on the part of the evaluator to imply that all command personnel assigned to direct tactical operations are unqualified and incapable of so doing. This would be an absurd implication. But by the same token, some command personnel, though highly capable and effective within other areas of law enforcement operations, may find it difficult, if not impossible, to function effectively within the tactical environment, where life and death decisions may have to be made with little consultation and time for contemplation. Instead, the evaluator's intention is to strongly suggest that only those command personnel who are qualified by virtue of training and experience and possess the proven ability to make decisions under pressure be utilized to direct tactical operations. To do otherwise is to increase both risk and liability, to say nothing of inviting disaster.

Fortunately, the incidence of tragedy and failure of tactical operations has been remarkably low. But, oftentimes, success has sadly been achieved in spite of command, not because of it. These are admittedly strong words. However, they are uttered not out of ignorance, but instead out of sincere concern, rooted in many years of experience at both the operational and command levels of tactical operations. Of all the decisions which are made during crisis situations, none has more impact on a successful resolution than the selection of the commander. It is this person who will set the tone and tempo for the actions which are to follow (11:10).

It would be unfair to be critical of the existing BATF concept without offering alternative solutions. Consequently, the following suggestions for organizational and structural improvement are offered for consideration.

1. Develop a cadre of command personnel, presumably, but not necessarily, at the SAC level who are trained in crisis management and SRT operations, hopefully experienced (within or outside of BATF), and whose decision-making ability under pressure is proven.
In the event of a sector operation, and presuming the affected SAC is not a member of the cadre, a SAC who is a member would be assigned as the Incident Commander. The non-cadre SAC would assume the role of Deputy Incident Commander, and any other sector SACs would have no command responsibility or assignment. Note: The temptation to allow unassigned sector SACs to participate as observers at the Command Post, or elsewhere, should be avoided. Their presence could have an adverse effect on the decision-making process, and encourage the practice of "decision by committee", which, in the opinion of the evaluator, has little, if any, place in law enforcement tactical operations. The obvious possibility of friction occurring between the assigned Incident Commander and the SAC of the affected division must be anticipated, and dealt with through tact and diplomacy. Hopefully, as the benefits of the concept are realized, acceptance will result.

2. Develop a similar cadre, presumably, but not necessarily, at the ASAC level to staff the position of Tactical Coordinator. The same training required of the Incident Command cadre would be required of this group, but special emphasis should be placed upon tactical operations.
The procedure for assigning these personnel would be identical to that described for the assignment of Incident Commanders.

Following initial training, both groups would be required to participate in formal in-service training, at least quarterly.

Suggestions 1 and 2 presume the retention of division SRTs as presently constituted.

3. Develop full-time SRT teams at the sector level. These multi-functional teams would respond according to specific written criteria, and all division offices would be mandated to request their services if the planned operation met the stated criteria. Sector teams *would not* assume the day-to-day responsibilities carried out by division SRT teams. The teams would possess their own chain of command, including staffing the positions of Incident Commander and Tactical Coordinator during activations. The affected division SAC would assume the role of Deputy Incident Commander, and logically, his personnel would staff support positions.

    Full-time sector teams would be equipped with all contemporary weapons and logistics believed necessary to carry out their assigned mission. Their munitions inventory would include flash/sound diversionary devices and a full range of chemical agents, as well as other less-lethal devices. Teams would be required to train a minimum of twenty-five percent of their on-duty time (generally, once each week). This concept would include integrated negotiation, EMS, and forward observer (countersniper) capabilities. In major metropolitan areas, where sector teams might be required to respond, agreements should be reached with civilian law enforcement teams to reduce the possibility of friction or jurisdictional disputes.

    Implementation of full-time sector SRT teams would undoubtedly impact existing divisional teams. Although the intention of this suggestion is not to eliminate divisional teams, availability of acceptable personnel to staff six sector teams may well require the dissolution of most. Were this to occur, affected divisions would undoubtedly find it necessary to rely upon local law enforcement teams for assistance in handling those situations not justifying the request of a sector team — much as they have done in the past.

Whether or not this concept is adopted, all SACs and ASACs should receive comprehensive training in tactically related crisis management. Division SRT teams not dissolved in the adoption of the full-time sector team concept should be allocated additional training time to equal at least two times per month. Of course, if the full-time concept is not adopted, then all division teams should receive the additional training time.

The sophistication and perishable nature of skills necessary to perform effectively within the contemporary tactical environment require that adequate time be allotted for their maintenance. Training conducted twice each month should be considered the absolute minimum.

The practice of maintaining an SRT team within one division, supervised by a Team Leader from another should be reviewed. Although nothing was originally developed to indicate this is posing a problem, there is a possibility that it could in the future. It is presumed this situation developed because of a void of interested or qualified personnel within the affected divisions. Assigning a Team Leader from another division places that person in the position of not being able to directly influence his team, except during the minimal training time presently allotted, and actual deployment. In addition, the caseload at his division of assignment would add to the difficulties of supervising and directing team activities.

Also, as a part of the overall review of the SRT program, it may be of benefit to evaluate the existing selection criteria, as well as the SRT training curriculum, to ensure they are in line with contemporary law enforcement tactical team standards.

Lastly, it is strongly suggested that SRT Team Leaders and Tactical Coordinators, under either the present or modified/new system, meet at least annually with their counterparts from other Federal agencies. These meetings could be hosted by a different agency each session, and that agency's members would be responsible for organizing the program and scheduling presenters. These meetings would ensure that teams share information, develop enhanced interagency cooperation, and remain contemporary within the field of tactical operations. It is important that guest speakers from civilian law enforcement teams be periodically included as presenters, so that attendees can share in their experience and expertise as well.

Many additional factors and details would have to be addressed prior to implementing either of the programs suggested, but it should be emphasized that command and control issues must be viewed as critical if maximum effectiveness is to be realized. Adoption of any of the suggestions noted would, of course, require changes and modifications to the existing BATF National Response Plan.

OPERATIONS SECURITY

The concept of Operations Security, or OPSEC, was defined and labeled during the Vietnam conflict. Whether applied formally or informally, OPSEC is a process of looking at specific programs or operations from the perspective of an adversary. Operations security is threat driven. Therefore, if there are no perceived threats, there are no perceived vulnerabilities, and the OPSEC process is not needed (6:19).

Like other governmental agencies, i.e., FBI, Secret Service, etc., the BATF subscribes to the OPSEC concept, and has used it in the past. The unprecedented scope of Operation Trojan Horse clearly called for the implementation of the OPSEC concept at all levels and phases of the operation. However, it would appear that while everyone involved in planning and preparation believed in and supported the OPSEC process, the magnitude and requirements of the operation often caused other priorities to take precedence. The most critical information to be protected during Operation Trojan Horse was, of course, the fact that the BATF was going to effect service of search and arrest warrants at the Branch Davidian Compound at a particular date and time. The following list of possible indicators from which the Branch Davidians or their supporters could have predicted the intended actions of the BATF expose deficiencies in the application of OPSEC principles:

- **The lodging of all support personnel in Waco.**
  Even though personnel were scheduled to arrive at staggered dates and times, the possibility of local residents, hotel, and other business people noticing the influx was presumably high. The City of Waco (population over 103,000) is certainly large enough to absorb the number of support personnel lodged there, especially since a number of hotels were used. Be that as it may, their presence, combined with other indicators, may have increased detection of the impending warrant service. Perhaps some of the support personnel could have been lodged south of Waco, in Temple, Texas.

- **Departure of the raid force from Fort Hood.**
  As mentioned elsewhere in this report, the long line of government and rental cars moving in convoy caused great concern to those involved in operational planning. Buses could have been used to reduce, if not eliminate, this concern. If for some reason this was not possible, vehicles should have been incrementally scheduled to depart Fort Hood.

- **Selection of the Bellmead Staging Area.**
  Although the Bellmead site was spacious, convenient, and comfortable, the accumulation of vehicles, both during arrival and after, combined with personnel dressed in tactical uniforms, had to peak the interest of anyone who observed these activities. While it is not known if those who saw

the activity at the Staging Area were Branch Davidian members or supporters, the fact remains that this information could have found its way to the Compound, or at the very least, local media. The utilization of bus transportation from Fort Hood might have reduced congestion at the Bellmead site, but as suggested earlier, an area adjacent to the T.S.T.I. Command Post might have been more secure.

- **Briefing at the Waco Best Western Hotel.**
  The briefing conducted at the Best Western Hotel the evening of February 27, 1993, was attended by an estimated 75-100 personnel representing Federal, state, and local agencies. The location of the site, and the number of personnel and agencies attending, would seem to reflect a high risk of detection. Operations security might have been better served by scheduling the briefing at a law enforcement or other government facility.

- **Multi-agency involvement.**
  There is always a risk of an inadvertent or intentional breach of security when multiple agencies become involved in a joint operation. This is not to say that local law enforcement or civilian support agencies in Waco were untrustworthy. The intent is only to identify possibilities.

- **Meetings with the media.**
  The area of media involvement will be addressed separately in this report. However, suffice it to say that meetings held with the Waco Tribune-Herald were a calculated risk that violated operations security.

- **FAA airspace restriction.**
  The evaluator has no knowledge of BATF or National Guard policy relative to the restriction of airspace prior to an operation. If policy requires restriction, then it was necessarily followed. However, lacking a policy requirement, it is suggested that airspace should not have been restricted. The published restriction of airspace in an area as rural as that in which the Compound was located would seem to unnecessarily increase suspicion in the minds of local pilots. In point of fact, one of the cult members was a pilot.

- **Counter-intelligence capabilities of David Koresh.**
  Though perhaps not possessing a formal counter-intelligence network, there seems little doubt that David Koresh had the capability to gather intelligence from cult members outside the Compound, as well as supporters. This capability undoubtedly included the use of computers.

It is well established that the rural mailman, a cult member himself, was an often-used source of information.

- **Contacts with local businesses.**
  The influx of support personnel into the Waco area created a corresponding necessity for them to utilize local facilities, i.e., restaurants, cocktail lounges, markets, etc. Although they were cautioned about the need for operations security, it is possible that suspicion could have been created in the minds of local patrons by something said, or not said, by support personnel. The same can be said for local law enforcement and civilian support personnel, who may have confided information to friends or relatives.

By reviewing the indicators listed previously from the perspective of an adversary, it can readily be seen that the existence of effective operations security for Operation Trojan Horse was highly unlikely.

It is apparent that improvement in the area of OPSEC is necessary to increase the chance of success in future sensitive operations.

MEDIA INVOLVEMENT

Law enforcement activities comprise a significant portion of information released by the press, and recent large-scale incidents, including Operation Trojan Horse, have generated a great deal of concern over how the media covers these events. Today, networks have the technological capability to present events live — any time, any place. The electronic media in the United States live or die by their ratings. As a result, each network wants to be the first with the most on any big story (12:15).

It goes without saying that there must be a cooperative effort on the part of both law enforcement and the media to provide basic information to the public without glorifying the perpetrators of crime, jeopardizing the public safety, or compromising tactical operations.

In the recent past, the BATF initiated a program of selectively inviting the news media to accompany their personnel on warrant services. This was done in the spirit of cooperation to improve and maintain a positive relationship with the press. Long-term, sensitive investigations requiring tightly controlled security to decrease the chance of compromise were the exception. In these situations, the media representatives were made aware of the operation following its conclusion. This was the posture taken by the BATF for Operation Trojan Horse. A Public Information Officer assigned for that purpose would be responsible for preparing a press release at the conclusion of the operation, and notifying appropriate print and electronic media.

Unfortunately, late in the investigation it became known that the Waco Tribune-Herald newspaper was preparing to release a seven-part article on David Koresh, his followers, and their activities. Concerned that these articles, depending upon their content, might compromise the operation, or at least cause David Koresh to become more suspicious, the decision was made to contact the newspaper in an attempt to persuade them to delay publication of the articles. The first meeting with the Tribune-Herald proved of little value, because the BATF mistakenly believed the newspaper was amenable to delaying the story. A subsequent meeting a few days before the planned raid proved equally unproductive. The Incident Commander was basically told that the seven-part article would be published as soon as it was ready, and that the most important issue was the "public's right to know." The position of the Waco Tribune-Herald in refusing to delay publication is difficult to justify. They must have realized the calculated risk BATF was taking by confiding in them to begin with, and since one of their complaints was that law enforcement was doing nothing to deal with the problems at the Compound, logic would dictate they would want to cooperate. Waiting until the warrants were served at the Compound could only strengthen the story when it was published. Their reliance on the well-worn adage of the "public's right to know" is without substance. They were not being asked to withhold information from the public, only to delay providing it in the interest of safety, both of the agents involved and cult members.

Interestingly, in an editorial published by the Tribune-Herald as a supplement to their reprint of the original seven-part article, the Editor admitted the newspaper received information from a "confidential source" on Saturday, February 27, that the ATF raid would take place on Sunday, February 28. He then went on to deny the rumor that someone at the paper had alerted the Davidians about the raid on February 28 (13). It is unfortunate that this issue cannot be explored further. However, pending litigation precludes additional discussion of the Herald-Tribune's possible role in the outcome of Operation Trojan Horse.

In retrospect, it seems apparent that the contacts with the Tribune-Herald should not have been made. As a result of media involvement before, during, and subsequent to Operation Trojan Horse, and allegations of media notification prior to the raid, the need for a review of the BATF press policy is evident.

Previously, the necessity for cooperation between law enforcement and the media was emphasized. It must also be emphasized that cooperation, by definition, involves a joint effort on the part of the involved entities. In the opinion of the evaluator, if law enforcement must concede to the media the unrestrained First Amendment right to freedom of the press, then the media should concede that they will exercise this right in a responsible way. Unfortunately, as Katherine Graham, Chairman of the Board of the Washington Post Company, said during an address before the American Newspaper Publishers Association in 1986, "high standards of professionalism do not guide every media organization nor every reporter." "And," she continued, "I regret to say that once one of these less scrupulous or less careful people reports some piece of information, all the media feel compelled to follow. Thus it is true: The least responsible person involved in the process could determine the level of coverage."

It would seem that, while the public certainly does have a right to know, whomever is charged with determining what the public is told (and it is usually the media) ought to make this determination in a responsible manner, with due consideration for the safety and well being of those affected. As Katherine Graham concluded, "I believe having experienced people at the helm, exercising sound judgment on the basis of high professional standards, is the best we can ask for. But I also believe it is all we should ask for."

Chapter 3

CONCLUSIONS AND RECOMMENDATIONS

CONCLUSIONS

The results of this project are believed to support the following conclusions:

1. BATF personnel involved in planning Operation Trojan Horse were dedicated, experienced law enforcement professionals.

2. Much time and effort was expended in planning and preparing for Operation Trojan Horse.

3. Planners relied upoand trusted intelligence information which, in many cases, lacked corroboration.

4. A lack of knowledge existed on the part of both command and operational personnel concerning the proper utilization and deployment of countersniper (Forward Observer Team) personnel.

5. Insufficient attention was directed by command personnel to the Operations Security (OPSEC) process.

6. There was an apparent lack of supervision over the intelligence gathering mechanism in terms of direction, coordination, corroboration, dissemination and control.

7. Though well intentioned, contacts initiated by command personnel with the **Waco Tribune-Herald** violated basic principles of operations security.

8. No media contacts should have been initiated by BATF before the operation's conclusion.

9. Command personnel lacked experience and training in directing major tactical operations.

10. The Incident Commander should have been located at the designated command post to facilitate communication and control.

11. Once information had been received and corroborated that the operation had

been compromised through the loss of surprise, command personnel should have aborted the mission.

12. There was no planned alternative course of action to be taken if the mission was aborted.

13. Following the negotiation of a cease fire to remove and evacuate the dead and wounded, perimeter positions should not have been abandoned until relief personnel had assumed them.

14. Had the operation not been compromised, there was a high probability that the tactical plan would have succeeded.

15. Sufficient oversight was exercised by BATF Headquarters during all phases of Operation Trojan Horse.

16. Numerous acts of heroism were displayed by the men and women of the BATF during, and subsequent to, the extensive firefight with the Branch Davidians.

RECOMMENDATIONS

The conclusions addressed above are believed to constitute justification for considering the following recommendations:

1. Assign personnel to command positions (Incident Commander, Tactical Coordinator, Deputy Tactical Coordinator) based upon qualifications — not rank or position.

2. Develop and provide tactical crisis management training for those assigned to these positions.

3. Explore the feasibility of selecting and training an on-call cadre of personnel with proven decision-making and leadership ability to assume the roles of Incident Commander and Tactical Coordinator.

4. Ensure that all command and supervisory personnel understand their joint responsibility to abort an operation if circumstances justify doing so.

5. Increase the training time of Division Special Response Teams to a minimum of twice a month.

6. Explore the feasibility of establishing regional, full-time Special Response Teams for deployment during major operations.

7. Review and modify, as necessary, the criteria for selecting Special Response Team members.

8. Review and modify, as necessary, the curriculum of Special Response Team training.

9. Establish a Tactical Emergency Medical Support (TEMS) program and formally assign EMS-trained personnel to each Special Response Team.

10. Develop and implement a hostage negotiation program as an integral part of Special Response Team operations.

11. Evaluate existing Special Response Team equipment based on contemporary standards within the tactical community (to include chemical agents).

12. Review the organization, structure, and functions of the Technology and Tactical Issues Committee to ensure the timely evaluation and approval of tactical equipment and procedures.

13. Conduct meetings, at least annually, of Federal special operations team leaders and command personnel (BATF, FBI, Marshals, Customs) to discuss past tactical analyses and contemporary procedures. Emphasize necessity for interagency cooperation and training.

14. Ensure familiarity with guidelines related to requesting and utilizing air support.

15. Review and modify, as necessary, OPSEC training for all command and operational personnel.

16. Review and modify the media notification process.

17. Review and modify the BATF National Response Plan.

18. Pursue legislation enabling electronic surveillance and monitoring under circumstances such as existed at the Branch Davidian Compound.

19. Empanel a committee comprised of representatives from affected BATF

entities to review these and other recommendations made by the Tactical Advisory Expert Panel.

The purpose of objectively analyzing any tactical incident is not to be critical of another agency's performance, but rather to learn from what occurred. The death of a comrade demands that our coordinated efforts be directed toward reducing the recurrence of similar tragedies. Certainly, the analysis which forms the basis of this report was conducted with the utmost care to ensure this belief was not violated. Hopefully, the results of this and other inquiries will provide enlightened guidance, rather than restrictive policies and procedures.

Lastly, the extensive effort expended in preparing this report is sincerely dedicated to the brave men and women of the BATF, who found themselves at the Branch Davidian Compound on February 28, 1993, under the gravest of circumstances.

REFERENCES

BOOKS

1. Kolman, John A. <u>A Guide to the Development of Special Weapons and Tactics Teams</u>. Springfield, Ill.: Charles C Thomas, Publisher, 1982.

2. Plaster, John L. Maj. <u>The Ultimate Sniper</u>. Boulder, Colo.: Paladin Press, 1993.

3. Roberts, Wes. <u>Leadership Secrets of Atilla The Hun</u>. New York: Warner Books, Inc., 1987.

GOVERNMENT PUBLICATIONS

4. International Association of Chiefs of Police. <u>A Compilation of Model Policies</u>, Hostage/Barricaded Subject Incidents; Concepts and Issues paper. Alexandria, Va.: I.A.C.P. 1991.

PERIODICALS

5. Ishimoto, Wade. "Intelligence Support of SWAT Operations", <u>The Tactical Edge</u>, (Winter, 1984), 7-11.

6. Keith, Ed. "Operations Security in the Tactical Environment", <u>The Tactical Edge</u>, (Summer, 1993), 19-22.

7. Rasumoff, David, M.D., and Carmona, Richard, M.D. "Inside The Perimeter", <u>The Tactical Edge</u>, (Winter, 1990), 56.

8. Rasumoff, David, M.D., and Carmona, Richard, M.D. "Essentials of Tactical Emergency Medical Support", <u>The Tactical Edge</u>, (Summer, 1990), 55.

9. Tate, Jerry. "ATF's SRT Program", <u>The Tactical Edge</u>, (Spring, 1993), 38-41.

UNPUBLISHED WORKS

10. Higgins, Stephen E. Testimony before the U.S. House of Representatives Committee on Appropriations Subcommittee on Treasury, Postal Service, and General Government. June 9 and 10, 1993.

11. Heal, Sid. "A Scientific Approach to Tactical Decisions". Unpublished Independent Study Project, California State Polytechnic University at Pomona, 1993.

NEWSPAPERS

12. Graham, Katherine. "Terrorism and the Media", <u>Los Angeles Daily Journal, Daily Journal Report</u>, May 2, 1986, 10-16.

13. Lott, Bob. "Serving our obligation to a free society", <u>Waco Tribune-Herald</u>, February 27 - March 1, 1993, follow-up coverage, March - May, 1993.

A Tactical Analysis
of the
Bureau of Alcohol, Tobacco & Firearms

Raid of The Branch Davidian Compound
in Waco, Texas

Prepared By
George Morrison

PREFACE

Although my role in the Waco Administrative Review (the "Review") was limited to performing a critical assessment of the entry plan and the process that created it, I am satisfied that the Review's conduct of this aspect of the investigation was thorough, professional and objective. I was provided with all documents and assistance that I requested. I was also given access to those individuals who developed the plan. It is my assumption that the specific issues and details relative to the investigation of Mr. David Koresh and the cult Branch Davidian compound and the decision to conduct a tactical raid of the facility outside Waco, Texas, are thoroughly revealed by the Treasury Department investigation team report. Further, I assume the specific actions and participation by personnel of the B.A.T.F. and other persons germane to the case investigation, intelligence task, planning and tactics involved in this incident are thoroughly documented by the investigation team report.

The six "Central Issues To Be Addressed By Waco Review" that was provided to each of the tactical experts focused on the raid as to preparation, execution, and post incident action. To address those issues the investigation and analysis required consideration of B.A.T.F. policy, procedures and organizational structure in place at the time of the raid. Preliminary analysis revealed the need to further expand the investigative scope, analysis and research to include the supervisory and management "mind set" and individual awareness of contemporary law enforcement standards, i.e. standard operating procedures and accepted levels of management/organization performance currently utilized in United States law enforcement.

The rational for expanding the investigation and for acquiring documents relating to policy, procedure, training and organization was to learn how such an apparent major investigation and high profile/high risk forced entry arrest/search warrant raid received only minimal management review, oversight and control.

The immediate issue became: Who approved the operation and by what incident command methodology?

> NOTE: My first concern was to ask for the arrest and search warrant affidavits to see whether the facts were supported in the court documents. The second concern was that if the court documents described the dangerous and exigent conditions described in the initial briefings by the Review, how did the raid approval proceed without greater management review and acceptable standards of command and control?

After additional preliminary inquiry and research by the Review it was clear that the Review's concerns were the same as mine. Brave and dedicated B.A.T.F. agents and supervisors were allowed or directed to go in harm's way by substantial management and organizational deficiencies and in some cases, an abdication of authority and responsibility by mid and top level managers.

SUMMARY

The incident of the February 28, 1993, raid in Waco, by the B.A.T.F. focused national attention on Mr. David Koresh, the cult Branch Davidian, and federal law enforcement. Fifty days after the unsuccessful and personally tragic raid conducted by the B.A.T.F., the standoff between the cult leadership and federal law enforcement concluded in an abortive assault and a virtually all-consuming fire of the cult structure(s). The subsequent critique, investigation and analysis of what occurred immediately before and during the B.A.T.F. raid were conducted separately and without the benefit of personal and physical evidence from within the cult and cult compound. The current criminal investigation and trial will add some insight as to the actions of cult members during the raid, but will not substantially change the Review's documentation of the case investigation and raid plan and execution.

In retrospect, there are several obvious critical concerns regarding the raid plan and execution. The analysis of those concerns is factually and emotionally impacted by the tragic 28 injuries and 4 deaths of B.A.T.F. agents who demonstrated courage and resolve when confronted by superior firepower and a tactical reaction from the cult members not anticipated by the raid plan.

Perhaps the primary concern is why the raid in the first place? The question goes to the core issue of the incident review. What was the role of B.A.T.F. management in the investigative and intelligence gathering process leading up to the point where a decision was made to tactically and dynamically serve an arrest\search warrant? And, although not the primary charge of the post incident investigation, why the apparent absence of case management standards and audits which critically impacted the raid planning?

The investigation readily identified substantial personnel and operational component breakdowns in several areas of day to day B.A.T.F. operations. Whether in or out of the context of the raid, a management/organization audit of B.A.T.F. would be in order because of the expanding operations and role the B.A.T.F. has undertaken in the last five to ten years. The investigation and review of the Waco incident supports the propriety of a directive from Treasury for a strategic plan and (in the process) "accountability charting" for personnel and entities within the B.A.T.F.

The actual Koresh case development and review resulted in an investigative report that did not pursue or produce an acceptable level of intelligence and case investigation follow-up and verification. Those deficiencies were aggravated by a "selective investigation information summary" which was submitted to the planners as "accurate and complete."

The absence of appropriate supervisory and management level review for the raid plan indicated weak B.A.T.F. policy and procedure and no definition of responsibility and authority. Probably the two most critical observations were:
1.) the absence of evidence that a deliberate and knowledgeable management review was made to determine the appropriateness and exigent conditions(s) for a raid (as opposed to alternatives), and
2.) the absence of evidence of a "buy off" of the actual raid plan.

The critique of the raid plan requires a diligent research and analysis of B.A.T.F. policy and procedure specifically as applied to supervision and management. To isolate on the planning efforts and actions of tactical teams members (and S.R.T.s) out of context of the B.A.T.F.'s bureau "management environment" adversely impacts analysis and support for change recommendations.

CASE MANAGEMENT AND DAILY ACTIVITIES

The volume of investigations and the expansion of missions indicates the need for a top level strategy session to insure that the B.A.T.F. organizational structure can control the activities of the field agents. The Bureau's activities, expectations and daily performance of personnel appear to have exceeded the ability of the existing management and organization structure to properly audit, inspect, supervise and manage. The apparent unregulated and unaudited autonomy of S.A.I.C.s allows excessive span of control and lack of accountability.

>   NOTE: This was clearly evident by the work load allowed and self imposed on the A/SAC Houston.

When this occurs on the basic and routine Bureau mission it can be corrected, but it can become exaggerated in non-routine and emergency operations. I firmly believe consideration of a secondary or emergency organization modification should be advanced as a recommendation for management realignment in major case investigations or major tactical missions.

THE RAID PLAN

Specifically, the raid plan did not establish or provide for adequate **communications, command** and **control**. The **logistic** support was arbitrarily limited, denied or inadequate for the mission objective. The tactical plan lacked **contingency planning**, counter measures, **readiness control** and **abort** conditions **recognition**. These observations are based on information known to the raid planners and the acknowledged management review and approval chain.

COMMAND AND CONTROL

The absence of an actual command and control concept and structure in and of itself contributed more to the tragic results of the raid than any other aspect of the plan and actions of the 48 hours leading up to and including the raid and the 8 hours immediately after the "cease-fire". The operational standards for "tactical raid-high risk" require an effective, conditioned and flexible command and control function to **manage** the incident plan, execution and recovery. Operation standards, **if understood and utilized by a qualified command** would have aborted the plan (as allegedly prepared and approved--and as "extracted" from witness interviews by the investigative team) at any one of several **"red flags"** prior to the committed point.

The raid plan as submitted to the Review and as enhanced by interviews indicated a disjointed assembly of component tactics and logistic support that was not reviewed by all the key players and decision makers.

> CRITICAL ISSUE: There was no single briefing for all the supervisors of each raid component, e.g., aviation, logistics, intelligence. Therefore, no chance to ask questions or clarify information presented.

The communications net established for the raid was untested and as designed did not support the alleged command and control This defect was evident to the commanders before the raid commitment. It was underscored during the fire fight and withdrawal. The command element did not know what was occurring tactically prior, during or after withdrawal commenced.

The element of surprise was <u>totally</u> lost prior to raid commitment and was known to command. To compound the strategic aspect of loss by surprise, the raid plan was not followed with regard to:
1.) **diversion element** (helicopters were not on station) 2.) **forward observation** posts/counter snipers (posts were not in position to report or cover) 3.) **airborne observation** and communication (communications ineffective and not on station, and

4.) **departure from time table** (advanced without concurrent countermeasures and "red light" parameters to abort).

In spite of the raid plan organization chart (National Response Plan) **NO ONE PERSON WAS IN CHARGE**. Mission leadership was compromised by this critical breakdown in the standard concept of command and control.

INTELLIGENCE

Intelligence was compromised from the start point of the investigation up to and including the hour before the raid and the ability of the command structure to effect a withdrawal and containment of the incident site. The critical points of intelligence control centered on the absence of analysis, management review and operational continuity. The absence of operational intelligence continuity negatively impacted the raid and the withdrawal of the dead and injured.

   NOTE: The absence of management review led to a serious breach of integrity...falsification of documents.

The selection of improperly trained and conditioned personnel for the intelligence function and the failure to debrief them negatively impacted case preparation, raid planning and raid execution.

The tactical team leaders went into the raid blind as to activity and conditions. Critical operational intelligence was "inadvertently" denied to raid planners.

NOTE: I will differ to TAG member Wade Ishimoto for an in-depth advisor's analysis and recommendation to correct the intelligence issues.

LOGISTICS

The logistics problems connected to the raid were evident prior to initial planning. The SRT mission was compromised by B.A.T.F. "policy" and a lack of adequate equipment. "Policy" must have a provision for <u>reasonable</u> and <u>top management approved</u> exceptions, e.g. use of automatic weapons, diversion grenades, chemical agents and armored vehicles. Special incident managers must be trained **to ask** for available equipment necessary to successfully and safely complete a mission. That is **their duty** and responsibility and **should be in writing if necessary**. Management review then has the <u>hard choice</u> to approve or deny <u>and</u> to accept responsibility and accountability for the decision which can include modification of the tactical plan! That was not done in preparation for Waco; there was compromise after compromise.

The **arbitrary decision** not to use Customs Service aircraft and instead use Texas National Guard helicopters was a disaster in and of itself. Customs aviation resources and experienced personnel were ideally suited for this mission and could have contributed substantially to the plan.

NOTE: That action further reinforces two observations. 1.) That the raid plan was disjointed, lacked management oversight and should have been comprehensively briefed; and 2.) B.A.T.F. needs to incorporate the Incident Command System into major tactical plans.

The reference to an emergency medical plan was shallow, defective and non-operational. Any competent incident manager would have insisted and verified a medical contingency plan, particularly considering the remote location of the raid. There was no alternative to the need for an on-site, in-field capable, triage trauma capability.

The weapons of choice and authorization did not consider **contingency planning** for **ambush, explosives and superior firepower.** The intelligence available to the planners and most certainly known to the managers required a contingency plan. The use and deployment of observation posts was minimized to the extent of being ineffective. **Counter sniper** considerations were not adequately presented in the plan and **were never fully deployed** even as planned. That oversight was fatal.

Once again this component of planning points to ineffective management and command and control.

> **The absence of accountability charting throughout the B.A.T.F. resulted in errors, omissions and failures in the investigation, intelligence, approval, planning and incident management of the Waco incident.**

CONDITIONS OF COMPLIANCE AND INTEGRITY

I will address an issue that is dependent on the summary of and response to the investigation. I consider this a side issue because of potential liability and internal discipline concerns.

There is an immediate need to develop and implement changes in organizational structure, strategy and tactics, investigation case management, logistics and accountability charting with B.A.T.F.

RECOMMENDATION

Upon conclusion of the investigative review, including the observations of the tactical advisors, a concurrent task group, composed of experienced technical and management personnel to implement issues of critique and the recommendations to enhance the structure and management of the B.A.T.F. should be integrated with the current management structure. This task group would insure a rational and prompt integration of change without disrupting on-going operations or any personnel reorganization. Additionally, the task group can develop and implement change without "personality intervention."

The task group mission, guideline and tenure should be developed and directed by the Assistant Secretary for (law enforcement).

The task group members(s) should not have operational authority or supervision, but may have audit and inspection authority. This recommendation would enhance continuity of the review process by ensuring that any recommendations can be implemented immediately upon approval by the Secretary of Treasury. The task group could be charged with preparing responses to the Secretary of Treasury.

SPECIFIC RECOMMENDATION SUMMARY

1. Review and revise the B.A.T.F. National Response Plan to include sub tasks of:
    A. S.R.T. reorganization to include Special Operation Capable/High Risk, Special Operations Group command, and
    B. Incident Command System to provide Inter Agency coordination, and
    C. Consideration of a centralized S.R.T., and
    D. A specific special incident command organizational structure from S.A.I.C. field office to Director, B.A.T.F., and
    E. A clear, concise policy and procedure statement approved at least at the Assistant Secretary (for law enforcement) level.

2. Establish a supervisory and management course for:
    A. Major case investigation.
    B. Major incident preparation/response control.

3. Establish a supervisory/management procedures manual for case review, approval, audit, and control including formats.

4. Review current law enforcement standards for investigative training and administration procedures for:
   A. Administrative systems and controls.
   B. Review of investigative progress and report approval.
   C. Report and file maintenance.
   D. References to administrative systems and controls.
   E. Case progress logs.
   F. Daily report books.
   G. Investigation activity summary.
   H. Extraordinary cases/multiple law enforcement agency involved cases.
   I. Record checks, inquiries, documents, controls and inventory.
   J. Due Diligence.
   K. Case transfer (for cause).

5. Conduct a management seminar on interagency assets, capability and access (to include the Director of Military Support, D.O.D.).

6. Pursue Title III application to specific major cases in B.A.T.F.

7. If not currently authorized and functional - establish an Inspection and Control section at the Director/Assistant Director level to audit and trouble shoot intra bureau management.

8. Under the direction of the Assistant Secretary (L.E.) and the Director conduct a 2 or 3 day management retreat to address B.A.T.F.'s strategic issues and future planning.

9. Consider an intra-Treasury Department (Law Enforcement) management council and Incident Command System-Special Operations Capable.

WACO ADMINISTRATIVE REVIEW

Brief
    Submitted

                                    by

                            John J. Murphy

WACO ADMINISTRATIVE REVIEW

Introductory Overview

The undersigned respectfully submits an assessment of the February 28, 1993, Bureau of Alcohol, Tobacco and Firearms execution of Search Warrant and Warrant for Arrest at the Branch Davidian compound, in Waco, Texas.

Over the last several weeks, I and five others with experience in major city police departments or the military have met in Washington D.C. as part of the Department of the Treasury's Waco Administrative Review, seeking to determine what happened during the Bureau of Alcohol, Tobacco and Firearms operation and why.

I believe that the report the Administrative Review will be submitting to the President will be comprehensive and impartial, and based on a complete and thorough investigation of the events prior to and on February 28, 1993. Ronald Noble, Assistant Secretary for Enforcement, who has supervised the investigation, has given me and my five colleagues complete access to the Review's work. The staff assembled under Secretary Noble and Project Director Geoffrey Moulton, has provided us with all interviews, reports, diagrams, regulations, plans and the like, without hesitation and in a most timely fashion.

My assessment will touch upon the many issues that jumped out at me as I reviewed information, heard from witnesses, listened to the results of investigatory efforts, and participated in exchanges with other panel members. It is not my intention to place blame on particular individuals, but rather to identify critical issues and to bring about change and improvement. The Bureau of Alcohol, Tobacco and Firearms, as is appropriate, will hold its members responsible and accountable for their actions and direction. The law enforcement community, in my experience, has always been able to draw lessons from tragedies and improve operations in the future. I have every expectation that the Bureau of Alcohol, Tobacco and Firearms will move forward from this occurrence with an enhanced and enlightened management and continue to carry out its mandate with a truly dedicated and professional workforce.

Bureau of Alcohol, Tobacco and Firearms Case

The actions of members of the Bureau of Alcohol, Tobacco and Firearms on February 28, 1993 were the result of a lengthy and inclusive investigation over several months that led to the issuance of a Search Warrant for Mount Carmel Center or the Branch Davidian compound and, a Warrant for Arrest of Vernon Wayne Howel a/k/a "David Koresh." Special Agent Davy Aguilera, the case agent, did a professional job in conducting the investigation and providing the necessary information to attain the approval of a judicial officer. The affidavit that Aguilera submitted provided a wealth of information concerning the Branch Davidians, their leader, and their philosophies. It also made quite clear how massive an undertaking it would be to execute the warrants.

Foundation Issues

Aguilera's affidavit highlighted the issues that should have been critical to the management of the investigation and its direction:

- the weaponry and firepower within the compound

- the size of and accessibility to the compound

- the fortress-like location of the compound

- the Messiah complex and teachings of the leader David Koresh

- the religious cult mentality of the Branch Davidians

- the number of innocent children, women and men of the cult in the compound

- the shootout takeover by Koresh of the compound from former leader Roden

Any effort to address these issues would be made more difficult:

- by the Bureau's lack of experience in dealing with firepower of the magnitude expected to be present in the compound

- by the possibility that a military solution would be needed in a civilian law enforcement environment

- by the sensitivity of a religious issue

- by the potential media and political involvement

- by the risk that any move against the compound could turn into a hostage situation involving many of its inhabitants

The Bureau's hierarchy (it's "overhead"), from immediate case supervisor to the Director, must take responsibility for not recognizing at the outset that this was an extraordinary case, requiring special resources and supervision. Instead, the investigation was allowed to proceed like any ordinary case in the field where a field-level agent is usually charged with bringing a case to conclusion, regardless of the obstacles. In the absence of specific direction from overhead - - which could have asked the hard questions, demanded to know the risks of a course of action, and insisted on possible alternatives - - this investigation moved forward with insufficient attention to the risks presented.

Praise

Before continuing in my comments, I think it is appropriate to praise the professionalism and actions the members of the Bureau of Alcohol, Tobacco and Firearms who came under heavy and constant gunfire for 30 minutes. These men and women were courageous under the most difficult and trying circumstances that members of law enforcement can face. Their response to the firepower was measured and proper; their energies and heroics were directed to protecting each other and addressing their wounded comrades. The slain agents have made the supreme sacrifice in the performance of duty, which will always be remembered, and my heartfelt condolences goes to their families and loved ones.

A special thanks goes to Agents Buford, King, Petrelli and Williams who voluntarily appeared before our panel to give a first-hand account of their involvement as Team Leaders in executing the warrants. They also gave a very candid presentation of their roles in the investigation and particularly as the raid planners. Their planning efforts were knowledgeable and professional as they attempted to prepare for the many contingencies of the operation. The training and practice at Fort Hood was very much on target; it prepared the teams for their mission, and most probably minimized the fatalities and injuries sustained. When the operation went bad, there was the expected immediate confusion. Within a short time leadership came to the front and response to the situation became organized and fruitful.

Critical Issues

No investigation in any law enforcement agency is able to satisfy every objective. Mistakes will be made, issues not addressed, and contingencies not planned for. My intention is to address those issues that I think may have changed the outcome had they been addressed in a different fashion. These critical comments are designed to encourage changes in how these issues will be addressed in future investigations and tactics. To be candid, hindsight is easy, but it is the way to learn and move forward.

Information/Intelligence

A tremendous amount of information was developed in this case, but it was not sufficiently analyzed or properly used in the planning of the raid. Many red flags should have been recognized and properly dealt with. Instead, it seems that many of these red flags were overlooked because those planning the raid adopted a mindset that the Compound had to be taken down, and that the only way to proceed was with a dynamic, high-risk entry.

The planners conducted interviews that were used to support the raid action. Contradictory information was available from equally knowledgeable persons, but the planners seem to have discounted or not properly assessed it.

As the case began to develop, it was deemed "sensitive," a designation which should have led to better monitoring by Headquarters to keep appropriate hierarchy informed.

In January, 1993 the undercover house was established to obtain intelligence and find out more about Compound routines. This critical operation broke down and never supplied the proper information to the planners, who selectively used what was obtained. All sides of the compound should have been kept under surveillance. Instead, because a proposal that agents watch utilizing bales of hay was rejected for fear that they would be seen, the agents never had 360-degree coverage.

Pen registers, tapes, and communication monitoring were considered, but never came to fruition.

Agents attempted to conduct photographic monitoring from the undercover house and pole cameras, but they had little skill and achieved minimum results. It should also be noted that a picture was taken in January that showed a female pointing a rifle from a compound door; this intelligence was never assessed.

An undercover agent was able to gain access into the compound on several occasions resulting in substantial intelligence, but there was no attempt to plan a deep undercover.

On March 6 to March 9, 1992, after Koresh mistook the SWAT training that several police departments conducted in the area for ATF activity, security at the compound was immediately heightened and arms purchases substantially increased. This information was not assessed by the planners.

The staging area in Waco and the use of hotels violated the basic tenets of operational security.

The job of reviewing and assessing all intelligence and directing the raid planning was simply too great to be given to a single person. Instead of saddling Houston ASAC Sarabyn with all of these responsibilities, ATF should have used a case management system better suited to such a large operation.

Options

Ruse

Originally, the planners attempted to use the Department of Human Services, which was investigating child abuse allegations, to get Koresh away from the Compound and place him under arrest; were Koresh not present when the compound was searched, it was thought that resistance would not occur. When the Department of Human Services would not cooperate, this tactical approach was dropped, and no other innovative attempts were developed. Information and intelligence reporting that Koresh would not leave the Compound, although not conclusively accurate, influenced the planners to look at other options.

Siege

The planners next looked to develop a siege plan based on the flat terrain surrounding the compound and the consequent lack of cover, the firepower of the Branch Davidians, and their possible use of sentries. The siege option was eliminated because of the time and manpower that it would require, and the fact that ATF did not have negotiators and expertise for a siege. I also believe that the planners' selective use of intelligence, particularly the reported possibility of mass suicide, led them not to pursue the siege option.

Raid

The raid planners now moved to develop a dynamic, high-risk entry as the appropriate vehicle to execute the arrest and search warrants and preserve evidence. They developed entry tactics according to their interpretation of ongoing intelligence. The planning sessions did not include Houston SAC Chojnacki or the other SACs who had committed their Special Response Teams; once a plan was formulated the concurrence of ATF headquarters was sought and obtained. The plan evolved around the element of surprise and a 10 a.m. execution, even though surprise is generally achieved by going in darkness just before light. The tactical plan called for three Special Response Teams, each with specific assignments that would isolate or contain everyone present in the Compound and secure the arms room. The undercover house would observe the Compound to insure normalcy. The undercover would enter the compound, exit an hour before raid and report conditions. Helicopters would provide a diversion a distance from the Compound, just prior to the arrival of the Special Response Teams.

Evaluation

The plan was well-conceived to address the intelligence developed. If the element of surprise had been maintained, there is every likelihood that the raid would have been successful. It should be noted, however, that contingency plans are as critical to an operation's success as a raid plan itself; insufficient attention was given to contingency planning here.

Raid Implementation Analysis

Criticism must be directed at the way the raid plan was carried out.

Critical to a successful operation on this day was the element of surprise. This advantage was not maintained because of several important tactical shortcomings.

Forward observers might have helped ensure that surprise was maintained, had they been positioned to have full-circle coverage of the Compound, and had they been given a developed plan of operation. Observer and sniper teams should have been in place for twelve hours prior to the raid. This kind of coverage would have allowed ATF to see the armed Branch Davidians who apparently went to the Compound's "spider holes" during the hour before the raid; a report that Compound residents had taken these positions would have required that the raid be cancelled.

The role of the helicopters was to create a diversion immediately prior to arrival of the raid force. Had command and control accurately directed and communicated the diversion, firing at the helicopters by Branch Davidians might have provided the signal that the raid should be aborted.

The use of Waco as the staging area and the number of media vehicles active in the area prior to the raid should have received careful and in-depth assessment.

The most important occurrence on raid day was undercover Agent Rodriguez's report from the Compound. The assessment of his information should have mandated cancellation of the raid. The element of surprise had been lost, and the possibility that the Branch Davidians would seek to repulse the raid was too quickly discounted. Rodriguez's report that no resistance was being planned inside the Compound should not have been expected to remain valid for very long -- certainly not for the time it would take to bring agents to the Compound. The significance of this report and the fact that the agents would arrive before the men were due to work in the field were not properly considered when the issue of surprise was assessed.

There was command and control framework in place on raid day, but it was not sufficient to direct the operation. The Incident Commander should have been at the command post to assess information and make decisions from a somewhat removed perspective.

Evaluation Summary

There were many problem areas that affected the raid and that should have led ATF to consider alternatives to going forward. Execution was plagued by failures in evaluating information relating to a cult mentality, and the potential firepower in the Compound. The process used by the ATF commanders in making their decisions illustrates the need for crisis management training.

In essence, the one major cause for this failed operation would have to be "the human element" -- from the entire "overhead" to the working field agents of the Bureau; a combination of human errors in addressing a monumental task can be deemed the reason for "What went wrong."

Recommendations

The Bureau must address the substantial damage done to its organization and, in particular, to the morale of its agents.

The aftermath,

- from the many avenues and aspects of self-inspection and examination
- from the extraordinary media attention and coverage
- and from the interest of the citizenry throughout the country

mandates a complete and thorough reorganization with the objectives of improving delivery of day-to-day operations and insuring that such an occurrence can never happen again. The organization must be prepared to handle another Waco investigation down the road.

Closing Comment

I salute the Bureau of Alcohol, Tobacco and Firearms as an organization of dedicated professionals who satisfy a most difficult mission in law enforcement. I encourage leadership to take the members forward with heads held high.

Respectfully submitted,

John J. Murphy
Deputy Chief
New York City Police Department
Commanding Officer
Special Operations Division

ROD PASCHALL　　　**1320 GEORGETOWN CIRCLE**　　　**CARLISLE, PA 17013**

August 23, 1993

Ronald K. Noble
Assistant Secretary for Enforcement
Department of Treasury, Room 4330
1500 Pennsylvania Ave., N.W.
Washington, D.C. 20220

SUBJECT: Waco Review Report

SUMMARY: The February 1993 Bureau of Alcohol Tobacco and Firearms (BATF) raid at Waco, a failure due to multiple causes, demonstrated a few commendable aspects, but in the main, revealed systemic defects in the preparation, planning, and execution of multiple Special Response Team (SRT) actions. Deficiencies included: a flawed National Response Plan; inadequate oversight for high-risk, sensitive operations; a defective tactical intelligence training program; an inadequate selection, training and administration program for personnel engaged in multiple SRT actions (particularly those charged with command and control responsibilities); subpar procedures in identifying and gaining appropriate specialized military support; and inadequate intelligence gathering means to support dangerous tactical operations. Most, if not all of these deficiencies still exist. The disastrous outcome at Waco could have happened anywhere and can reoccur at any time. The Treasury Department, facing trends indicating a future higher incidence rate for these types of law enforcement actions, cannot assume an improved performance in coming, similar operations and should implement changes. Unfortunately, the review of this event also revealed Treasury lacks analytical, enforcement focused studies, studies that could be of use as decision aids to make changes leading to the more effective execution and management of the Department's statutory responsibilities.

The Department should institute immediate, interim and long term measures to increase its capacity for the safe and professional execution of hazardous operations. This phased approach can be accompanied with a series of studies designed to provide Treasury's decision makers and concerned Congressional committees with management and evaluation tools to guide successive enforcement improvements. Recommended immediate measures include: commending deserving BATF personnel; revision of the National Response Plan and gaming the result; improving tactical intelligence training; achieving a better understanding of the capabilities and limitations of military support in domestic law enforcement efforts; and, the conduct of two studies, one designed to present options the United States might select for reducing the public threat posed by the increasing numbers of assault weapons in civilian hands, the other examining the benefits, dangers and past record of dynamic entry-type operations.

Recommended interim measures include: gaining Title III authority in cases involving illegal automatic weapons or explosives; reversal of BATF's media policy and the elimination of its field public information structure; and, the conduct of two additional studies, one aimed at defining Treasury's future law enforcement environment, the second designed to evaluate the cost/effectiveness of Special Agent Gerald Petrilli's thoughtful April 27, 1993 suggestion to revise BATF's SRT structure.

Recommended long-term measures include: the establishment of a multi-use Department level law enforcement response team; coordination with the Department of Justice and the Office of International Criminal Justice to sponsor a series of multi-national law enforcement conferences aimed at gaining a better understanding of armed cults and the newly emerging characteristics of terrorism, defining promising techniques to deal with trafficking in illegal or black market items; and, exploring the possibilities of gaining a more accessible international criminal justice data base.

FINDINGS AND RECOMMENDATIONS: Suggested, specific corrective actions, phased into immediate, interim and longer term measures, are identified in bold text below. The rationale for each recommendation is provided in following bracketed text and incorporates the undersigned's Waco Review findings and observations.

Immediate Measures

Commend selected BATF personnel, including J. William Buford, Gerald T. Petrilli, Curtis D. Williams, and Kenny King, for bravery, dedication to duty and uncommon poise under fire.

[Rationale: The action at Waco involved a number of incidents where BATF personnel demonstrated an extraordinary degree of personal courage and disregard for their own lives in the execution of their duties. The assault team leaders were particularly conspicuous in their heroism, but there were others who risked their own safety. For example, some agents exposed themselves to withering fire in order to administer first aid to the wounded. These, and other acts were marked by an unusual degree of coolness and professionalism on the part of BATF personnel. Such exemplary behavior should not go unremarked or unrewarded by the Treasury Department.]

Revise the National Response Plan, relieving Field Division Special Agents in Charge and their Assistants of tactical command responsibilities for multiple SRT raids, temporarily replacing them with HQ BATF Special Operations Division personnel, clarifying the division of duties between the Incident Commander and the Tactical Coordinator, and testing the results by means of an exercise at the BATF National Command Center.

[Rationale: Field division SACs and ASACs are not selected for their abilities to conduct large-scale, complex special operations, nor do they have the time or training opportunities to become proficient in such functions. Since the current National Response Plan directs these officers to handle such operations, it ensures, at best, an inadequate performance at the command and control level. Hindsight analysis of the Waco incident reveals numerous mistakes made by both the Houston Special Agent in Charge and his assistant, however, there is no indication that any other field office within BATF was trained and prepared to produce better results. A two-week exposure to the SRT course is insufficient to qualify an officer for the tactical command of sizeable, multi-faceted operations. By revising the Plan to designate

HQ BATF Special Operations Division personnel to perform critical tactical command and control tasks for multiple SRT actions, officers possessing day-to-day familiarity with such operations will be temporarily controlling the direct application of force in these occasional events. There is no reason that the field division SAC cannot retain overall responsibility for the action and the current title: incident commander.

This revision will have the additional effect of addressing another deficiency exposed by the Waco raid. There was clearly a difference between what Washington-level authorities believed to be the criteria for the raid's initiation and what officials at Waco assumed. Placing a Washington-based element in tactical command will encourage more rigorous high-level scrutiny over the planning and execution of large-scale operations, that by their very nature demand close attention. While this solution is not optimum, it provides a near-term fix until a more satisfactory, long-term solution discussed below is examined and developed. Experience (2-4 multiple BATF SRT raids in the past 2-3 years) indicates the actual implementation of this temporary recommendation will be infrequent.

The command and control sections of the National Response Plan are ambiguous. During Director Higgins' testimony before a Congressional panel on June 9, 1993, he stated the Houston Field Division Special Agent in Charge was the tactical commander of the raid at Waco. The three Special Response Team leaders, interviewed by the undersigned during July 1993, stated they considered the Assistant SAC of the Houston Field Office to be the tactical commander. This confusion can be explained by examining the portion of the National Response Plan designating the ASAC as the "Tactical Coordinator," while charging that person with "directing" SRT employment. Directing and coordinating are two entirely different functions. This ambiguity can be eliminated by changing the title, "tactical coordinator," to read "tactical commander" while retaining those portions of the plan that assign the overall responsibility for such operations to the Field Division Special Agent in Charge.

Once these changes have been made, a National Command Center exercise should be conducted to test the new provisions, familiarize key personnel with their duties and identify the need for adjustments, if necessary. It is recommended that appropriate Treasury Department officials participate in the exercise. In order to gain the maximum benefit from the exercise, it is recommended that key Treasury and BATF personnel be unaware of the its nature when play begins. Therefore, the exercise should be written, administered and evaluated by outsiders: Department of Justice personnel, contractors, consultants or a combination of all three.]

Establish a 4-5 day required training course for Intelligence Research Specialists, a course wholly devoted to tactical intelligence.

[Rationale: Among the several reasons for the failure at Waco, inadequate intelligence loomed large. In some cases, raid planners failed to use available intelligence. For example, a pre-raid photo that might have indicated Davidian women were trained in the use of rifles was disregarded and some film taken from the undercover house was apparently not even developed. But, existing intelligence was not corroborated, challenged, analyzed or presented with a view towards tactical utility. On the other hand, intelligence was rather well handled and expertly used to establish probable cause. A review of the training for BATF intelligence research specialists, indicated such training is primarily devoted to standard law enforcement investigative techniques, name traces, etc., and is not sufficiently augmented with tactical intelligence techniques and procedures, subjects of increasing value to BATF field offices. A four to five-day remedial or fundamentals course for BATF intelligence research specialists presented by HQ BATF special operations personnel could provide the Bureau with improved tactical intelligence practices in field offices. Some of the instruction should be devoted to camera work and graduates of the course should be expected to pass on their camera expertise to field agents. It is suggested the course utilize case history methods, including the incident at Waco, to demonstrate the difference between quality and inadequate intelligence for SRT operations.]

Meet with the Director of Military Support, Department of Defense, to obtain an inventory of available military expertise, facilities, equipment, training and augmentation to Treasury Department law enforcement agencies along with an understanding of the capabilities and limitations of such support and the procedures to acquire such advice and assistance, and, compare these services with what is already available within the Department.

[Rationale: The Waco incident indicated the BATF and possibly the Department of Treasury as a whole, has an incomplete understanding of the capabilities and limitations of military support available to law enforcement agencies. Field agents obtained advice from the 3rd Special Forces Group, a unit with no experience or particular expertise in dynamic entry techniques or with effective communications plans associated with close quarters assaults. A superior solution would have been to gain the advice of the Army's Delta Force, an organization that has developed the country's best techniques for such operations. BATF SRT leaders requested, but were unable to obtain smoke grenades, devices that would have been of high utility in masking vulnerable agents from the Davidians' fire. Some federal officers were struck by fire from the compound as they lay wounded on the ground. Smoke grenades should have been provided from military stocks and made available to the BATF. There is no reason the Department cannot have some on hand, avoiding unreasonable delays. Additionally, it is likely Customs helicopters and crews would have been of greater help than those of the Texas National Guard. There are legal limitations placed on military personnel, including aviation crews, in support of domestic law enforcement operations. For instance, military crews would have probably been legally prohibited from picking up the wounded while under fire. Conversely, Customs operates under a different charter and could have made the pick-up. Then, too, the U.S. military has a general lack of experience in this field. Gaining a better understanding of the capabilities and limitations of available military support is essential to the Department's efforts in improving its own capabilities--for all of its law enforcement organizations.]

Conduct a study of ways and means to minimize America's growing problem with assault weapons.

[Rationale: One of the outstanding features of and prime reasons for the BATF failure at Waco was the presence and use of assault rifles. Indeed, it is probable that the warrant would have not been sought if Vernon Howell had not acquired these weapons and given the clear indication that he was converting them to fire automatically. During the initial seconds of the attempted entry into the Davidian compound, federal officers were suddenly exposed to an overwhelming tactical disadvantage. When Howell and his followers opened a devastating barrage of automatic fire, most officers had no choice but to rely on basic instincts and seek cover. As the fight progressed, these officers had little opportunity to retrieve the wounded because their own semi-automatic weapons could not provide the volume of covering firepower essential to temporarily overcome the Davidians' fire. In those conditions, rescues of the exposed and helpless could not be attempted unless a wholly unusual degree of physical courage was called upon.

The BATF policy of prohibiting its agents from using automatic weapons may be laudable, but it is not logical. The incident at Waco will likely prove of critical importance. Howell's example (the bizarre cult association aside) is indicative of a greater trend. Assault weapons, both pistol and rifle versions, are becoming prevalent throughout America. These weapons have no place in sport hunting or pleasure in either their semi-automatic or fully automatic forms. Their purpose for being is either purely military or purely criminal. They exist to gain an advantage over an armed adversary, usually to provide suppressive fire (forcing the opponent to seek cover) in support of the user's maneuver or escape. Their sole intended use is, therefore, combat. Growing numbers of law enforcement officers face this threat and are at as much of a disadvantage as the BATF agents were at Waco. The next tragedy where law enforcement officers are outgunned by them and killed will, as a matter of common sense, provoke a drumbeat among the nation's policemen asking for automatic weapons in defense of their own lives. The country may therefore face a ludicrous arms race between cops and criminals.

Surely, there must be a way for the federal government to, at most, ban the civilian possession of these military tools or, at least, inhibit their sale and conversion. Such worthy goals are deserving of a serious study. It is recommended that a firm with a strong public policy and technological background be commissioned to conduct the study under the supervision of the Department.]

Initiate a study of past, dynamic entry-style law enforcement operations, along with a confidential survey of police attitudes toward them so that guidelines and tips for future such operations can be identified and used, particularly in SRT-type training.

[**Rationale:** There are good arguments, both for and against dynamic entry techniques in domestic law enforcement situations. In an official setting, most law enforcement officers support such operations. However, in private, the undersigned has often heard an opposing view from experienced officers. Reservations include the resultant "storm trooper" image that these actions portray, especially from nationally telecast commercial programs that gain an audience from the dramatic display of brute force. Additionally, some officers are deeply troubled by some cases where there was great injustice done to innocents, citizens whose only fault was being in the wrong place at the wrong time. This phenomenon appears to warrant a confidential survey of American police officers. Additionally, there appears to be a problem with federal law enforcement actions centered on a rural crime site. During the Waco review, this latter factor was discussed and a number of controversial past actions that bore some resemblance to the Davidian operation were identified. A study of these actions, one done with an examination of comparative urban incidents and sieges may yield helpful corrective measures for use in the future. The logical setting where these lessons could be taught is in tactical police team training sessions.]

Interim Measures

Pending the favorable outcome of a cost/effectiveness study, implement Special Agent Gerald Petrilli's April 27, 1993 Regional Special Response Teams suggestion.

[Rationale: Petrilli's suggestion involves eliminating district teams in favor of fewer regional teams and establishing a numerical, scored system for determining when to employ a SRT. While appearing to offer a more professional SRT capability to the Bureau while decreasing some costs and creating helpful criteria for SRT raids, Treasury and BATF officials do not currently have enough empirical data to make a rational appraisal. What is known is that SRT training detracts from essential man power available to Regional and District SACs in the daily execution of their enforcement duties. If there is a relationship (as common sense would seem to indicate) between arrest and conviction rates and available BATF special agents in the field, changes in the Bureau's SRT structure will impact on the overall accomplishment of BATF's mission. An analytical examination of Petrilli's idea may reveal that it is even more attractive than it appears. There may be a potential increase in BATF's effectiveness since implementation of the proposal would release about 200 (almost half) of the Bureau's current SRT members for continuous assignment to day-to-day field duties. Additionally, this concept would eliminate some travel and instructional time for those agents involved in teaching duties at Ft. McClellan. These latter factors, impacting on both the costs and effectiveness of the Bureau should be calculated and considered with other factors, such as safety, prior to a decision. A competent, impartial analytical studies firm could produce a product that would establish the relationship between the Bureau's effectiveness and its personnel strength directly engaged in arrests and convictions. The study could then calculate mandays and money costs, applying these factors to Petrilli's concept. Such a study would likely prove a valuable, rational decision aid to the BATF Director and interested Congressional committees in this and in other difficult choices centered on the Bureau's policy alternatives.]

Review Title III laws as they apply to cases involving the illegal possession of automatic weapons or explosives, identify why BATF rarely requests such authority, and, if necessary, propose additional legislation to the Congress.

[Rationale: BATF Director Higgins, in his testimony before Congress implied that the Bureau does not have the authority to use this form of intelligence gathering as a matter of course in enforcing the laws BATF is charged with. On the other hand, during the review, lawyers who were queried by the undersigned stated such authority can be granted under current law. If there is a misty understanding of the law in Washington, there is likely only a foggy notion of its meaning outside of the nation's capital.

Because of their unique skills, Treasury Department law enforcement organizations are often the agencies of "last resort" in specialized, high-hazard cases. For example, both Texas law enforcement officials and the FBI were unable to develop probable cause against Vernon Howell despite expressed Congressional and media interest in the case. In contrast, the BATF was competent to develop probable cause against Howell--without Title III authority. However, once that hurdle was overcome, the next step, presentation of the warrant, involved a reasonable chance that Howell and his followers might use the illegal weapons they were suspected to possess.

This situation is typical of many BATF cases and explains why the Bureau is prone to serve warrants in similar instances by the use of dynamic entry techniques. As the 578 SRT deployments prior to the Waco incident may indicate, use of dynamic entry provides some promise of preserving the lives of both federal law enforcement officers and the subjects of their investigations. But, the tragedy at Waco also points to the need for using additional law enforcement tools. If there had been wire taps or electronic surveillance of the Davidian compound, it is likely the actual extent of Howell's preparations to resist the raid would have been known. Several lives might have been preserved. Although electronic surveillance constitutes another regrettable increase in the invasion of privacy, it is not difficult to imagine other, future cases where life and limb might be saved with the use of this technique.]

Revise BATF media relations policy, abolish field public information officer positions, return the incumbents to law enforcement duties and assign the resulting, freed-up positions to HQ BATF Special Operations Division.

Taxpayer benefits, if any, gained by the expanded, proactive BATF public relations program of the past two years are, at best, obscure, and even if such a program had been of some demonstrable value, the pre-Waco media environment for the Bureau was a dramatically different one from the arena the BATF finds itself in today. With the grim video images of the failure at Waco burned into the memories of both the media and the public, the BATF is not likely to garnish its reputation, or even present itself in the best light through the commercial-style ritual of employing its corps of public relations experts to develop close and friendly relations with local press and broadcast functionaries. Public interests would likely be better served if the Bureau's image makers were pressed into its ongoing struggle to safely increase arrest and conviction rates.

The Bureau might learn from the experience of the Department of Defense during the Gulf War. Following the Vietnam War, the Armed Services, at considerable expense, developed a cadre of professionally trained public information officers. At the outset of the Gulf War, these officers were used to put the best face on American military efforts, appearing on national television and conducting print media interviews. Within two weeks, when these specialists proved incapable of delivering the detail and authoritative statements the modern American media demanded, they were replaced by senior operational staff officers, and in some instances, by field commanders. Following this change, the U.S. Armed Services enjoyed an excellent public image. It is likely that BATF's senior field agents are capable of conducting unaided interviews and delivering announcements with as much skill and success as their military counterparts--at a savings to the taxpayer.

It is doubtful that the Bureau's special operations can in any way benefit from the current BATF policy of proactive media relations. In essence, the aims of special operations elements and media organs are antithetical. A successful special operation hinges on secrecy, surprise, and speed. A successful media effort depends on beating the competition to publish or broadcast news to the broadest possible audience. At Waco, BATF officers, operating under a Washington-level directive demanding proactive media relations, were unable to influence the Waco Tribune staff in the suppression of the story about Vernon Howell and it would be unlikely to see any newsroom abandon its reason for being to satisfy the needs of a law enforcement organization. While the undersigned has seen or heard no proof that the relationship between the press and BATF's Houston office resulted in a compromise of the operation, there is little doubt that such contacts can prove disastrous.

There is another reason to reverse the Bureau's proactive media policy. An aggressive policy like the current one, inevitably results in competition with other law enforcement agencies, one-upmanship, unseemly turf battles and unhealthy professional relationships. By adopting a style of quiet competence and substance over image, the Bureau is apt to gradually gain the increased respect of its peers, an attitude that will undoubtedly be discovered by discriminating journalists. As an example, the Secret Service enjoys an excellent reputation among law enforcement agencies, the media, and the public--all the while shunning publicity.]

Initiate an analytical study to project the Department's probable law enforcement environment in the next four to five years.

[**Rationale:** (Note: The following unsolicited comments may be considered outside the immediate considerations of the events in Waco.) Institutional modifications, influenced by a reasonable projection of tomorrow's conditions, are superior to those anchored in past events. Any changes in BATF's methods of operation, staffing or procedures are likely to affect other law enforcement elements under the purview of the Treasury Department. Customs, BATF and the Secret Service often augment one another and any action that focuses on one of the agencies takes essential oversight and administration from the other two. Thus the potential impact of changes in one bureau should be considered in the light of possible future effects on the others. Additionally, although outyear and even next week's events cannot be accurately predicted, decision makers are apt to make better changes if they are aware of trends and alternative futures.

The undersigned was unable to find any law enforcement futures studies within the BATF and was given the indication there were no such studies of a recent nature within Treasury. A cursory analysis of the Department's areas of law enforcement interest indicates an ominous growth of Treasury related criminal activity and a dramatic rise in likely legislation that will substantially increase the Department's policing workload:

> ▸ The nature of terrorism appears to be changing. During the Cold War era, terrorist organizations were often state supported, foreign governments supplying explosives, weapons, instructions and training. As the recent New York City World Trade Center bombing demonstrated, terrorists may now have to rely on their own initiatives to acquire weapons or manufacture explosives. The FBI will undoubtedly

remain as the country's lead agency and first line of defense against domestic terrorism. But the BATF may well play a growing role in identifying terrorist activity, albeit in some cases inadvertently. Additionally, the Trade Center incident showed the modern terrorist has a bent for political assassination, a phenomenon that was mostly avoided during the Cold War due to tacit, unwritten agreements between competing nations. This new and alarming situation could well make the duties of the Secret Service even more difficult than they already are.

▸ Hate crimes are on the increase, particularly those associated with the country's rapidly expanding skinhead groups. The Anti-Defamation League states 78 percent of all hate murders during the past six years have occurred in the last three. And, the Alabama based Klanwatch claims the majority of racist violence is now caused by skinheads. While this criminal activity is another responsibility of the FBI, there is a greater likelihood that the BATF will, as a normal matter, be involved. The FBI's traditional adversaries in this arena, members of the Ku Klux Klan, rarely resorted to automatic weapons--skinheads are a different breed and the BATF is likely to be increasingly involved in these types of investigations and arrests.

▸ It is now clear that Customs' role in waging part of America's drug war is larger than previously thought. No one knows for certain the precise means by which illegal drugs are imported, but any number of recent indicators point to substantial deliveries under the guise of commercial, cross-border trade. High-ranking military officers have stated that less than five percent of illegal drug traffic pass through the nation's air defense zones and seaborne interceptions have all but vanished. On the other hand, the two largest illegal drug finds in the nation's history were both associated with large capacity trucks that entered the United States from Mexico, through Customs inspection points. Commercial truck traffic through these Southern border facilities has grown five-fold in the past six years, and that growth continues. Since $500 worth of cocaine or heroin in Mexico can fetch $100,000 in the United States, there is no end of incentives to increase this illicit trade. In June, 200 lbs of cocaine concealed in a Columbian shipment of bananas was brought to the attention of Florida based Custom's officers by a commercial vendor. Drug traffickers often protect their goods with heavy weaponry, therefore the work of Customs may be more hazardous in future than in the past.

▸ BATF officials state there have been few necessary enforcement actions associated with the Bureau's tobacco responsibilities, but that happy circumstance may soon disappear. The July confrontation between the Paugussett Indian tribe and the State of Connecticut over the State's right to collect a 47 cent per-pack tax on cigarettes may be a harbinger of things to come for federal officials. The Connecticut confrontation was an armed one, the tribal chief and his AK-47 toting guards were determined to protect their growing cigarette business, growth due to a $4.00 per-carton savings for his customers. Apparently, there is already enough profit in defying the law on cigarette taxes to risk arrest. It is all but certain that the Congress will pass a heavy cigarette tax in the fall in order to partially off-set the cost of the forthcoming national health legislation, a cost that some estimate will amount to about $50 billion in increased annual federal outlays. Estimates for the add-on federal tax on cigarettes range from $1.00 to $1.75 a-pack. A rough estimate of Treasury's take from this new levy is from $15 to $20 billion per year. Therefore, BATF's ability to enforce the tobacco sales statutes will assume a wholly new significance in the near future. It is likely some of the country's 50-60 million smokers will support criminal, tax-free trade in tobacco when the new federal cigarette tax takes effect. BATF's work and its need for resources is bound to expand.

- Another sin tax associated with the coming health bill, an increase in the federal levy on alcoholic beverages, is also probable. Since there is considerable resistance to a beer add-on, the bulk of this tax is likely to fall on spirits, another BATF concern. The manufacture of and trade in illegal whiskey has traditionally been protected by weapons in the United States, and there is no reason to expect that this age-old American custom will not continue--and, flourish. It would be naive to believe that the federal campaign against moonshiners is not about to enter a new chapter.

- Finally, there is the matter of guns themselves. A Spring, 1993 national poll provided what the pollster, Louis Harris, described as the first firm indication that the country is now prepared for significant, new federal firearms legislation. The incident at Waco may have had something to do with this change in public attitude. Currently, there are eight pieces of proposed legislation in the Congress. Most tax ammunition and firearms, some as much as 1000 percent. One is keyed to the emerging national health bill, raising the cost of guns by imposing a 20 percent tax, collections neatly destined for the nation's trauma centers. Whatever the results, in the end, Treasury will be charged with enforcement.

In the case of the above mentioned likely legislation, the Department should be in a position to advise lawmakers of the impact such legislation will have on Treasury's ability to enforce the laws, ideally before such legislation is passed. Such a study should be conducted in the light of the changing nature of crime in America, not only to better advise lawmakers, but to serve Treasury Department decision makers as they adjust the duties, procedures and methods of operation within the Department's law enforcement organizations. Any number of competent firms can produce such a study within a period of 60 to 90 days for as little as

$200,000, a paltry sum considering what is at stake.]

Long-Term Measures

Create a full-time, Treasury-wide recruited, Treasury controlled, multi-purpose response team of 50-60 members that will conduct the Department's high-risk, high-profile, complex and dangerous law enforcement operations and other assigned tasks.

[**Rationale:** There are better ways to conduct large-scale, complicated special operations than the methods used in February. The Waco incident clearly demonstrated the hazards of employing part-time special operations personnel in a large-scale, difficult operation. Although the agents at Waco had conducted long hours of rehearsals at Ft. Hood, interviews with some of the participants indicated their understanding of specific duties and the overall concept was a bit vague. Response team members that work together on a full-time basis would have likely been more cognizant of the plan and its individual parts. The Waco debacle was not only costly in human life, the action and its aftermath was terribly costly in dollar terms to the U.S. taxpayer. Rather than ignore the possibilities of repeat performances, it would be advisable to invest in a solution that promises improved execution in these operations. People whose day-to-day duties are aimed at special operations have a better opportunity to conduct well planned, expertly controlled actions than those who can only devote a part of their time to such efforts. And, well planned, expertly controlled actions have a better chance of success than operations conceived and executed in an ad hoc fashion by people who may never have worked together before.

A high-profile, sensitive operation is best developed and controlled from the beginning by high-level authorities--in the end, it is they who will be held accountable. The raid at Waco, involving sizeable numbers of both women and children, the delicate matter of religion, issues of child sexual abuse, polygamy and the presence of large numbers of illegal automatic weapons and explosives, had headlines-grabbing, national-level significance from its very inception. Yet, it was handled by the Bureau of Alcohol, Tobacco and Firearms as a regional concern, deserving of only a cursory notification to responsible Treasury officers on the eve of execution. When the advisability of the raid was raised at Treasury, a hasty series of phone calls between officials resulted in confusion over what constituted the criteria for the raid's initiation. A superior arrangement would have Treasury officials involved at a much earlier stage. Placement of the responsibility to execute the National Response Plan at a higher level within the national administration will ensure such operations are developed and controlled with a more appropriate level of oversight.

The Department should consider the U.S. Army's experience in creating a satisfactory counterterrorist capability in developing Treasury's own organization to execute large-scale, high-profile law enforcement operations. Initially, in the mid-1970s, the Army's counterterrorist force was a single Special Forces battalion, a unit that had several other responsibilities. That inadequate solution was quickly discarded and the choice of placing the responsibility with a larger unit, a Special Forces Group, was made. Later, this, too, was cast aside and an organization with Army-wide recruiting authority, one controlled and overseen at a much higher level was finally selected. At each successive step in this process, the organization gained a better opportunity to select from a wider range of talent. And, at each step, time-consuming, confusion-producing levels of command and control were eliminated. The end result provides the country with a full-time, highly capable team whose characteristics and operations are in full view of the officials who must bear the responsibility for the team's support and employment.

A full-time Treasury response team would provide the Department with more options in situations such as the one at Waco. One of the unadmitted, but obvious determinants that influenced the Incident Commander and his assistant to initiate the assault despite learning the raid was expected, was that changing the approach to a siege would deprive much of the American Southwest of BATF manpower for an undetermined length of time. A full-time response team, with no other compelling duties, would be more likely to opt for a siege if the tactical situation lent itself to that solution. A part-time special operations force does well if it can master the fundamentals of dynamic entry--a technique that was fully developed by counterterrorist teams in the 1970s. This technique relies on an overpowering, surprise, simultaneous assault staged through multiple entry points. A full-time special operations force is likely to have mastered dynamic entry and have more options such as selective, clandestine penetration of critical areas, up its sleeve. A full-time team is more apt to develop ruses and lures to accomplish missions without resorting to either chancy armed assaults or lengthy, expensive sieges.

A full-time response team will be able to use better technology and weaponry than a part-time team is capable of handling. For example, when the Waco assault team leaders were asked about the possibility of BATF using automatic weapons to even the odds in special circumstances, they stated they would not recommend such a practice for a variety of reasons--one of which was that SRT personnel do not have the essential firing practice time to gain proficiency. A full-time team would not have that limitation. SRTs do not have the capability to use low order, non-fragmenting explosives for shock entry, a highly effective technique that gains an initial advantage for assault elements at an extremely critical moment. A full-time team would have that edge--and more.

A full-time team would be more likely to ensure that the principles of operational security are observed in the conduct of planning and preparing for an action. At Waco, there were countless opportunities for Vernon Howell to learn of the impending assault: interviews with family members of Davidians during the investigative phase that may have provoked phone calls to the compound; contacts with the media; coordination with a variety of local agencies, law enforcement and otherwise, any one of which could have compromised the operation; the large number of support personnel that arrived in Waco long prior to the arrival of the assault teams; and, pre-assault radio transmissions, some of which were in the clear. Additionally, there was no officer who had operational security as his or her sole function. A full-time team would have such a person or persons, vested with authority to take immediate, corrective action to prevent compromise.

A full-time Treasury response team need not be a seldom-used, single purpose organization and it need not be of the size that was used at Waco. It could and should have multiple tasks and responsibilities. For example, once it is organized, equipped and trained, it should have the responsibility to train BATF's SRTs, relieving current instructors who must temporarily abandon pressing duties in their own regions and districts. It should be forward deployed and placed at the disposal of the Secret Service when the President or other Treasury protectees are exposed to potential danger. It should be employed as a back-up or augmentation force for Customs' more difficult operations. Also, Treasury should make this force available when the Justice Department's law enforcement elements, the FBI, DEA and the Marshal's Service are in need of assistance, particularly when Treasury-specific expertise is required. And, if sizeable manpower is required, on the scale of that used at Waco, it could be augmented by BATF's SRTs.]

In conjunction with the Department of Justice and the Office of International Criminal Justice, sponsor a series of international conferences on law enforcement actions against armed cults, the changing face of terrorism, the control of automatic weapons and explosives, the suppression of trade in illegal drugs, tobacco and liquor, and improvements in obtaining information on international criminals and suspects.

[**Rationale:** The United States Government should not consider its experience with such groups as the Davidians or skinheads as unique. Nor should it attempt to only learn from its own experience in dealing with terrorists, automatic weapons, and illegal substances. Additionally, the WACO experience as well as the Trade Center bombing, involving a number of aliens, pointed once again to the inescapable fact that law enforcement officers in America are increasingly dependent on international assistance and information. The federal government should be interested in a more accessible international data base on criminals and their activities. It should share its experience and needs with its friends and allies abroad and learn from their ideas, mistakes and proven techniques. The Chicago-based Office of International Criminal Justice, a non-profit organization with offices in several foreign countries, is well qualified to administer and manage international conferences devoted to these subjects, bringing to the U.S. any number of foreign law enforcement experts as speakers. OICJ conducts approximately six such conferences on a wide range of criminal justice subjects per year, often publishing conference papers.]

End Report

Rod Paschall

ASSESSMENT OF WACO RAID PLAN

BY

LIEUTENANT ROBERT A. SOBOCIENSKI

NEW YORK CITY POLICE DEPARTMENT

EMERGENCY SERVICES UNIT

WACO REVIEW COMMITTEE

On February 28, 1993 one of if not THE most difficult undertakings in law enforcement history was conducted in Waco, Texas. On that day members of various Special Response Teams of the Bureau of Alcohol, Tobacco and Firearms were joined together in an effort to carry out the mandates of the U.S. District Court of Texas and arrest Vernon Wayne Howell, A.K.A. David Koresh. A.T.F. members were also directed to search for and seize illegal weapons and explosive devices as per a search warrant on the 77 acre Branch Davidian compound which this male controlled. Personally, I am not aware of a bigger, more complex and difficult assignment in police work.

CASE HISTORY - AN OVERVIEW

The events of February 28, 1993 were the result of an exhaustive investigation which began with a case referral by Chief Deputy Dan Weyenberg of the McLennan County Sheriff's office to the Bureau of A.T.F. in late May of 1992. As the case progressed A.T.F. agents came to know that Howell was in the process of purchasing an enormous amount of firearms, weapons and ammunition. Based on their experience and further investigation, they came to the realization that Howell was engaged in the unlawful manufacture and possession of explosive devices and machine guns. This entire cache of arms and munitions was believed to be stockpiled at his Mount Carmel compound in Waco, Texas. The matter was complicated by several other factors. The subject had a prior history of violent behavior. He was also the leader of a religious cult. The Branch Davidian compound which Howell operated was known to be inhabited by a sizeable number of followers consisting of men, women and children.

As the investigation progressed through the initial stage, it became apparent that this was to become a unique case. Shortly thereafter it became a headquarters monitored case.

ORIGINAL PLAN

Initially the plan called for some type of ruse to be used in an effort to lure Howell and as many of his leaders as possible away from the compound where they would be taken into custody. It was felt that, with Koresh under arrest, there would not be a strong influence for cult members to resist law enforcement personnel in the execution of the warrant. The objective was then to safely enter the Mount Carmel Center and a second location called the "Mag Bag" to search for evidence of the manufacture of explosives and machine guns. Unfortunately, "information, observation and intelligence" determined Koresh had not left the compound in months and was not planning to leave his Davidian stronghold. With this in mind, attempts to apprehend Koresh away from his base of power were terminated.

SIEGE PLAN

In <u>late December</u> of 1992 discussion was given to the formalization of a SIEGE PLAN. Several ex-cult members were interviewed. Intelligence was gathered relative to the firearms and military training given to members of the compound as well as any alert system, defensive positions and fortifications. Inquiries were also made relative to an area called "The Tower" on the compound. Questions were asked relative to Koresh's expected reaction to a potential siege. Interviews revealed that Koresh had a deep hatred for A.T.F. He did not wish to go to jail. He repeatedly had boasted he had enough provisions on hand to sustain members for three months. Some ex-cult members believed that a mass suicide was a definite possibility. With the belief that Koresh was prepared to remain inside of his bunker indefinitely, the prospect of mass suicide, and the possibility of a long standoff ultimately ending with a massive display of force, the concept of surrounding the compound and announcing their intention to enforce a warrant was discarded by A.T.F. agents.

RAID PLAN

Due to the likelihood of a prolonged standoff with heavily armed cult members, and the fear of a mass suicide in the event of a siege, A.T.F. members began developing a TACTICAL PLAN. Agents began to compile "facts" relative to the daily routine within the compound. Intelligence discovered that, unlike times in the past, there presently were no guards on duty within the compound. It was also determined that "The Tower" was not used for surveillance purposes. Reportedly it was a area where women and children slept in addition to the second floor. Male cult members were restricted to and slept on the first floor. Agents learned of the presence of an armory on the second floor. This location was next to Howell's bedroom and reportedly contained the bulk of all munitions stored on the compound. It was believed this section would be locked to prevent children or mutinous cult members from gaining admittance and obtaining weapons. Intelligence determined. members would arise around 6:00 a.m., have breakfast, then attend a worship service between the hours of 8:00 to 10:00 a.m. After the prayer session ended, the women would care for the children as the men, weather permitting, would begin working outside in a pit area, unarmed. This work area was at the opposite side of the compound from the armory.

UNDERCOVER HOUSE

On January 11, 1993 an undercover surveillance house was established by the Bureau of A.T.F. It was situated across from the long driveway which led into the compound itself. Originally, it was scheduled to be in operation for 24 hours a day, 7 days a week. The case agent requested that the eight man team assigned to the house document significant events as well as the traffic coming and going through the compound. It was hoped surveillance would aid in the identification of persons frequenting or living in the compound as well as establish day-to-day activities and patterns. It was hoped that an undercover agent could be introduced, gain entry and begin to frequent the Davidian leader's stronghold. This becomes a reality when on January 28, 1993 an undercover agent establishes rapport with Vernon Howell himself.

NATIONAL RESPONSE PLAN

The tactical plan called for three Special Response Teams of A.T.F. to be used in this operation. The enormity of the undertaking dictates that a newly developed and as yet untested A.T.F. National Response Plan would go into effect. Rather than conduct the raid under cover of darkness (during early morning hours), the plan centers on the information relative to activities at 10:00 a.m. During this time the men will be separated from the weapons as they work in the outside pit area.

The plan would begin prior to entering the compound with the placement of forward observer/sniper teams. One team would be placed in an area north of the compound. Another team would be placed in the undercover house. This was also the best spot available to monitor activities in both the front of the compound and the pit area. The placement of a third team was eliminated due to fear of discovery prior to the raid because of the 10:00 a.m. hour.

On the morning of the raid the undercover agent was to gain admittance to the compound. Once in place he was to make observations, look for weapons and determine the readiness of cult members. Upon leaving the compound the undercover would report these results back to a supervisor in the undercover house and to the Tactical Coordinator of the raid. If it was determined to be "business as usual" in the compound, the green light would be given for the raid to commence.

As SRT members approached the scene a helicopter diversion would be staged. This event would take place in a distant area of the compound on the opposite side of the main road leading into the Mount Carmel Center. The diversion would be visible to cult members working in the outside pit area. With all observers on the alert looking for a display of weapons or unusual activity by cult members, agents would be transported to the compound surreptitiously in horse trailers. These trailers were commonly used in this part of the country and should not arouse suspicion.

After receiving an all clear signal from the Deputy Tactical Coordinator in the undercover house, all members would converge on the compound armed with the element of surprise.

The Houston SRT Team would exit the cattle trailers, enter the front of the compound and clear it. It was also their function to clear the pit area and take control of the men in this work area before they could reach any weapons.

The Dallas SRT Team was responsible for entering the front door of the compound and securing the second floor except for Koresh's quarters. They were also to clear the towers.

The New Orleans SRT Team had dual roles. Half the team would enter the compound from the front door. They would clear and pass through the chapel, go up the stairs, secure the arms room and the adjacent bedroom belonging to Koresh. The second part of the team would exit the trailers, ascend ladders and climb to the roof of the compound. At this point authorized personnel would toss a distraction device into the arms room prior to entering and secure it as well as the rear storage room. However, since the undercover couldn't confirm the existence of an inside stairwell, the plan was changed. The entire New Orleans team entered the east side of the dwelling and second floor roof by ladder in an effort to enter Koresh's bedroom and adjacent armory simultaneously.

Ideally, if all went according to the script, all SRT teams would be able to "exit the transportation vehicles in eight seconds, get into position and make entry at the front door in approximately 33 seconds." By catching cult members completely off guard, highly trained and equipped A.T.F. members felt they could safely take control of the compound and its inhabitants without incident.

That, basically, was the Plan. Had the events of February 28, 1993 ended peacefully, few people would have ever heard of or known the story of David Koresh and his Davidian cult members in a compound in Waco, Texas. From the exhaustive information put together by the investigation team, as well as interviews conducted by the review panel, I would like to discuss some topics and offer some opinions and suggestions relative to the warrant execution on that day. It is hoped that all law enforcement personnel will gain additional insight and understanding as the events of Waco are studied.

Many questions have been raised in the aftermath of the law enforcement activities at Waco, Texas. One of the most perplexing is whether ANY law enforcement agency is adequately prepared to handle a similar assignment. I cannot answer that question. I can only caution against the thought of military intervention in a like situation. Unlike the military, in civilian law enforcement there can never be consideration given to any acceptable casualty losses. Occurrences of this type are nightmares for every police planner, manager and chief.

ANALYSIS OF PLAN

After dissecting A.T.F.'s involvement with the Vernon Howell investigation, it is my feeling that the raid on the Mount Carmel Center was doomed to fail even before the first highly trained SRT member stepped out of the cattle trailers on February 28, 1993.

One of the key ingredients to any successful plan is intelligence gathering. Good, sound, correct and up to the minute information is essential for any raid plan, not to mention the mammoth undertaking in Waco. This was an area in need of major improvement in the A.F.T. investigation.

It is my opinion that the case agent did his homework. I believe he conducted as thorough an investigation as was possible within the bureaucratic framework at A.T.F. There was mention of the fact that he only had five years experience in investigations and that this was his first big case. The fact remains, he developed the investigation and obtained critical information to substantiate probable cause, which led to the arrest warrant for Howell and search warrants for the compound and the "Mag Bag."

There was, however, a lot of missing information and poor intelligence gathered before the raid and on the raid day itself. Added to this was the fact that vital intelligence was overlooked, discarded or not used. This information was obtained by a host of A.T.F. personnel.

Examples of this can be seen when former cult members are interviewed and, apparently, much if not all of their statements are reported to be facts. No thought is given to the idea that these ex-cult members had been away from the compound for some time, or to their individual biases, or if they had an ax to grind with present cult members.

Another weak link in the investigation was the undercover house set up to monitor and track cult activities. From the beginning we learn agents assigned do not have a strong sense of mission. Team members were inexperienced, had no direction or supervisor. They state they did not know what to look for or what was expected of them. Did they ask?

Originally the undercover house was intended to operate on a full time basis. Within a short period it appears as if the undercover agents adjust observation times on their own. There is no 24-hour watch. Agents fail to see Howell one critical time as he left the compound. Surveillance equipment is faulty or misused. Members report there are 75 members living in the compound. The fact is 127 people are present on the day of the raid. A supervisor is brought in to take charge of operations but little changes. Why? Little useful information is gained from efforts prior to undercover agent Rodriguez making contact with the compound leader.

On the day of the raid Agent Rodriguez gets into the compound and exits after hearing Koresh say "A.T.F. and the National Guard are coming. They won't get me, they'll never get me." The undercover reports this and other useful information to the Deputy Tactical Coordinator at the undercover house. Rodriguez is instructed to call and brief the Tactical Coordinator at the rear command post. After asking the undercover several sterile questions, the Tactical Coordinator consults with the Incident Commander and another supervisory agent, then decides to speed the raid up. He disregards all the significant factors to the plan and accelerates its timetable which was based on 10:00 a.m. as being the point for entry into the compound. SRT members are instructed to dress quickly for their assignment. They are loaded onto cattle trailers and rushed to the compound.

During this time radio communications begin to break down within the raiding party. The helicopters get to the scene behind schedule. A group of observers are not in place. Added to this is the fact that forward observers at the undercover house are unfamiliar with the daily routine in the compound. They don't know what to look for. They fail to recognize that no signs of life or movement by cult members means danger. They do not report back that there are no men working in the pit. That was the critical element of the plan, SURPRISE, and the ability to separate the men from the weapons. All is lost.

As all this is happening, the leaders of the raid have inadvertently quarantined themselves from any new information. They assume tactically incorrect positions. They are not centralized. This helped make the coordination of efforts very difficult. As the response teams roll up to the front of the compound they are sitting ducks. Had it not been for the extensive training which members received at Fort Hood in preparation for this event, I feel many more agents would have been killed or injured.

Questions have been asked in the days since the initial raid on the compound. Was the plan sound? Was there consideration given to alternatives? Was the choice for a dynamic entry a reasonable call?

Based on my 25 years of experience with the New York City Police Department, if all the given facts which led to the decision to conduct the entry were true, I believe the plan had a reasonable chance of success. Members considered alternatives, but their "FACTS" led them to believe a raid on the compound could be successfully achieved. Strictly as a Monday morning quarterback, I would have opted for a siege plan. It should be noted that a plan of this nature was ultimately unsuccessful in Waco.

I believe the three-day training and other preparation conceived at Fort Hood was excellent and well thought out. Improvement in tactical situations by all members concerned was evident as displayed in the training tapes.

I disagree with A.T.F.'s policy of using the Tactical Coordinators as investigators to gain information from cult members. It put them too close to the case. I believe they lost objectivity relative to the plan. Had the investigation been done by others, tactical leaders would have questioned these so-called "facts" more closely. The decision to siege or go tactical should not be decided solely by tactical members. They are the can do, must do when all else fails people of the organization. It should be their responsibility to formulate a plan which should be analyzed, scrutinized and questioned by supervisors from above before sanctioning it. This acts as a check valve and ensures that those putting the plan together have all the facts available and that the plan holds up when challenged.

Other major flaws with this case were the way members became desensitized to the amount of arms which were reportedly in the compound and this group's fanatic hatred of A.T.F. Supervising agents failed to either realize or appreciate the magnitude of firepower that they would be up against if a fire fight erupted. Early in the case this investigation was marked "sensitive." This designation meant that A.T.F. Headquarters would automatically begin monitoring its progress. Surprisingly, there was little input or direction from above. Nobody up or down the supervisory chain of command asked tough or unpopular questions relative to the plan. No one questioned its poor case management, the improper utilization of surveillance equipment or the availability of other resources. Could agents get a warrant and put a tap on phones in the compound? Could A.T.F. not monitor CB communications coming and going to the center? No one decided to ask for or send in specialists when called for. The final decision to go/no go was ultimately left in the overtaxed hands of the Tactical Coordinator. As the decision to go forward progressed, leaders failed to properly evaluate the information learned from Agent Rodriguez. They failed to recognize that the element of surprise and its tactical significance had been lost. They underestimated their target and his unseen ambush by overestimating the intimidating appearance of 86 agents dressed in full SWAT gear.

No discussion of the events of February 28th could be complete without mention of problems encountered with the media. On December 15, 1992 case agent Aguilera learned the Waco Tribune-Herald was obtaining information about the cult, its leader and the Davidian compound for a possible article. As time went on, members of A.T.F. attempted to persuade Tribune officials to delay publication of an upcoming series featuring the cult, citing the ongoing investigation and likelihood of a potential raid. Not only did the paper refuse to comply, but the first article "The Sinful Messiah" appeared a day before the actual raid.

On the day of the raid at least seven media vehicles were in the vicinity of the compound. The Texas Rangers report of investigation details how a reporter unwittingly leaked details of a potential A.T.F. raid to a cult member who returned to the compound and alerted Koresh.

CONCLUSION

In conclusion, I would like to thank Mr. Ronald K. Noble, Assistant Secretary for Enforcement, for the leadership, candor and enthusiasm which he brought to his position. Congratulations go to all members of his team for their varied skills, straight forwardness and dedication to duty during the arduous task of gathering the information for the review panel. A word of praise as well for fellow members of the review panel. It was an honor and privilege to serve with persons of such varied backgrounds, experience and knowledge.

It is always easier to criticize, second guess and punch holes into a plan rather than construct one. No plan is or will ever be perfect. Under pressure mistakes were made. Enough cannot be said for the courage and fortitude exhibited by all A.T.F. members who risked their lives at a previously unknown compound in Texas. Despite this incident, there can be no doubt why the Bureau of Alcohol, Tobacco and Firearms is thought of, so highly by the law enforcement community.

My extreme gratitude goes to those members from A.T.F. who volunteered to meet with and discuss openly and freely the events of Waco with the review panel. To my knowledge this was an unprecidented event. Their wish and mine is that lessons can be learned from this tragic incident and that the mistakes made will not be repeated in the future.

The events in Waco should bring about a change in philosophy and create interaction between federal, state and local law enforcement and encourage the sharing of ideas equipment and training which will be beneficial to all.

Appendix B

Explosives Experts
(alphabetically by author)

Paul W. Cooper

Joseph T. Kennedy

REPORT on EXPLOSIVES QUESTIONS
RELATED to the
WACO ADMINISTRATIVE REVIEW

Paul W. Cooper
August 5, 1993

EXECUTIVE SUMMARY

A review was made of documents describing items and materials purported to have been delivered to the Branch Davidian Compound near Waco, Texas. These items and materials could, in the author's opinion, be combined in any of several ways to construct explosive destructive devices. It is shown that abundant literature is readily available which instructs the reader in the fabrication and use of such devices. It is further shown that in the United States, each year, a great number of such devices have actually been illegally fabricated and used, as reported by both the BATF and the FBI.

INTRODUCTION

This report is in response to three major questions which were posed to me by the Waco Administrative Review[Ref.1]. These were (in reference to materials/chemicals contained in an ATF Report of Investigation[Ref.2]):
  1. "Do any of these entities when combined, in any manner or quantity, constitute an explosive?"
  2. "From your experience, could any of these entities when combined, in any manner or quantity, be utilized as an explosive in an improvised explosive device?"
  3. "From your experience, what explosive or improvised explosive devices could be manufactured from the referenced entities?"

In addition to these questions, I will add three others:
  4. How many explosive devices (re: question 3) could be manufactured from the referenced entities?
  5. If the referenced entities could be made into an explosive device, would the methods of doing that exist as reference or instructional material, and if so, how available are such instructional materials?
  6. Have explosive mixtures and/or improvised explosive devices which could be fabricated from the reference entities and described in the available instructional literature ever actually been made and or used?

The report which follows will first discuss the referenced entities, and then answer each question in technical depth.

THE REFERENCE ENTITIES

The materials/chemicals described above as the reference entities and which are pertinent to the making of explosives and explosive devices (quoted from Reference 2) are:

1. "Large quantity of black powder."
    (In reference 3 this is described as "black gun powder", and also is given as 40 to 50 pounds. This may be smokeless gun powder and not black powder. The reason for suspecting this is because no shipping documents are referenced for this item but this was based, in Ref.3, upon testimony of the UPS driver. The two different gun powders are often confused by many people or not even thought to be different and therefore the names are often interchanged.).
2. "Ninety (90) pounds of powder aluminum metal and 30 to 40 card board tubes; 24" in length by 1 1/4 to 1 1/2 in diameter."
3. "Fifty (50) M-31 practice rifle grenades."
4. "One hundred fifty (150) M-31 practice rifle grenades."
5. "Potassium Nitrate (oxidizer)."
    (This is given as 30 pounds in Reference 3)
6. "Ignitor Cord (Class "C" explosive)."
    (This is given as one pound in Reference 3.).
7. "Magnesium Metal (Flammable solid)."
    (This is described as "Magnesium metal powder" and given as five pounds in Reference 3.).

In addition to the above, but not mentioned in Ref. 2, are:
8. Two boxes of practice ("pineapple type") hand grenades (about 50 hand grenades), assumed to be empty or inert[Ref.3]. This description fits the U.S. Army M21 Practice Hand Grenade.
9. Over 138,000 rounds of various small arms ammunition[Refs.3,4,5]. These are mentioned here because the smokeless powder with which each cartridge is loaded is easily removed. The total amount of smokeless powder in this number of small arms cartridges is approximately 840 pounds.

QUESTION 1

"Do any of these entities when combined, in any manner or quantity, constitute an explosive?"

Yes.

The black powder by itself is an explosive. The black powder can be combined with the aluminum powder to give it an intensified incendiary effect. The black powder can be combined with the potassium nitrate to increase its gas output when it explodes.

The smokeless powder by itself is an explosive, and like the black powder can have aluminum or magnesium powder added to it to give it an enhanced incendiary effect.

The potassium nitrate can be combined with either the aluminum powder or the magnesium powder or a mixture of the two metal powders to form an explosive.

QUESTION 2

"From your experience, could any of these entities when combined, in any manner or quantity, be utilized as an explosive in an improvised explosive device?"

Yes.

When confined in a metal case the powders and mixtures described in the answer to question 1 (above) can, when ignited, explode violently, bursting or fragmenting the casing and producing potentially lethal high velocity fragments in addition to the blast and fireball.

If confined lightly, such as in a card board tube, the powders and mixtures described above may explode sufficiently to produce a blast wave and also produce a fireball or incendiary effect.

The ignitor cord can be used not only to ignite the explosive filler of an explosive device, but can also be used to provide a delay element in a fusing train such as the burning fuse in a firework, or delay element in a hand grenade fuse.

QUESTION 3

"From your experience, what explosive or improvised explosive devices could be manufactured from the referenced entities?"

The practice hand grenade parts could be loaded with the mixtures described above and fused (have a fuse or fusing mechanism attached). The blank vent hole in the base of the practice grenade would have to be sealed by either welding or threading and plugging with a metal bung, thus making working grenades.

The mixtures described above could be loaded into metal pipes or pipe nipples, sealed at each end with pipe caps, and fused with the ignitor cord, thus making pipe bombs.

The mixtures could be loaded into card board tubes, sealed at each end, and fused with the Ignitor cord, thus making a blast and incendiary device. Such a device could be lethal from the blast effects if exploded close to or in contact with a person.

QUESTION 4

How many explosive devices (re: question 3) could be manufactured from the referenced entities?

The M21 practice grenade can hold approximately 40 to 50 cubic centimeters of powder. All of the powders mentioned above have approximately the same loose pour bulk density (approximately 0.9 g/cc), therefore each grenade would hold about 35 to 45 grams of powder. There is sufficient quantity of powder of each type described above to fill more than 250 grenades (there were at least 50 grenade bodies purported to have been delivered).

The number of pipe bombs which could have been filled would depend upon the size and length of pipes used. As an example, standard two inch pipe cut to five inches length and capped with standard end caps would hold approximately a half pound of loose poured powder. Therefore as many as 70 or more such pipe bombs could have been made from the stated quantities of any of the powders.

The 30 to 40 each 24 inch long cardboard tubes shipped with the aluminum powder could each be loaded with approximately three quarters of a pound of loose poured powder. This would fill all of the tubes and leave over some powder.

QUESTION 5

If the referenced entities could be made into an explosive device, would the methods of doing that exist as reference or instructional material, and if so, how available are such instructional materials?

Yes. Instructional material in the form of books, pamphlets, and instruction sheets are readily available in book shops, gun shows, through mail order, and even on computer bulletin boards.

References Nos. 6 through 10 of this report are examples which were recently purchased at a local gun show in Albuquerque NM. All of these references mention the REFERENCED ENTITIES in a number of admixtures and in a number of explosive devices. Reference 9 in particular describes using these exact materials loaded into modified practice hand grenades and gives methods of modifying and reloading the grenade fuses as well as manufacturing improvised fuses for the practice grenades.

QUESTION 6

Have explosive mixtures and/or improvised explosive devices which could be fabricated from the reference entities and described in the available instructional literature ever actually been made and or used?

Yes. A review of recent FBI and BATF annual reports[Refs.11,12] show a large number of cases involving pipe bombs as well as modified military ordnance (the latter includes practice grenades). The two agencies utilize somewhat different yet overlapping data bases, and report the data somewhat differently. However, a good overall picture of the usage of the referenced explosives in pipe bombs and modified military ordnance can be seen in figures 1 through 4.

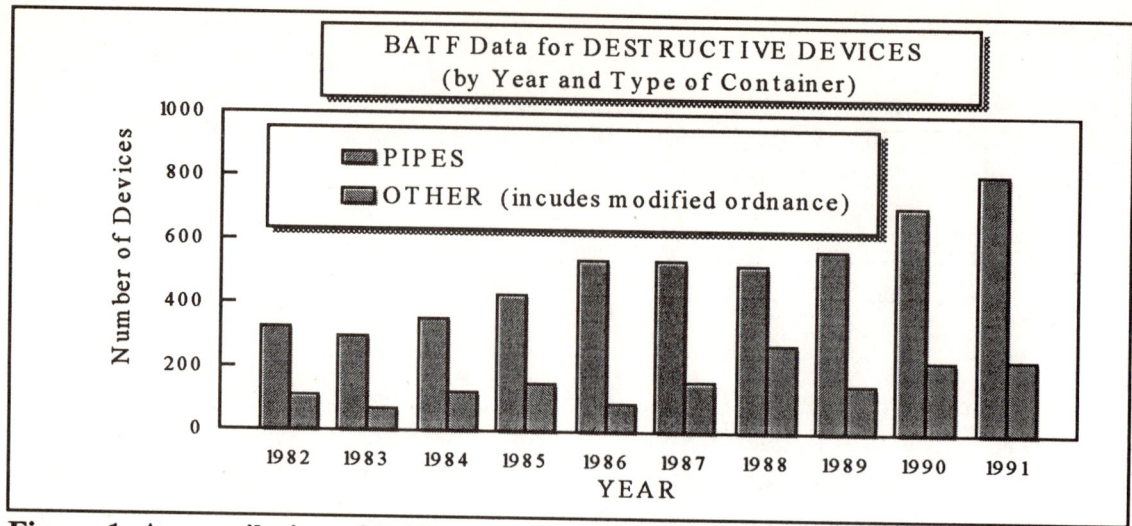

Figure 1. A compilation of BATF data for a ten year period, showing number of reported pipe bombs and modified military ordnance (these include but are not limited to modified practice grenades) regardless of filler explosive.

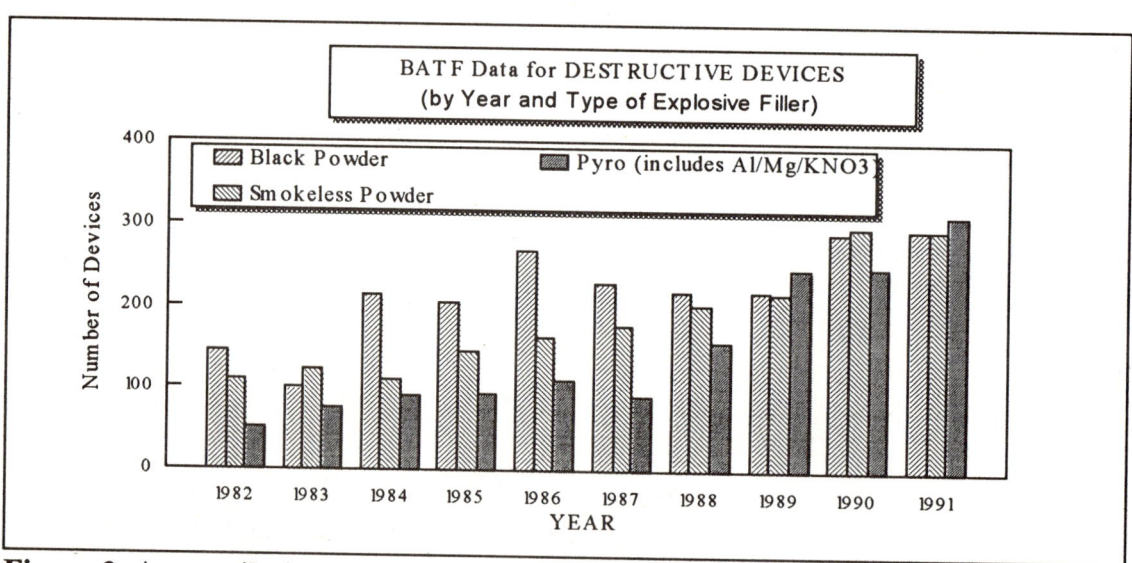

Figure 2. A compilation of BATF data for a ten year period, showing number of reported destructive devices by the type of explosive filler. These fillers are black powder, smokeless powder, and pyrotechnics (the latter include but are not limited to mixtures containing aluminum, magnesium, and potassium nitrate).

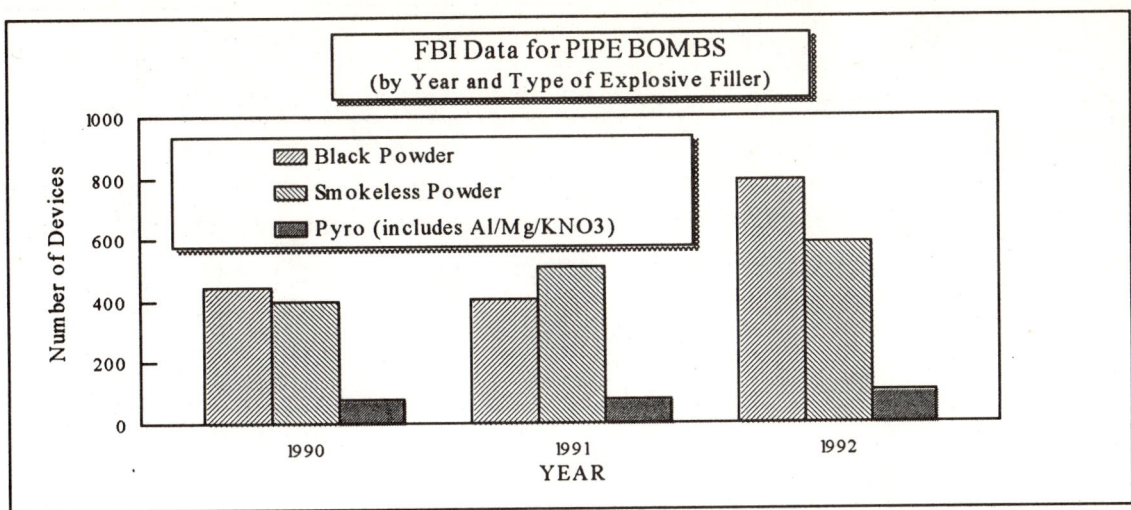

Figure 3. A compilation of FBI data for a three year period, showing number of reported pipe bombs utilizing various explosive fillers.

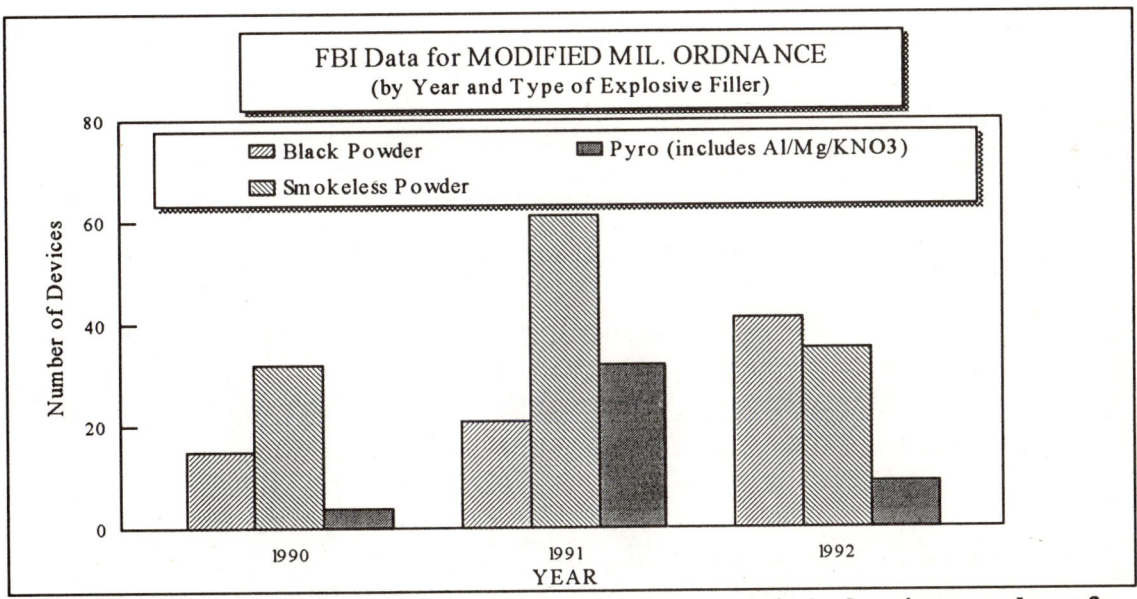

Figure 4. A compilation of FBI data for a three year period, showing number of reported modified military ordnance items (these include but are not limited to practice grenades) utilizing various explosive fillers.

CONCLUSIONS

The materials purportedly delivered to the Branch Davidians as stated in the referenced documents can, in the opinion of this author, be combined in several ways to make explosive materials and destructive explosive devices. In particular, all of the materials were present to modify and fabricate functioning fragmentation hand grenades, as well as pipe bombs, and blast and incendiary devices.

Respectfully submitted,

Paul Cooper 8/5/93

Paul W. Cooper

REFERENCES

1. "Questions for Explosives Experts", a query by the Waco Review presented to me on 7 July 1993 (copy attached as Appendix I).
2. ATF Report of Investigation, No. 53110-92-1069-X, 22 July 1992.
3. Application and Affidavit for Search Warrant, U.S. District Court, Western District of Texas, (marked W93-15M), Filed 26 Feb. 1993.
4. A Spreadsheet, titled "Deliveries to Mag-Bag", 5 pages (copy attached as Appendix II).
5. A Spreadsheet, untitled, 2 pages, (copy attached as Appendix III)
6. "CIA Field Expedient Incendiary Manual", The Combat Bookshelf, Desert Publications, Phoenix AZ, 1977.
7. "The Poor Man's James Bond", Kurt Saxon, Atlan Formularies, Eureka CA, 1972.
8. "Special Forces Demolition Techniques", Extract from Army Field Manual FM 31-20 (December 1965), Paladin Press, Boulder CO, (no date)
9. "OSS Sabotage & Demolition Manual", Paladin Press, (no date)
10. "Unconventional Warfare Devices and Techniques, INCENDIARIES", US Army TM 31-201-1 (May 1966).
11. Bu. ATF, Annual Explosives Incidents Reports:
    1985 (10 year Retrospective, 1976-1985) and all reports 1986 through 1991.
12. FBI Annual Bomb Summaries:
    1990 through 1992.

Appendix I

QUESTIONS FOR EXPLOSIVE EXPERTS

Reference the materials/chemicals contained in ATF Report of Investigation, 53110-92-1069X, dated 7/22/92.

Do any of these entities when combined, in any manner or quantity, constitute an explosive?

From your experience, could any of these entities when combined, in any manner or quantity, be utilized as an explosive in an improvised explosive device?

From your experience, what explosives or improvised explosive devices could be manufactured from the referenced entities.

Appendix II

DELIVERIES TO "AG BAG"
ROUTE 7, BOX 555, WACO, TEXAS
March 26 thru August 12, 1992
I. N. 53110-92-1069X

PAGE NO.: 1

SHIPPED FROM	DATE	INVOICE #	QUANT.	COST	DESCRIPTION
ALPHA TRADING COMPANY	06/17/92	NO INVOICE	20	$1,200.00	100 RD., AK-47 MAGAZINES
ALPHA TRADING COMPANY	08/06/92	NO INVOICE	200	$540.00	USED AR-15 30 MAGAZINES
ALPHA TRADING COMPANY	08/12/92	NO INVOICE	30	$150.00	USED M14 MAGAZINES
CENTEC FIRE SYSTEMS, INC.	07/17/92	NO INVOICE		$411.29	UNKNOWN (CONT #309912, SHIP #409992)
CENTURY INTERNAT'L ARMS	07/06/92	NO INVOICE			1M - 7.62 (#026529, PIECE #026529)
FOX FIRE CO.	06/05/92	NO INVOICE			90 LBS-POWDER, ALUM.METAL & 30-40 CARDBOARD TUBES
JONATHAN ARTHUR CIENER	07/08/92	NO INVOICE			.22 LR CONV. KITS - AR15,MINI-14 & AK47 (#451221)
JONATHAN ARTHUR CIENER	07/08/92	NO INVOICE			M203 LAUNCHERS, SUPPRESSORS, BELT FEED - AR-15
KENGS FIREARM SPECIALTY	07/09/92	NO INVOICE	2	$290.56	UNKNOWN (SHIPPING #383833, CONTROL #039756)
L & N SHOOTERS	08/07/92	NO INVOICE		$280.50	2800 RDS, 9MM AMMUNITION
NESARD GUN PARTS CO.	05/14/92	NO INVOICE		$720.00	UNKNOWN (SHIPPING #622836, CONT. #443693)
NESARD GUN PARTS CO.	05/26/92		2	$620.00	EZ KIT (M16) W/AZ, 20" BBL
NESARD GUN PARTS CO.	05/26/92		2	$550.00	CAR KIT (M16)
NESARD GUN PARTS CO.	05/26/92		1	$10.00	REVERSE FLASHHIDER (FLASH SUPPRESSOR)
NESARD GUN PARTS CO.	06/19/92	NO INVOICE	1		M-76 GRENADE LAUNCHER
NESARD GUN PARTS CO.	07/09/92	NO INVOICE		$1,250.65	UNKNOWN (SHIPPING #622836, CONT. #473126)

Appendix II-(continued)

DELIVERIES TO "...AG BAG"
ROUTE 7, BOX 555, WACO, TEXAS
March 26 thru August 12, 1992
I. N. 53110-92-1069X

PAGE NO.: 2

SHIPPED FROM	DATE	INVOICE #	QUANT.	COST	DESCRIPTION
OLYMPIC ARMS, INC.	03/26/92	A43880	5	$1,215.00	K1B, 16"
OLYMPIC ARMS, INC.	03/26/92	A43878	5	$1,215.00	K1B, 16"
OLYMPIC ARMS, INC.	03/26/92	A43879	1	$10.00	H18
OLYMPIC ARMS, INC.	03/26/92	A43879	5	$1,215.00	K1B, 16"
OLYMPIC ARMS, INC.	03/30/92	A43911	4	$972.00	K1B
OLYMPIC ARMS, INC.	03/30/92	A43911	4	$1,152.00	K2B W/EZ & AZFS
OLYMPIC ARMS, INC.	03/30/92	A43911	4	$1,152.00	K2B, W/EZ & AZFS
OLYMPIC ARMS, INC.	03/30/92	A43911	4	$972.00	K1B
OLYMPIC ARMS, INC.	03/30/92	A43923	5	$1,215.00	K1B, 16" W/AZFS
OLYMPIC ARMS, INC.	03/30/92	A43922	5	$1,215.00	K1B, 16" W/AZFS
OLYMPIC ARMS, INC.	03/30/92	A43923	5	$1,215.00	K1B, 16", W/AZFS
OLYMPIC ARMS, INC.	04/02/92	A43929	3	$879.00	K1B, W/EZ, UPPER
OLYMPIC ARMS, INC.	04/02/92	A43929	1	$243.00	K1B, 16"
OLYMPIC ARMS, INC.	04/02/92	A43929	1	$243.00	K1B, 16"
OLYMPIC ARMS, INC.	04/02/92	A43929	2	$516.00	K2B, 20 W/EZ UPPER & AZFS FLASH SUPPRESSOR
OLYMPIC ARMS, INC.	04/02/92	A43929	3	$879.00	K1B, 16" W/EZ, UPPER

Appendix II-(continued)

DELIVERIES TO "AG BAG"
ROUTE 7, BOX 555, WACO, TEXAS
March 26 thru August 12, 1992
I. N. 53110-92-1069I

PAGE NO.: 3

SHIPPED FROM	DATE	INVOICE #	QUANT.	COST	DESCRIPTION
OLYMPIC ARMS, INC.	04/02/92	A43929	2	$576.00	K2B, 20" W/EZ UPPER & AZFS
OLYMPIC ARMS, INC.	04/24/92	A45210	4	$1,228.00	K2B, W/EZ
OLYMPIC ARMS, INC.	04/24/92	A45211	4	$1,304.00	CAR-9 UNITS W/16" BBL (4 K10'S)
OLYMPIC ARMS, INC.	04/24/92	A45210	2	$598.00	K1B, W/EZ
OLYMPIC ARMS, INC.	04/24/92	A45231	4	$1,232.00	K2B, W/EZ
OLYMPIC ARMS, INC.	04/24/92	A45211	4	$1,304.00	CAR-9 UNITS W/16" BBL
OLYMPIC ARMS, INC.	04/24/92	A45210	4	$1,228.00	K2B, W/EZ
OLYMPIC ARMS, INC.	04/24/92	A45210	2	$598.00	K1B, W/EZ
OLYMPIC ARMS, INC.	04/28/92	A45233	2	$620.00	K1B, W/16" & EZ
OLYMPIC ARMS, INC.	04/28/92	A45233	8	$2,104.00	K1B, W/16"
OLYMPIC ARMS, INC.	04/28/92	A45233	2	$620.00	K1B, W/16" & EZ
OLYMPIC ARMS, INC.	04/28/92	A45233	8	$2,104.00	K1B, W/16"
OLYMPIC ARMS, INC.	04/28/92	A45231	4	$1,232.00	K2B, W/EZ
OLYMPIC ARMS, INC.	07/13/92	A47046	2	$616.00	CAR-45 UNIT
OLYMPIC ARMS, INC.	07/13/92	A47046	2	$586.00	CAR-9 UNIT
OLYMPIC ARMS, INC.		NO INVOICE		$2,500.00	.223 AMMUNITION (MARCH 92)

Appendix II-(continued)

PAGE NO.: 4

DELIVERIES TO "..AG BAG"
ROUTE 7, BOX 555, WACO, TEXAS
March 26 thru August 12, 1992
I. N. 53110-92-1069I

SHIPPED FROM	DATE	INVOICE #	QUANT.	COST	DESCRIPTION
OLYMPIC ARMS, INC.		NO INVOICE		$280.50	9MM AMMUNITION - 2800 RDS. (AUG. 92)
P. L. & T. TIFFIN KNIVES	08/03/92	NO INVOICE		$374.00	KNIVES
ROCK ISLAND ARMORY, INC.	06/17/92	104722	50	$162.50	M31 PRACTICE RIFLE GRENADES
ROCK ISLAND ARMORY, INC.	06/29/92	104818	150	$487.50	M31 PRACTICE RIFLE GRENADES
SARCO, INC.	05/26/92	A43318	1	$274.95	M16 PARTS SET KIT "A" W/SLING & MAG (NO LWR.RCVR.)
SARCO, INC.	06/18/92	A45276	2	$249.50	M261 RIFLE CONVERSION KITS
SARCO, INC.	06/18/92	A45276	3	$30.00	COMBO WRENCH
SARCO, INC.	06/18/92	A45276	3	$824.85	M16 KIT "A" (SPECIAL OFFERINGS)
SARCO, INC.	06/18/92	A45276	6	$49.95	.22 CONVERSION UNIT MAGS
SARCO, INC.	06/18/92	A45276	4	$79.80	M203 HANDGUARDS
SHOOTERS EQUIPMENT CO.	07/16/92	NO INVOICE		$387.51	UNKNOWN (CONT #833766, SHIP #227471, PKG 4199)
SHOOTERS EQUIPMENT CO.	07/17/92	NO INVOICE		$68.88	UNKNOWN (CONT #833722, SHIP #277471, ID SEC-T-68)
SHOOTERS EQUIPMENT CO.	07/20/92	NO INVOICE		$122.76	UNKNOWN (CONT #833674, SHIP #227471, ID SEC-T-73)
TAPCO, INC.	06/30/92	0022292	2	$299.90	FLARE LAUNCHER W/C.A.R. MOUNT
TAPCO, INC.	07/14/92	NO INVOICE		$1,386.86	UNKNOWN (CONT #578336, SHIP #393495)
TAPCO-SPECIALIZED WEAPONS	06/15/92		2	$44.00	M203 M16 HANDGUARDS

Appendix II-(continued)

DELIVERIES TO "AG BAG"
ROUTE 7, BOX 555, WACO, TEXAS
March 26 thru August 12, 1992
I. N. 53110-92-1069X

PAGE NO.: 5

SHIPPED FROM	DATE	INVOICE #	QUANT.	COST	DESCRIPTION
TAPCO-SPECIALIZED WEAPONS	06/15/92		2	$355.50	CM-2037 FLARE LAUNCHER
TAPCO-SPECIALIZED WEAPONS	06/15/92		2	$65.50	M203 H.G. SIGHT ASSEMBLY
UNKNOWN	06/08/92	NO INVOICE	60		M-16/AR-15 MAGAZINES
UNKNOWN	06/18/92	NO INVOICE			CHEMICALS, INSTRUMENTS & GLASSWARE
UNKNOWN		NO INVOICE			PRACTICE GRENADES (2 CASES) & BLACK POWDER
UNKNOWN (UPS SHIPMENT)	07/02/92	NO INVOICE			POTASSIUM NITRATE, 30 LBS. (OXIDIZER) ID #UNI486
UNKNOWN (UPS SHIPMENT)	07/02/92	NO INVOICE			MAGNESIUM METAL, 5 LBS.
UNKNOWN (UPS SHIPMENT)	07/02/92	NO INVOICE			IGNITER CORD, 1 LB. (CLASS C EXPLO.)

TOTAL COST: $44,325.46

E N D O F R E P O R T

Appendix III

Feb 1992	March 5 - 9, 1992	March 5 - 9, 1992	April 1992	May 1992	June 1992
18 Firearms Purchased: 13 Assault Rifles, 1 Pistol and 4 Shotgun	Team Training held at house 500 Yards East of "Mag Bag" towards Compound. These SWAT Teams from five different law enforcement agencies held all day SWAT Team entries.	2 Firearms Purchased: 2 Assault Rifles	67 Firearms Purchased: 56 Assault Rifles and 11 Pistols	35 Firearms Purchased: 31 Assault Rifles and 4 Pistols.	18 Firearms Purchased: 18 Assault Rifles.
		Fatta buys ground sensors and night vision 3/9/92.	Purchased 6 Walkie Talkies 4/15/92.	1 Case 7.62 ammo 5/10/92.	90 Pounds Aluminum Powder 6/5/92.
		Little orders chemicals to build explosive devices and hand grenades 3/10/92.	11 SWG Lower Receivers for building machineguns M-16 4/1/92.	6 SWG Lower Receivers for building machineguns M-16 5/12/92.	Repairs Water Well in Compound 6/5/92.
	Howell believes this is a large ATF SWAT Team who are practicing for a raid on the Compound.	Howell orders CA Davidians to come to Texas Compound and 40 members arrive from England in mid-March.	15 SWG Lower Receivers for building machineguns M-16 4/7/92.	6 SWG Lower Receivers for building machineguns M-16 5/18/92.	12 SWG Lower Receivers for building machineguns 6/7/92.
	Howell makes call to arms at Compound in preparation for what he believes is an impeding search and arrest by ATF.	Michael Schroeder orders and receives conversion kits to make machineguns: 3/11/92 29 machinegun kits 4/1/92 20 machinegun kits 5/18/92 34 machinegun kits 7/16/92 37 machinegun kits	100 Magazines 7.65 cal, 30 round; 30 Cases 7.62 ammo 4/22/92.	48 cases 7.62 x 39 steel core ammo on 5/22/92.	3 SWG Lower Receivers for building machineguns 6/9/92.
		Upper receivers to make 100 AR-15/M-16 Assault Rifles arrive by 4/28/92.	5 SWG Lower Receivers for building machineguns M-16 4/30/92.	144 webb belts 4/22/92	200 M-31 Rifle Grenades (Attempt to Activate) 6/10/92
		60 Cases of 7.62 ammo, 20 Cases of .308 ammo received in March and April. (1200 rounds per case)		50 vests, 4 pouches each for AK-47, 30 round magazines on 5/14/92.	
		100 Magazines 7.62 cal 30 round 3/26/92			

* * FIREARMS DATA OBTAINED THROUGH VERIFIED RECORDS/SOURCES. UNDOCUMENTED FIREARMS ARE NOT INCLUDED IN DATA.

B-151

Appendix III-(continued)

	July	Aug 1992	Sept 1992	Oct 1992	Nov 1992	Dec 1992	1993	Feb 1993	TOTALS
14 Firearms Purchased: 13 Assault Rifles and 1 Pistol.	2 Firearms Purchased: 3 Assault Rifles and 9 Pistols.	No Activity	2 Firearms Purchased: 2 Pistols	20 AK-47 Magazines 100 Round 11/23/92.	1 Firearm Purchased: 1 Pistol	No Activity	No Activity	Prior to March 5, 1992 80 Firearms were purchased.
8 SWG Lower Receivers for building machineguns M-16 7/20/92.	200 AR-15/ M-16 Magazines 30 round 8/6/92.			20 AK-47 100 round magazines on 11/23/92.				After March 5, 1992 236 Additional Firearms were purchased (153 Assault Rifles included).
2 SWG Lower Receivers for building machineguns M-16 7/27/92.	2800 Rounds 9mm ammo 8/7/92.							120 Conversion kits for Assault Rifles.
	30 M-14 Magazines .308 cal 20 rounds 8/12/92.							
	9 Cases .308 ammo 8/18/92.							

* * THIS REPORT DOES NOT INCLUDE FIREARMS THAT WERE PURCHASED AND/OR ACQUIRED WITHOUT RECORDS BEING MADE (CASH SALES AT GUN SHOWS AND ELSEWHERE)

 **TECHMATICS, Inc.**   Three Crystal Park, 2231 Crystal Drive, Suite 1000, Arlington, Virginia 22202-3742
(703) 521-3818

July 23, 1993

Department of the Treasury
Waco Review Office, Room 4311
1500 Pennsylvania Avenue, N.W.
Washington, D.C.   20220

ATTN: Mr. Joseph A. Masonis

Subj: Waco Review Independent Explosive Report

Dear Sir:

   The enclosed report constitutes my individual assessment relative to the chemicals and materials reported to be involved in the Waco, Texas incident.
   I sincerely appreciate the opportunity to be of service and if there are any question regarding the substance of this report please call me.

Sincerely,

Joseph T. Kennedy
Captain USN (Ret)

Enclosure: Waco Review Independent Explosive Report w/2 annexes

Corporate Headquarters: Fair Lakes II, 12450 Fair Lakes Circle, Suite 800, Fairfax, Virginia 22033 • (703) 802-8300

WACO REVIEW INDEPENDENT EXPLOSIVE REPORT

PURPOSE. The purpose of this report is to provide an independent judgment whether the list of materials and chemicals contained in the <u>ATF Report of Investigation, 53110-92-1069x, dated 7/22/92</u>, could be used singly or in combination to fabricate an improvised explosive device (IED).

BACKGROUND/DEFINITIONS. The following ingredients contained in the report could be made into an IED: black powder, potassium nitrate, aluminum powder, magnesium powder, ignitor cord and the M-21 practice hand grenades. Of these materials the following are included in the U.S. military <u>Explosive Ordnance Disposal (EOD) -60 series</u> publications as "Typical Improvised Device Materials":

Material	Hazard	Remarks/Precautions
Black Powder	Friction, spark, flame, shock, or static electricity.	Use nonsparking tools and packing materials. Protect against reaction elements.
Potassium Nitrate	Produces toxic oxides when burned.	Increases flammability of combustible materials.
Aluminum Powder	Respiratory and eye irritant.	Used primarily to increase temperatures in explosive and incendiary mixtures.
Magnesium powder	Respiratory and eye irritant.	Used to increase temperatures in explosive and incendiary mixtures.

Ignitor cord, a class C explosive, generally consists of a center wire coated with a burning compound contained by layered wrappings which is used to cause ignition or provide a delay regulated by the speed of burn designed into the compound. All these materials could also be used in an improvised incendiary device. M-21 practice grenades with some modification can be used as a container to provide containment for these materials.

EXPERIENCE. I would be able to construct an IED by modifying the grenades to permit loading of the black powder. Black powder could be used alone or mixed with small amounts of potassium nitrate and either aluminum or magnesium powder. Aluminum and magnesium powders would serve to increase temperature while potassium nitrate, an oxidizer, would enhance combustion.

M-21 practice grenades are designed with a smooth hole in the bottom containing a stopper plug which can be blown out when the ignitor initiates the small amount of black powder. To modify this into an explosive grenade, the smooth hole could be threaded to accept a closure plug thereby sealing the bottom of the grenade and providing containment for the explosive mixture. Practice grenades normally contain a fuse resembling the operational model. The fuse consists of a primer that, when struck by the spring loaded striker mechanism, emits a spark to ignite a small charge of black powder. This generates a puff of smoke to provide realism in a training exercise. This fuse could be easily modified to provide a delay channel using time fuse or ignitor cord which would accept the primer's spark and burn with a short delay (approximately 5 seconds) to then ignite the black powder or black powder mixture.

Annex A, taken from the <u>Expedient Hand Grenades</u> publication listed in Annex B, is just one example of this type of delay fuse. If a practice fuse was not available, time fuse or ignitor cord could be used in a more rudimentary way through a stuffing tube in the top of the grenade to provide delay and ignition of the black powder. This same application is typically found in pipe bombs except the fuse is introduced through a drilled hole in one end cap on a piece of pipe. Fabricating an improvised device is one thing and having it function as desired is another. While their safety and quality are usually suspect, their consistency and effectiveness can provide insight into the maker's subject knowledge.

The quantities of materials listed in the report would support conversion of the two cases of practice grenades (30-40 grams each) as well as a large quantity of pipe bombs or incendiary devices.

KNOWLEDGE. While someone with the proper educational background or appropriate training in explosives from military or commercial sources can build an improvised explosive device, the ability to produce an IED is essentially limited only by one's ability to read. Numerous publications on the open market not only describe the chemistry in detail but provide a step by step description to build explosive and incendiary devices. The appendix to this report includes a small sampling of publications that are available in newsstands, gun shows, and public libraries. Additionally, there are periodicals such as <u>Soldier of Fortune</u> magazine that occasionally have "how to" articles as well as an advertisement for many of the books in the appendix.

I determined the availability of information for the construction of improvised explosive devices by visiting the Library of Congress, a local bookstore, and newsstand in

Alexandria, VA. At the Library of Congress, I used an access terminal in the Adams Building's Science and Technology Reading Room to search on the keyword "explosives." This identified the book titles included in the bibliography, Annex B. Paladin Press, which specializes in this genre, has several pages of book advertisement in two recent editions of <u>Soldier of Fortune</u> magazine and continues its production of <u>The Poor Man's James Bond</u>, one of the original classics. The newest source of information is computer bulletin boards. Anyone with a computer and telephone modem, and knowledge to access networks can dial in and find this information on the "bulletin board." As a test case, I dialed in and found numerous articles on how to manufacture explosives and make improvised explosive and incendiary devices.

CONCLUSION. The ingredients referenced in the reports and discussed above could be fabricated into an explosive or incendiary device.

Respectfully submitted _____
                                        Joseph T. Kennedy
                                        Captain USN (Ret)

ANNEX A
EXPEDIENT HAND GRENADES

STRIKER ACTUATED EXPEDIENT TYPE HAND GRENADE FUZE

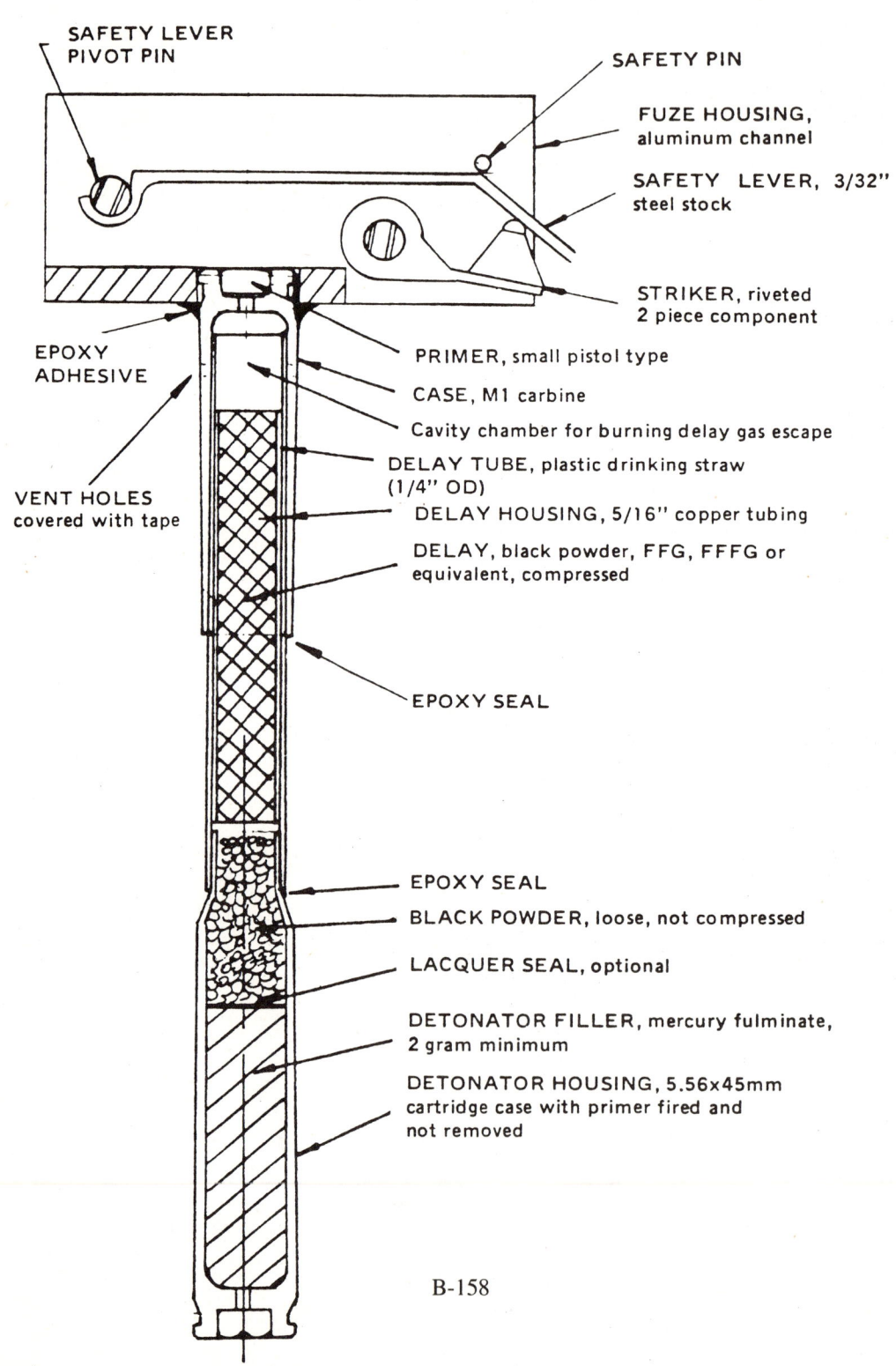

ANNEX B

<u>The Anarchist Arsenal: Improvised Incendiary and Explosives Techniques</u>, by David Harber, published by Paladin Press, Boulder CO, 1990 (Keyword was "Explosives--Amateurs' manuals").

<u>The Anarchist Handbook</u>, by Robert Wells, published by J. Flores, Rosemead CA, 1985 (keyword was "Explosives, Military--Handbooks, manuals, etc.").

<u>Bomb Squad: Defining and Defusing Terrorist Explosives</u>, published by Paladin Press, Boulder CO, 1990 (keyword was "Paladin Press").

<u>Deadly Brew: Advanced Improvised Explosives</u>, by Seymour Lecker, published by Paladin Press, Boulder CO, 1987 (keyword was "Explosives--Handbooks, manuals, etc.").

<u>EOD Improvised Explosives Manual</u>, published by Paladin Press, Boulder CO, 1990 (keyword was "Explosives--Handbooks, manuals, etc.").

<u>Expedient Hand Grenades</u>, by G. Dmitrieff, published by Desert Publications, El Dorado AR, 1984.

<u>Improved Explosives: How to make your own</u>, by Seymour Lecker, published by Paladin Press, Boulder CO, 1985 (keyword was "Explosives, Military--Handbooks, manuals, etc.").

<u>Improvised Munitions Black Book</u>, published by Desert Publications, El Dorado AZ, 1982 (Keyword was "Explosives--Amateurs' manuals").

<u>The Poisoner's Handbook</u>, by Maxwell Hutchkinson, published by Loompanics, Port Townsend WA, 1988 (keyword was "Explosives--Miscellanea").

<u>The Poor Man's James Bond</u>, by Kurt Saxon, published by Atlan Formularies, Eureka CA.

<u>Ragnar's Guide to Home and Recreational Use of High Explosives</u>, by Ragnar Benson, published by Paladin Press, Boulder CO, 1988 (Keyword was "Explosives--Amateurs' manuals").

Appendix B

Firearms Experts

(alphabetically by author)

Wm. C. Davis

Charles R. Fagg

TIOGA ENGINEERING COMPANY, INC.
P.O. Box 913, 13 Cone Street
Wellsboro, PA 16901

WM. C. DAVIS, JR., P.E.
REGISTRATION 453K, Pa.

TELEPHONES:
(717) 724-3533
(717) 662-2730
FAX (717) 662-3347

LETTER REPORT

SUBJECT: Review of BATF Operations in the Matter of David Koresh and the Branch Davidian Cult at Waco, Texas

FOR: Joseph A. Masonis
Waco Review Team
U. S. Treasury Department
1500 Pennsylvania Avenue NW
Washington, DC 20220

DATE: 3 August 1993

1. BACKGROUND:

1.1 As is now well known, agents of the Bureau of Alcohol, Tobacco and Firearms (BATF), attempting to execute a search warrant on 28 February 1993 at the compound of the so-called "Branch Davidian" cult which was led by Vernon W. Howell (aka: David Koresh) near Waco, Texas, were met by armed resistance. The initial encounter resulted in the shooting deaths of both BATF agents and cult members; the ensuing confrontation, which lasted until 19 April 1993, resulted finally in the death of Koresh and many members of his cult. A review of all aspects of this operation is now in progress. One part of that review is to address the question of whether the evidence available to the BATF, before the raid on 28 February 1993, was sufficient to support a reasonable inference that Koresh and his followers inside the compound were assembling automatic weapons ("machine guns") in violation of provisions of the National Firearms Act.

1.2 This writer has agreed to serve and has been appointed as a technical consultant to review independently the evidence that was available to the BATF prior to the raid on 28 February 1993, and to formulate an opinion, if possible, as to whether the BATF had reasonable cause to obtain a search warrant and attempt to execute it on the premises of the "Branch Davidian" cult on 28 February 1993.

2. ITEMS OF EVIDENCE EXAMINED:

2.1 Inclosure 1 herewith is a compiled list of military and/or paramilitary materiel, including firearms, ammunition, etc., procured by Koresh and his followers from about February 1992 to December 1992. The names of items listed in Inclosure 1 were taken from several different source documents that were made available to me for review, as shown at Inclosure 2. The items listed on the various source documents were entered into a computer data base so that they could be sorted and grouped according to various criteria for analysis. Inclosure 1 is a printout of the data base. Because of overlapping dates and inconsistencies in nomenclature used in the source documents, there are some uncertainties in their interpretation. It follows, therefore, that there may be some inaccuracies in the data base compiled from the source documents. It is possible that some of the individual items found in the source documents have been either omitted entirely or have been counted twice in compiling the data base. I believe, however, that the number of such discrepancies is relatively small, and would have no significant effect on the overall conclusions to be drawn from the data.

2.2 Another point of information that is important, in my opinion, to the analysis of the data on acquisition of materiel by Koresh and his followers, is the kind of machine tools available to them. In response to my inquiries on this point, I have been informed that at least an engine lathe and a milling machine were known to be available inside the compound.

3. OBSERVATIONS:

3.1 None of the many pieces of information available to me is sufficient, by itself, to answer the question as to whether Koresh and his followers inside the compound were engaged in assembling automatic weapons in violation of the National Firearms Act. However, these pieces of information, taken together, form a context in which that overall question should be addressed. The evidence indicates that the BATF had acquired the following information by about the end of December 1992, approximately two months before the attempt to execute the search warrant at the "Branch Davidian" compound.

3.1.1   Between February 1992 and December 1992, Koresh and his followers had acquired the items listed below:

> 3.1.1.1   Approximately 136 weapons described as "assault rifles", 29 pistols, 4 shotguns, 786 magazines for firearms, and 211,000 rounds of small-arms ammunition.
>
> 3.1.1.2   In addition to these purchases of complete firearms, Koresh and his followers also had purchased 110 AR15/M16 upper receivers (with barrels) and 68 AR15/M16 lower-receiver

assemblies, indicating that at least 110 AR15/M16 rifles were to be assembled.

3.1.1.3   Additional firearms-related items procured by Koresh and his followers included grenade-launcher attachments for AR15/M16 rifles, and a modification that reportedly allowed the AR15/M16 rifle to be loaded and fired using belts of ammunition (a typical characteristic of true machine guns) instead of loading and firing ammunition fed from magazines, as it is commonly done for rifles.

3.1.1.4   Koresh and his followers also had purchased more than 400 empty M31 Practice rifle grenades, unspecified quantities of blackpowder, and various materials that may be used in making explosive and/or pyrotechnic compounds, including 30 pounds of potassium nitrate, 5 pounds of magnesium metal, 90 pounds of powdered aluminum, and one pound of igniter cord (a Class C explosive).

3.1.2   The items enumerated above include only those known to have been delivered to Koresh and his followers in recorded transactions. They do not include items that might have been purchased directly from vendors or from private parties within the state of Texas, or otherwise in unrecorded transactions.

3.2 It seems virtually certain that most of the parts obtained by Koresh and his followers for assembly into AR15/M16 rifles were of the military M16 configuration, some of which differ significantly from those of the semiautomatic AR15 rifle. In particular, the bolt carrier, selector, trigger, hammer and disconnector of M16 configuration differ significantly from those of the semiautomatic AR15 rifle. These parts of M16 configuration can be installed in a semiautomatic AR15 rifle, but they do not convert the rifle to automatic fire, except in combination with an **automatic sear**. There is no automatic sear listed in the accounting above, so the question now arising is whether it is reasonably probable that Koresh and his followers had possession of automatic sears for use in assembling automatic rifles from the AR15/M16 parts that they had obtained.

3.2.1   It is perhaps significant that Koresh and his followers elected to purchase parts for assembly into AR15/M16 rifles, rather than buying the assembled weapons themselves. One might speculate that buying parts to assemble the firearms was an economy measure, but the savings realized would not have been very great in comparison with the cult's total expenditures on armament during this period. The alternative and more plausible explanation seems to be that firearms of the type they preferred could not have been legally procured because they are automatic weapons. Furthermore, it seems unlikely that the cult would have purchased parts sufficient to assemble more than 100 rifles unless they knew in advance that they had access to all the parts required to complete the weapons, including automatic sears.

3.2.2 Automatic sears are of two types. The automatic sear used in military M16 automatic rifles is specifically designed for installation and functioning in the lower receiver of the M16 automatic rifle, and the lower receiver of the M16 automatic rifle is designed to accommodate the automatic sear. The lower receiver of the non-military AR15-type semiautomatic rifle is purposefully designed so as to <u>prevent</u> the installation of the military automatic sear, but the AR15-type receiver can, by a person sufficiently skilled and having access to a milling machine with appropriate tooling, be altered to allow installation of a military automatic sear.

3.2.3 The so-called "drop-in" automatic sear was specifically designed and intended for installation in the unmodified lower receiver of the AR15 semiautomatic rifle. The "drop-in" automatic sear will, when used in combination with certain military M16-type parts that are readily available, provide the capability for genuine automatic fire from the rifle. The "drop-in" automatic sear was available from various sources and was not subject to special controls before 1986. It has since 1986 been subject to the same controls imposed by the NFA on automatic weapons ("machine guns"), but there are undoubtedly unregistered specimens of the "drop-in" sear still in existence. Given one specimen as a pattern, a skilled machinist, having access to a milling machine with appropriate tooling, could produce serviceable "drop-in" automatic sears.

4. CONCLUSIONS:

4.1 It is my conclusion that the quantities and types of military and/or paramilitary items purchased by Koresh and his followers between February 1992 and December 1992 indicate that he was preparing for what he perceived would be all-out armed conflict against the forces of civil authority. If that is so, he would probably have perceived some advantage in arming his followers with automatic weapons for the occasion, and he would have had little concern for the comparatively trivial infraction of violating the National Firearms Act by assembling automatic weapons.

4.2 It is also my conclusion, based on the aforementioned records of purchases made by Koresh and his followers, that they had by January 1992 acquired all of the parts necessary, with the possible exception of automatic sears, for assembling a substantial number of M16-type automatic rifles. Furthermore, it is my conclusion that Koresh and his followers had equipment capable of modifying the lower receivers of AR15-type semiautomatic rifles to accept the M16-type automatic sears, and also equipment capable of making "drop-in" automatic sears for use in unmodified AR15-type lower receivers.

4.3 In summary, it is my conclusion that the information available to the BATF on or before 31 December 1992 was sufficient to justify a reasonable inference that Koresh and his followers in the compound of the cult were engaged in the assembly of automatic weapons, in violation of the National Firearms Act.

SUBMITTED: _____
Wm. C. Davis, Jr., P.E.

Incls:
1. Compilation of data on materiel acquired.
2. Source documents from which data were compiled.

8/04/93　　　　　　　　　　　　　　DELIVERIES
　　　　　　　　　　　　　　　　　(DESC. SORT)

Date	Desc	Qty	From	Cost
4/30/92	AMMUNITION, .308 (1200 RDS PER CASE-20 CASES)	24000	UNKNOWN	
8/18/92	AMMUNITION, .308 (1200 RDS PER CASE-9 CASES)	10800	UNKNOWN	
7/06/92	AMMUNITION, 7.62 (#026529, PIECE #026529)	1000	CENTURY INTERNATIONAL ARMS	
5/10/92	AMMUNITION, 7.62 (1200 RDS PER CASE-1 CASE)	1200	UNKNOWN	
4/22/92	AMMUNITION, 7.62 (1200 RDS PER CASE-30 CASES)	36000	UNKNOWN	
3/31/92	AMMUNITION, 7.62 (1200 RDS PER CASE-60 CASES)	72000	UNKNOWN	
5/22/92	AMMUNITION, 7.62 X 39 STEEL CORE(1200 RDS PER CASE-48 CASES)	57600	UNKNOWN	
8/07/92	AMMUNITION, 9MM	2800	L & N SHOOTERS	280.50
8/01/92	AMMUNITION, 9MM	2800	OLYMPIC ARMS, INC	280.50
8/07/92	AMMUNITION, 9MM	2800	UNKNOWN	
2/01/92	ASSAULT RIFLES	13	UNKNOWN	
3/09/92	ASSAULT RIFLES	2	UNKNOWN	
4/01/92	ASSAULT RIFLES	56	UNKNOWN	
5/01/92	ASSAULT RIFLES	31	UNKNOWN	
6/01/92	ASSAULT RIFLES	18	UNKNOWN	
7/01/92	ASSAULT RIFLES	13	UNKNOWN	
8/01/92	ASSAULT RIFLES	3	UNKNOWN	
7/08/92	BELT FEED (AR15)		JONATHAN ARTHUR CIENER	
5/26/92	CAR. KIT, M16	2	NESSARD GUN PARTS CO.	550.00
3/10/92	CHEMICALS FOR EXPLOSIVE DEVICES & HAND GRENADES		UNKNOWN	
'92	CHEMICALS, INSTRUMENTS & GLASSWARE		UNKNOWN	
2	CLEANING KIT, M16	1	OLYMPIC ARMS, INC	10.00
7/__/92	CONVERSION KIT, .22LR, AR15,MINI14 & AK47 (#451221)		JONATHAN AARTHUR CIENER	
6/18/92	CONVERSION KITS, AR15/M16, (M261 RIFLE CONVERSION KITS)	2	SARCO, INC	249.50
6/18/92	CONVERSION, AR15/M16 KIT, (EXCEPT LOWER RECEIVER)	3	SARCO, INC	824.85
5/26/92	EZ KIT, M16, W/AZ, 20" BBL	2	NESSARD GUN PARTS CO.	620.00
6/10/92	GRENADES, M-31 RIFLE	200	UNKNOWN	
6/17/92	GRENADES, M31 PRACTICE RIFLE	50	ROCK ISLAND ARMORY, INC	162.50
6/29/92	GRENADES, M31 PRACTICE RIFLE	150	ROCK ISLAND ARMORY, INC	487.50
	GRENADES, PRACTICE (CASES)	2	UNKNOWN	
3/09/92	GROUND SENSORS & NIGHT VISION EQUIPMENT		UNKNOWN	
6/18/92	HANDGUARDS, M203	4	SARCO, INC	79.80
6/15/92	HANDGUARDS, M203 FOR M16	2	TAPCO-SPECIALIZED WEAPONS	44.00
7/02/92	IGNITER CORD, 1 LB (CLASS C EXPLOSIVE)		UNKNOWN	
8/03/92	KNIVES		P.L. & T. TIFFIN KNIVES	374.00
6/15/92	LAUNCHER, FLARE CM-2037	2	TAPCO-SPECIALIZED WEAPONS	355.50
6/30/92	LAUNCHER, FLARE W/C.A.R. MOUNT	2	TAPCO, INC	299.90
6/19/92	LAUNCHER, GRENADE, M76	1	NESSARD GUN PARTS CO.	
7/08/92	LAUNCHERS, M203		JONATHAN ARTHUR CIENER	
6/07/92	LOWER RECEIVERS, SWG	12	UNKNOWN	
6/09/92	LOWER RECEIVERS, SWG	3	UNKNOWN	
4/01/92	LOWER RECEIVERS, SWG (M16)	11	UNKNOWN	
4/07/92	LOWER RECEIVERS, SWG (M16)	15	UNKNOWN	
4/30/92	LOWER RECEIVERS, SWG (M16)	5	UNKNOWN	
5/12/92	LOWER RECEIVERS, SWG (M16)	6	UNKNOWN	

8/04/93   DELIVERIES
                             (DESC. SORT)

Date	Desc	Qty	From	Cost
5/18/92	LOWER RECEIVERS, SWG (M16)	6	UNKNOWN	
7/20/92	LOWER RECEIVERS, SWG (M16)	8	UNKNOWN	
7/27/92	LOWER RECEIVERS, SWG (M16)	2	UNKNOWN	
6/18/92	MAGAZINES, .22 CONVERSION, (FOR G.I. M261 CONVERSION UNIT)	6	SARCO, INC	49.95
3/26/92	MAGAZINES, 7.62, (30 RD)	100	UNKNOWN	
4/22/92	MAGAZINES, 7.65 (30 RD)	100	UNKNOWN	
11/23/92	MAGAZINES, AK47, 100 RD	20	UNKNOWN	
11/23/92	MAGAZINES, AK47, 100 RD	20	UNKNOWN	
6/17/92	MAGAZINES, AK47, 100 RD.	20	ALPHA TRADING COMPANY	1,200.00
8/06/92	MAGAZINES, AR15/M16, (30-RD)	200	UNKNOWN	
8/12/92	MAGAZINES, M14, (.308 CAL, 20-RD)	30	UNKNOWN	
6/08/92	MAGAZINES, M16/AR15	60	UNKNOWN	
8/06/92	MAGAZINES, USED AR15,30	200	ALPHA TRADING COMPANY	540.00
8/12/92	MAGAZINES, USED M14	30	ALPHA TRADING COMPANY	150.00
7/02/92	MAGNESIUM METAL, 5 LBS		UNKNOWN	
5/26/92	PARTS, M16, SET KIT "A", W/SLING & MAG (NO LOWER RECEIVER)	1	SARCO, INC	274.95
2/01/92	PISTOL	1	UNKNOWN	
4/01/92	PISTOL	11	UNKNOWN	
5/01/92	PISTOL	4	UNKNOWN	
7/01/92	PISTOL	1	UNKNOWN	
8/01/92	PISTOL	9	UNKNOWN	
10/ /92	PISTOL	2	UNKNOWN	
/ /92	PISTOL	1	UNKNOWN	
7/ /92	POTASSIUM NITRATE, (OXIDIZER), (LBS.)	30	UNKNOWN	
6/05/92	POWDER, ALUMINUM		UNKNOWN	
6/05/92	POWDER, ALUMINUM METAL (LBS.) (& 30-40 CARDBOARD TUBES)	90	FOX FIRE CO.	
	POWDER, BLACK		UNKNOWN	
2/01/92	SHOTGUN	4	UNKNOWN	
6/15/92	SIGHT ASSEMBLY, M203 H.G.	2	TAPCO-SPECIALIZED WEAPONS	65.50
5/26/92	SUPPRESSOR, FLASH, REVERSE FLASHHIDER	1	NESSARD GUN PARTS CO.	10.00
7/08/92	SUPPRESSORS		JONATHAN ARTHUR CIENER	
7/16/92	UNKNOWN		SHOOTERS EQUIPMENT CO.	387.51
7/17/92	UNKNOWN		SHOOTERS EQUIPMENT CO.	68.88
7/20/92	UNKNOWN		SHOOTERS EQUIPMENT CO.	122.76
7/14/92	UNKNOWN		TAPCO, INC	1,386.86
7/17/92	UNKNOWN (CONT #309912, SHIP #409992)		CENTEC FIRE SYSTEMS, INC	411.29
7/09/92	UNKNOWN (SHIPPING #383833, CONTROL #039756)	2	KENGS FIREARM SPECIALTY	290.56
7/09/92	UNKNOWN (SHIPPING #622836, CONT. #473126)		NESSARD GUN PARTS CO.	1,250.65
5/14/92	UNKNOWN, (SHIPPING #622836, CONT. #443693)		NESSARD GUN PARTS CO.	720.00
4/24/92	UPPER ASSEMBLY, 16" BBL, CAR-9 (9MM)	4	OLYMPIC ARMS, INC	1,304.00
4/24/92	UPPER ASSEMBLY, 16" BBL, CAR-9 (9MM)	4	OLYMPIC ARMS, INC	1,304.00
7/13/92	UPPER ASSEMBLY, CAR-45 (.45AUTO)	2	OLYMPIC ARMS, INC	616.00
7/13/92	UPPER ASSEMBLY, CAR-9 (9MM)	2	OLYMPIC ARMS, INC	586.00
4/02/92	UPPER RECEIVER, 16" BBL	1	OLYMPIC ARMS, INC	243.00
4/02/92	UPPER RECEIVER, 16" BBL	1	OLYMPIC ARMS, INC	243.00
4/28/92	UPPER RECEIVER, 16" BBL	8	OLYMPIC ARMS, INC	2,104.00

8/04/93   DELIVERIES
                         (DESC. SORT)

Date	Desc	Qty	From	Cost
4/28/92	UPPER RECEIVER, 16" BBL	8	OLYMPIC ARMS, INC	2,104.00
3/30/92	UPPER RECEIVER, 16" BBL, (W/AZFS)	5	OLYMPIC ARMS, INC	1,215.00
3/30/92	UPPER RECEIVER, 16" BBL, (W/AZFS)	5	OLYMPIC ARMS, INC	1,215.00
3/30/92	UPPER RECEIVER, 16" BBL, (W/AZFS)	5	OLYMPIC ARMS, INC	1,215.00
4/28/92	UPPER RECEIVER, 16" BBL, (W/EZ)	2	OLYMPIC ARMS, INC	620.00
4/28/92	UPPER RECEIVER, 16" BBL, (W/EZ)	2	OLYMPIC ARMS, INC	620.00
3/26/92	UPPER RECEIVER, 16" BBL, ASSEMBLED & TEST FIRED	5	OLYMPIC ARMS, INC	1,215.00
3/26/92	UPPER RECEIVER, 16" BBL, ASSEMBLED & TEST FIRED	5	OLYMPIC ARMS, INC	1,215.00
3/26/92	UPPER RECEIVER, 16" BBL, ASSEMBLED & TEST FIRED	5	OLYMPIC ARMS, INC	1,215.00
3/30/92	UPPER RECEIVER, 16" BBL, ASSEMBLED & TEST FIRED	4	OLYMPIC ARMS, INC	972.00
3/30/92	UPPER RECEIVER, 20 "MATCH BBL, (W/EZ & AZFS)	4	OLYMPIC ARMS, INC	1,152.00
3/30/92	UPPER RECEIVER, 20" MATCH BBL, (W/EZ & AZFS)	4	OLYMPIC ARMS, INC	1,152.00
4/24/92	UPPER RECEIVER, 20" MATCH BBL, (W/EZ)	4	OLYMPIC ARMS, INC	1,228.00
4/24/92	UPPER RECEIVER, 20" MATCH BBL, (W/EZ)	4	OLYMPIC ARMS, INC	1,232.00
4/28/92	UPPER RECEIVER, 20" MATCH BBL, (W/EZ)	4	OLYMPIC ARMS, INC	1,232.00
4/02/92	UPPER RECEIVER, 20" MATCH BBL,(W/EZ UPPER & AZFS FLASH SUPP)	2	OLYMPIC ARMS, INC	516.00
4/02/92	UPPER RECEIVER, 20" MATCH BBL,(W/EZ UPPER & AZFS)	2	OLYMPIC ARMS, INC	576.00
4/24/92	UPPER RECEIVER, 20" MATCH BBL,(W/EZ)	4	OLYMPIC ARMS, INC	1,228.00
4/02/92	UPPER RECEIVER, BBL, (W/EZ, UPPER)	3	OLYMPIC ARMS, INC	879.00
3/30/92	UPPER RECEIVER, BBL, ASSEMBLED & TEST FIRED	4	OLYMPIC ARMS, INC	972.00
4/24/92	UPPER RECEIVER, BBL,(W/EZ)	2	OLYMPIC ARMS, INC	598.00
/92	UPPER RECEIVER, BBL,(W/EZ)	2	OLYMPIC ARMS, INC	598.00
/92	UPPER RECEIVER, BBL,(W/EZ, UPPER)	3	OLYMPIC ARMS, INC	879.00
/14/92	VESTS, 4-POUCH EACH FOR AK47, 30 RD. MAGAZINES	50	UNKNOWN	
4/15/92	WALKIE-TALKIES	6	UNKNOWN	
4/22/92	WEB BELTS	144	UNKNOWN	
6/18/92	WRENCH, COMBO (FOR AR15/M16)	3	SARCO, INC	30.00

Feb 1992	March 5 - 9, 1992	After March 5 - 9, 1992	April 1992	May 1992	June 1992
18 Firearms Purchased: 13 Assault Rifles, 1 Pistol and 4 Shotgun	Team Training held at house 500 Yards East of "Mag Bag" towards Compound. These SWAT Teams from five different law enforcement agencies held all day SWAT Team entries. Howell believes this is a large ATF SWAT Team who are practicing for a raid on the Compound. Howell makes call to arms at Compound in preparation for what he believes is an impeding search and arrest by ATF.	2 Firearms Purchased: 2 Assault Rifles. Fatta buys ground sensors and night vision 3/9/92. Little orders chemicals to build explosive devices and hand grenades 3/10/92. Howell orders CA Davidians to come to Texas Compound and 40 members arrive from England in mid-March. Michael Schroeder orders and receives conversion kits to make machineguns: 3/11/92 29 machinegun kits 4/1/92 20 machinegun kits 5/18/92 34 machinegun kits 7/16/92 37 machinegun kits Upper receivers to make 100 AR-15/M-16 Assault Rifles arrive by 4/28/92. 60 Cases of 7.62 ammo, 20 Cases of .308 ammo received in March and April. (1200 rounds per case) 100 Magazines 7.62 cal 30 round 3/26/92	67 Firearms Purchased: 56 Assault Rifles and 11 Pistols. Purchased 6 Walkie Talkies 4/15/92. 11 SWG Lower Receivers for building machineguns M-16 4/1/92. 15 SWG Lower Receivers for building machineguns M-16 4/7/92. 100 Magazines 7.65 cal, 30 round; 30 Cases 7.62 ammo 4/22/92. 5 SWG Lower Receivers for building machineguns M-16 4/30/92.	35 Firearms Purchased: 31 Assault Rifles and 4 Pistols. 1 Case 7.62 ammo 5/10/92. 6 SWG Lower Receivers for building machineguns M-16 5/12/92. 6 SWG Lower Receivers for building machineguns M-16 5/18/92. 48 cases 7.62 x 39 steel core ammo on 5/22/92. 144 webb belts 4/22/92. 50 vests, 4 pouches each for AK-47, 30 round magazines on 5/14/92.	18 Firearms Purchased: 18 Assault Rifles. 90 Pounds Aluminum Powder 6/5/92. Repairs Water Well in Compound 6/5/92. 12 SWG Lower Receivers for building machineguns 6/7/92. 3 SWG Lower Receivers for building machineguns 6/9/92. 200 M-31 Rifle Grenades (Attempt to Activate) 6/10/92.

** FIREARMS DATA OBTAINED THROUGH VERIFIED RECORDS/SOURCES. UNDOCUMENTED FIREARMS ARE NOT INCLUDED IN DATA.

July 92	Aug 92	Sept 1992	Oct 1992	Nov 1992	Dec 1992	1993	Feb 1993	TOTALS
14 Firearms Purchased: 13 Assault Rifles and 1 Pistol.	2 Firearms Purchased: 3 Assault Rifles and 9 Pistols.	No Activity	2 Firearms Purchased: 2 Pistols	20 AK-47 Magazines 100 Round 11/23/92.	1 Firearm Purchased: 1 Pistol	No Activity	No Activity	Prior to March 5, 1992 80 Firearms were purchased.
8 SWG Lower Receivers for building machineguns M-16 7/20/92.	200 AR-15/ M-16 Magazines 30 round 8/6/92.			20 AK-47 100 round magazines on 11/23/92.				After March 5, 1992 236 Additional Firearms were purchased (153 Assault Rifles included).
	2800 Rounds 9mm ammo 8/7/92.							
2 SWG Lower Receivers for building machineguns M-16 7/27/92.	30 M-14 Magazines .308 cal 20 rounds 8/12/92.							120 Conversion kits for Assault Rifles.
	9 Cases .308 ammo 8/18/92.							

* THIS REPORT DOES NOT INCLUDE FIREARMS THAT WERE PURCHASED AND/OR ACQUIRED WITHOUT RECORDS BEING MADE (CASH SALES AT GUN SHOWS AND ELSEWHERE)

DELIVER TO "AG BAG"
ROUTE 7, BOX 555, WACO, TEXAS
March 26 thru August 12, 1992
I.N. 53110-92-1069X

SHIPPED FROM	DATE	INVOICE #	QUANT.	COST	DESCRIPTION
ALPHA TRADING COMPANY	06/17/92		20	$1,200.00	100 RD., AK-47 MAGAZINES
ALPHA TRADING COMPANY	08/06/92		200	$540.00	USED AR-15 30 MAGAZINES
ALPHA TRADING COMPANY	08/12/92		30	$150.00	USED M14 MAGAZINES
CENTEC FIRE SYSTEMS, INC.	07/17/92	NO INVOICE		$411.29	UNKNOWN (CONT #309912, SHIP #409992)
CENTURY INTERNAT'L ARMS	07/06/92	NO INVOICE			1M - 7.62 (#026529, PIECE #026529)
FOX FIRE CO.	06/05/92	NO INVOICE			90 LBS-POWDER, ALUM.METAL & 30-40 CARDBOARD TUBES
JONATHAN ARTHUR CIENER	07/08/92	NO INVOICE			.22 LR CONV. KITS - AR15,MINI-14 & AK47 (#451221)
JONATHAN ARTHUR CIENER	07/08/92	NO INVOICE			M203 LAUNCHERS, SUPPRESSORS, BELT FEED - AR-15
KENGS FIREARM SPECIALTY	07/09/92	NO INVOICE	2	$290.56	UNKNOWN (SHIPPING #383833, CONTROL #039756)
L & N SHOOTERS	08/07/92	NO INVOICE		$280.50	2800 RDS, 9MM AMMUNITION
NESARD GUN PARTS CO.	05/14/92	NO INVOICE		$720.00	UNKNOWN (SHIPPING #622836, CONT. #443693)
NESARD GUN PARTS CO.	05/26/92		2	$620.00	EZ KIT (M16) W/AZ, 20" BBL
NESARD GUN PARTS CO.	05/26/92		2	$550.00	CAR KIT (M16)
NESARD GUN PARTS CO.	05/26/92		1	$10.00	REVERSE FLASHHIDER (FLASH SUPPRESSOR)
NESARD GUN PARTS CO.	06/19/92	NO INVOICE	1		M-76 GRENADE LAUNCHER
NESARD GUN PARTS CO.	07/09/92	NO INVOICE		$1,250.65	UNKNOWN (SHIPPING #622836, CONT. #473126)

DELIVER.. TO ..AG BAG"
ROUTE 7, BOX 555, WACO, TEXAS
March 26 thru August 12, 1992
I. N. 53110-92-1069X

PAGE ..o.: 2

SHIPPED FROM	DATE	INVOICE #	QUANT.	COST	DESCRIPTION
OLYMPIC ARMS, INC.	03/26/92	A43880	5	$1,215.00	K1B, 16"
OLYMPIC ARMS, INC.	03/26/92	A43878	5	$1,215.00	K1B, 16"
OLYMPIC ARMS, INC.	03/26/92	A43879	1	$10.00	H18
OLYMPIC ARMS, INC.	03/26/92	A43879	5	$1,215.00	K1B, 16"
OLYMPIC ARMS, INC.	03/30/92	A43911	4	$972.00	K1B
OLYMPIC ARMS, INC.	03/30/92	A43911	4	$1,152.00	K2B W/EZ & AZFS
OLYMPIC ARMS, INC.	03/30/92	A43911	4	$1,152.00	K2B, W/EZ & AZFS
OLYMPIC ARMS, INC.	03/30/92	A43911	4	$972.00	K1B
OLYMPIC ARMS, INC.	03/30/92	A43923	5	$1,215.00	K1B, 16" W/AZFS
OLYMPIC ARMS, INC.	03/30/92	A43922	5	$1,215.00	K1B, 16" W/AZFS
OLYMPIC ARMS, INC.	03/30/92	A43923	5	$1,215.00	K1B, 16", W/AZFS
OLYMPIC ARMS, INC.	04/02/92	A43929	3	$879.00	K1B, W/EZ, UPPER
OLYMPIC ARMS, INC.	04/02/92	A43929	1	$243.00	K1B, 16"
OLYMPIC ARMS, INC.	04/02/92	A43929	1	$243.00	K1B, 16"
OLYMPIC ARMS, INC.	04/02/92	A43929	2	$516.00	K2B, 20 W/EZ UPPER & AZFS FLASH SUPPRESSOR
OLYMPIC ARMS, INC.	04/02/92	A43929	3	$879.00	K1B, 16" W/EZ, UPPER

DELIVERIES TO "AG BAG"
ROUTE 7, BOX 555, WACO, TEXAS
March 26 thru August 12, 1992
I. N. 53110-92-1069X

PAGE NO.: 3

SHIPPED FROM	DATE	INVOICE #	QUANT.	COST	DESCRIPTION
OLYMPIC ARMS, INC.	04/02/92	A43929	2	$576.00	K2B, 20" W/EZ UPPER & AZFS
OLYMPIC ARMS, INC.	04/24/92	A45210	4	$1,228.00	K2B, W/EZ
OLYMPIC ARMS, INC.	04/24/92	A45211	4	$1,304.00	CAR-9 UNITS W/16" BBL (4 K10'S)
OLYMPIC ARMS, INC.	04/24/92	A45210	2	$598.00	K1B, W/EZ
OLYMPIC ARMS, INC.	04/24/92	A45231	4	$1,232.00	K2B, W/EZ
OLYMPIC ARMS, INC.	04/24/92	A45211	4	$1,304.00	CAR-9 UNITS W/16" BBL
OLYMPIC ARMS, INC.	04/24/92	A45210	4	$1,228.00	K2B, W/EZ
OLYMPIC ARMS, INC.	04/24/92	A45210	2	$598.00	K1B, W/EZ
OLYMPIC ARMS, INC.	04/28/92	A45233	2	$620.00	K1B, W/16" & EZ
OLYMPIC ARMS, INC.	04/28/92	A45233	8	$2,104.00	K1B, W/16"
OLYMPIC ARMS, INC.	04/28/92	A45233	2	$620.00	K1B, W/16" & EZ
OLYMPIC ARMS, INC.	04/28/92	A45233	8	$2,104.00	K1B, W/16"
OLYMPIC ARMS, INC.	04/28/92	A45231	4	$1,232.00	K2B, W/EZ
OLYMPIC ARMS, INC.	07/13/92	A47046	2	$616.00	CAR-45 UNIT
OLYMPIC ARMS, INC.	07/13/92	A47046	2	$586.00	CAR-9 UNIT
OLYMPIC ARMS, INC.		NO INVOICE		$2,500.00	.223 AMMUNITION (MARCH 92)

DELIVE.. TO ..AG BAG"
ROUTE 7, BOX 555, WACO, TEXAS
March 26 thru August 12, 1992
I. N. 53110-92-1069X

PAGE NO.: 4

SHIPPED FROM	DATE	INVOICE #	QUANT.	COST	DESCRIPTION
OLYMPIC ARMS, INC.		NO INVOICE		$280.50	9MM AMMUNITION - 2800 RDS. (AUG. 92)
P. L. & T. TIFFIN KNIVES	08/03/92	NO INVOICE		$374.00	KNIVES
ROCK ISLAND ARMORY, INC.	06/17/92	104722	50	$162.50	M31 PRACTICE RIFLE GRENADES
ROCK ISLAND ARMORY, INC.	06/29/92	104818	150	$487.50	M31 PRACTICE RIFLE GRENADES
SARCO, INC.	05/26/92	A43318	1	$274.95	M16 PARTS SET KIT "A" W/SLING & MAG (NO LWR.RCVR.)
SARCO, INC.	06/18/92	A45276	2	$249.50	M261 RIFLE CONVERSION KITS
SARCO, INC.	06/18/92	A45276	3	$30.00	COMBO WRENCH
SARCO, INC.	06/18/92	A45276	3	$824.85	M16 KIT "A" (SPECIAL OFFERINGS)
SARCO, INC.	06/18/92	A45276	6	$49.95	.22 CONVERSION UNIT MAGS
SARCO, INC.	06/18/92	A45276	4	$79.80	M203 HANDGUARDS
SHOOTERS EQUIPMENT CO.	07/16/92	NO INVOICE		$387.51	UNKNOWN (CONT #833766, SHIP #227471, PKG 4199)
SHOOTERS EQUIPMENT CO.	07/17/92	NO INVOICE		$68.88	UNKNOWN (CONT #833722, SHIP #277471, ID SEC-T-68)
SHOOTERS EQUIPMENT CO.	07/20/92	NO INVOICE		$122.76	UNKNOWN (CONT #833674, SHIP #227471, ID SEC-T-73)
TAPCO, INC.	06/30/92	0022292	2	$299.90	FLARE LAUNCHER W/C.A.R. MOUNT
TAPCO, INC.	07/14/92	NO INVOICE		$1,386.86	UNKNOWN (CONT #578336, SHIP #393495)
TAPCO-SPECIALIZED WEAPONS	06/15/92		2	$44.00	M203 M16 HANDGUARDS

DELIVER TO "AG BAG"
ROUTE 7, BOX 555, WACO, TEXAS
March 26 thru August 12, 1992
I. N. 53110-92-1069X

PAGE NO.: 5

SHIPPED FROM	DATE	INVOICE #	QUANT.	COST	DESCRIPTION
TAPCO-SPECIALIZED WEAPONS	06/15/92		2	$355.50	CM-2037 FLARE LAUNCHER
TAPCO-SPECIALIZED WEAPONS	06/15/92		2	$65.50	M203 H.G. SIGHT ASSEMBLY
UNKNOWN	06/08/92	NO INVOICE	60		M-16/AR-15 MAGAZINES
UNKNOWN	06/18/92	NO INVOICE			CHEMICALS, INSTRUMENTS & GLASSWARE
UNKNOWN		NO INVOICE			PRACTICE GRENADES (2 CASES) & BLACK POWDER
UNKNOWN (UPS SHIPMENT)	07/02/92	NO INVOICE			POTASSIUM NITRATE, 30 LBS. (OXIDIZER) ID #UNI486
UNKNOWN (UPS SHIPMENT)	07/02/92	NO INVOICE			MAGNESIUM METAL, 5 LBS.
UNKNOWN (UPS SHIPMENT)	07/02/92	NO INVOICE			IGNITER CORD, 1 LB. (CLASS C EXPLO.)

TOTAL COST: $44,325.46

E N D   O F   R E P O R T

TIOGA ENGINEERING COMPANY, INC.
P.O. Box 913, 13 Cone Street
Wellsboro, PA 16901

Charles R. Fagg
REGISTRATION 40239 TX.

TELEPHONES:
(717) 724-3533
(717) 662-2730
FAX (717) 662-3347

August 5, 1993

LETTER REPORT

Subject:

Investigation of the Circumstances Leading to the February 28, 1993 Raid and Subsequent Siege of the Branch Davidian Compound, Waco, Texas.

To:

Joseph A. Masonis
1500 Pennsylvania Avenue, N. W., Rm. 4121
Washington, D.C. 20220

Background:

In the Spring of 1993, virtually every television and radio station in America broadcast the events which occurred at the Branch Davidian Compound at Waco, Texas. This extensive coverage, coupled with the tragic ending, raised questions in the minds of both the American people and the Government responsible to those people. In order to provide answers to these questions, the Government has mounted a massive investigation into the events which led to the raid, and into the execution of that raid. Mr. William C. Davis, Jr. and the undersigned, both of Tioga Engineering Co., Wellsboro, PA, were asked to participate in this investigation. To provide the necessary information and an understanding of the part we were to play, Mr. Joseph A. Masonis, of the Treasury Department, provided a briefing on July 1, 1993, at the test facilities of Tioga Engineering. At that briefing, we were provided written information and verbal direction. This took the following form.

1. The written material consisted of lists of the firearm and explosive-related materials known to have been received prior to February, 1993, by the "Mag Bag Corp.", a mailing address of the Branch Davidians.

2. The verbal direction consisted of an overview of the investigation and a clear delineation of the scope of our involve-

ment. My understanding of this direction was that Mr. Davis and I were to independently review the information available to the Bureau of Alcohol, Tobacco and Firearms prior to the incident, and to determine if they acted reasonably in seeking and executing a search warrant.

Information Provided

1. A five-page list of deliveries to "Mag Bag Corp." from March 26 through August 12, 1992, This document is undated but contains the number I. N. 53110-92-1069X. (see Appendix 1.)

2. Olympic Arms, Inc. retail catalog, dated January, 1992. (example not enclosed)

3. A two-page document "Firearms Technology Branch Report of Technical Examination" dated Dec. 15, 1992. This document refers to 53110-92-1069 X, and lists some of the same materials listed in document number 1., above. (see Appendix 2.)

4. A two-page, undated document purported to provide a history of weapon-related transactions of certain members of the Branch Davidians from February, 1992 to February, 1993. (see Appendix 3.)

5. A two-page "Report of Investigation (Law Enforcement)", dated 23 July, 1992, referring to Investigation No. 53110-92-1069-X (see 1. and 3. above). This document lists the known firearms parts and accessories received by "Mag Bag Corp." from March, 1992 to July, 1992, and requests an evaluation as to whether Vernon Howell and Mike Schroeder were "possibly converting or manufacturing Title II weapons". (see Appendix 4.)

6. A list containing the names, addresses and telephone numbers of other parties involved in the investigation. (copy not included)

7. A written outline and verbal review of the overall scope of the investigation. (copy not included)

8. At a later date, in response to a verbal request for further information, Mr. Masonis reported that an engine lathe and a milling machine were known to be within the compound.

Comments

Though the information upon which this study is based was prepared by the organization under scrutiny, there is no reason to doubt its accuracy or objectivity.

The lists of materials are difficult to interpret because they often, but not always, include the same equipment as duplicate entries. Some items appear on more than one list, and others do not. In document number 4., lower receivers are listed as "lower receivers" in the monthly acquisitions, but are listed as "firearms" in the totals. Whether or not the "lower receivers" are also counted among the monthly firearms acquisitions is unclear. To overcome these problems, only approximate quantities are included in the recap list below.

Since the ammunition acquisitions are sometimes listed in case lots without indication of the size of these cases, and since the 5.56 mm ammunition is listed only by dollar value, it is impossible to establish the exact amount of ammunition received. Here, again, quantities are estimated.

Partial List of Materials Present:

The following is an approximate recap of the firearm and explosive-related materials known to be within the complex by 28 February, 1993.

1. 249 firearms (over 60 % of military derivation)
2. Parts to construct an additional 68 AR-15 rifles
3. Incomplete parts kits to construct 52 AR-15 rifles
4. One belt-fed AR-15 rifle
5. 260 magazines for AR-15 rifles
6. 20 100-round magazines for AK-47 rifles
7. 100 magazines for 7.62 mm weapons (probably AK-47 rifles)
8. 6 caliber .22 conversion unit magazines
9. 30 magazines for M14 rifles
10. M203 Grenade launcher (quantity unknown)
11. 1 M76 (?) grenade launcher
12. 6 Walkie Talkies
13. Kits for converting AR-15, AK-47 and MINI-14 to fire cal. .22 Rimfire ammunition (quantity unknown)
14. 2 kits for converting AR-15 to fire cal. .45 ammunition
15. 10 kits for converting AR-15 to fire 9 mm ammunition
16. 4 Flair Launchers
17. Over 200,000 rounds of assorted ammunition
18. 200 M31 practice rifle grenades
19. 2 cases of practice grenades (quantity and type unknown)
20. 5 manuals for activating M31 practice rifle grenades
21. Black powder (quantity unknown)
22. 90 pounds of aluminum powder
23. 5 pounds of Magnesium (assumed to be powder)
24. 30 pounds of potassium nitrate
25. An engine lathe and a milling machine

Rationale:

The above is an approximate list of the firearm and explosive-related materials known to have been acquired by the Branch Davidians before Feb. 28, 1993. Most had been acquired between March 26, 1992 and Aug. 12, 1992. During this brief period of 4

1/2 months, their expenditures for weapon-related materials was in excess of $43,000. Had they been functioning as dealers, had they been acquiring collector-type materials, or had the firearms market been such as to make investment lucrative, these acquisitions might be explained as some form of peaceful endeavor, but when none of these conditions exist, the only logical explanation is that the Branch Davidians were preparing for a massive, armed confrontation.

Particularly revealing is their acquisition of practice rifle grenades, manuals for activation of these grenades, black powder and materials for manufacturing explosives. This, more than any other item of information, indicates their willingness to modify material to enhance their capability of armed resistance.

Having concluded that the Branch Davidians were arming, and that they were willing to modify materials to meet their needs, it is reasonable to assume that they were also contemplating means of increasing the effectiveness of other weapons. Since it is popularly believed that the combat effectiveness of automatic weapons is superior to that of semiautomatic weapons, it is highly probable that attempts were being made to convert some, or all, of their semiautomatic weapons to fire automatically. To do so, and at the same time retain acceptable reliability, requires the installation of some form of automatic sear, and an appropriate selection of parts of M16 configuration. Except for automatic sears, the remaining M16 configuration internal parts are easily and legally obtainable. Appendix 5. indicates the ease with which these parts may be obtained. While not specifically stipulated in Appendix 3., the 120 parts kits called "machinegun kits" probably consisted of such parts.

Automatic sears for the AR-15 or M16 rifle are of two basic types. The military-type and the drop-in type. Unless modified through the use of machine tools, specifically a milling machine, the design of the lower receiver of the AR-15 rifle prevents installation of the military-type automatic sear. The drop-in automatic sear, however, is specifically designed to function in conjunction with the aforementioned M16 parts, but to be capable of installation in an unmodified, AR-15, lower receiver. They are a simple assembly, and can be installed or removed in less than one minute by an inexpert craftsman.

The material made available does not indicate that the Branch Davidians received shipments containing automatic sears. However, with the machine tools known to exist within the compound, a knowledgeable and motivated individual could easily modify AR-15 lower receivers for installation of military-type automatic sears, or fabricate automatic sears of the drop-in type.

Conclusions:

Applying the above rationale leads to the following conclusions.

The Branch Davidians were arming with the intent of entering into an armed confrontation.

In their pursuit of arms, they were attempting to activate grenades through use of black powder or other crude explosives.

In an attempt to increase the combat effectiveness of the weapons available to them, it is highly probable that they were attempting to convert semiautomatic weapons to fire automatically, and it is possible that they had succeeded.

In view of the information available prior to February 28, 1993, the Bureau of Alcohol, Tobacco and Firearms was fully justified in seeking and attempting to execute a search warrant at the Branch Davidian Compound in Waco, Texas.

Respectfully submitted,

Charles R. Fagg, P. E.

DELIVERIES TO "..AG BAG"
ROUTE 7, BOX 555, WACO, TEXAS
March 26 thru August 12, 1992
I. N. 53110-92-1069X

SHIPPED FROM	DATE	INVOICE #	QUANT.	COST	DESCRIPTION
ALPHA TRADING COMPANY	06/17/92		20	$1,200.00	100 RD., AK-47 MAGAZINES
ALPHA TRADING COMPANY	08/06/92		200	$540.00	USED AR-15 30 MAGAZINES
ALPHA TRADING COMPANY	08/12/92		30	$150.00	USED M14 MAGAZINES
CENTRIC FIRE SYSTEMS, INC.	07/17/92	NO INVOICE		$411.29	UNKNOWN (CONT #309912, SHIP #409992)
CENTURY INTERNAT'L ARMS	07/06/92	NO INVOICE			1M - 7.62 (#026529, PIECE #026529)
FOX FIRE CO.	06/05/92	NO INVOICE			90 LBS-POWDER, ALUM.METAL & 30-40 CARDBOARD TUBES
JONATHAN ARTHUR CIENER	07/08/92	NO INVOICE			.22 LR CONV. KITS - AR15,MINI-14 & AK47 (#451221)
JONATHAN ARTHUR CIENER	07/08/92	NO INVOICE			M203 LAUNCHERS, SUPPRESSORS, BELT FEED - AR-15
KENGS FIREARM SPECIALTY	07/09/92	NO INVOICE	2	$290.56	UNKNOWN (SHIPPING #383833, CONTROL #039756)
L & N SHOOTERS	08/07/92	NO INVOICE		$280.50	2800 RDS, 9MM AMMUNITION
NESARD GUN PARTS CO.	05/14/92	NO INVOICE		$720.00	UNKNOWN (SHIPPING #622836, CONT. #443693)
NESARD GUN PARTS CO.	05/26/92		2	$620.00	EZ KIT (M16) W/A2, 20" BBL
NESARD GUN PARTS CO.	05/26/92		2	$550.00	CAR KIT (M16)
NESARD GUN PARTS CO.	05/26/92		1	$10.00	REVERSE FLASHHIDER (FLASH SUPPRESSOR)
NESARD GUN PARTS CO.	06/19/92	NO INVOICE	1		M-76 GRENADE LAUNCHER
NESARD GUN PARTS CO.	07/09/92	NO INVOICE		$1,250.65	UNKNOWN (SHIPPING #622836, CONT. #473126)

Appendix 1-(continued)

DELIVERI... ...NG BAG"
ROUTE 7, BOX 555, WACO, TEXAS
March 26 thru August 12, 1992
I. N. 53110-92-1069X

page no.: 2

SHIPPED FROM	DATE	INVOICE #	QUANT.	COST	DESCRIPTION
OLYMPIC ARMS, INC.	03/26/92	A43880	5	$1,215.00	K1B, 16"
OLYMPIC ARMS, INC.	03/26/92	A43878	5	$1,215.00	K1B, 16"
OLYMPIC ARMS, INC.	03/26/92	A43879	1	$10.00	H18
OLYMPIC ARMS, INC.	03/26/92	A43879	5	$1,215.00	K1B, 16"
OLYMPIC ARMS, INC.	03/30/92	A43911	4	$972.00	K1B
OLYMPIC ARMS, INC.	03/30/92	A43911	4	$1,152.00	K2B W/EZ & AZFS
OLYMPIC ARMS, INC.	03/30/92	A43911	4	$1,152.00	K2B, W/EZ & AZFS
OLYMPIC ARMS, INC.	03/30/92	A43911	4	$972.00	K1B
OLYMPIC ARMS, INC.	03/30/92	A43923	5	$1,215.00	K1B, 16" W/AZFS
OLYMPIC ARMS, INC.	03/30/92	A43922	5	$1,215.00	K1B, 16" W/AZFS
OLYMPIC ARMS, INC.	03/30/92	A43923	5	$1,215.00	K1B, 16", W/AZFS
OLYMPIC ARMS, INC.	04/02/92	A43929	3	$879.00	K1B, W/EZ, UPPER
OLYMPIC ARMS, INC.	04/02/92	A43929	1	$243.00	K1B, 16"
OLYMPIC ARMS, INC.	04/02/92	A43929	1	$243.00	K1B, 16"
OLYMPIC ARMS, INC.	04/02/92	A43929	2	$516.00	K2B, 20 W/EZ UPPER & AZFS FLASH SUPPRESSOR
OLYMPIC ARMS, INC.	04/02/92	A43929	3	$879.00	K1B, 16" W/EZ, UPPER

B-185

Appendix 1-(continued)

DELIVERIES TO "AG BAG"
ROUTE 7, BOX 555, WACO, TEXAS
March 26 thru August 12, 1992
I. N. 53110-92-1069X

PAGE NO.: 3

SHIPPED FROM	DATE	INVOICE #	QUANT.	COST	DESCRIPTION
OLYMPIC ARMS, INC.	04/02/92	A43929	2	$576.00	K2B, 20" W/EZ UPPER & AZFS
OLYMPIC ARMS, INC.	04/24/92	A45210	4	$1,228.00	K2B, W/EZ
OLYMPIC ARMS, INC.	04/24/92	A45211	4	$1,304.00	CAR-9 UNITS W/16" BBL (4 K10'S)
OLYMPIC ARMS, INC.	04/24/92	A45210	2	$598.00	K1B, W/EZ
OLYMPIC ARMS, INC.	04/24/92	A45231	4	$1,232.00	K2B, W/EZ
OLYMPIC ARMS, INC.	04/24/92	A45211	4	$1,304.00	CAR-9 UNITS W/16" BBL
OLYMPIC ARMS, INC.	04/24/92	A45210	4	$1,228.00	K2B, W/EZ
OLYMPIC ARMS, INC.	04/24/92	A45210	2	$598.00	K1B, W/EZ
OLYMPIC ARMS, INC.	04/28/92	A45233	2	$620.00	K1B, W/16" & EZ
OLYMPIC ARMS, INC.	04/28/92	A45233	8	$2,104.00	K1B, W/16"
OLYMPIC ARMS, INC.	04/28/92	A45233	2	$620.00	K1B, W/16" & EZ
OLYMPIC ARMS, INC.	04/28/92	A45233	8	$2,104.00	K1B, W/16"
OLYMPIC ARMS, INC.	04/28/92	A45231	4	$1,232.00	K2B, W/EZ
OLYMPIC ARMS, INC.	07/13/92	A47046	2	$616.00	CAR-45 UNIT
OLYMPIC ARMS, INC.	07/13/92	A47046	2	$586.00	CAR-9 UNIT
OLYMPIC ARMS, INC.		NO INVOICE		$2,500.00	.223 AMMUNITION (MARCH 92)

Appendix 1-(continued)

DELIVERIES TO "..AG BAG"
ROUTE 7, BOX 555, WACO, TEXAS
March 26 thru August 12, 1992
I. N. 53110-92-1069X

SHIPPED FROM	DATE	INVOICE #	QUANT.	COST	DESCRIPTION
OLYMPIC ARMS, INC.		NO INVOICE		$280.50	9MM AMMUNITION - 2800 RDS. (AUG. 92)
P. L. & T. TIFFIN KNIVES	08/03/92	NO INVOICE		$374.00	KNIVES
ROCK ISLAND ARMORY, INC.	06/17/92	104722	50	$162.50	M31 PRACTICE RIFLE GRENADES
ROCK ISLAND ARMORY, INC.	06/29/92	104818	150	$487.50	M31 PRACTICE RIFLE GRENADES
SARCO, INC.	05/26/92	A43318	1	$274.95	M16 PARTS SET KIT "A" W/SLING & MAG (NO LWR.RCVR.)
SARCO, INC.	06/18/92	A45276	2	$249.50	M261 RIFLE CONVERSION KITS
SARCO, INC.	06/18/92	A45276	3	$30.00	COMBO WRENCH
SARCO, INC.	06/18/92	A45276	3	$824.85	M16 KIT "A" (SPECIAL OFFERINGS)
SARCO, INC.	06/18/92	A45276	6	$49.95	.22 CONVERSION UNIT MAGS
SARCO, INC.	06/18/92	A45276	4	$79.80	M203 HANDGUARDS
SHOOTERS EQUIPMENT CO.	07/16/92	NO INVOICE		$387.51	UNKNOWN (CONT #833766, SHIP #227471, PKG 4199)
SHOOTERS EQUIPMENT CO.	07/17/92	NO INVOICE		$68.88	UNKNOWN (CONT #833722, SHIP #277471, ID SEC-T-68)
SHOOTERS EQUIPMENT CO.	07/20/92	NO INVOICE		$122.76	UNKNOWN (CONT #833674, SHIP #227471, ID SEC-T-73)
TAPCO, INC.	06/30/92	0022292	2	$299.90	FLARE LAUNCHER W/C.A.R. MOUNT
TAPCO, INC.	07/14/92	NO INVOICE		$1,386.86	UNKNOWN (CONT #578336, SHIP #393495)
TAPCO-SPECIALIZED WEAPONS	06/15/92		2	$44.00	M203 M16 HANDGUARDS

Appendix 1-(continued)

DELIVERED TO "MAG BAG"
ROUTE 7, BOX 555, WACO, TEXAS
March 26 thru August 12, 1992
I. N. 53110-92-1069X

PAGE NO.: 5

SHIPPED FROM	DATE	INVOICE #	QUANT.	COST	DESCRIPTION
TAPCO-SPECIALIZED WEAPONS	06/15/92		2	$355.50	CM-2037 FLARE LAUNCHER
TAPCO-SPECIALIZED WEAPONS	06/15/92		2	$65.50	M203 H.G. SIGHT ASSEMBLY
UNKNOWN	06/08/92	NO INVOICE	60		M-16/AR-15 MAGAZINES
UNKNOWN	06/18/92	NO INVOICE			CHEMICALS, INSTRUMENTS & GLASSWARE
UNKNOWN		NO INVOICE			PRACTICE GRENADES (2 CASES) & BLACK POWDER
UNKNOWN (UPS SHIPMENT)	07/02/92	NO INVOICE			POTASSIUM NITRATE, 30 LBS. (OXIDIZER) ID #UNI486
UNKNOWN (UPS SHIPMENT)	07/02/92	NO INVOICE			MAGNESIUM METAL, 5 LBS.
UNKNOWN (UPS SHIPMENT)	07/02/92	NO INVOICE			IGNITER CORD, 1 LB. (CLASS C EXPLO.)

TOTAL COST: $44,325.46

E N D O F R E P O R T

Appendix 2

DEPARTMENT OF THE TREASURY
BUREAU OF ALCOHOL, TOBACCO AND FIREARMS

Firearms Technology Branch
Report of Technical Examination

Law Enforcement
Washington, D.C. 20226

Phone: (202) 927-7910

(Use window envelope. Begin typing between dots.)

DATE: 12/15/92

YOUR: 53110-92-1069 X

Special Agent Davy Aguilera
Bureau of Alcohol, Tobacco and Firearms
P.O. Box 20-2828
Austin, TX 78720-2828

RE: Howell, V.W. et.al.

OUR: 3-184-CHB

DATE EXHIBITS RECEIVED: 12/15/92

DELIVERED BY: Fax.

TYPE OF EXAMINATION REQUESTED:

Classification

EXHIBITS:

Description of firearm parts and components including the following:

From Olympic Arms:

1. 9mm and .45 ACP upper assemblies/receivers/conversion units.
2. Barrel units and upper receiver assemblies.
3. Heavy match barrel units with assault handguards and upper receiver assembly.
4. Flash suppressors.
5. K-1B 16" with AZFS.
6. K-2B with EZ and AZFS.
7. Car 9 units.

From Sarco Inc.:

1. M16 parts set kit with sling and magazine.
2. Bolt catch extractor pin and buttcap screw.
3. M16 "A" kits.
4. M-261 rifle conversion kits.
5. M-203 handguards.

From Nesard Gun Parts Co.:

1. M16 Car kits.
2. M16 EZ Car kits.
3. Flash suppressor.

B-189

Appendix   2-(continued)

Special Agent Davy Aguilera

53110-92-1069 X
3-184-CHB
page 2

From unknown company:

    1.   M16/AR15 magazines.

FINDINGS: Based on the description provided the above items are consistent with component parts and accessories for AR-15 rifles or M16 machineguns.

CONCLUSION: The described parts and accessories are not firearms as defined in 18 U.S.C. Chapter 44, or 26 U.S.C. Chapter 53.

[signature]
Curtis H.A. Bartlett
Firearms Enforcement Officer

Appendix 3

Feb 1992	March 5 - 9, 1992	R March 5 - 9, 1992	April 1992	May 1992	June 1992
18 Firearms Purchased: 13 Assault Rifles, 1 Pistol and 4 Shotgun	Team Training held at house 500 Yards East of "Mag Bag" towards Compound. These SWAT Teams from five different law enforcement agencies held all day SWAT Team entries.	2 Firearms Purchased: 2 Assault Rifles	67 Firearms Purchased: 56 Assault Rifles and 11 Pistols	35 Firearms Purchased: 31 Assault Rifles and 4 Pistols.	18 Firearms Purchased: 18 Assault Rifles.
		Fatta buys ground sensors and night vision 3/9/92.			90 Pounds Aluminum Powder 6/5/92.
	Howell believes this is a large ATF SWAT Team who are practicing for a raid on the Compound.	Little orders chemicals to build explosive devices and hand grenades 3/10/92.	Purchased 6 Walkie Talkies 4/15/92.	1 Case 7.62 ammo 5/10/92.	Repairs Water Well in Compound 6/5/92.
		Howell orders CA Davidians to come to Texas Compound and 40 members arrive from England in mid-March.	11 SWG Lower Receivers for building machineguns M-16 4/1/92.	6 SWG Lower Receivers for building machineguns M-16 5/12/92.	12 SWG Lower Receivers for building machineguns 6/7/92.
	Howell makes call to arms at Compound in preparation for what he believes is an impeding search and arrest by ATF.	Michael Schroeder orders and receives conversion kits to make machineguns: 3/11/92 29 machinegun kits 4/1/92 20 machinegun kits 5/18/92 34 machinegun kits 7/16/92 37 machinegun kits	15 SWG Lower Receivers for building machineguns M-16 4/7/92.	6 SWG Lower Receivers for building machineguns M-16 5/18/92.	3 SWG Lower Receivers for building machineguns 6/9/92.
		Upper receivers to make 100 AR-15/M-16 Assault Rifles arrive by 4/28/92.	100 Magazines 7.65 cal, 30 round, 30 Cases 7.62 ammo 4/22/92.	48 cases 7.62 x 39 steel core ammo on 5/22/92.	200 M-31 Rifle Grenades (Attempt to Activate) 6/10/92.
		60 Cases of 7.62 ammo, 20 Cases of .308 ammo received in March and April. (1200 rounds per case)	5 SWG Lower Receivers for building machineguns M-16 4/30/92.	144 webb belts 4/22/92.	
		100 Magazines 7.62 cal 30 round 3/26/92		50 vests, 4 pouches each for AK-47, 30 round magazines on 5/14/92.	

** FIREARMS DATA OBTAINED THROUGH VERIFIED RECORDS/SOURCES. UNDOCUMENTED FIREARMS ARE NOT INCLUDED IN DATA.

Appendix 3.

Appendix 3

July 92	Aug 92	Sept 1992	Oct 1992	Nov 1992	Dec 1992	Jan 1993	Feb 1993	TOTALS
14 Firearms Purchased: 13 Assault Rifles and 1 Pistol.	2 Firearms Purchased: 3 Assault Rifles and 9 Pistols.	No Activity	2 Firearms Purchased: 2 Pistols	20 AK-47 Magazines 100 Round 11/23/92.	1 Firearm Purchased: 1 Pistol	No Activity	No Activity	Prior to March 5, 1992 80 Firearms were purchased.
	200 AR-15/ M-16 Magazines 30 round 8/6/92.			20 AK-47 100 round magazines on 11/23/92.				After March 5, 1992 236 Additional Firearms were purchased (153 Assault Rifles included).
8 SWG Lower Receivers for building machineguns M-16 7/20/92.	2800 Rounds 9mm ammo 8/7/92.							120 Conversion kits for Assault Rifles.
2 SWG Lower Receivers for building machineguns M-16 7/27/92.	30 M-14 Magazines .308 cal 20 rounds 8/12/92.							
	9 Cases .308 ammo 8/18/92.							

* THIS REPORT DOES NOT INCLUDE FIREARMS THAT WERE PURCHASED AND/OR ACQUIRED WITHOUT RECORDS BEING MADE (CASH SALES AT GUN SHOWS AND ELSEWHERE)

Appendix 4

DEPARTMENT OF THE TREASURY- BUREAU OF ALCOHOL, TOBACCO AND FIREARMS

REPORT OF INVESTIGATION (Law Enforcement)

1. INVESTIGATION IS: [X] ROUTINE [ ] SENSITIVE [ ] SIGNIFICANT

Page 1 of 2 pages

TO: Chief, Firearms Technology Branch, Washington, D.C.

3. MONITORED INVESTIGATION INFORMATION (Number and Branch):
CIP: HOUSTON FY-92
FIREARMS VIOLATIONS
REPORT 002

TITLE OF INVESTIGATION: Howell, Vernon Wayne et.al...

5. INVESTIGATION No. (Include Suspect No.): 53110-92-1069-X

TYPE OF REPORT (Check applicable boxes):
- [X] COLLATERAL (Request)

7. BUREAU PROGRAM:
- [X] TITLE I — FIREARMS
- [X] TITLE II — FIREARMS
- [X] TITLE XI — EXPLOSIVES

8. PROJECT(S):
- [X] OTHER (Specify): GENERAL

DETAILS:

This collateral request relates to an investigation initiated in response to a "Referral" from the McLennan County Sheriff's Department, Waco, Texas, concerning the alleged illegal possession and or illegal conversion/manufacturing of Title II, NFA weapons and explosives by Vernon W. Howell, AKA: David Koresh, Route 7, Box 471-B, Waco, McLennan County, Texas.

Assorted firearm parts and accessories have been shipped to the "Mag Bag" corporation, addressed to Vernon Howell and Mike Schroeder from March of 1992, to the present. Additional firearm parts currently being shipped to the "Mag Bag" corporation are being closely monitored and documented. It is requested that following documented firearm parts and accessories received by the "Mag Bag" corporation be evaluated, to determine if, that with these parts, the aforementioned subjects are possibly converting or manufacturing Title II weapons:

Shipped from: Olympic Arms Inc.
624 Old Pacific Hwy., S.E.,
Olympia, Wa.
(206) 456-3471

1) Four (4) 9mm and .45, ACP upper assemblies/receivers/conversion units.
2) Twenty-three (23) Barrel units and upper receiver assembly.
3) Eighteen (18) heavy match barrel units with assault handguards and upper receiver assembly.
4) Eleven (11) flash suppressors.
5) Twenty-five (25) K-1B 16", with AZFS.
6) Fourteen (14) K-2B with EZ and AZFS.

SUBMITTED BY (Name): Davy Aguilera
11. TITLE AND OFFICE: Special Agent, Austin
12. DATE: 07/23/92

REVIEWED BY (Name): Larry E. Sparks
14. TITLE AND OFFICE: Resident Agent in Charge
15. DATE: 7/23/92

APPROVED BY (Name): Phillip J. Chojnacki
17. TITLE AND OFFICE: Special Agent in Charge
18. DATE: / /

Appendix 4-(continued)

DEPARTMENT OF THE TREASURY
BUREAU OF ALCOHOL, TOBACCO AND FIREARMS

REPORT OF INVESTIGATION - CONTINUATION SHEET
(Law Enforcement)

PAGE 2 OF 2 PAGES

INVESTIGATION: ll, Vernon Wayne et.al... (Continued)

INVESTIGATION NO.: 53110-92-1069-X

Four (4) Car-9 units.

ipped from: Sarco Inc.
              Union Street
              Stirling, N.J.
              (908) 647-3800

One (1) set of M-16 parts set kit with sling and magazine.
One (1) bolt catch extractor pin and buttcap screw.
Three (3) M-16 "A" kits.
Two (2) M-261 rifle conversion kits.
Four (4) M-203 handguards.

ipped from: Nessard Gun Parts Co.
              27 W. 990 Industrial Rd.
              Barrington, Ill.
              (708) 381-7629

Two (2) M-16 car kits, which contain everything that an M-16 contains, to include a 16" barrel, with out the lower receiver.
Two (2) M-16 EZ car kits, which contain everything that an M-16, with the 20" barrel, with out the lower receiver.
One (1) flash suppressor.

ipped from: Unknown Company at this time.

Two (2) boxes containing a total of M-16/AR-15 magazines, 30 in each box.

has been recently learned that the "Mag Bag" Corporation have also been ceiving other firearm parts and accessories from the following companies at have not yet been identified:

ooters Equipment Co.   Center Fire Systems Inc.
O. Box 517   102 Fieldview
chland, S.C. 29765   Versailies, Ky. 40383

tached are copies of invoices for your assistance and information.

ould you have any questions regarding this request, please contact ecial Agent Davy Aguilera at (512) 482-5333. Please submit the results your evaluation to:

              Bureau of Alcohol, Tobacco and Firearms
              ATTN: Special Agent Davy Aguilera
              P.O. Box 20-2828
              Austin, Texas 78720-2828

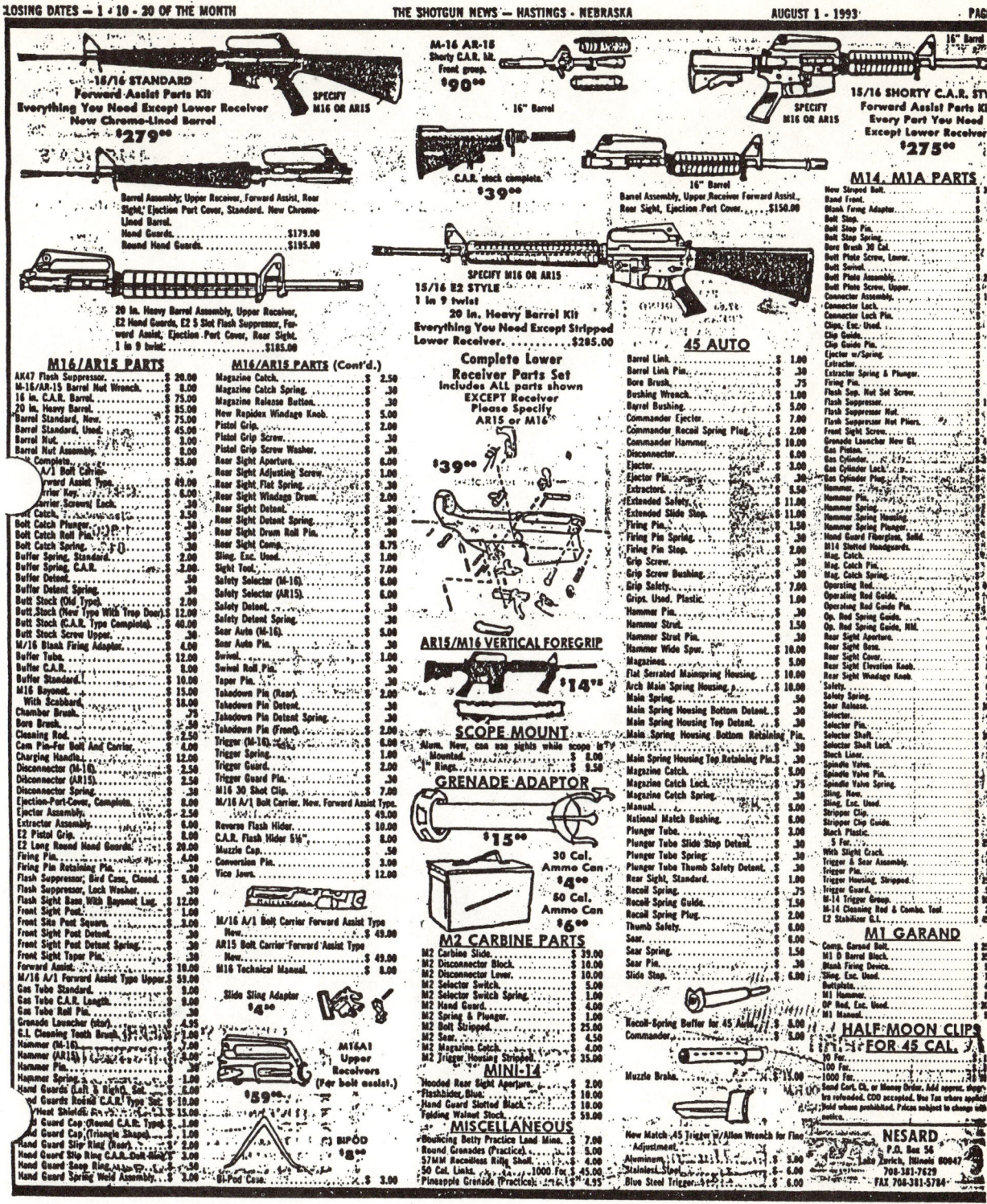

Appendix C

ATF Operations Plans

Original Operations Plan

February 25, 1993

OPERATIONS PLAN

1. SITUATION:

A. CIRCUMSTANCES:
On March 1, 1993 a Federal Search Warrant will be executed on the premises known as the residence of Vernon Wayne Howell, AKA: David Koresh, and others, along with all outbuildings and appurtenances and vehicles located on the premises.

B. TERRAIN:
The premises is in a rural setting, located on an approximate 77 acre tract of land, nearly 14 miles north and east of Waco, Texas. The premises contains the residences of approximately eighty (80) men, women and children, along with storage buildings and other structures.

C. TARGET:
Howell is the leader of a religious cult known as Branch Davidian and the premises has been named the Mount Carmel Center. For the past several years Howell has been receiving firearms parts which, if combined, could constitute the manufacture of machineguns. Also, he has been receiving shipments of chemicals and explosive materials which, if combined, could constitute the manufacture of explosive devices. These deliveries have been made through a cult operated mail drop known as the "Mag Bag". Additionally, nearby neighbors have reported hearing what they believe to be the sound of automatic weapons being fired in the nighttime coming from the Howell residence.

D. SUBJECT:
Vernon Wayne Howell is a white, male, born on August 17, 1959. He first took control of the Mount Carmel Center in early 1988 after an armed assault on the previous occupant in November of 1987. Howell, according to credible witnesses, depicts himself as Jesus Christ incarnate, requires all cult members to turn over all of their personal belongings to him, and he also sexually appropriates all of the female cult members for himself exclusively, to include female children as young as thirteen. Howell has surrounded himself with a group of approximately ten male cult members who have either criminal records and/or special skills which might precipitate violence during the execution of the search warrant.

2. MISSION:

The objective of the operation is to safely enter the premises of the Mount Carmel Center, to search the entire premises (to include the upper level residence of Howell and all other living quarters) for evidence of the manufacture of machineguns and explosive devices and for the machineguns and devices which may have already been manufactured. Personal identification of all persons on the premises will be accomplished and any persons who have outstanding warrants and/or immigration violations will be detained pending release to proper authorities. All others will be allowed to either leave the premises or to remain, as they may desire, once the search has been concluded.

3. EXECUTION:

A. HOW THE OBJECTIVE WILL BE ATTAINED:
Utilizing a number of facilities and the services of a wide array of Federal, State and local agencies, ATF will accomplish the mission. On Sunday, February 28, 1993, at approximately 8:30 p.m., an undercover ATF special agent will admit the Deputy Tactical Coordinator into an undercover residence which is across the road from the premises where the warrant will be served. Sometime prior to 8:30 a.m., on Monday, March 1, 1993, the undercover agent will position Forward Observers outside the premises, front and rear, in semi-concealed locations. At 9:00 a.m., Monday, March 1, 1993, the Tactical Coordinator will gather the tactical elements at a large parking lot site approximately eight miles away from the premises. The Tactical Coordinator will advise the undercover special agent by STU phone that the tactical elements are in position at which time the undercover special agent will visit the premises and identify the location of Howell and other principals. He will also check for recent changes at the premises and for any barriers or obstructions which may have recently been erected which might deter entry.

After his check of the premises, the undercover special agent will return to the undercover residence across the road and he will advise the Deputy Tactical Coordinator of his findings. The Deputy Tactical Coordinator will advise the Tactical Coordinator by STU phone of the conditions at the premises. Once the premises site has been determined to be functioning normally, the Tactical Coordinator will advise the three road block sites to begin their road blocks and he will deploy his tactical force of approximately seventy SRT special agents into two cattle trailers being pulled by civilian trucks and being driven by qualified special agents. The Tactical Coordinator will ride as a passenger in one of the trucks pulling a cattle trailer. He will be accompanied by an EMT trained special agent assigned to the SRT. As the Tactical Coordinator deploys, he will notify the Deputy Tactical Coordinator, who will then broadcast a radio message to the Command Post, air support units, the road block units and the standby ambulance unit that the tactical operation has begun.

Following a prearranged flight schedule, the three helicopters participating in the operation as well as the fixed wing aircraft, will depart from their staging area and will proceed to approach and hold a position at the rear of the premises. Their arrival at the rear of the premises will coincide with and cause a diversion for the entry by the SRT trailers at the front entrance to the premises. One of the helicopters will be occupied by the Incident Commander or his Deputy to provide an overall assessment of the tactical operation from his vantage point.

The New Orleans Division SRT will lead the entry into the main structure of the premises and will push straight ahead toward the interior staircase. They will proceed to the third level and will contain all persons found at that location. Next in line of entry will be the Houston Division SRT which will split in to two separate groups. The first group will make entry to the main structure immediately behind the New Orleans SRT and will spread to the left which is a series of bedrooms. The second group will disperse around the perimeter of the premises and contain any persons found. The Dallas Division SRT will immediately follow the Houston SRT which entered the structure and will spread to the right and to the rear.

Once all persons on the premises have been located, they will be assembled in the central area of the structure. Vernon Howell will be segregated from the rest of the group so as to minimize any attempt on his part to exhort his followers to some action. Once facilities have been erected outside the structure on the premises, all persons will be removed to those outside facilities to be identified and interviewed. Simultaneous with the structure being cleared of the cult members, a search of the entire premises will begin by those who have been designated to perform this function. Perimeter and internal security duties will be performed by additional ATF special agents until such time as the scene can be released.

B. CONTINGENCIES:
On February 28, 1993, a Texas Air National Guard aircraft will overfly the premises and will photograph the entire area. This reconnaisance will provide information regarding any late changes at the site of the tactical operation which will take place the following day.

On March 1, 1993, an ambulance will be positioned at the site of the road block closest to the premises. This ambulance will be manned by qualified Emergency Medical Technicians and will provide nearly immediate response to any injuries sustained in the tactical operation.

At the airfield at TSTC, immediately adjacent to the CP, a Careflight helicopter with a registered nurse aboard will be standing by in the event that an aerial evacuation of an injured person from the premises is required.

4. ADMINISTRATION AND LOGISTICS:

A. ASSIGNMENTS AND LODGING:
On February 23, 1993 the case agent will appear before the United States Magistrate and have the Federal Search Warrant Affidavit approved and the Federal Search Warrant signed.

On February 24, 1993 the Tactical Coordinator, the Deputy Tactical Coordinator, and the ATF SRT Team Leaders and their assistants will travel so as to arrive at Fort Hood, Texas by 1400 hours. Lodging will be arranged in the military barracks at Fort Hood to accomodate twenty (20) persons.

On February 24, 1993 the Incident Commander, the Deputy Incident Commander, the Support Coordinator, and his support staff will travel to the Texas State Technical College (TSTC), Waco, Texas to set up the Command Post

(CP). Accomodations will be arranged in a Waco motel for eleven (11) persons.

On February 24, 1993, two Communications Specialists will assist in the set up of the CP. Once the CP has been established, they will depart for Temple/Belton, Texas where they will establish a radio repeater site and be lodged in a motel. The Temple/Belton location is equidistant between Fort Hood and Waco and the repeater site at this location will facilitate radio transmissions between the SRT elements at Fort Hood and the CP at TSTC in Waco.

On February 25, 1993, the thirty-seven (37) Sector SRT members arrive at Fort Hood, Texas by 1400 hours and they are initially briefed by the Incident Commander and his staff. They will be lodged in the military barracks at Fort Hood to accomodate what is now a group of fifty-seven (57) persons.

On February 26, 1993, thirty-four (34) ATF special agents from the Houston, New Orleans, and Dallas Divisions arrive at Fort Hood, Texas by 1400 hours. These special agents represent auxiliary personnel who will be utilized in the identification and interviewing of detainees at the site of the warrant execution. They will be lodged in the military barracks at Fort Hood to accomodate what has now become a group of ninety-one (91) persons.

On February 26, 1993, one ATF special agent/pilot and two Texas Air National Guard pilots arrive in Waco at TSTC with their aircraft. They are lodged in a Waco motel and their presence increases the number of operational personnel in Waco to fourteen (14) persons.

On February 27, 1993, the Sector SRT personnel and other special agents assigned to the tactical operation will practice the tactics of the warrant execution at Fort Hood, Texas.

On February 27, 1993, two Public Information Officers (PIO) will arrive at the CP at TSTC in Waco. They will be lodged in Waco and will increase the number of personnel at this location to sixteen (16) persons.

On February 27, 1993, the Project Alliance Coordinator will arrive at the Temple/Belton, Texas location where he will meet with the Communications Specialists, bringing the number of operational personnel in this location to three (3).

On February 28, 1993, the ninety-one (91) Sector SRT members and additional support special agents will travel from Fort Hood, Texas to Waco, Texas. The Communications Specialists and the Project Alliance Coordinator in Temple/Belton, Texas will relocate to Waco, Texas. A representative from the Tactical Response Branch, Special Operations Division, Bureau Headquarters will arrive in Waco. Two (2) representatives from the Explosives Technology Branch will arrive in Waco and two (2) fingerprint examiners from the ATF Laboratory will also arrive in Waco. On this date ten (10) Texas National Guard Aviation support personnel will arrive in Waco as well as twenty-five (25) additional ATF special agents from the Houston and Dallas Divisions. The total number of operational personnel lodged in Waco this night will be one hundred-fifty (150) persons.

On March 1, 1993 the Federal Search Warrant will be executed as outlined in section 3A of this plan.

B. EQUIPMENT:
The following special equipment, beyond what is normally carried by SRT members, was authorized for purchase during this tactical operation:
    100 Flex Cuffs
    250 Hospital ID Bracelets
      2 Inertial Rams
      1 Bolt Cutters
      2 "Hooligan" pry bars, 30 inch
     31 Sets of knee and elbow pads
     26 Pair of Protective Goggles
      3 Halon type, 13 lb, fire extinguishers

5. COMMAND AND SIGNALS:

A. COMMAND POST:
The Command Post (CP) will be physically located at the Airport Manager's Building, immediately adjacent to the airfield at the Texas State Technical College (TSTC), approximately eight (8) miles north of Waco, Texas. The CP will be the operational headquarters for the Incident Commander, the Deputy Incident Commander, and the Support Coordinator and his staff.

B. SIGNALS:
The CP will provide the Incident Commander with point-to-point Coded DES communications between all elements of the tactical operation and the National Command Center. These communications capabilities are: handheld radios, mobile radios, fixed site equipment, satellite cellular communication with secure STU III and Secure/Clear FAX. This will be accomplished through the installation of a Motorola Micor 100 watt repeater in the airfield control tower, an antenna installed on top of the airfield control tower, a portable System Saber base station and a secure STU III telephone unit with Secure/Clear FAX capability along with four secure point-to-point deskset telephones.

C. COMMANDS:

Modified Operations
Plan

Provided to
Texas Rangers

on
March 11, 1993

OPERATIONS PLAN

1. SITUATION:

   A. CIRCUMSTANCES:

   On February 28, 1993 a Federal Search Warrant will be executed on the premises known as the residence of Vernon Wayne Howell, AKA: David Koresh, and others, along with all outbuildings and appurtenances and vehicles located on the premises. (Annex B, Affidavit for Federal Search Warrant)

   B. TERRAIN:

   The premises is in a rural setting, located on an approximate 77 acre tract of land, nearly 14 miles north and east of Waco, Texas. The premises contains the residences of approximately eighty (80) men, women and children, along with storage buildings and other structures. (Annex C)

   C. TARGET:

   Howell is the leader of a religious cult known as Branch Davidian and the premises has been named the Mount Carmel Center. For the past several years Howell has been receiving firearms parts which, if combined, could constitute the manufacture of machineguns. Also, he has been receiving shipments of chemicals and explosive materials which, if combined, could constitute the manufacture of explosive devices. These deliveries have been made through a cult operated mail drop known as the "Mag Bag". Additionally, nearby neighbors have reported hearing what they believe to be the sound of automatic weapons being fired in the nighttime coming from the Howell residence. (Annex D, Deliveries to Mag Bag)

   ▓ Shaded area represents text that was added to the original operations plan.

   Underlined sentences represent original text which was moved to a different part of the operations plan.

D. SUBJECT:

Vernon Wayne Howell is a white, male, born on August 17, 1959. He first took control of the Mount Carmel Center in early 1988 after an armed assault on the previous occupant in November of 1987. Howell, according to credible witnesses, depicts himself as Jesus Christ incarnate, requires all cult members to turn over all of their personal belongings to him, and he also sexually appropriates all of the female cult members for himself exclusively, to include female children as young as thirteen. Howell has surrounded himself with a group of approximately ten male cult members who have either criminal records and/or special skills which might precipitate violence during the execution of the search warrant. The subject has not left the compound in months and has made statements that he does not plan to leave. (Annex E)

2. MISSION:

The objective of the operation is to safely enter the premises of the Mount Carmel Center, to search the entire premises (to include the upper level residence of Howell and all other living quarters) for evidence of the manufacture of machineguns and explosive devices and for the machineguns and devices which may have already been manufactured. The women, men and firearms are kept in different areas in the structure. Usually at approximately 10:00 a.m. in the morning, the majority of the males and Howell should be in the underground area. SRT teams have been divided to handle the areas listed above. Personal identification of all persons on the premises will be accomplished and any persons who have outstanding warrants and/or immigration violations will be detained pending release to proper authorities. All others will be allowed to either leave the premises or to remain, as they may desire, once the search has been concluded.

3. EXECUTION:

A. CONCEPT OF OPERATION:

Utilizing a number of facilities and the services of a wide array of Federal, State and local agencies, ATF will accomplish the mission. On Sunday, February 27, 1993, at approximately 8:30 p.m., an undercover ATF special agent will admit the Deputy Tactical Coordinator into an undercover residence which is across the road from the premises where the warrant will be served. Sometime prior to 8:30 a.m., on Sunday, February 28, 1993, the undercover agent will position Forward Observers outside the premises, front and rear, in semi-concealed locations. At 9:00 a.m., Sunday, February 28, 1993, the Tactical Coordinator will gather the tactical elements at a large parking lot site approximately thirteen miles away from the premises. The Tactical Coordinator will advise the undercover special agent by STU phone that the tactical elements are in position at which time the undercover special agent will visit the premises and identify the location of Howell and other principals. He will also check for recent changes at the premises and for any barriers or obstructions which may have recently been erected which might deter entry.

After his check of the premises, the undercover special agent will return to the undercover residence across the road and he will advise the Deputy Tactical Coordinator of his findings. The undercover special agent will advise the Tactical Coordinator by STU phone of the conditions at the premises. Once the premises site has been determined to be functioning normally, the Tactical Coordinator will advise the three road block sites to begin their road blocks and he will deploy his tactical force of approximately eighty SRT special agents into two cattle trailers being pulled by civilian trucks and being driven by qualified special agents. The Tactical Coordinator will ride as a passenger in one of the trucks pulling a cattle trailer. He will be accompanied by an EMT trained special agent assigned to the SRT.

As the Tactical Coordinator deploys, he will notify the Deputy Tactical Coordinator, who will notify him if the operation is a go until they reach the residence. The Deputy Tactical Coordinator then will broadcast a radio message to the Command Post, air support units, the road block units and the standby ambulance unit that the tactical operation has begun. (Annex F, Block Map)

Following a prearranged flight schedule, the three helicopters participating in the operation as well as the fixed wing aircraft, will depart from their staging area and will proceed to approach and hold a position at the rear of the premises. Their arrival at the rear of the premises will coincide with and cause a diversion for the entry by the SRT trailers at the front entrance to the premises. One of the helicopters will be occupied by the Incident Commander or his Deputy to provide an overall assessment of the tactical operation from his vantage point.

The New Orleans Division SRT will lead the entry to the right side of the main structure of the premises and will make entry from the roof into the second floor windows of the Arms room and Koresh's room. They will proceed to the rear of the structure and will contain all persons found at that location after entry. Next in line of entry will be the Houston Division SRT which will split into two separate groups. The first group will make entry to the main structure front door area and will spread to the left which is a series of mens bedrooms.

[handwritten margin note: 2cd HFD SRT will actually enter underground area to prevent split and retreat into dormitory area.]

The second group will disperse around the perimeter of the premises and contain those persons found in the underground area. The Dallas Division SRT will immediately follow the Houston SRT which entered the structure and will go upstairs and clear 2nd, 3rd, and 4th floor areas which contains the womens bedrooms. Two outside teams of non-SRT team members will provide outside cover on all sides of the structure. A third team of non-SRT team members will be used for custody control of people.

C-18

Once all persons on the premises have been located, they will be assembled in the central area of the structure. Vernon Howell will be segregated from the rest of the group so as to minimize any attempt on his part to exhort his followers to some action. Once facilities have been erected outside the structure on the premises, all persons will be removed to those outside facilities to be identified and interviewed. Simultaneous with the structure being cleared of the cult members, a search of the entire premises will begin by those who have been designated to perform this function. Perimeter and internal security duties will be performed by additional ATF special agents until such time as the scene can be released.

B.   CONTINGENCIES:

On February 28, 1993, a Texas Air National Guard aircraft will overfly the premises and will photograph the entire area. This reconnaissance will provide information regarding any late changes at the site of the tactical operation which will take place the following day.

On February 28, 1993, an ambulance will be positioned at the site of the road block closest to the premises. This ambulance will be manned by qualified Emergency Medical Technicians and will provide nearly immediate response to any injuries sustained in the tactical operation.

At the airfield at TSTC, immediately adjacent to the CP, a Careflight helicopter with a registered nurse aboard will be standing by in the event that an aerial evacuation of an injured person from the premises is required.

4. ADMINISTRATION AND LOGISTICS:

A. ASSIGNMENTS AND LODGING:
On February 23, 1993 the case agent will appear before the United States Magistrate and have the Federal Search Warrant Affidavit approved and the Federal Search Warrant signed.

On February 24, 1993 the Tactical Coordinator, the Deputy Tactical Coordinator, and the ATF SRT Team Leaders and their assistants will travel so as to arrive at Fort Hood, Texas by 1400 hours. Lodging will be arranged in the military barracks at Fort Hood to accommodate twenty (20) persons.

On February 24, 1993 the Incident Commander, the Deputy Incident Commander, the Support Coordinator, and his support staff will travel to the Texas State Technical College (TSTC), Waco, Texas to set up the Command Post (CP). Accommodations will be arranged in a Waco motel for eleven (11) persons.

On February 24, 1993, two Communications Specialists will assist in the set up of the CP. Once the CP has been established, they will depart for Temple/Belton, Texas where they will establish a radio repeater site and be lodged in a motel. The Temple/Belton location is equidistant between Fort Hood and Waco and the repeater site at this location will facilitate radio transmissions between the SRT elements at Fort Hood and the CP at TSTC in Waco.

On February 25, 1993, the thirty-seven (37) Sector SRT members arrive at Fort Hood, Texas by 1400 hours and they are initially briefed by the Incident Commander and his staff. They will be lodged in the military barracks at Fort Hood to accommodate what is now a group of fifty-seven (57) persons.

On February 26, 1993, thirty-four (34) ATF special agents from the Houston, New Orleans, and Dallas Divisions arrive at Fort Hood, Texas by 1400 hours. These special agents represent auxiliary personnel who will be utilized in the identification and interviewing of detainees at the site of the warrant execution. They will be lodged in the military barracks at Fort Hood to accommodate what has now become a group of ninety-one (91) persons.

On February 26, 1993, one ATF special agent/pilot and two Texas Air National Guard pilots arrive in Waco at TSTC with their aircraft. They are lodged in a Waco motel and their presence increases the number of operational personnel in Waco to fourteen (14) persons.

On February 27, 1993, the Sector SRT personnel and other special agents assigned to the tactical operation will practice the tactics of the warrant execution at Fort Hood, Texas.

On February 27, 1993, two Public Information Officers (PIO) will arrive at the CP at TSTC in Waco. They will be lodged in Waco and will increase the number of personnel at this location to sixteen (16) persons.

On February 27, 1993, the Project Alliance Coordinator will arrive at the Temple/Belton, Texas location where he will meet with the Communications Specialists, bringing the number of operational personnel in this location to three (3). <u>Two (2) representatives from the Explosives Technology Branch will arrive in Waco and two (2) fingerprint examiners from the ATF Laboratory will also arrive in Waco. On this date ten (10) Texas National Guard Aviation support personnel will arrive in Waco as well as twenty-five (25) additional AFT special agents from the Houston and Dallas Divisions. The total number of operational personnel lodged in Waco this night will be one hundred-fifty (150) persons.</u>

On February 28, 1993, the ninety-one (91) Sector SRT members and additional support special agents will travel from Fort Hood, Texas to Waco, Texas to the staging area from which point they will prepare to execute the search warrant as outlined in Section 3A of this plan.

    B.   EQUIPMENT:

The following special equipment, beyond what is normally carried by SRT members, was authorized for purchase during this tactical operation:

100 Flex Cuffs
250 Hospital ID Bracelets
2 Inertial Rams
1 Bolt Cutters
2 "Hooligan" pry bars, 30 inch
31 Sets of knee and elbow pads
26 Pair of Protective Goggles
3 Halon type, 13 lb, fire extinguisher

5.   COMMAND AND SIGNALS:

    A.   COMMAND POST:

The Command Post (CP) will be physically located at the Airport Manager's Building, immediately adjacent to the airfield at the Texas State Technical College (TSTC), approximately eight (8) miles north of Waco, Texas. The CP will be the operational headquarters for the Incident Commander, the Deputy Incident Commander, and the Support Coordinator and his staff. (Annex G, Reporting Instructions)

B. SIGNALS:

The CP will provide the Incident Commander with point-to-point Coded DES communications between all elements of the tactical operation and the National Command Center. These communications capabilities are: handheld radios, mobile radios, fixed site equipment, satellite cellular communication with secure STU III and Secure/Clear FAX. This will be accomplished through the installation of a Motorola Micor 100 watt repeater in the airfield control tower, an antenna installed on top of the airfield control tower, a portable System Saber base station and a secure STU III telephone unit with Secure/Clear FAX capability along with four secure point-to-point deskset telephones. (Annex H, Common Plan)

Final Raid Plan incorporating the handwritten changes from March 11, 1993 version. This document was provided to Texas Rangers on March 22, 1993 and later to the Review

OPERATIONS PLAN

1. SITUATION:

    A.   CIRCUMSTANCES:

        On February 28, 1993 a Federal Search Warrant will be executed on the premises known as the residence of Vernon Wayne Howell, AKA: David Koresh, and others, along with all outbuildings and appurtenances and vehicles located on the premises.
(Annex B, Affidavit for Federal Search Warrant)

    B.   TERRAIN:

        The premises is in a rural setting, located on an approximate 77 acre tract of land, nearly 14 miles north and east of Waco, Texas. The premises contains the residences of approximately eighty (80) men, women and children, along with storage buildings and other structures. (Annex C)

    C.   TARGET:

        Howell is the leader of a religious cult known as Branch Davidian and the premises has been named the Mount Carmel Center. For the past several years Howell has been receiving firearms parts which, if combined, could constitute the manufacture of machineguns. Also, he has been receiving shipments of chemicals and explosive materials which, if combined, could constitute the manufacture of explosive devices. These deliveries have been made through a cult operated mail drop known as the "Mag Bag". Additionally, nearby neighbors have reported hearing what they believe to be the sound of automatic weapons being fired in the nighttime coming from the Howell residence. (Annex D, Deliveries to Mag Bag)

▒ Shaded text represents the handwritten notes of the incdent commander incorporated into operations plan.

D. SUBJECT:

Vernon Wayne Howell is a white, male, born on August 17, 1959. He first took control of the Mount Carmel Center in early 1988 after an armed assault on the previous occupant in November of 1987. Howell, according to credible witnesses, depicts himself as Jesus Christ incarnate, requires all cult members to turn over all of their personal belongings to him, and he also sexually appropriates all of the female cult members for himself exclusively, to include female children as young as thirteen. Howell has surrounded himself with a group of approximately ten male cult members who have either criminal records and/or special skills which might precipitate violence during the execution of the search warrant. The subject has not left the compound in months and has made statements that he does not plan to leave. (Annex E)

2. MISSION:

The objective of the operation is to safely enter the premises of the Mount Carmel Center, to search the entire premises (to include the upper level residence of Howell and all other living quarters) for evidence of the manufacture of machineguns and explosive devices and for the machineguns and devices which may have already been manufactured. The women, men and firearms are kept in different areas in the structure. Usually at approximately 10:00 a.m. in the morning, the majority of the males and Howell should be in the underground area. SRT teams have been divided to handle the areas listed above. Personal identification of all persons on the premises will be accomplished and any persons who have outstanding warrants and/or immigration violations will be detained pending release to proper authorities. All others will be allowed to either leave the premises or to remain, as they may desire, once the search has been concluded.

3. EXECUTION:

    A.   CONCEPT OF OPERATION:

Utilizing a number of facilities and the services of a wide array of Federal, State and local agencies, ATF will accomplish the mission. On Sunday, February 27, 1993, at approximately 8:30 p.m., an undercover ATF special agent will admit the Deputy Tactical Coordinator into an undercover residence which is across the road from the premises where the warrant will be served. Sometime prior to 8:30 a.m., on Sunday, February 28, 1993, the undercover agent will position Forward Observers outside the premises, front and rear, in semi-concealed locations. At 9:00 a.m., Sunday, February 28, 1993, the Tactical Coordinator will gather the tactical elements at a large parking lot site approximately thirteen miles away from the premises. The Tactical Coordinator will advise the undercover special agent by STU phone that the tactical elements are in position at which time the undercover special agent will visit the premises and identify the location of Howell and other principals. He will also check for recent changes at the premises and for any barriers or obstructions which may have recently been erected which might deter entry.

After his check of the premises, the undercover special agent will return to the undercover residence across the road and he will advise the Deputy Tactical Coordinator of his findings. The undercover special agent will advise the Tactical Coordinator by STU phone of the conditions at the premises. Once the premises site has been determined to be functioning normally, the Tactical Coordinator will advise the three road block sites to begin their road blocks and he will deploy his tactical force of approximately eighty SRT special agents into two cattle trailers being pulled by civilian trucks and being driven by qualified special agents. The Tactical Coordinator will ride as a passenger in one of the trucks pulling a cattle trailer. He will be accompanied by an EMT trained special agent assigned to the SRT.

As the Tactical Coordinator deploys, he will notify the Deputy Tactical Coordinator, who will notify him if the operation is a go until they reach the residence. The Deputy Tactical Coordinator then will broadcast a radio message to the Command Post, air support units, the road block units and the standby ambulance unit that the tactical operation has begun (Annex F, Block Map)

Following a prearranged flight schedule, the three helicopters participating in the operation as well as the fixed wing aircraft, will depart from their staging area and will proceed to approach and hold a position at the rear of the premises. Their arrival at the rear of the premises will coincide with and cause a diversion for the entry by the SRT trailers at the front entrance to the premises. One of the helicopters will be occupied by the Incident Commander or his Deputy to provide an overall assessment of the tactical operation from his vantage point.

The New Orleans Division SRT will lead the entry to the right side of the main structure of the premises and will make entry from the roof into the second floor windows of the Arms room and Koresh's room. They will proceed to the rear of the structure and will contain all persons found at that location after entry. Next in line of entry will be the Houston Division SRT which will split into two separate groups. The first group will make entry to the main structure front door area and will spread to the left which is a series of mens bedrooms.

The second group will enter the underground area, contain those persons found in the underground area, in order to keep them from returning through the "tunnel" into the men's dormitory area encountering the Houston SRT. The Dallas Division SRT will immediately follow the Houston SRT which entered the structure and will go upstairs and clear 2nd, 3rd, and 4th floor area which contains the womens bedrooms. Two outside teams of non-SRT team members will provide outside cover on all sides of the structure. A third team of non-SRT team members will be used for custody control of people.

Once all persons on the premises have been located, they will be assembled in the central area of the structure. Vernon Howell will be segregated from the rest of the group so as to minimize any attempt on his part to exhort his followers to some action. Once facilities have been erected outside the structure on the premises, all persons will be removed to those outside facilities to be identified and interviewed. Simultaneous with the structure being cleared of the cult members, a search of the entire premises will begin by those who have been designated to perform this function. Perimeter and internal security duties will be performed by additional ATF special agents until such time as the scene can be released.

B. CONTINGENCIES:

On February 28, 1993, a Texas Air National Guard aircraft will overfly the premises and will photograph the entire area. This reconnaissance will provide information regarding any late changes at the site of the tactical operation which will take place the following day.

On February 28, 1993, an ambulance will be positioned at the site of the road block closest to the premises. This ambulance will be manned by qualified Emergency Medical Technicians and will provide nearly immediate response to any injuries sustained in the tactical operation.

At the airfield at TSTC, immediately adjacent to the CP, a Careflight helicopter with a registered nurse aboard will be standing by in the event that an aerial evacuation of an injured person from the premises is required.

4. ADMINISTRATION AND LOGISTICS:

A. ASSIGNMENTS AND LODGING:
On February 23, 1993 the case agent will appear before the United States Magistrate and have the Federal Search Warrant Affidavit approved and the Federal Search Warrant signed.

On February 24, 1993 the Tactical Coordinator, the Deputy Tactical Coordinator, and the ATF SRT Team Leaders and their assistants will travel so as to arrive at Fort Hood, Texas by 1400 hours. Lodging will be arranged in the military barracks at Fort Hood to accommodate twenty (20) persons.

On February 24, 1993 the Incident Commander, the Deputy Incident Commander, the Support Coordinator, and his support staff will travel to the Texas State Technical College (TSTC), Waco, Texas to set up the Command Post (CP). Accommodations will be arranged in a Waco motel for eleven (11) persons.

On February 24, 1993, two Communications Specialists will assist in the set up of the CP. Once the CP has been established, they will depart for Temple/Belton, Texas where they will establish a radio repeater site and be lodged in a motel. The Temple/Belton location is equidistant between Fort Hood and Waco and the repeater site at this location will facilitate radio transmissions between the SRT elements at Fort Hood and the CP at TSTC in Waco.

On February 25, 1993, the thirty-seven (37) Sector SRT members arrive at Fort Hood, Texas by 1400 hours and they are initially briefed by the Incident Commander and his staff. They will be lodged in the military barracks at Fort Hood to accommodate what is now a group of fifty-seven (57) persons.

On February 26, 1993, thirty-four (34) ATF special agents from the Houston, New Orleans, and Dallas Divisions arrive at Fort Hood, Texas by 1400 hours. These special agents represent auxiliary personnel who will be utilized in the identification and interviewing of detainees at the site of the warrant execution. They will be lodged in the military barracks at Fort Hood to accommodate what has now become a group of ninety-one (91) persons.

On February 26, 1993, one ATF special agent/pilot and two Texas Air National Guard pilots arrive in Waco at TSTC with their aircraft. They are lodged in a Waco motel and their presence increases the number of operational personnel in Waco to fourteen (14) persons.

On February 27, 1993, the Sector SRT personnel and other special agents assigned to the tactical operation will practice the tactics of the warrant execution at Fort Hood, Texas.

On February 27, 1993, two Public Information Officers (PIO) will arrive at the CP at TSTC in Waco. They will be lodged in Waco and will increase the number of personnel at this location to sixteen (16) persons.

On February 27, 1993, the Project Alliance Coordinator will arrive at the Temple/Belton, Texas location where he will meet with the Communications Specialists, bringing the number of operational personnel in this location to three (3). Two (2) representatives from the Explosives Technology Branch will arrive in Waco and two (2) fingerprint examiners from the ATF Laboratory will also arrive in Waco. On this date ten (10) Texas National Guard Aviation support personnel will arrive in Waco as well as twenty-five (25) additional AFT special agents from the Houston and Dallas Divisions. The total number of operational personnel lodged in Waco this night will be one hundred-fifty (150) persons.

On February 28, 1993, the ninety-one (91) Sector SRT members and additional support special agents will travel from Fort Hood, Texas to Waco, Texas to the staging area from which point they will prepare to execute the search warrant as outlined in Section 3A of this plan.

B. EQUIPMENT:

The following special equipment, beyond what is normally carried by SRT members, was authorized for purchase during this tactical operation:

100 Flex Cuffs
250 Hospital ID Bracelets
2 Inertial Rams
1 Bolt Cutters
2 "Hooligan" pry bars, 30 inch
31 Sets of knee and elbow pads
26 Pair of Protective Goggles
3 Halon type, 13 lb, fire extinguisher

5. COMMAND AND SIGNALS:

A. COMMAND POST:

The Command Post (CP) will be physically located at the Airport Manager's Building, immediately adjacent to the airfield at the Texas State Technical College (TSTC), approximately eight (8) miles north of Waco, Texas. The CP will be the operational headquarters for the Incident Commander, the Deputy Incident Commander, and the Support Coordinator and his staff. (Annex G, Reporting Instructions)

B.   SIGNALS:

The CP will provide the Incident Commander with point-to-point Coded DES communications between all elements of the tactical operation and the National Command Center. These communications capabilities are: handheld radios, mobile radios, fixed site equipment, satellite cellular communication with secure STU III and Secure/Clear FAX. This will be accomplished through the installation of a Motorola Micor 100 watt repeater in the airfield control tower, an antenna installed on top of the airfield control tower, a portable System Saber base station and a secure STU III telephone unit with Secure/Clear FAX capability along with four secure point-to-point deskset telephones.   (Annex H, Common Plan)

Appendix D

Chronology of Events

WACO REVIEW TIMELINE OF EVENTS

DATE	EVENT	REMARKS
OCT/NOV, 1987	VERNON HOWELL AND SEVERAL OF HIS ASSOCIATES PURCHASED SEVERAL RIFLES AT LOCAL PALESTINE, TEXAS AREA GUN SHOPS. THESE WEAPONS WERE USED BY HOWELL AND HIS ASSOCIATES FOR A RAID ON MT. CARMEL.	
11/3/87	VERNON WAYNE HOWELL AND SEVEN OF HIS GROUP ARE ARRESTED FOR ATTEMPTED MURDER OF GEORGE BUCHANAN RODEN.	
11/4/87	HOWELL IS RELEASED ON BAIL ($50,000) AND AWAITS TRIAL.	
4/25/88	A MISTRIAL IS DECLARED (JURY DEADLOCKED) IN HOWELL'S TRIAL - HOWELL IS NOT TRIED AGAIN. HIS SEVEN ASSOCIATES RECEIVE ACQUITTALS.	
11/4/88	THE CHARGE AGAINST HOWELL IS DISMISSED.	
11/7/88	THE COURT ORDERS ALL PROPERTY SEIZED RETURNED TO HOWELL.	THIS INCLUDES A SUBSTANTIAL NUMBER OF GUNS AND AMMUNITION.
1988-1989	GEORGE RODEN IS INCARCERATED FOR SIX MONTHS FOR CONTEMPT OF COURT, AFTER HIS RELEASE, HE KILLS A MAN AND IS COMMITTED TO AN MENTAL INSTITUTION.	THIS ALLOWS HOWELL AND HIS ASSOCIATES TO GAIN CONTROL OF MT. CARMEL.
9/90	WACO FBI RECEIVES INQUIRY ABOUT "CYRUS" PRODUCTIONS PROMOTING "SHAM" MARRIAGES WITH AUSTRALIAN CITIZENS. DISCUSSION WITH AUSA, WACO DETERMINE NO FEDERAL VIOLATION, INQUIRY IS CLOSED.	FBI DETERMINES "CYRUS" PRODUCTIONS TO BE A MUSICAL GROUP LED BY KORESH.
2/27/92	TEXAS DEPARTMENT OF PROTECTIVE AND REGULATORY SERVICES (DPRS) VISIT THE MT. CARMEL COMPOUND RE: ACCUSATIONS OF CHILD ABUSE.	
3/5-9/92	DAVID KORESH, AKA, VERNON WAYNE HOWELL, VISITS THE WACO OFFICE OF THE DPRS AND SPEAKS WITH JOYCE SPARKS REGARDING THE CHILD ABUSE ALLEGATIONS. LOCAL LAW ENFORCEMENT CONDUCT SWAT TRAINING NEAR "MAG BAG". DAVID KORESH, AKA, VERNON HOWELL, REACTS BY: 1) BRINGING BACK MEMBERS FROM CALIFORNIA AND ENGLAND; 2) MAKING LARGE PURCHASES OF WEAPON PARTS; 3) ACQUIRING CHEMICALS WHICH CAN BE USED TO MAKE EXPLOSIVES; 4) PURCHASING NIGHT VISION SCOPES AND SENSORS; AND, 5) ACCUMULATING LARGE SUPPLIES OF AMMUNITION.	ATF DOES NOT LEARN OF THE SWAT TRAINING UNTIL AFTER 2/28/93. PRIOR TO MARCH 5, COMPOUND BELIEVED TO HAVE APPROX. 80 FIREARMS, AFTER MARCH 5, AN ADDITIONAL 143 (MOSTLY ASSAULT RIFLES) ARE ACQUIRED.

4/92	WACO TRIBUNE-HERALD REPORTER MARK ENGLAND BEGINS INVESTIGATION OF BRANCH DAVIDIANS AFTER HEARING REPORTS OF POSSIBLE MASS SUICIDE OVER DAVIDIAN PASSOVER.	
4/6/92	WACO FBI OPENS CASE ON KORESH FOR INVOLUNTARY SERVITUDE.	
4/30/92	TEXAS DPRS VISITS COMPOUND RE: CHILD ABUSE.	
5/92	TEXAS DPRS VISITS THE COMPOUND REGARDING THE CHILD ABUSE ALLEGATIONS FOR THE LAST TIME AND SUBSEQUENTLY CLOSES IT'S INQUIRY.	JOYCE SPARKS CONTINUES TO HAVE TELEPHONE CONTACTS WITH KORESH.
	LT. COY JONES, McLENNAN COUNTY SHERIFF'S OFFICE CONTACTED BY UPS RE: DELIVERY OF LARGE AMOUNTS OF FIREARM PARTS TO THE MAG BAG.	UPS DRIVER GILBREATH REVEALS DELIVERIES MADE SINCE MARCH, 1992 AMOUNTED TO APPROX. $20,000 IN CASH
	CHIEF DEPUTY WEYENBERG CALLS SA CHARLES MEYER, AUSTIN TO REPORT UPS INFORMATION.	
	FBI CONTACTS TEXAS DEPARTMENT OF PROTECTIVE AND REGULATORY SERVICES, JOYCE SPARKS, RE: FBI INVESTIGATION.	SPARKS TELLS FBI SHE IS AWARE OF KORESH.
5/26/92	SA DAVY AGUILERA IS TOLD BY SA CHARLES MEYER TO CONTACT CHIEF DEPUTY WEYENBERG, McLENNAN CO SHERIFF'S OFFICE RE: UPS DELIVERIES. WEYENBERG ASSIGNS LT GENE BARBER TO WORK WITH AGUILERA	MEYER ORIGINALLY TOOK CALL FROM SHERIFF'S OFFICE, BUT CASE IS REFERRED TO AGUILERA BY MEYER.
6/92	JOYCE SPARKS' LAST CONTACT WITH DAVID KORESH.	
	FBI CLOSES INVESTIGATION OF KORESH FOR INVOLUNTARY SERVITUDE.	
6/4/92	AGUILERA MEETS FIRST W/AUSA BILL JOHNSTON, THEN WITH BARBER. BARBER SHARES HISTORY OF BRANCH DAVIDIANS, DELINEATES NATURE AND AMOUNT OF UPS DELIVERIES TO "MAG BAG".	BARBER DESCRIBES METHOD UPS DELIVERIES ARE MADE AND ABOUT A HAND GRENADE CASING FALLING OUT OF A DELIVERY PACKAGE.
6/9/92	AGUILERA SUBMITS INITIATING REPORT TO HOUSTON VIA AUSTIN.	INCLUDES INFORMATION PROVIDED BY BARBER, SKINNER AND GILBREATH
6/17/92	SAC CHOJNACKI NOTIFIES RAC LARRY SPARKS, AUSTIN VIA HANDWRITTEN FAXED NOTES, INVESTIGATION CLASSIFIED AS SENSITIVE. INVESTIGATION CONTINUES.	SENSITIVE CLASSIFICATION DENOTES HEADQUARTERS MONITORING OF CASE.
6/19/92	ATF HEADQUARTERS (HQ) BECOMES AWARE OF INVESTIGATION IN WACO.	BECOMES A HQ MONITORED CASE (SIGNIFICANT)
7/92	TACTICAL OPERATIONS OFFICER, MARK HANDLEY RECOMMENDS TO AGUILERA USE OF POLE CAMERA AND PEN REGISTER AS INVESTIGATIVE TOOLS.	

7/22/92	AGUILERA REQUESTS OPINION FROM ATF HQ RE: EXPLOSIVE MANUFACTURING AND AUTOMATIC WEAPONS MANUFACTURING/CONVERSION BASED ON COMPONENTS KNOWN TO BE IN POSSESSION OF DAVIDIANS.	
7/30/92	COMPLIANCE INSPECTION OF HENRY MCMAHON BY AGUILERA AND JIM SKINNER REVEALS APPROX 65 LOWER RECEIVERS FOR AR-15s MISSING, MCMAHON SAYS STORED AT PREACHER'S (DAVID KORESH), ADDITIONALLY SAYS 36 FIREARMS SOLD TO VERNON HOWELL. DOES NOT ACKNOWLEDGE OR OFFER THEY ARE SAME PERSON.	SKINNER FINDS COMPLIANCE VIOLATIONS, BUT DOES NOT CITE, IN ORDER TO MAINTAIN INVESTIGATION INTEGRITY.
8/5/92	RAC LARRY SPARKS, AUSTIN IS ADMINISTRATIVELY REMOVED FROM AUSTIN OFFICE FORMER RAC EARL DUNAGAN IS MADE ACTING RAC OF AUSTIN.	SPARKS IS LATER FIRED FROM THE ATF AND HAS APPEALED THIS ACTION.
8/8/92	SKINNER RETURNED TO MCMAHON'S PLACE OF BUSINESS AND PROVIDES HIM WITH INFORMATION ON PROPER RECORD KEEPING AND FEDERAL EXCISE TAXES.	
8/11/92	ATF INSTALLED POLE CAMERA, FAILED TO GET IT TO WORK UNTIL DECEMBER 11, 1992.	ATF ATTEMPTED TWICE IN OCTOBER TO GET THE CAMERA TO WORK.
SEPT. & OCT.	CASE AGENT AGUILERA ASSIGNED TO USSS PROTECTIVE DETAILS AT THREE WEEK INTERVALS.	DURING USSS DETAIL, HE IS UNABLE TO PURSUE THE INVESTIGATION.
10/92	SARABYN IS TEMPORARILY ASSIGNED TO HQ TO PREPARE NATIONAL RESPONSE PLAN (SECTOR PLAN).	
10/92	HARTNETT APPROVES FORWARD OBSERVER PROGRAM.	SUBSEQUENT TRAINING OCCURS FOR SIX TEAMS IN NOV., 1992
OCT./NOV 1992	WACO TRIB REPORTER, DARLENE MCCORMICK CALLS AUSA JOHNSTON RE: DAVIDIANS AND LEGALITY OF FIREARMS.	
10/92	DUNAGAN TELLS AGUILERA TO START WORK ON AFFIDAVIT FOR SEARCH/ARREST WARRANTS AND RECEIVES AUTHORIZATION TO SET UP AN U/C HOUSE.	
11/92	SRTs FROM HOUSTON, DALLAS AND NEW ORLEANS MEET IN HOUSTON.	
	DIVISION MEETING AT HQ, DETAILS OF INVESTIGATION AND TACTICAL PLANNING FOR SEARCH WARRANT DISCUSSED, HARTNETT AND CONROY WANT MORE INTELLIGENCE INFORMATION. TOLD DIVISION CHIEFS TO SLOW DOWN TACTICAL PLANNING....	
11/2/92	ATF HQ OPINES NOT ENOUGH EVIDENCE TO SUPPORT SEARCH WARRANT RE: EXPLOSIVE MATERIAL LIST SUBMITTED JULY 22ND.	TECH PARKER, ATF HQ, RENDERS THIS OPINION.
11/3/92	AGUILERA GOES TO CALIFORNIA TO INTERVIEW ISABELLA ANDRADE, JAYLENE OJENA, AND SAUNDRA LEAKE RECEIVES INFORMATION FROM LAVERNE, CA PD ABOUT DAVIDIANS LIVING IN CALIFORNIA.	

11/5,6 & 7/92	ANDRADE AND OJENA VISIT ANDRADE DAUGHTERS LIVING IN THE COMPOUND AND ARE DEBRIEFED BY AGUILERA.	
11/20/92	AUSA JOHNSTON REVIEWED PC TO DATE AND OPINES ENOUGH INFORMATION FOR A HISTORICAL SEARCH WARRANT.	DUNAGAN AND SARABYN PRESENTED FACTS OF CASE.
12/4/92	HQ PERSONNEL BEGAN TO ATTEND MEETINGS IN HOUSTON. (CHOJNACKI, ROYSTER, CAVANAUGH, BUFORD, PETRILLI, LATIMER, LEWIS, CARTER, HENRY, CURTIS WILLIAMS, LTC WALKER, DUNAGAN, AND AGUILERA) LOGISTICS FOR OPERATION DISCUSSED, INVESTIGATIVE REQUESTS MADE AND TACTICAL PLANNING CONTINUES. MEDIA INTEREST IN THE DAVIDIANS IS DISCUSSED, CHOJNACKI THINKS ATF CONTACT SHOULD BE INITIATED, CAVANAUGH ADAMANTLY OPPOSES CONTACT.	SARABYN WAS IN WDC WORKING (ON NRP AT THE TIME) AND TEACHING A CLASS. BUFORD SELECTED AS FOCAL POINT FOR SRT INVOLVEMENT. AGUILERA TOLD TO CONCENTRATE ON INVESTIGATION AND ESTABLISHING PC FOR WARRANTS. NEITHER A PEN REGISTER NOR TRAP AND TRACE WERE USED DURING THIS INVESTIGATION.
12/7/92	AGUILERA RECEIVED INFORMATION FROM SPARKS RE: CHILD ABUSE. SHE PROVIDES FLOOR PLANS OF COMPOUND.	
12/9/92	SUBPOENA TO PHONE COMPANY FOR SUBSCRIBER AND TOLL INFORMATION AND IDENTIFICATION OF ALL TELEPHONE NUMBERS ASSOCIATED WITH COMPOUND. TELEPHONE COMPANY COULD NOT PROVIDE LATTER.	
12/11/92	SA VIEGRA MEETS WITH TEXAS NATIONAL GUARD TO LEARN WHAT TYPE OF MILITARY SUPPORT IS AVAILABLE TO ATF. IS TOLD BY TEXAS NATIONAL GUARD, A DRUG NEXUS IS NECESSARY FOR NON REIMBURSABLE NATIONAL GUARD SUPPORT. AGUILERA LEARNS FROM SGT. HACKWORTH, LAVERNE PD, ABOUT ROBYN, JEANINE, DAVID AND DEBORAH BUNDS AND MARC BREAULT. POLE CAMERA STARTS TO WORK, BUT IS INEFFECTIVE, BECAUSE OF THE DISTANCES INVOLVED.	
12/14/92	NATIONAL GUARD RECEIVES FAX REQUEST FROM DUNAGAN FOR AERIAL PHOTOS OF COMPOUND AND MIL SUPPORT. DOES NOT MENTION DRUG NEXUS.	LT. JUSTICE NOTES LACK OF DRUG NEXUS, PHOTOS APPROVED BY LTC PETIT.

12/15/92	AGUILERA CALLS BREAULT AND ASKS NOT TO SHARE INFORMATION WITH WACO TRIBUNE. BREAULT AGREES TO DEAL SOLELY WITH AGUILERA.	THIS IS FIRST ATF CONTACT WITH BREAULT. IN SPITE OF ATF REQUEST TO STOP, HE CONTINUES HIS CONTACT WITH THE WACO TRIBUNE.
	AGUILERA RECEIVES VERBAL (AND LATER WRITTEN) OPINION FROM ATF FIREARM TECHNICAL BRANCH THAT THE LIST OF THE PARTS AND ACCESSORIES SUBMITTED FOR OPINION WERE CONSISTENT WITH COMPONENT PARTS, WHICH IF USED TO MAKE AN M-16 MACHINE GUN, THAT MACHINE GUN WOULD BE ILLEGAL TO POSSESS.	PARTS AND ACCESSORIES IN AND BY THEMSELVES, ARE NOT TECHNICALLY FIREARMS AS DEFINED BY LAW.
12/16/92	AGUILERA RECEIVES FAX FROM BREAULT, GIVES INFORMATION RE: METHAMPHETAMINE LAB PRESENT WHEN KORESH TOOK OVER CONTROL OF THE COMPOUND FROM RODEN, IN APRIL, 1988.	BREAULT NAMES JEAN SMITH, FORMER CULT MEMBER AS BEING ABLE TO CORROBORATE INFORMATION ON METHAMPHETAMINE LAB.
	AGUILERA AND C. WILLIAMS OVERFLY COMPOUND IN CUSTOMS AIRCRAFT AND OBTAIN INFRARED PHOTOS OF COMPOUND.	
12/17/92	DEA NOTIFIED OF POSSIBLE DRUG NEXUS BY ATF.	
12/18/92	SECOND FAX RECEIVED BY NATIONAL GUARD FROM DUNAGAN, MENTIONS "POSSIBLY NARCOTICS" AND ASKS FOR PHOTO OF MAG BAG.	FIRST TIME DRUG NEXUS NOTED VIA WRITTEN REQUEST FROM ATF.
	MEETING IN HOUSTON WITH KALISTER, LTC WALKER, CHOJANCKI, ROYSTER, SARABYN, PETRILLI, DUNAGAN, CAVANAUGH, LATIMER, CURTIS WILLIAMS, JOHN WILLIAMS, SHIDLER, HANDLEY, DIBETTA, WHITE, TERRY ANDERSON AND AGUILERA.	DECISION MADE TO INSERT SAs IN U/C HOUSE AND DESIGNATE TSTC AIRPORT OPS BUILDING AS ATF CP. CONCEPT FOR TACTICAL PLAN WAS FOR SIEGE AT THIS TIME.
12/24/92	MEETING AT HQ (HARTNETT, CONROY, GARNER, TROY, BROWN, VITA, TATE AND KALISTER) RE: GENERAL BRIEFING ON CASE. VITA APPOINTED TO MONITOR THE INVESTIGATION. MENTION OF POSSIBLE USE OF U/C HOUSE TO CORROBORATE PC AND GATHER INTELLIGENCE FOR TACTICAL PLAN. HARTNETT/CONROY WANT MORE PC DEVELOPED IN CASE AND TO "SLOW" DOWN TACTICAL OPS. PLANNING.	TATE AND KALISTER DO THE GENERAL BRIEF.
12/27/92	McMAHON LOSES LEASE ON PLACE OF BUSINESS AND MOVES TO FLORIDA.	
12/28-30/92	MEETING IN AUSTIN. AGUILERA, DUNAGAN, FROST, BRZOZOWSKI, LATTIMER, KING, PETRILLI, SARABYN, C. WILLIAMS, BUFORD, AND CAVANAUGH WENT TO WACO TO VIEW THE COMPOUND AND NEGOTIATE WITH PEERY FOR USE OF U/C HOUSE.	CHOJNACKI IS OFF. DURING THIS PERIOD OF TIME. WILLIAMS MAINTAINS AT THIS POINT PLAN WAS FOR SIEGE. AGUILERA TASKED TO INTERVIEW BREAULT AND OTHERS WITH MEMBER OF SRT.

12/92 FOR MONTH OF DECEMBER	KORESH OBSERVED OFF THE COMPOUND IN DECEMBER, 1992 BY JOGGING BY RESIDENCE SEVERAL TIMES; JONES, EMPLOYEE AT STRING WORLD; DONNEL, PRACO PAWN SHOP; AND, DULACK, ELK GENERAL STORE.	ALTHOUGH KORESH REPORTED OFF COMPOUND IN NEWS MEDIA AFTER DECEMBER, ONLY TWO SIGHTINGS WERE CONFIRMED, 1) AUTO REPAIR JAN. 29 AND 2) VISIT TO SPOON'S RESIDENCE, LATE DECEMBER, EARLY JAN.
1/4/93	PAT PIAZZA, OWNER STRING WORLD MUSIC STORE, SAID HE TALKED WITH KORESH AT LOCAL WACO DAIRY QUEEN.	PIAZZA BASES HIS RECOLLECTION ON DATE HE RECEIVES SPEAKERS HE AND KORESH TALK ABOUT.
1/6/93	NATIONAL GUARD OVERFLY COMPOUND AND MAG BAG TAKE AERIAL PHOTOS AND INFRARED IMAGING PICTURES. THERMAL IMAGING SYSTEM PICKS UP "HOT SPOT" INSIDE COMPOUND AND IDs THREE SENTRIES TO REAR OF COMPOUND. REPORT FROM TAYLOR, ATF, EXPLOSIVES ENFORCEMENT OFFICER, (WALNUT CREEK, CA) OPINING KORESH PURCHASING CHEMICALS AND EXPLOSIVE MATERIALS FOR ILLEGAL USE. PRELIMINARY WORK ON TSTC COMMAND POST BEGINS.	TEXAS NG UC-26 IS USED. FIRST FLIGHT. NO OFFICIAL INTERPRETATION OF "HOT SPOT" PROVIDED TO ATF BY NG.
1/7-9/93	AGUILERA AND BUFORD CONDUCT INTERVIEWS OF THE BUNDS, BREAULT, ANDRADE AND OJENA. TELEPHONE LINES, RADIO AND COMPUTERS INSTALLED AT TSTC COMMAND POST. THIS SITE USED BY THE U/C HOUSE AGENTS AS OFFICE.	PURPOSE OF INTERVIEWS TO GAIN INTELLIGENCE FOR TACTICAL PLANNING AND GAIN INSIGHT INTO KORESH'S STATE OF MIND.
1/11/93	U/C HOUSE BEGINS OPERATION. O'FLAHERTY, BRZOZOWSKI, VIEGRA, RODRIGUEZ, BRIGANCE, SEALE, TINKER AND BROWN STAFF THE HOUSE. U/C HOUSE IS VISITED BY DAVIDIANS, DAVID JONES, WAYNE MARTIN AND NEIL SCHROEDER.	
1/13/93	ATF INTERNAL MEMORANDUM REGARDING USE OF NATIONAL GUARD PERSONNEL SIGNED BY HARTNETT. THAT IS, NG PERSONNEL AND SPECIALIZED EQUIPMENT TO BE USED AGAINST COMMON AREAS, NOT SPECIFIC INDIVIDUALS, VEHICLES, OR AREAS.	

1/14/93	SECOND NG OVERFLIGHT (RF4-C A) TAKES OBLIQUE AERIAL PHOTOS. ALSO NG UC-26 OVERFLIES MAG BAG AND COMPOUND. NUMEROUS AERIAL AND INFRARED IMAGING PHOTOS TAKEN AND SUBSEQUENTLY DELIVERED TO ATF ON OR ABOUT JAN. 21, 1993.	DUNAGAN THANKS NATIONAL GUARD FOR ASSISTANCE SPECIFICALLY FOR INTERPRETATION AND EVALUATION OF PHOTOS. NATIONAL GUARD INFORMS W.A.R. ANY INTERPRETATIONS OR EVALUATIONS BY ANY NATIONAL GUARD PERSONNEL WOULD BE DEEMED UNOFFICIAL.
1/18/93	U/C AGENTS TOLD BY SPOONS, DAVIDIANS SUSPECT OCCUPANTS OF U/C HOUSE TO BE FBI AGENTS, THAT KORESH THOUGHT POLICE WERE WATCHING THEM AND THAT KORESH WAS EXPECTING A VISIT FROM THE FBI.	
1/19/93	SARABYN VISITS U/C HOUSE. HE AGREES WITH U/C AGENTS TO DISCONTINUE SURVEILLANCE DURING THE NIGHT TIME HOURS. HE FURTHER CHANGED THE PRIORITY FROM SURVEILLANCE TO INFILTRATION OF THE COMPOUND VIA UNDERCOVER MEANS. TEAMS TOLD NOT TO PUT EVERYTHING IN LOGS, ONLY SIGNIFICANT THINGS.	PRIOR TO SARABYN'S VISIT, SURVEILLANCE WAS AT 100% LEVEL. CHANGED TO MONITOR UNUSUAL ACTIVITY AT ALL TIMES. BUT, VISUAL SURVEILLANCE WAS LIMITED TO DAYLIGHT HOURS.
1/21/93	POLE CAMERA REMOVED, DUE TO SECURITY LEAK BY POWER COMPANY EMPLOYEE. REQUEST BY LTC. WALKER/SARABYN TO MILITARY FOR EQUIPMENT TO SUSTAIN A SIEGE (INCLUDING SEVEN BRADLEY FIGHTING VEHICLES) IS MADE.	NOTHING OF EVIDENTIARY OR INTELLIGENCE NATURE WAS GAINED FROM THIS EQUIPMENT. PLAN FOR SIEGE IS CONFIRMED BY THIS REQUEST.
1/22/93	SA PALI CONTACTS DEA LIAISON, TO OPERATION ALLIANCE, WILLIAM ROSHEN AND DISCUSSES DRUG NEXUS. ROSHEN OFFERS DEA TECHNICAL ASSISTANCE FOR SUSPECTED METHAMPHETAMINE LAB AT THE COMPOUND.	
1/25/93	AGUILERA AND BUFORD INTERVIEW DAVID BLOCK. SUPPOSED TO HAVE MOST CURRENT INTELLIGENCE ON COMPOUND, HAVING LEFT THE COMPOUND AROUND MAY, 1992. BLOCK INFORMED: TOWER NOT USED FOR SURVEILLANCE, BUT, FOR WOMEN'S SLEEPING AREA, MEN SEGREGATED FROM WOMEN, GAVE ROUTINE, GAVE LOCATION OF ARMORY (SAID IT WAS LOCKED), MEN OCCASIONALLY KEPT GUNS UNDER BED AND A FEW MEN ALLOWED TO RETAIN PRIVATE WEAPONS OF SMALL CALIBER, KORESH OBSESSED WITH POSSIBILITY OF SIEGE, HAD VAST QUANTITY OF FOOD (MREs), THREE .50 CALIBER WEAPONS IN COMPOUND, AND, POSSIBLE "STEN" GUN BEING MADE IN COMPOUND.	THIS AND OTHER INFORMATION, TO INCLUDE A DISCUSSION OF A POSSIBLE MASS SUICIDE, PROVIDED BY PREVIOUS INTERVIEWS OF FORMER CULT MEMBERS LIKELY MOVES TACTICAL PLANNERS FROM SIEGE TO DYNAMIC ENTRY APPROACH.

D-9

1/27-29/93	MEETINGS IN HOUSTON. C. WILLIAMS, LATIMER, LITTLETON, PETRILLI, KING, WHITE, DUNAGAN, AGUILERA, BETTERTON, HONNYCUTT, CHOJNACKI, SARABYN, ROYSTER, AND MASTIN. BUFORD PRESENTS INFORMATION GLEANED FROM INTERVIEWS. U/C HOUSE REPORTS NO SENTRIES VISIBLE AND A ROUTINE WHERE MEN AND WOMEN ARE SEGREGATED AND MEN AWAY FROM GUNS. DISCUSSION OF SIEGE VS. DYNAMIC ENTRY HELD. IT IS CONCLUDED, BASED ON INTELLIGENCE GATHERED, TO GO WITH DYNAMIC ENTRY. MEDIA INTEREST IN COMPOUND DISCUSSED, MOST AGREE A MEETING WITH A REPRESENTATIVE FROM THE WACO TRIBUNE IS WARRANTED. A COIN FLIP DETERMINES DEPUTY INCIDENT COMMANDER POSITION FOR OPERATION. MASTIN WINS AND IS NAMED DEPUTY. ROYSTER NO LONGER PARTICIPATES IN SUBSEQUENT PLANNING SESSIONS.	DURING THIS PHASE THE TACTICAL PLANNERS BEGIN IN EARNEST TO DEVELOP AN OPERATIONAL PLAN PREFACED ON A DYNAMIC ENTRY.
1/27/93	SA MEDRANO IN U/C ROLE (UPS TRAINEE) VISITS MAG BAG AND COMPOUND.	
1/28/93	SA ROBERT RODRIGUEZ AND SA WADE BROWN MAKE FIRST SUSTAINED CONTACT WITH COMPOUND MEMBERS, INCLUDING KORESH.	CONTACT LASTS ONE HOUR, AND IS CONDUCTED OUTSIDE THE COMPOUND BUILDINGS.
1/29/93	KORESH LEAVES COMPOUND TO PICK UP PARTS FOR HIS CAMARO AT MICHAEL BARNARD'S PLACE OF BUSINESS, PERFORMANCE AUTOMOTIVE MACHINE, AXTELL, TX.	NOT OBSERVED BY U/C SURVEILLANCE.
2/1/93	SARABYN AND DUNAGAN MEET WITH BARBARA ELMORE, WACO TRIBUNE.	APPROXIMATE DATE OF ATF ACTION GIVEN.
2/2/93	ANDRADE AND OJENA VISIT ANDRADE'S DAUGHTERS AT THE COMPOUND. THEY RETURN TO THE COMPOUND ON THE 2ND AND 3RD. THEY ARE NOT DEBRIEFED BY ATF.	
	RODRIGUEZ GOES TO COMPOUND, BUT IS TOLD KORESH IS ILL AND TO RETURN.	
	OPERATION ALLIANCE SUPPORT AUTHORIZED, BASED ON ATF SUBMISSION OF A DRUG NEXUS PRESENTED BY SA PHIL LEWIS AT EL PASO.	
	ROCHEN, DEA, OFFERS DEA CLANDESTINE CERTIFIED LABORATORY TEAM TO ATF.	
2/4/93	JOINT COMMAND PLANNING SESSION WITH CHOJNACKI, SARABYN AND REPRESENTATIVES FROM THE NATIONAL GUARD, JTF-6 AND SPECIAL FORCES.	SARABYN ANSWERS QUESTION's REGARDING DRUG NEXUS.
2/5/93	RODRIGUEZ ATTENDS FIRST BIBLE STUDY AT COMPOUND, INTENSE ONE ON ONE SESSION WITH KORESH.	
2/9/93	CHUCK ROCHNER, COX ENTERPRISES, CALLS CHOJNACKI AND SAYS HE IS THE WACO TRIBUNE'S LIAISON WITH ATF.	ROCHNER SAYS CHOJNACKI TOLD HIM ACTION TO OCCUR 3/1/93.
	CHOJNACKI MAKES REQUEST TO HQ TO ACTIVATE THE (NRP) SECTOR PLAN.	

2/11/93	BRIEFING AT HQ. INVESTIGATORS AND TACTICAL PLANNERS BRIEF HARTNETT ET AL. PROBABLE CAUSE DISCUSSED AS WELL AS TACTICAL PLAN IN DEPTH.	SOME SAY DELAY IN THIS MEETING CAUSED DELAY IN THE OPERATION'S PLANNED DATE FEB. 22, 1993.
2/12/93	BRIEFING AT HQ FOR HIGGIN'S BENEFIT. SAME ISSUES DISCUSSED AS PREVIOUS DAY. AUSA's JOHNSTON AND PHINIZY AND SA DUNAGAN MEET WITH WACO DISTRICT ATTORNEY, ELIZABETH TOBIN TO DISCUSS LOCAL ARREST WARRANT FOR KORESH FOR CHILD ABUSE.	WANTED TO USE WARRANT TO GET KORESH AWAY FROM COMPOUND.
2/16/93	HARTNETT ACTIVATES SECTOR PLAN PER ATF ORDER 3350.10	
2/17/93	FOUR OF EIGHT U/C AGENTS SENT HOME FROM U/C HOUSE. RODRIGUEZ ATTENDS BIBLE STUDY (2.5 HRS). CHOJNACKI CALLS ROCHNER AND VIA MESSAGE INVITES ROCHNER TO VIEW ATF TRAINING AT FORT HOOD. PALI BRIEFS TEXAS GOVERNOR'S REPRESENTATIVE TO THE TEXAS NARCOTICS CONTROL PROGRAM, JAMES WILLBORN ABOUT THE HOWELL INVESTIGATION.	KORESH TELLS RODRIGUEZ HE DOES NOT LEAVE COMPOUND OFTEN.
2/18/93	RODRIGUEZ ATTENDS BIBLE STUDY (3 HRS) IN COMPOUND. NATIONAL RESPONSE PLAN - ATF ORDER 3350.10 IS FORMALIZED.	RODRIGUEZ ARRANGES TO SHOOT WITH KORESH NEXT DAY.
2/19/93	RODRIGUEZ AND BRZOZOWSKI SHOOT WITH KORESH IN REAR OF COMPOUND. KORESH NOTES HE HAS OBSERVED U/C AGENTS SHOOTING, TALKS ABOUT DROP IN SEARS. RODRIGUEZ AND BRZOZOWSKI TAKEN THROUGH COMPOUND BUILDING TO REAR AREA. CURTIS WILLIAMS CANCELS U.S. CUSTOMS SUPPORT REQUEST.	
2/21/93 MONDAY	KORESH ASKS RODRIGUEZ TO COME TO COMPOUND TO LISTEN TO MUSIC. INVITES RODRIGUEZ TO BECOME MEMBER OF HIS GROUP.	RODRIGUEZ AGREES TO BEGIN BIBLE STUDY TO START MARCH 1, 1993.

2/22/93 TUESDAY	AGUILERA & DUNAGAN BRIEF McLENNAN SHERIFF'S OFFICE RE: RAID SUPPORT REQUESTS.	RAID DATE GIVEN AS MARCH 1, 1993.
	DUNAGAN SAID HE CALLED ELMORE AND TOLD HER WITH SARABYN'S PERMISSION, RAID DATE MOVED TO MARCH 1, 1993.	ELMORE SAID CALL CAME IN SOMETIME EARLY TO MID FEB.
	AGUILERA ACCOMPANIES A FEMALE MINOR TO DISTRICT ATTORNEY TOBIN'S OFFICE FOR INTERVIEW.	THE FEMALE MINOR DECLINES TO TESTIFY AGAINST KORESH, SO TOBIN CONCLUDES STATE CANNOT PROCEED AGAINST KORESH FOR CHILD ABUSE.
2/24/93 WED:	CHOJNACKI MEETS WITH EDITORIAL STAFF OF WACO TRIBUNE-HERALD IN AN ATTEMPT TO DELAY PUBLICATION OF ARTICLE.	
	PREDDY MAKES TENTATIVE DECISION TO PRINT SERIES STARTING SATURDAY.	
	WITHERSPOON TELLS STAFF ABOUT HIS "TIP" GIVING RAID DATE FOR MONDAY, 3/1/93.	
	BLANSETT ASSIGNS THREE REPORTERS TO COVER ANTICIPATED RAID ON MONDAY, 3/1/93.	
	SARABYN TRAVELS TO FT. HOOD TO COMMENCE SRT TRAINING FOR OPERATION. SRT LEADERS, ASSIST. TEAM LEADERS AND FORWARD OBSERVERS PRESENT.	HARTNETT, AFTER BEING BRIEFED BY CHOJNACKI, AGREES TO SUNDAY RAID DATE.
	CHOJNACKI ASKS SARABYN IF RAID COULD BE MOVED UP TO SATURDAY, IS TOLD NO, DECISION IS MADE TO MOVE RAID TO SUNDAY, 2/28/93.	
	TSTC COMMAND POST STAFF ARRIVE IN WACO AND BEGIN TO SET UP CP.	
	NOTIFICATIONS GO OUT TO ATF PERSONNEL, MOVING UP REPORTING DATES TO FORT HOOD/WACO.	
	ATF REQUEST TO THE NATIONAL GUARD FOR MILITARY SUPPORT IS SUBSTANTIALLY DIFFERENT FROM THE JAN. 21 REQUEST, ELIMINATING ITEMS NECESSARY FOR A SIEGE, INCLUDING THE BRADLEY FIGHTING VEHICLES.	
2/25/93 THURS:	SRTs ARRIVE AT FORT HOOD AND BEGIN TRAINING:	
	MAGISTRATE GREEN SIGNS AFFIDAVITS FOR ARREST AND SEARCH WARRANTS.	
	WITHERSPOON TELLS MULLONY ABOUT ATF RAID ON MT CARMEL TO OCCUR ON MARCH 1, 1993.	

2/26/93: FRIDAY:	SA CUYLER PROVIDES TREASURY WITH ONE PAGE MEMORANDUM RE: ATF'S PLANNED ACTION AGAINST THE DAVIDIANS. TREASURY EXPRESSES CONCERN ABOUT RAID, AT FIRST CANCELS RAID, THEN, AFTER FURTHER DISCUSSION WITH HIGGINS, RESCINDS ORDER TO CANCEL RAID. 3:00PM - ROCHNER TELLS CHOJNACKI ARTICLE TO COME OUT ON SATURDAY, NO MENTION OF ATF IN ARTICLE. DUNAGAN ADVISES SHERIFF'S OFFICE AND OTHERS ABOUT NEWS ARTICLE AND THAT RAID IS MOVED UP TO SUNDAY MORNING, 2/28/93.	A NUMBER OF CALLS ARE MADE TO INFORM SUPPORT PEOPLE OF THE CHANGE IN RAID DATE BY ATF AND COY JONES AND GENE BARBER.

FEBRUARY 27, 1993 (SATURDAY)

1:00AM	-	PEROT/GRAY GET ADVANCE PUBLICATION OF WACO TRIBUNE HERALD AND DELIVER COPY TO CHOJNACKI.
8:00AM	-	RODRIGUEZ JOINS CHURCH SERVICES IN COMPOUND.
??:??AM	-	WITHERSPOON'S INFORMANT TELLS HIM RAID CHANGED TO SUNDAY.
	-	WITHERSPOON CALLS BLANSETT AND SAYS INFORMANT GAVE CHANGE IN RAID DATE TO SUNDAY.
12:00N	-	RODRIGUEZ LEAVES COMPOUND AND RELATES INFORMATION TO CHOJNACKI ON THE REACTION OF KORESH TO THE ARTICLE. SARABYN AND CHOJNACKI INDICATE RODRIGUEZ OBSERVES NO OVERT CALL TO "ARMS" BY KORESH, MOREOVER, CHOJNACKI REPORTS TO HARTNETT ONLY CONCERN OF KORESH IS WHAT ARTICLE WILL DO TO FUND RAISING. DURING AFTERNOON BRIEF OF CHOJNACKI, RODRIGUEZ ONLY RECALLS CHOJNACKI ASKING IF RODRIGUEZ HAD SEEN GUNS OR PREPARATIONS. RODRIGUEZ IN W.A.R. INTERVIEW STATES, KORESH TOLD FOLLOWERS "THEY" WERE COMING FOR HIM AND SHOULD THIS HAPPEN, THE FOLLOWERS SHOULD NOT GET HYSTERICAL AND REMEMBER WHAT HE HAD TOLD THEM TO DO. CHOJNACKI OR SARABYN NOT TOLD THIS BY RODRIGUEZ.
	-	PREDDY, BLANSETT, LOTT AND ROCHNER MEET AT PAPER TO DISCUSS WITHERSPOON'S INFORMATION. DECISION IS MADE TO COVER THE RAID. BLANSETTE CHANGES THE NUMBER OF PERSONNEL ASSIGNED TO COVER THE RAID, FROM 3 TO 9.
	-	HELMSTETTER GETS FROM GLOVER RAID TO OCCUR ON SUNDAY, AND TELLS MULLONY.
3:00PM	-	MULLONY AND WITHERSPOON PLAY RACQUETBALL AND DISCUSS CHANGE OF RAID DATE.
	-	BLANSETT, LOTT, AND ROCHNER DRIVE BY COMPOUND, ON WAY BACK TO PAPER OBSERVE HELICOPTER FLY TOWARDS TSTC, PROCEED TO TSTC AIRPORT AND SEE HELICOPTER AND PEOPLE, SOME IN UNIFORMS. ROCHNER THINKS STAGING AREA FOR ATF.
5:00PM	-	RODRIGUEZ RE-ENTERS COMPOUND, LISTENS TO KORESH'S ASSESSMENT OF THE WACO TRIBUNE'S ARTICLE "SINFUL MESSIAH".
	-	SCHNEIDER CALLS BLANSETT AND ASKS FOR INTERVIEW RE: NEWS ARTICLE. BLANSETT CALLS ENGLAND AND ROCHNER. ROCHNER CALLS CHOJNACKI AND ASKS IF SAFE TO SEND REPORTER INTO COMPOUND FOR INTERVIEW. ENGLAND DECLINES OPPORTUNITY TO PERSONALLY INTERVIEW KORESH OR SCHNEIDER.
	-	BLANSETT NOTIFIES REPORTERS/PHOTOGRAPHERS TO MEET SUNDAY AT 8:00AM AT PAPER.
7:00PM	-	BRIEFING FOR SUPPORT PERSONNEL AT WACO BEST WESTERN HOTEL. BRIEFING CONDUCTED BY SARABYN.
9:00PM	-	FORWARD OBSERVERS INSERTED INTO U/C HOUSE, CAVANAUGH IS INSERTED LATER....
12:00MN	-	RODRIGUEZ EXITS COMPOUND AND RELATES OBSERVATIONS TO SARABYN. IS TOLD BY SARABYN HE WILL HAVE TO GO BACK INTO THE COMPOUND NEXT AM. RODRIGUEZ IS NOT HAPPY ABOUT HAVING TO REENTER THE COMPOUND ON SUNDAY MORNING.

OTHER EVENTS OCCURING ON 2/27/93 (SATURDAY)

AGENTS AT FORT HOOD CONTINUE TRAINING, ARE TOLD RAID MOVED UP TO SUNDAY....MANY READ THE ARTICLE ON THE DAVIDIANS.
ATF SUPPORT AGENTS, ARRIVE AT WACO AND ARE BRIEFED THAT NIGHT WITH OTHER LOCAL LAW ENFORCEMENT AND NATIONAL GUARD, AT THE BEST WESTERN HOTEL.
PIO WHEELER CONTACTS LOCAL DALLAS MEDIA FOR WEEKEND NUMBERS.
NATIONAL GUARD HELICOPTERS PRACTICE RAID AT FORT HOOD, THEN PROCEED TO TSTC AIRPORT AND STAGE HELICOPTERS, ARRIVING THERE AT APPROXIMATELY 4:00PM. (ABOUT THE TIME BLANSETT, LOTT AND ROCHNER OBSERVE THEM)
ATF BOMB TRUCKS TRANSPORTED FROM HOUSTON AND DALLAS AND PARKED AT THE TSTC AIRPORT COMPLEX.

RAID DAY FEB. 28, 1993 (SUNDAY)

4:30AM	-	REAR COVER FORWARD OBSERVER (FO) TEAM AND COVER SRT MEMBERS DEPART FORT HOOD.
6:00AM	-	ATF CARAVAN DEPARTS FORT HOOD.
7:30AM	-	REAR COVER FORWARD OBSERVER TEAM AND COVER SRT ARRIVE TSTC COMMAND POST.
		KWTX (MULLONY, PEELER, McLEMORE AND BRADFIELD) MEET AT STATION.
		ATF CONVOY ARRIVES AT BELLMEAD CIVIC CENTER.
7:45AM	-	REAR COVER FORWARD OBSERVER TEAM AND COVER SRT, LEAVE TSTC FOR HAY BARN, TRANSPORTED BY BRZOZOWSKI.
		KWTX (MULLONY AND McLEMORE) ARRIVE COMPOUND AREA (FR2491). PEELER IS LOST IN THE AREA OF OLD MEXIA ROAD.
8:00AM	-	RODRIGUEZ ENTERS COMPOUND.
		SARABYN GIVES SHORT UPDATE AT BELLMEAD CIVIC CENTER.
		ATF NATIONAL COMMAND CENTER IS MANNED BY VITA/GARNER (9:00EST)
		WACO TRIB REPORTERS MEET AT PAPER OFFICES.
8:30AM	-	PEELER TELLS MULLONY VIA CELLULAR PHONE, HE CAN'T TALK TO MULLONY, SINCE HE IS TALKING TO A POSTMAN.

D-15

RAID DAY FEB. 28, 1993 (SUNDAY) CONTINUED.

8:45AM	—	DAVID JONES RETURNS TO THE COMPOUND AND ALERTS KORESH ABOUT RAID.
8:46AM	—	TRIB REPORTERS (3 CARS) ARRIVE COMPOUND AREA. TRIBUNE PHOTOGRAPHER, SANCHEZ ARRIVES TSTC AIRPORT.
	—	SANCHEZ CALLS BLANSETT AND REPORTS HELICOPTERS AND POLICE VEHICLES AT TSTC AIRPORT.
9:00AM	—	SARABYN RETURNS TO TSTC CP.
9:05AM	—	RODRIGUEZ DEPARTS COMPOUND
	—	RODRIGUEZ TALKS TO CAVANAUGH.
	—	RODRIGUEZ CALLS SARABYN, WHO IS AT THE TSTC COMMAND POST.
	—	SARABYN, CHOJNACKI AND ROYSTER DISCUSS RODRIGUEZ' INFORMATION AND DECIDE TO "GO".
	—	SARABYN DRIVES TO BELLMEAD
	—	RODRIGUEZ LEAVES U/C HOUSE FOR TSTC COMMAND POST.
9:10AM	—	CHOJNACKI CALLS THE NATIONAL COMMAND CENTER (NCC) IN WASHINGTON, D.C. AND INFORMS THE OPERATION IS A GO.
9:13AM	—	SANCHEZ REPORTS VEHICLES AT TSTC WERE STARTING TO LINE UP AS IF TO MOVE.
9:25AM	—	SARABYN ARRIVES BELLMEAD AND ANNOUNCES OPERATION TO PROCEED.
	—	ATF AGENTS BOARD THE CATTLE TRAILERS AND PREPARE FOR THE RAID.
9:29AM	—	SANCHEZ REPORTS TO BLANSETT, HELICOPTERS ON THE WAY.
9:30AM	—	SARABYN CALLS CAVANAUGH ON CELLULAR PHONE AND GETS UPDATE ON COMPOUND ACTIVITY AND TELLS CAVANAUGH, THEY ARE ON THE WAY TO MT. CARMEL.
9:35AM	—	O'FLAHERTY AND BRZOZOWSKI GO TO SPOON RESIDENCE TO SECURE.
9:41AM	—	SANCHEZ IS PULLED OVER BY ATF AGENTS AFTER TRYING TO PASS THE CATTLE TRAILERS ON FR 2491. HE SEES ATF AGENTS AND CALLS BLANSETT TELLS HIM THEY ARE ON THE WAY.
9:45AM	—	"MAG BAG" SEARCH TEAM DEPART TSTC EN ROUTE "MAG BAG"
	—	MULLONY/McLEMORE AT FR 2491 AND DOUBLE E SEE, THEN FOLLOW CATTLE TRAILERS INTO COMPOUND, STOPPING AT BUS.

D-16

	–	ENGLAND AND DOE FOLLOW MULLONY/McLEMORE DOWN DOUBLE E ROAD, BUT PASS THE MT. CARMEL DRIVEWAY AND PARK BY AYDELOTTE'S CAR, ON DOUBLE E ROAD.
	–	WITHERSPOON ASKS O'FLAHERTY IF HE CAN FILM FROM SPOON PROPERTY, IS TOLD NO, AS CAR WITHERSPOON ARRIVED IN IS BACKING OUT ONTO DOUBLE E ROAD, THEY SEE CATTLE TRAILERS ENTER COMPOUND DRIVEWAY.
9:47AM	–	SARABYN AND CAVANAUGH END THEIR CELLULAR TELEPHONE CALL.
	–	REAR FO TEAM MOVE INTO POSITION BEHIND COMPOUND AND ARE IMMEDIATELY TAKEN UNDER FIRE BY POSITION/S TO THEIR LEFT.
	–	HELICOPTERS ARRIVE IN SIGHT OF COMPOUND AND ARE TAKEN UNDER FIRE.
	–	RAID BEGINS....AGENTS TAKEN UNDER FIRE. MEDIA ON DOUBLE E ROAD ARE SHOT AT. KWTX CAMERA CREW HALF WAY DOWN MT. CARMEL DRIVEWAY HEAR SHOTS AND TAKE COVER BEHIND BUS, AND VIDEO RAID.
	–	"MAG BAG" SEARCH TEAM CALLED BACK TO TSTC.
9:48AM	–	911 RECEIVES CALL FROM WAYNE MARTIN REPORTING RAID ON MT. CARMEL. GUNSHOTS ARE HEARD IN BACKGROUND. HE REMAINS ON THE LINE BRIEFLY, THEN LEAVES THE PHONE OFF HOOK.
9:52AM	–	911 ATTEMPTS TO CONTACT ATF TO REPORT OPEN LINE INTO COMPOUND. ATTEMPTS CONTINUE (19 TIMES) TO REACH ATF. CONTACT IS FINALLY ESTABLISHED VIA TSTC PATROLMAN "197" AT 10:20AM.
9:55AM	–	NCC IS NOTIFIED BY THE TSTC COMMAND POST, WARRANT EXECUTED, AGENTS RECEIVING HEAVY GUNFIRE.
	–	NCC NOTIFIES DADLE CONROY, WHO NOTIFIES ADLE HARTNETT, WHO NOTIFIES DIRECTOR HIGGINS.
	–	911 HAS OPEN LINE INTO COMPOUND, BUT, NO ONE IS ON THE LINE. 911 CONTINUES TO HEAR GUNSHOTS.
10:02AM	–	CALL TO 911 IS TERMINATED BY COMPOUND.
10:03AM	–	911 CALLS COMPOUND, ESTABLISHES OPEN LINE. WAYNE MARTIN AND OTHERS CONVERSE ON SPEAKER PHONE TO LT. LYNCH. LYNCH STARTS NEGOTIATION WITH MARTIN.
10:15AM	–	DYER TAKES 12 INDIVIDUALS FROM TSTC COMMAND POST AND ATTEMPTS TO SET UP AN OUTER PERIMETER.
10:20AM	–	911 MAKES CONTACT WITH ATF VIA SHERIFF'S RADIO FREQUENCY. CHOJNACKI AND ROYSTER PARTICIPATE IN NEGOTIATIONS FOR CEASE FIRE THROUGH LT. LYNCH.
10:30AM	–	HARTNETT TELLS CONROY TO GO TO WACO.

10:34AM	-	KORESH CALLS 911 VIA CELLULAR PHONE.
10:40AM	-	KORESH'S CALL IS DISCONNECTED.
10:42AM	-	KORESH CALLS 911 AGAIN ON CELLULAR PHONE, TALKS TO LYNCH.
10:43AM	-	KORESH'S CALL DISCONNECTS.
10:46AM	-	SCHNEIDER CALLS 911 ON CELLULAR PHONE, TALKS TO LYNCH, KORESH GETS ON LINE THEY TALK ABOUT CEASE FIRE.
10:49AM	-	SCHNEIDER'S CALL DISCONNECTS.
	-	LYNCH PASSES TO ATF AT TSTC THE TELEPHONE NUMBER FOR KORESH/SCHNEIDER'S CELLULAR PHONE AND ADVISES KORESH WANTS ATF TO CALL DIRECT. ROYSTER PASSES TELE # TO CAVANAUGH AT U/C HOUSE.
10:59AM	-	ATF ESTABLISHES HARD TELEPHONE LINE CALL INTO 911. ROYSTER AND LYNCH CONDUCT NEGOTIATIONS WITH MARTIN/SCHNEIDER FOR CEASE FIRE.
11:27AM	-	CAVANAUGH CALLS INTO COMPOUND VIA CELLULAR PHONE AND CONTINUES TO NEGOTIATE FOR CEASE FIRE.
11:30AM	-	HARTNETT ARRIVES NCC (12:30PM EASTERN TIME) AND GETS FURTHER BRIEF ON EVENTS AT WACO.
	-	"MAG BAG" SEARCH TEAM TOLD TO GO TO "MAG BAG" AND SECURE PERIMETER, WERE TOLD NOT TO EXECUTE SEARCH WARRANT.
	-	HARTNETT UNILATERALLY REQUESTS FBI HRT SUPPORT.
11:39AM	-	AGENTS START TO MOVE TO PICKUP SA KING AND OTHERS. ONLY FOUR AGENTS ARE ALLOWED TO REMOVE KING.
11:44AM	-	MARTIN TELLS LYNCH ATF GOT ONE WOUNDED FROM BACK OF COMPOUND BUILDING (K. KING).
11:46AM	-	MARTIN SAYS ATF CAN GET WOUNDED FROM FRONT OF COMPOUND.
11:54AM	-	AMBULANCE MOVES INTO COMPOUND TO PICK UP WOUNDED AND DEAD AGENTS.
12:01PM	-	ROYSTER TELLS LYNCH TWO AGENTS ON ROOF ARE DEAD.
12:12PM	-	ROYSTER TELLS LYNCH, "IT'S NOW A STANDOFF", ALL AGENTS (WOUNDED AND DEAD) HAVE BEEN REMOVED FROM THE COMPOUND AND ALL OTHER AGENTS ARE SAFE.
12:37PM	-	SCHNEIDER DEMANDS CONTACT WITH ATF, JIM (CAVANAUGH), LYNCH GIVES SCHNEIDER CAVANAUGH'S CELLULAR TELEPHONE NUMBER.

12:53PM	-	LYNCH CONFIRMS WITH MARTIN THAT SCHNEIDER IS TALKING WITH CAVANAUGH.
	-	CAVANAUGH LEAVES U/C HOUSE FOR TSTC.
	-	CAVANAUGH REESTABLISHES CONTACT WITH SCHNEIDER/KORESH.
2:00PM	-	HIGGINS ARRIVES THE NATIONAL COMMAND CENTER AND TELLS HARTNETT TO PROCEED TO WACO.
4:00PM	-	REAR FORWARD OBSERVER TEAM AND COVER SRT WITH DYER, BRIGANCE AND APPELT COME UNDER FIRE WHILE MOVING FROM THE HAY BARN TO EVACUATION POINT. SCHROEDER KILLED, NASH ARRESTED, KENDRICK ESCAPES.
5:00PM	-	HARTNETT DEPARTS WASHINGTON, D.C. WITH THE FBI HOSTAGE RESPONSE TEAM (HRT).
5:30PM	-	FBI SAC JAMAR ARRIVES TSTC ATF COMMAND POST.
	-	ROYSTER CONDUCTS FIRST PRESS CONFERENCE.
8:30PM	-	CONROY ARRIVES TSTC COMMAND POST.
10:00PM	-	HARTNETT ARRIVES TSTC AIRPORT VIA FBI HRT PLANE.

MARCH 1, 1993 (MONDAY)

1:00AM	-	HARTNETT AND CONROY ARE TAKEN TO THEIR HOTEL.
6:00AM	-	HARTNETT ADVISED BY TREASURY, FBI, HRT TO ASSUME CONTROL OF OPERATION.
10:00AM	-	MEETING WITH NONPOSTED ATF AGENTS, HARTNETT INFORMS THEM FBI TO BE IN CHARGE.

Appendix E

ATF Advisory

to

Treasury Office of Enforcement

T R E A S U R Y   I N T E R O F F I C E   M E M O R A N D U M

```
                              Date:   26-Feb-1993 02:27pm EST
                              From:   Christopher Cuyler
                                      CUYLERC
                              Dept:   Asst Sec Enforcement
                              Tel No:
```

TO: Michael D. Langan   (LANGAN)

Subject: ATF Special Operation

Mike, be advised that ATF will be executing both arrest warrants and search warrants on Sunday, February 28, 1993, at the compound of the Branch Davidian Seventh-day Adventists, a religious cult near Waco, Texas. The leader of this cult is Vernon Wayne Howell and they are housed on a 70 acre compound in rural Waco. It is believed there are approximately 75 people (men, women and children) currently on the compound.

ATF has an arrest warrant for Howell and search warrants for the main compound and a second storage site about two miles from the compound. Howell has a history of violence and has been acquitted of attempted murder in the past. Members of this cult come from all over the world and it is believed that many are aliens unlawfully in this country. INS will participate in this raid.

Automatic weapons fire has been heard from this compound and ATF has undercover agents that have gained access to the compound. It is known that UPS has delivered enough firearms parts to convert 200 AR-15's (semi-auto) to M-16's (full auto). Howell has an unknown quantity of explosives on site and in the past has been involved in a shootout with a rival religious cult.

When a member joins the Branch Davidian, he turns over all possessions, including his wife and any daughters. Howell is the only male allowed to have sexual relations with any of the women, and in general the women are not allowed outside the main compound. Howell strips these people of all dignity and his treatment of them is atrocious across the board - from eating habits to sanitary depravation.

On Sunday, February 28, 1993, at 11 AM, ATF, assisted by State, local and military authorities, will raid this compound. Our Special Response Teams from Houston, Dallas and New Orleans will be used, along with a host of other law enforcement officers. A well-reasoned, comprehensive plan has been approved which allows for all contingencies. ATF's National Command Center at Bureau Headquarters will be on-line for this operation at 9 AM Sunday morning.

It is felt this operation will generate considerable media attention, both locally (Texas) and nationally. If necessary, I can be contacted over the weekend at my residence or on my pager (1-800-759-7243 -- PIN 595-3161).

End of message.

Appendix F

Mission Charter

CHARTER

POST - WACO ADMINISTRATIVE REVIEW

Mission:

There is established a comprehensive, impartial investigation into the planning, decisions, and related issues leading to the events occurring in Waco, Texas, on February 28, 1993. The purpose of this administrative inquiry is to determine whether the procedures followed by the Bureau of Alcohol, Tobacco and Firearms were correct and appropriate to the law enforcement situation, whether the operational decisions were correct based on the available intelligence and whether the tactical planning and execution met generally accepted law enforcement standards. The Review will be carefully planned in order to ensure effective and regular coordination with the criminal investigations and prosecutions underway. The inquiry will be completed as quickly as possible, and no later than six months after its inception, a report will be presented to the Secretary of Treasury and the President.

Organization:

The Review Team: The administrative investigation will be conducted by a dedicated, full-time team of investigators, analysts and administrative staff detailed from several bureaus and offices within Treasury. (The Secret Service, IRS - Criminal Investigative Division, The Customs Service, the Office of General Counsel, and the Office of the Inspector General). The review team will be organizationally located within the Office of Enforcement. The Director of the review team will be selected from outside Treasury. He will develop the investigative plan and supervise the day to day investigation and analysis of the events as well as the development of the draft report. The Review Team Director will be under the overall supervision of the Assistant Secretary for Enforcement.

The Review Board: In order to provide effective oversight and guidance to the administrative inquiry, an independent Review Board will be established. It will be comprised of a Chairman and four other members from outside the Federal Government. The Assistant Secretary for Enforcement will serve, ex officio, as a sixth member of the Board. Its membership will include individuals of unparalleled expertise, independence and integrity. It will be responsible for two distinct roles during the pendency of the review. First, it will provide advice and guidance during the review process. Following the completion of the investigation, it will provide a complete and independent assessment of the process and findings. Specifically the Review Board will have the following responsibilities:

1. Review the investigative plan developed by the Review Team Director and provide guidance on its adequacy in terms of both scope and depth.

2. Evaluate the investigative and analytical materials developed by the Review Team throughout the investigation and meet as a Board at the times and locations as determined by the Review Board.

3. Provide guidance and direction to the Assistant Secretary for enforcement (or the project review team?) including the identification of outside experts or additional interviews which should be undertaken to ensure a comprehensive and balanced inquiry. Only in cases where the Assistant Secretary for Enforcement determines that such direction may adversely affect the interests of the criminal investigation and prosecution or the ability of the Review team to meet the report deadlines, will such guidance not be followed.

4. Finally, the Review Board will be expected to provide the Secretary and the President its judgment regarding the quality of the administrative inquiry including, but not limited to, the substance of the report, the nature of the investigation and the procedures followed in conducting the review. It will also concur or dissent with the recommendations in the report and provide separate findings and conclusions if it determines this is necessary. The Review Board's independent assessment will be made a part of the final report.

Expert Consultants: In order to further ensure that the Treasury Department has the broadest available expertise in conducting its review, outside expert consultants will be engaged to address such areas as law enforcement tactical operations, crisis decision-making, management of law enforcement intelligence, media relations, etc. Expert consultants may be identified by the Review Board or the Review Team and made available to advise both.

Concluding Guidance:

It is expected that a comprehensive, impartial Report will be completed and delivered to the Secretary of the Treasury and the President no later than six months after the inception of the review. The report will analyze the actions taken by the Bureau of Alcohol, Tobacco and Firearms (ATF) from the outset of its investigation of David Koresh and the Davidians through and including the events occurring on February 28, 1993. The report will be based on the interviews of participants in the events as well as independent analysis of standard law enforcement practices and procedures in order to determine the adequacy of ATF training, procedures and practices. The Review Board will ensure that the review is unbiased, comprehensive and forthright. If problems occur that cannot be reconciled, it is the obligation of the Chairman of the Review Board to report them to the Secretary. To the extent that certain investigative paths were <u>not</u> followed because of potential interference with the concurrent criminal investigations, the final report must explain the reports shortcomings and recommend further investigation as appropriate.

Appendix G

A Brief History
of
Federal Firearms Enforcement

A BRIEF HISTORY OF FEDERAL FIREARMS ENFORCEMENT

Frederick S. Calhoun, Ph.D.
Historian
Federal Law Enforcement Training Center

The Bureau of Alcohol, Tobacco, and Firearms (ATF) is a relatively young law enforcement organization, having been created formally in 1972. Yet, measured by the federal laws related to the regulation and taxing of alcohol, tobacco, and firearms — the laws ATF now enforces — the history of the bureau's duties and responsibilities stretches across the full two centuries of American history. As early as 1791, revenue acts taxed both alcohol and tobacco and created the offices of tax inspector, collector, and supervisor. During the next century, the offices changed names as frequently as the tax rates changed, but the federal interest in raising revenues from alcohol and tobacco remained strong. Indeed, the formal organization of an independent bureau within the Department of Treasury specializing in alcohol, tobacco, and firearms law enforcement belatedly recognized the distinct need for such an agency.

After the Civil War, revenue agents battled moonshiners throughout the South in some of the bloodiest opposition ever to federal law enforcement. Revenue agents and deputy U.S. marshals by the score were killed as they roamed the hills and hollows searching out illicit stills. Prohibition changed the government's focus from taxing whiskey to banning it, yet the revenue agent's job remained as dangerous. After experimenting in social adjustment a dozen years, Prohibition was rescinded. Spawned by the 1933 repeal of Prohibition, the Alcohol Tax Unit was established as a tax-collecting branch within the Internal Revenue Service (IRS).

Continued concern over the violent, organized mobs that plagued the major cities compelled the federal government to try to curb the gangsters' ability to arm themselves. Rather than ban outright the purchase of machineguns and sawed-off shotguns — the weapons of choice for the mobsters — Congress in 1934 simply imposed a tax those weapons. Paying the tax required registering the weapon. The registration requirement was intended to discourage ownership of such weapons without outlawing them. No self-respecting gangster would want to register, much less pay the tax, on his Tommygun. Their evasion of the tax gave the government another legal tool to use in arresting the gangsters and breaking up the mobs.

Because it was a tax rather than a prohibition, it fell to Treasury to enforce the law as part of Treasury's role in collecting all funds due the government. Within Treasury, the Alcohol Tax Unit seemed the logical branch to enforce the new law. Registering and taxing stills required many of the same procedures and investigatory talents that would be needed to register and tax weapons. In the end, the new assignment proved comparatively easy. The unit was not overwhelmed with registrations nor by the 1940s were the investigations into evasions of the tax very time-consuming. As the gangsters declined in number and power, so did their use of machineguns and sawed-off shotguns. Enforcing the alcohol taxes again occupied most of the unit's attention.

In 1951, the Alcohol Tax Unit began enforcing federal taxes on tobacco, thus prompting a name change in 1952 to the Alcohol and Tobacco Tax Division. Once again, the logic seemed to be that collecting the tax on tobacco closely resembled the work necessary to collect the tax on alcohol, machineguns, and sawed-off shotguns. The 1968 passage of the Omnibus Crime Control and Safe Streets Act and the Gun Control Act expanded the IRS unit's jurisdiction to the criminal use of explosives and bombs. The new laws also defined specific federal offenses involving firearms, including transportation across state lines and use in organized crimes. In recognition of this new enforcement responsibility, the Alcohol and Tobacco Tax Division changed its name to the Alcohol, Tobacco, and Firearms Division (ATFD). Two years later, Congress passed the Explosives Control Act defining certain bombings and acts of arson as federal crimes. It assigned jurisdiction for enforcing this new law to ATFD.

With these expanded responsibilities, the Treasury Department on July 1, 1972 created the Bureau of Alcohol, Tobacco, and Firearms under the general oversight of the Assistant Secretary of the Treasury for Enforcement, Tariffs and Trade, and Operations. For the past twenty-one years, ATF has enforced the collection of federal taxes on alcohol and tobacco and the federal controls and regulations on firearms, with particular attention to their use by criminals. Although on its face the bureau seems a discordant collection of separate duties, the techniques for enforcing the taxes and ferreting out the illicit products, whether cases of whiskey, cartons of cigarettes, crates of automatic weapons, or containers of bombs, are strikingly similar.

Subsequent laws have expanded ATF's jurisdiction. The 1976 Arms Export Control Act focused the bureau's attention on international gun smuggling. The 1982 Anti-Arson Act gave ATF authority to investigate the destruction of property by fire as well as by explosives. Increased taxes on cigarettes and alcohol, and enhanced regulatory measures such as the 1978 Contraband Cigarette Act, have also enhanced the bureau's responsibility to ensure the government receives its lawful taxes.

The bureau has been an effective force in law enforcement. Supplies of illicit alcohol and smuggled tobacco have steadily decreased, and tax revenues have risen. During 1991, for example, ATF collected $7.7 billion in alcohol taxes and $4.8 billion in tobacco taxes. ATF agents have also focused on tracking down armed career criminals and criminal gang members. Investigations in Florida resulted in the arrest of 45 Warlock motorcycle gang members in 1991. Members of the Gullymen Posse, a gang of Jamaican drug dealers known for its propensity to commit murder, were arrested in New York by ATF agents in January 1991. Similarly, an ATF investigation into the activities of the Born to Kill gang culminated in the arrest of a dozen gang members in August 1991. Sixteen members of the San Diego chapter of the Hells Angels were convicted in 1992. As a result of these and similar investigations, ATF has become the nation's principal repository for gang-related information and intelligence. The bureau has also earned an excellent reputation for working well with federal, state, and local law enforcement agencies.

ATF agents also specialize in identifying anonymous bombers by their "signature" habits in making bombs. For example, in 1990, the assassin of Eleventh Circuit Court of Appeals Judge Robert Vance was ultimately identified by ATF agents who recognized the way the bomb was constructed. Similarly, in the midst of the tragedy in Waco, Texas, ATF agents investigating the World Trade Center bombing helped to identify the van that was used to hold the bomb. This early identification led FBI agents to the rental car company and thereafter to arrests of the terrorists before they could escape the country.

The bureau has developed considerable expertise in arson investigations. At the request of the National Fire Protection Agency, ATF began developing nationwide standards for fire investigators. The State Department's Diplomatic Security Service invited ATF to develop a protocol establishing an International Response Team of investigators trained to search blast scenes involving U.S. property abroad. Despite a rather eclectic array of duties, ATF has succeeded in developing considerable expertise in each area of its enforcement responsibilities.

The raid by ATF agents on the Branch Davidian compound resulted from its enforcement of contemporary federal firearms laws. In a larger sense, however, the raid fit within an historic, well-established and well-defended government interest in prohibiting and breaking up all organized groups that sought to arm or fortify themselves. The 1934 law taxing weapons was only the first time the federal government addressed private ownership of weapons; it was not the first federal effort to control firearms. From its earliest formation, the federal government has actively suppressed any effort by disgruntled or rebellious citizens to coalesce into an armed group, however small the group, petty its complaint, or grandiose its ambition. The collection of large arsenals by organized groups lent itself, ultimately, to the violent use of those weapons against the government itself or portions of its citizenry. Indeed, federal agents who tried to disband the groups frequently became the targets.

The discomfort over armed organizations predated the Constitution. The outbreak of what became known as Shays' Rebellion in 1786 gave added urgency to the establishment of a strong national government. During the rebellion, hundreds of angry Massachusetts farmers, most veterans of the Revolution and facing foreclosures on their farms, banded together to keep the courts from issuing any executions. Calling themselves Regulators, the farmers quickly organized into a small army. Significantly, their first foray was to capture the arsenal at Springfield. Although the Regulators failed, the specter survived. Five months, delegates from each of the thirteen states met in Philadelphia to design a new experiment in government.

The lesson of Shays' Rebellion was not forgotten, even after the new government was formed. In 1792, Congress passed a law empowering the president to call out the state militias to suppress insurrections if either an associate justice of the Supreme Court or a local district court judge certified that opposition to the laws was beyond the powers of the civil authority to suppress. Ironically, the first occasion to resort to that law grew out of the violent, organized, and armed resistance to the federal government's whiskey tax. Thus, two of the duties that ATF would later inherent — enforcing alcohol taxes and controlling firearms — combusted in 1794 into the Whiskey Rebellion, the first violent opposition to the new federal government.[1]

Across the next century, succeeding presidents had sporadic, though no less fearsome, occasion to dispatch the Army and the state militias to suppress various outbreaks of armed opposition to federal laws, taxes, and interests. In 1799, Fries Rebellion against a federal tax on houses forced President John Adams to muster the militia. Fugitive slave rescues during the 1850s prompted the government to call out the military. Organized resistance in Massachusetts, Pennsylvania, New York, Ohio, and Wisconsin raised a troublesome specter. "The main opposition," President Millard Fillmore warned Congress in December 1851, "is aimed against the Constitution itself." At the end of the decade, John Brown's ill-fated raid on

---

[1] Bowen, *Miracle at Philadelphia*, p. 287; Frederick S. Calhoun, *The Lawmen: United States Marshals and Their Deputies, 1789-1989*, (Washington, D.C.: Smithsonian Institution Press, 1990), p. 32.

Harper's Ferry, Virginia, sparked the government to decisive action. Brown chose Harper's Ferry because of the federal arsenal there. His intent was to distribute the weapons among Southern slaves and lead them in revolt for their freedom. Federal troops, however, thwarted the plan.[2]

After the Civil War, the federal government battled unrepentant Southerners to protect the rights of the freedmen. Nonetheless, federal officials acted only after the innumerable Klan-style attacks were finally perceived as organized. "Outrages of various descriptions," Attorney General George Williams advised southern U.S. Attorneys and Marshals in 1874, "and in some cases atrocious murders have been committed in your district by bodies of armed men, sometimes in disguise and with the view it is believed of overawing and intimidating peaceable and law abiding citizens and depriving them of the rights guaranteed to them by the Constitution and laws of the United States." The attorney general ordered his attorneys and marshals "to detect, expose, arrest, and punish the perpetrators of these crimes."[3]

Throughout the western territories and along the Mexican border, the federal government found occasional need to suppress armed bands of outlaws, ganged together to steal cattle or rob the mails. General William Tecumseh Sherman, sent to the Arizona border in April 1882 to investigate the outlaw troubles there, advised President Chester A. Arthur that "the

---

[2] Fillmore quoted in W.U. Hensel, *The Christiana Rio and the Treason Trials of 1851: An Historical Sketch*, (New York: Negro Universities Press, 1911), pp. 92-3; Calhoun, *The Lawmen*, pp. 82-93.

[3] Attorney General George Williams, circular letter to U.S. Attorneys and Marshals, September 3, 1874, Attorney General Instruction Book E, Record Group 60, Records of the Department of Justice, National Archives.

Civil Officers have not sufficient forces to make arrests, to hold prisoners for trial or punish when convicted." The President promptly proclaimed on May 31 that the areas plagued by the outlaws were in a state of rebellion.[4]

The federal government looked no more kindly on the labor strikes that broke out in the closing years of the nineteenth century and the opening years of the twentieth. What seemed so dangerous about events such as the 1894 Pullman strike was not just the disruption of the mails, which was the legal basis on which the government relied to break the strike, but the fact that the mails were being violently disrupted by organized groups. "We have been brought to the ragged edge of anarchy," Attorney General Richard Olney frantically explained when he ordered that the trains be kept running. Eventually, Eugene Debs and his colleagues in the American Railway Union, which took the lead in the strike, were indicted and convicted. Once again, it was the volatile mixture of violence and organization — combinations determined difficult to suppress — that evoked the full power of the federal government.[5]

The passage of the National Firearms Act of 1934, the first federal effort to control private ownership of firearms, grew out of this historic fear of armed organizations. The various collections of gangsters that proliferated during Prohibition were the true targets of the law, which required a tax and registration on the sale of their weapons of choice — machineguns

---

[4] General William Tecumseh Sherman to Attorney General Benjamin Brewster, April 12, 1882, Source-Chronological Files, Record Group 60, National Archives; Calhoun, *The Lawmen*, p. 196; Larry Ball, *United States Marshals of Arizona and New Mexico, 1846-1912*, (Albuquerque, NM: University of New Mexico Press, 1978), pp. 125-6.

[5] Almont Lindsey, *The Pullman Strike*, (Chicago: University of Chicago Press, 1967), p. 245, 274-92; Calhoun, *The Lawmen*, 209, 214.

and sawed-off shotguns. Subsequent federal firearms laws have been of a piece. Other than the 1968 ban on mail-order sales, which was in direct, though delayed, response to the assassination of President Kennedy, federal gun laws have typically been concerned with the weapons of considerable destructive power generally preferred by organized groups — bombs, machineguns, and automatic weapons.

In recent times, the federal government has shown itself even less patient with armed groups than it had historically. Radical extremists of both the Right and the Left have been pursued aggressively once they began breaking the law. For instance, after the Symbionese Liberation Army (SLA) launched its self-styled "people's war" by kidnapping newspaper heiress Patty Hearst and committing a number of daring bankrobberies, the federal government dedicated its full resources to tracking the group down. Within approximately three months, FBI agents and Los Angeles police closed in on the group at a house just outside what was then known as Watts. During an intense gun battle and fire, every member of the SLA in the house was killed.[6]

Gordon Kahl, who stood at the opposite end of the political spectrum from the SLA, met a similar end. Kahl belonged to the Posse Comitatus which refused to recognize the authority of any government above the county level. Accordingly, Kahl consistently refused to pay his federal taxes, even after he served time in prison for not doing so. When U.S. Marshals attempted to arrest him for violating the terms of his probation, Kahl killed two of them. For the next five months, Kahl hid among his friends and sympathizers until FBI agents located him

---

[6] *Los Angeles Times*, May 18, 1974.

in a farmhouse just outside Smithville, Arkansas. After refusing to surrender, Kahl was killed, and the farmhouse was burned down.[7]

Robert Matthews, the head of a group of right-wing fanatics known as the Order, embraced many of Kahl's beliefs. Unlike Kahl, whose resistance was essentially passive until the marshals tried to arrest him, Matthews and the Order launched an aggressive private war against the country. Like the SLA, the Order committed a series of bank and armored car robberies, netting $3.6 million in one heist alone. The Order also assassinated Alan Berg, a radio talk show host in Denver, Colorado.

The FBI began an equally aggressive pursuit. After a brief, violent skirmish in Idaho and another in Portland, Oregon, FBI agents finally closed in on Matthews hiding out among three adjoining houses on Whidbey Island, some fifty miles north of Seattle. After negotiating his surrender for two days, Matthews began firing on an FBI Hostage Response Team that attempted to enter the house. Protected by a full suit of body armor, Matthews ran from the first floor to the second floor firing automatic weapons. The FBI dropped a magnesium flare from a helicopter. The flare landed on the roof of the house and burned through it to the room where Matthews had stored his ammunition and explosives. These ignited, setting off a roaring, exploding fire that consumed Matthews.[8]

---

[7] James Corcoran, *Bitter Harvest Gordon Kahl and the Posse Comitatus: Murder in the Heartland*, (New York: Viking Press, 1990).

[8] James Coates, *Armed and Dangerous: The Rise of the Survivalist Right*, (New York: Hill and Wang, 1987), pp. 41-76.

A year later, in the spring of 1985, ATF collected considerable evidence that an 80-member group styling itself the Covenant of the Sword and the Arm of the Lord (CSA) had stockpiled a large arsenal at its fortified compound in Arkansas. The group had collected over 150 firearms, (including 35 machineguns), two anti-personnel mines, three anti-aircraft rockets, 50 pounds of military plastic explosives, 300 blasting caps, 2,000 feet of detonating cord, and around 100 explosive devices. CSA had also stockpiled food, water, and supplies.

ATF led the assault on the CSA compound on April 20, 1985. CSA members retreated farther into the compound, barricading themselves behind their defenses. The agents set up a siege perimeter and settled in to wait. The group used the wait to destroy many of the weapons (and hence evidence) illegally obtained. Negotiators from the FBI arrived and began the tedious, frustrating process of talking the group out. Three days later, on April 22, 1985, James D. Ellison and the 75 members of the CSA surrendered.[9]

As both history and recent events clearly show, the United States has never tolerated armed groups residing within its borders. The intent of the particular organization, whether ideological or criminal, mattered little. If the group was building an illegal arsenal, the group was subject to a federal enforcement action. To this day, ATF's enforcement focus retains the flavor of that historic concern with armed organizations. The agency has developed considerable expertise and success in investigating the activities of motorcycle, street, and drug gangs, all of which share in common a proclivity to amass large arsenals of powerful weapons.

---

[9] James Coates, *Armed and Dangerous: The Rise of the Survivalist Right*, (New York: Hill and Wang, 1987), pp. 142-4.

The raid on the Branch Davidian compound occurred in the context of that historical background.

STAFFORD LIBRARY
COLUMBIA COLLEGE
1001 ROGERS STREET
COLUMBIA, MO 65216

ISBN 0-16-042025-3